Taiwan Film Directors

D1437865

FILM AND CULTURE / JOHN BELTON, GENERAL EDITOR

Emilie Yueh-yu Yeh and Darrell William Davis

Taiwan Film Directors

A TREASURE ISLAND

COLUMBIA UNIVERSITY PRESS / NEW YORK

COLUMBIA UNIVERSITY PRESS
Publishers Since 1893
New York   Chichester, West Sussex

Copyright © 2005 Emilie Yueh-yu Yeh and Darrell William Davis
All rights reserved

Library of Congress Cataloging-in-Publication Data
Yeh, Emilie Yueh-yu.
    Taiwan film directors : a treasure island / Emilie Yueh-yu Yeh and Darrell William Davis.
        p. cm. — (film and culture)
    Includes index.
    ISBN 0–231–12898–3 (alk. paper) — ISBN 0–231–12899–1 (pbk. : alk. paper)
    1. Motion picture producers and directors—Taiwan.   I. Davis, Darrell William. II. Title. III.
Series.
    PN1998.2.Y44   2005
    791.4302'33'092251249—dc22   2005041382

⊛

Columbia University Press books are printed
  on permanent and durable acid-free paper.

Printed in the United States of America

Columbia University Press acknowledges the Taipei Economic and Cultural Office for its generous
  assistance in the publication of this book.

Designed by Lisa Hamm
c 10 9 8 7 6 5 4 3 2 1
p 10 9 8 7 6 5 4 3 2

[Color photos on the title page also appear as figures 6.1 and 6.2.]

IN MEMORY OF OUR DEPARTED FAMILY,

Ke-haoYeh, Sylvia Hemingway, Virginia Ellison, and Ilah Thompson

Contents

Acknowledgments

Many people and organizations have lent their support, inspiration, and assistance to this project. In Taiwan, Peggy Chiao Hsiung-p'ing's encouragement led to a generous research grant awarded by the Chiang Ching-kuo Foundation for International Scholarly Exchange. We thank the filmmakers for taking time to answer our questions and share their insights with us: Wu Nianzhen, Wan Ren, Wang Tong, and Xu Ligong, all of whom provided valuable information at crucial stages. At the Taipei Film Archive, Jady Long and Xue Huiling helped to source many rare illustrations, and we thank Winston Lee, director of the Archive. Li Yamei of the Golden Horse International Film Festival provided key information and introductions. To Jennifer Jao, CMPC, Lin Mengshan, Liu Zhenxiang (Liu Chen-hsiang), and Hou Hsiao-hsien, we are grateful for your kind assistance. Still in Taiwan, we thank Robert Ru-shou Chen and Lin Wenchi for invitations to two conferences on Taiwan cinema, along with many stimulating discussions. In Australia, David Yuyi Wang provided translation and other valuable research assistance, under the auspices of a University of New South Wales Faculty Research Grant. Darrell Davis thanks his colleagues and students at the erstwhile School of Theatre, Film and Dance, especially the able administrative assistance of Kathy Arnold and Jennifer Beale. In Hong Kong, we acknowledge the research support of Hong Kong Baptist Uni-

ACKNOWLEDGMENTS

versity, and especially Monna Lau at the department of Cinema-TV for her technical dexterity. Thanks also to Georgette Wang, Chen Ling, and Huang Yu of Hong Kong Baptist University. Hwang Hua Information and Culture Center in Hong Kong supplied graphic materials and a key screening of *That Day, on the Beach*.

In the United States, we thank David Bordwell for his careful reading and suggestions on the manuscript. Likewise, John Belton, Sheldon Hsiao-peng Lu, and Gina Marchetti offered constructive comments and criticism. Dudley Andrew and James Tweedie graciously invited us to the excellent conference "Double Vision: Taiwan's New Cinema, Here and There" at Yale University in late 2003. Special thanks goes out to Michael Curtin and Nicole Huang of the University of Wisconsin–Madison, and Yang Yuanying of the Beijing Film Academy. Verdy Wai-yee Leung and Zero Yan-ling Yiu have helped us in too many ways to count. At Columbia University Press, we have enjoyed strong, consistent support from Jennifer Crewe, Juree Sondker, and the indefatigable copyediting of Roy Thomas.

All these people and many more have contributed their expertise and enthusiasm for a body of films that deserves more scholarly attention. We apologize to those we may have overlooked and we take full responsibility for errors in fact or emphasis. Finally, we extend deepest thanks to our families in Taiwan and in the United States for their unflagging support and patience.

Taiwan Film Directors

Introduction: Treasure Island

This is a study of selected Taiwan film directors. Since the mid-1980s, Taiwan cinema has enjoyed international exposure through the work of young filmmakers who were brought in to revitalize a declining film industry. Although it was not the intention to use these new filmmakers to win international prizes, their films attracted great acclaim at festivals worldwide. The international profile has emerged as a pivotal, controversial feature of Taiwan directors, who went on to acquire outstanding reputations in world cinema. Collectively, the work of these filmmakers, along with several others, was known as the Taiwan New Cinema, a movement detailing indigenous sociopolitical issues from local Taiwanese viewpoints. Hou Hsiao-hsien, Edward Yang, Wan Ren, Wang Tong, Wu Nianzhen, and a number of others made up the movement. New Cinema lost its momentum in the later 1980s. However, it created a space for further developments. Ten years on, Tsai Ming-liang and Ang Lee debuted with strong pictures on the festival and art house circuit, which they have followed up with increasingly ambitious work. Our study analyzes all these directors in depth, and several more, attempting to build up a picture of Taiwan's changing film culture. *Taiwan Film Directors* is historical and thematic, collective and individual, considering the formal strategies of the pictures in tandem with the media environment within which—and sometimes against which—these directors work.

Though the New Cinema may have seemed an exceptionally innovative movement, Taiwan directors did not come from nowhere. They all have deep and abiding roots in Taiwan, despite considerable exposure to overseas influence. These roots prompted many of the formal innovations of the New Cinema, which in turn generated such widespread international notice. Among the roots of the New Cinema are Taiwan's Mandarin-language films of the preceding decades. There were several pioneering directors in the 1960s and 1970s, such as Li Xing, Bai Jingrui, King Hu, and Li Hanxiang, regarded as "founding fathers" of Taiwan cinema. Their films in turn drew on earlier models of narrative, style, and industry organization, while most of their productions were funded by large state subsidies or transnational Chinese corporations. These directors represented a Taiwan cinema of firm industrial, generic, and ideological constraint. The constraints betokened a cultural policy of martial law (1947–1987), which even so yielded a productive, quality cinema; talented directors still managed to craft personal and distinctive works. This political backdrop nonetheless governed the prospects of New Cinema figures, both limiting and enabling projects of those just starting out, which testifies to a structure of negotiated creativity inherited by the New Cinema, one that took into account competing demands of the state, industry, and authorial assertion.

Today, more than twenty years since the burgeoning directorial triumphs of all these figures, Taiwan film has moved on to a "post–New Cinema" phase occasioned by the collapsing Taiwan film industry, and necessitating finance and production according to international sales patterns. The New Cinema celebrated its twentieth anniversary in 2002 at the Golden Horse Film Festival in Taipei.[1] Still, several of these directors are at the top of their form even though they often lack sufficient resources to maximize their creativity.

An important part of our study is to reconstruct some of the factors that supported, and then deflated, the heady promise of Taiwanese films and their makers, a "treasure island" of receding images and stories. At the same time, we want to emphasize that this is still a vibrant cinema albeit supported by global finance capital. In this book we write about artists who are still working. Taiwan cinema is therefore an irregular national cinema because of the interesting paradox that the New Cinema represents: the collapse of the commercial sector has been a catalyst for the growth of an artistically viable cinema for specialized events, such as festivals, cinematheques, and community activism. Taiwan New Cinema futhermore helped put Taiwan—an island without a political identity in the world—on the map. This book is about a contemporary cinema whose directors continue to revitalize their work, as well as a historically resonant cinema, touched by every kind of twentieth-century cultural force.

時代舊記憶　國片新浪潮

台灣新電影
二十年

20TH ANNIVERSARY OF TAIWANESE NEW CINEMA

Twentieth anniversary of the Taiwan New Cinema (Taipei, 2002)

(COURTESY TAIPEI GOLDEN HORSE FILM FESTIVAL)

History: Treasure Island, Island of Greed

Figuring Taiwan through its treasures is not difficult because of its history of usurpation. Taiwan may be understood in terms of at least two images. As *Formosa,* we have a "beautiful island" named by early sixteenth-century Portuguese traders sailing between Macao and Japan. The name encoded it as a paradise, but also as hinterland, its exotic, wild beauty, headhunting, and savagery signaling a lawless place. Despite its promise, Taiwan was always on civilization's edge, whether defined by Europe, China, Japan, or a would-be global imperium such as the United States. Taiwan is at once strategically important and marginal. Therefore it is a place prone to the pillage of outsiders, a stopping place, garrison, and temporary shelter marked by the sedimentation of successive occupations and adventures. To many, Taiwan remains an occupied place, full of enticing opportunities for exploration and exploitation. A British character in Edward Yang's *Mahjong* (1996) marvels at Taipei's fantastic wealth, on an island bursting with seemingly easy pickings for sharp expatriates.

It is not only a treasure island but an island of greed. For centuries, Taiwan has been a site for transient activity, extracting spoils to be taken away. It was seen as a place to pause and soon depart, not a place to build a home. Beginning in the 1620s, Taiwan was occupied by Spanish and Dutch traders because it was anonymous, belonging to no one except fishermen and aboriginal tribes. It was never formally regarded as Chinese territory when Europeans first set foot there. But Taiwan was still subject to China's influence. Zheng Chenggong (Koxinga) was a Chinese general who refused to surrender to the new Manchu rulers of the Qing dynasty. When he needed a refuge, he chose Taiwan. In 1661, Zheng led his army to attack the Dutch garrison in Tainan. Within several months of his blockade, the Dutch surrendered and Zheng became the new master of Formosa. Fifty years later, in order to eliminate the last remnants of the Ming dynasty, the Qing court launched a force and defeated the son of Zheng Chenggong. Only at this point did Taiwan fall under the governance of China in order to block further resistance to central control. Taiwan remained for a time a frontier Chinese territory. So when China lost its first major war to Japan in 1895, the island was ceded to Japan as compensation. Shocked by China's abandonment, Taiwan declared independence in order to defend itself against this betrayal. Japan easily took control despite military clashes at major ports. The modern history of Taiwan thus began with foreign occupation by force.

At this point Taiwan was turned into a colony proper, building on the settlement and agricultural base established by Chinese administration. Japanese occupation had the further purpose of demonstrating a campaign of colonial modernization equaling that of the Western powers. More important were substantial material interests in rice, sugar, camphor, timber, mines, and conscript labor, all monopolized by Japanese firms. When the Japanese were defeated in 1945, the mainland Nationalists took over the colonial reins and lost no time behaving as another usurper. Opportunistic officials and merchants summarily looted the island's resources in the name of continuing the civil war against the Communists. This resulted in island-wide rebellion and the crackdown over the February 28 Incident of 1947, which was a protest against Nationalist exploitation. In 1949 Taiwan became a refuge again, when the Communists drove the Nationalists out of China. It continues until now to be called a renegade province. The United States contributed its military and diplomatic assistance in order to contain the Red threat, though under the Nationalists' KMT (Kuomintang) party rule "Free China" was being leeched of its vitality. This situation changed with the policies of the 1970s, based on the same principles of export-oriented high growth as the Japanese economic miracle.

Taiwan as an "Island of Greed," along with Taiwan as a "Treasure Island," covers centuries of unruly, and mostly dubious, history. Serial occupation and plunder also have had a specifically political meaning, as dramatized in the gangster film *Island of Greed* (Hei jing, meaning "black gold"). This 1997 Hong Kong film, directed by Michael Mak Dong-kit, depicts Taiwan as a Chinese Sicily where politicians and ruthless triads (mafia-like organized gangs) are in cahoots. The gangsters need the politicians to legitimize their criminal activities and bleach their "black" money into green, while scrofulous politicians rely on this "black gold," or underground tender, to remain in office.

A few years before, Taiwanese director Chen Kuo-fu released a more stylish gangster-noir called *Treasure Island* (1993). "I just want to be with you, if for only a day" (Zhiyao weini huo yitian) is its Chinese title, and it takes place in Taipei, a city of temptation, fate, danger, and last chances. Here too, the paths of fabulously wealthy gangsters cross with those of shady politicians, petty kidnappers, and ordinary Taipei workers dazzled by the privileges of shadowy figures that turn society's wheels. Typically for director Chen, the film ends on apocalyptic overtones of borrowed time, dogged by natural and military cataclysms.

Film History: Authority and Authorship

What does all this have to do with Taiwan filmmakers and the cinema? Taiwan itself, as a "floating" treasury, represents a procession of would-be owners claiming legitimacy. From the war between the Dutch and Zheng Chenggong to the ongoing standoff between the Taiwan and Chinese governments, the history of Taiwan evolves around negotiations over patrimony. The struggle over patrimony is not just political but also cultural, linguistic, and ethnic. As a modern technology, cinema must draw on the cultural resources in which it is embedded. If culture in Taiwan is constituted by a series of residues left behind by various occupiers, what is the relation between Taiwan cinema and the shifting layers of modern colonial history? How do competing cultural and political patrimonies help shape and re-shape the cinema of Taiwan?

In the postwar period, cinema was used as an instrument of KMT's authority, eradicating Japanese remnants and bolstering an anti-Communist Chinese polity. Taiwan cinema in the following four decades sustained a political authority in Tai-wan and a cultural authority speaking on behalf of China as a whole. Censorship forces, as well as linguistic and tax policies, permitted commercial films to develop only on a limited scale, and it was difficult for creativity to flourish. The authorities in Taiwan were not really interested in developing film culture unless it served a political function.

Taiwan cinema changed when it shifted from a cinema of authority to a cin-ema of authorship. In the early 1980s, the relaxation of laws concerning films helped facilitate the New Cinema in which indigenous perspectives were assert-ed in the name of Taiwan nativism. The cinema that used to speak for the na-tion could now speak for personal and community history. This is an important turning point since Taiwan cinema, as a national cinema, was going nowhere. As national cinema its significance has declined, except as a sort of crooked branch of the PRC and Chinese-language cinema generally. Conversely, Taiwan cinema has become more visible due to the rise of internationally recognized names: Hou Hsiao-hsien, Edward Yang, Tsai Ming-liang, and Ang Lee. These Taiwan di-rectors enjoy substantial attention, not as figures within the accustomed national cinema model but as auteurs of the international cinema, navigating the cease-less roll of nation versus international, local versus global. Hence, the intention of this book is to bring together under a common rubric filmmakers whose col-lective work is rooted in the conjunction of a waning national and waxing inter-national cinematic tradition.

Directors now take precedence over national cinema and the nation-state. A personal voice and style is on offer since the experiments undertaken in the New Cinema. Their work entails rejection of an instrumental use of the medium and is based on dialogue with earlier founding filmmakers attempting to forge a personal style, attempts that were hampered by the old cinema of authority. As the authority begins to wane, authorship waxes. The works of these directors are rarely explicitly political, but in order to establish the authority of authorship, they must confront a cinematic and cultural patrimony. In this connection, old formats of storytelling (melodrama), familiar formulae of mass production (genre), patrilineal succession (apprenticeship) and, finally, cultural legacies like Confucianism are contested, re-vised, or phased out.

Imagine contemporary Taiwan filmmakers trying to reconcile with a number of different fathers, actual or metaphorical. Fatherhood is an overriding theme in the work of both Ang Lee and Tsai Ming-liang. Lee's best-loved films are known collectively as the "father-knows-best" trilogy, while Tsai dissects the evolving relations between the perennial Xiao Kang and his lugubrious father, Miao Tian. More broadly, Lee's films can be analyzed in terms of their cinematic ancestry, their references to and updates of Chinese literary and film classics. Tsai goes even further, incorporating segments of the Chinese canon into his film, *Goodbye, Dragon Inn* (2003), as well as the presence of Miao Tian and Shi Jun, both regulars in King Hu's stock company. Both Lee and Tsai grapple with the cinematic, historical, and ideological patrimony of the ancestors, particularly the traditional Confucian authority of father figures like King Hu and Li Hanxiang. Lee and Tsai are building on a Chinese canon but they do so critically, reviewing it with firm, sometimes severe, corrections.

It is possible also to think of fatherhood and patrimony in terms of formal conventions and norms. Hou Hsiao-hsien and Edward Yang are foremost among the New Cinema directors who asserted their authorship over the authority of genre, stars, and studio politics. In fact, Hou earned a share of opprobrium for turning his back on entertainment in favor of personal experiments in narrative authenticity. With the influence of talented collaborators like Zhu Tianwen and Wu Nianzhen, Hou pressed his formal innovations toward aesthetically rarefied, celebrated epics and historical adaptations. Today Hou is the doyen of Taiwan's film establishment, but his influence is exerted through cultural rather than commercial channels. Yang, on the other hand, has rejected Taiwan cinema outright. His international triumph, *Yi Yi, A One and a Two* (2000), has never been released in Taiwan though not for lack of commercial potential. Yang's experience with producers and distributors in Taiwan has been bitter ever since his seminal work on the New Cinema for Central Motion Picture Corporation. Before that, he had some training in the United States, but found it a waste of time. An autodidact, struggling to work with entrenched producers and crew on his early pictures, Yang has found an autonomous space to work since his challenging period piece, *A Brighter Summer Day* (1991). Appropriately, this film centers on the (de)formation of a teenager under the authority of a regimented school and an ineffectual father. This film has a level of formal sophistication rivaling any in the world, but Yang subsequently turned to easier genres. Now producing inventive animation shorts carried on his Web site, Yang represents an active rebellion against the film industry establishment. Hou, on the other hand, creatively reacted to it and has become an establishment figure himself.

With these newly minted authorships, Taiwan cinema was able to step out of its domestic confinement and walk into the wider world. But these authors were established at a time when commercial cinema plummeted. The Taiwan film market was left to Hong Kong films in the 1980s and then to Hollywood in the 1990s. Currently, the screens of Taiwan remain a place securely occupied by Hollywood. With regard to consumption, Hollywood is the de facto national cinema of Taiwan just as, politically, the United States guarantees Taiwan's liminal existence.

The shift from authority to authorship also stimulated a sea change in practical film studies in Taiwan. With the rise of the new authorship, articles on individual directors and their films dominated film publications. Peggy Chiao Hsiung-p'ing (Jiao Xiongping) and Huang Jianye were the most prolific and influential among a group of critics writing in the 1980s.[2] Through their review articles in newspapers and film magazines, young cinephiles learned to embrace the burgeoning local art cinema in directors such as Hou, Yang, Lee and Tsai. Peggy Chiao's key book on Taiwan New Cinema is largely organized by authorship, and Huang Jianye also published the first book-length study on Edward Yang.[3]

In Taiwan, the focus on directors and authorship continues with a slew of major European, American, and Asian awards falling into the hands of Hou, Yang, Lee, Tsai, and even Tsai's protégé Lee Kang-sheng. On the other hand, while academic film studies remains forever in a state of incubation, studies of the cinema are taken more seriously as part of a rising Taiwan identity as well as a sobering diagnosis of domestic production. In the early 1990s, government funds were made more available for researchers to conduct in-depth studies and interviews, especially on cinema during the Japanese occupation period, the Taiwanese-language films (*taiyu pian*), and the film industry in the immediate postwar years.[4] These topics were firmly out of bounds during martial law. This historiographical turn to Taiwan contravenes the earlier KMT literature, which was based on Sinocentric, right-wing discourse established on the mainland.[5] Apart from authorship and new historiography, quantitative analyses of political economy emerged in the 1990s. Funded by a national research grant, Lu Feiyi compiled a database on the policy, regulation, distribution, and exhibition of cinema in Taiwan since 1949. Lu summarized the copious data in a book called *Taiwan cinema, 1949–1994: politics, economy, and aesthetics*.[6] This book is a useful reference for continuing institutional analyses, especially in tackling the problem of domestic film production.[7] Subsequent to Lu's book, political-economic investigations on the New Cinema and its connection to global capital are on the rise. But the assumption of these works is that authorship is the culprit in the industry's collapse, and it is at the expense of the domestic audience that auteur directors are able to make international reputations for themselves.

While political-economic examination of Taiwan cinema is important to understand cultural and global finance capital at various levels, it provides little textual explanation of why the turn to authorship would bankrupt Taiwan cinema, assuming film auteurs should be embedded in a healthy domestic industry, preferably backed by government subsidy. What this diagnosis lacks is analysis of the most basic imperatives of the cinema—the films and filmmakers themselves. If authorship is seen as the villain in the development of a commercially viable Taiwan cinema, why do the authors' *films* fail to attract the domestic audience? Why do Taiwan-made art films travel around the world but fall flat at home? This is a question about reception and marketing, a crucial area in the development of Taiwan cinema, yet to be properly studied. While acknowledging this gap in the field, our book attempts to develop an alternative proposition, a thick description of contemporary Taiwan authorship. We argue that *precisely* because of authorship, Taiwan cinema remains alive and energetic, especially in the context of world cinema, constituting an alternative form of popularity as seen in various international circuits. Although *commercial* and *artistic* need not be antithetical, they may remain relatively separate; furthermore, in the writing of Taiwan film as an irregular national cinema, they may even be bracketed, held "at bay," as it were. This does not mean we are indifferent to the plight of domestic production, only that Taiwan film authorship goes some way toward compensating, in "export quality," for the drop in industrial quantity. Thus the book is complementary to, not opposing, political-economic analysis and audience studies. Where we depart from the literature is in our treatment of authorship as grounded in an institutional and historical tradition. Contemporary auteurs in Taiwan need to be understood within opportunities and constraints that have since disappeared with the demise of the commercial sector. As a study on directors, the priority is placed on films as cultural work, more than on the expression of individual artists. In the films of these authors, Taiwan is no longer a site for occupation and transplantation of the occupier's mentality, but the birthplace of contemporary cinematic virtuosity.

The Filmmakers

Given the international profiles of the filmmakers presented here, there should be no doubt over the importance of their work and its inclusion in this critical volume. But there are many others. We concede that important filmmakers have been left out. Among the missing are Chen Kuo-fu (Chen Guofu), Lin Qingjie (Lin Ching-jie), Lin Zhengsheng (Lin Cheng-sheng), Song Cunshou (Song Ts'un-shou), Yu Kanping (Yu K'an-p'ing), Zhu Yanping (Chu Yen-p'ing), Zhang Yi (Chang Yi), Zhang Zuoji (Chang Tso-ji), several directors working in the *taiyu pian*, and perhaps most regrettably Sylvia Chang (Zhang Aijia), the most active woman narrative filmmaker from Taiwan. Chang's 2004 film *20:30:40* represents her characteristically professional packaging of stars, not only from Taiwan but also from Hong Kong and Southeast Asia. It is significant too for its distribution by Columbia Pictures–Asia under the executive production of Chen Kuo-fu, based on the successful pattern of his own *Double Vision* (2002). Leaving so many figures out may be due to a smaller body of work, or because they have not yet received any exposure to Western audiences, as have the big name directors. Included are some Taiwan directors who are not completely of Taiwan, like Li Hanxiang and King Hu, both being transplants from Hong Kong Mandarin films but hailing originally from Beijing. These directors are more pan-Chinese, working in Hong Kong, South Korea, and in one instance on the mainland itself. But for the Cultural Revolution, these two giants would gladly have worked in China exclusively. Politics was against them. As a result, Li and Hu did some of their finest work in Taiwan, and had a lasting impact on the film industry there. If these filmmakers are only incidentally related to Taiwan, they nonetheless helped put Taiwan cinema on the map, as in King Hu's made-in-Taiwan prizewinner, *A Touch of Zen* (1970). Others are vitally important to Taiwan cinema but are virtually unknown outside. Major directors like Li Xing, Bai Jingrui, and Wan Ren made all their films within Taiwan. Even so, an English-language book on Taiwan directors should at least introduce some figures new to Western readers, so we do this by reference to key movements (like the New Cinema) or projects (such as Hou Hsiao-hsien's Taiwan trilogy).

A more pressing issue of inclusion may arise because readers may not find their favorite films discussed in this book. In the chapter on Ang Lee, for instance, we have left out almost all his English-language pictures, though these are just as meticulous and engaging as his Chinese-themed films. Hou Hsiao-hsien has made sixteen feature films plus many commercials and executive-produced projects. Not every film can be analyzed with the care it deserves; not every film or project is equally deserving of careful analysis. This book is a series of essays on the selected directors, and particularly their place in Taiwan film and those Chinese cultural traditions that impact on cinematic form. The rich productivity of these directors' careers leads to a difficult choice, one faced in every chapter. If every film were covered, the result would be much like a catalog. Should we write about every film made by each director? Or is it preferable to choose fewer films and discuss them in more depth, letting a more "thick description" stand for a range of films, or career phases. We opted for the latter choice, relinquishing exhaustiveness in favor of textual analysis that reveals a director's distinctive accomplishments, or failures. This book is therefore a somewhat eccentric monograph, not a reference work, about Taiwan film directors. We must be mindful of the director's work as process, through which the object-works come into being. We also must be forthright about our own aesthetic preferences; not every film in a director's portfolio interests us equally. But which films are chosen for extended discussion? We are guided by the following criteria:

- Is the film among a director's richest, especially in the use of style and narrative structure? Does the film represent a director's overall work in a given period?
- Does the film connect with preoccupations of other directors in Taiwan, either as a movement (like the New Cinema, of which Edward Yang was a leader) or as contemporaries (e.g., the opposite roads of Tsai Ming-liang and Ang Lee)?
- Does the film open up to a larger cultural framework, whether in film history, in criticism, or in the cultural politics of Taiwan itself?
- Sheer availability: can the film(s) be watched adequately, and in what format? They may be screened in 35mm or 16mm at film festivals, classrooms, or special events. On home video, they may or may not have subtitles, like King Hu's *Dragon Inn* (1967), which can be watched on a fine Japanese-made DVD—with Japanese subtitles. A corollary of this is the film's success at the box office, though a financially successful film does not always guarantee availability (e.g., *Dragon Inn*).

To the question of why these films and not others, we must reply because they speak to the preoccupations of the director, and because they represent for us the most intriguing innovations in Taiwan film culture. Besides, they are available, sometimes with a little patient fossicking and inquiries on the Internet.

Unlike most film books organized by thematic categories, this one is a series of essays with several interconnected arguments governing the organization of each chapter. Following a single director and his films, each tends to have its own focus and its own approach. Chapters can be read in any order, and they stand relatively independent of one another. However, they share some common themes. Authorship emerges as an issue not only with respect to individual directors, but as a structural problem in Taiwan cinema at different stages of continuity and transformation. Another theme is the idea of cinematic and cultural patrimony, the background material employed by every filmmaker. In the first two chapters it is the KMT with its expectation of conformity to conservative standards of sociopolitical morality. With Li Han-xiang and King Hu, as well as Edward Yang, Hou Hsiao-hsien, and Ang Lee, the patrimony is archival, in the sense that they draw on Chinese literary-autobiographical models. Tsai Ming-liang also incorporates autobiography, but his basic film treasury is more ethnographic, hidden in vernacular popular cultures, including—like Lee—the films of King Hu. Overall, the book moves from general historical description to close-up analyses of directorial style and film form.

The first two chapters seek a balance between historiography and authorship. Directors are framed within specific cinematic, political, and cultural contexts. Their works are seen as manifestations of their complicity or trouble with established modes of filmmaking. Major directors of the 1960s and the 1970s such as Li Xing and Bai Jingrui operated within a state-sponsored film style called *healthy realism*. But their activities during this period are not to be seen as entirely official, just as Taiwan cinema was not all propaganda. A thriving commercial cinema was well established by the late 1950s, with low-budget *taiyu pian*—Taiwanese-language pictures—produced by small companies and directors with various regional backgrounds. We propose the idea of "parallel cinema" to account for the conditions of Taiwan film production in the 1950s and the 1960s. The parallel tracks highlight the authorities' neocolonial policy toward local Taiwanese culture but, at the same time, leaves a market gap that allows alternatives to flourish. Although Li and Bai were celebrated as the foremost directors of healthy realism, they also made scores of other popular genre pictures with healthy box office.

The ambivalent status of Li Hanxiang and King Hu allows us to rethink their Taiwan achievements as famous transplants from China, via Hong Kong. Li and Hu belong to the Chinese diaspora in that neither was ever completely embedded in local Taiwan or Hong Kong culture. Their works have a strong period fetishism rooted in dynastic China, which proved essential to the development of martial arts and costume dramas in Taiwan, Hong Kong, and later in China.

The second chapter follows an identical setup as the first. It begins with a general historical analysis of the New Cinema, moving to close-up descriptions of some of its most important writers, producers, and directors, inspired by the literature of Taiwan nativism of the 1970s. We cover writer-producers Wu Nianzhen and Xiao Ye to provide a different view of the standard account of the New Cinema movement. It seems to us that the New Cinema should be seen not only as director-driven, but as a collective endeavor by lesser-known artists, critics, and the public. This impression is consistent with material collected in our interviews with some of the major New Cinema figures. In the last part of this chapter, we focus on Wang Tong and Wan Ren, two directors with distinctive approaches to Taiwan nativism. Wang and Wan tend to oscillate between individual style and commercial appeal. But we regard them as topical filmmakers who are more interested in Taiwan historical subjects, including autobiographical accounts, than in the quest for stylistic consistency or innovation.

With chapter 3 we move into single-director studies. Edward Yang is a master of intricately plotted films that dazzle with their juggling of time, space, and cognitive games. We discuss Fredric Jameson's account of Yang, which raises a number of problems in relation to Taiwan cinema's canonization in the West. Readers unfamiliar with Jameson or uninterested in methodology might wish to skip the coda and reprise at the end of this chapter. Here, we offer a different analysis of the famous film *The Terrorizers* (1986). A handful of films by some directors are representatives of a generation, as outstanding cinematic contributions from Taiwan. The exceptional *A Brighter Summer Day* is one of these, and receives extended treatment for its visual strategies, organized under a figure of style called "tunnel visions." These strategies, placed in a context of perceptual and phenomenological film theories, also carry over into works by other Taiwan directors. Yang's more recent comedies are comparatively modest, satirical and humanist reflections on cosmopolitan Taipei, a city presented as a motley conglomeration of colliding values. Within highly entertaining packages, Yang explicitly addresses a distorted Confucianism under the trappings of Western-style rationalization.

Chapter 4 advances the authorship-historiography framework. It uses Hou Hsiao-hsien, Taiwan's preeminent director, to map Taiwan film culture's trajectory. Hou's career is trisected into three episodes—the commercial past, the explorative New Cinema period, and the experiments of the historical national trilogy. Hou's personal development is taken as a microcosm of the transformations of Taiwan cinema. Following the second chapter's argument that the New Cinema movement is a collective endeavor, we look at crucial interventions in Hou Hsiao-hsien's most important texts. Accordingly, Hou's films fit within a framework of autobiography. A number of literary and historical figures provided Hou with vital raw materials. Hou's collaborators Zhu Tianwen and Wu Nianzhen offered their autobiographies to Hou's *Summer at Grandpa's* (1984) and *Dust in the Wind* (1986). The eminent Chinese author Shen Congwen inspired Hou to make his own autobiographical *The Time to Live and the Time to Die*. Taiwan's national treasure, Li Tianlu, portrayed himself in Hou's biographical *The Puppetmaster* (1993). Hou's finest achievements are a succession of "borrowed" autobiographies, and explore cultural patrimony in Taiwan cinema via autobiographical acts.

Another figure preoccupied with the Chinese patrimony is Ang Lee. We advance the proposition that Lee may be "Confucianizing" Hollywood, not just as alignment of American genres around family hierarchies, but in the injection of sincerity and diligent craftsmanship. This is exemplified by Lee's *Crouching Tiger, Hidden Dragon* (2000), the most successful non-English language picture ever. We consider *Crouching Tiger's* production background, its embodiment of martial arts, as well as its narrative structure and literary source by Wang Dulu. Another Chinese-language Lee picture, *Eat Drink Man Woman* (1994), is a transposition of a Hong Kong classic from the 1950s, not a simple remake. In both of these extended examples, we see Lee coming to terms with his ancestral patrimony, weighing the alternate attractions of submission and rebellion.

Chapter 6 is probably the weirdest in its dealings with the enigmatic Tsai Ming-liang. Strictly speaking, Tsai is not a Taiwan director because he too is a transplant, from provincial Malaysia, but he certainly has become an intriguing Taiwan auteur. Unlike King Hu or Li Hanxiang, Tsai is deeply embedded in Taiwan's vernacular culture. The queer affection toward local working-class life allows us to bring camp aesthetics to the discussion of Tsai's distinct authorship. Camp is rarely used in analyzing Asian film directors, but we find it a powerful strategy to account for many extraordinary things in Tsai's films. Household utensils, low-brow décor, working-class environments, clothes, antiques, and pseudo-political paraphernalia are all part of the Tsai camp. By way of camp, we also trace a couple of aged vernacular histories that continue to haunt Tsai's creation. Sultry popular music and cinemas of a bygone era serve as potent sources of arousal for Tsai. In this respect, Tsai also works within the line of a pan-Chinese cultural patrimony.

■ ■ ■ ■ ■

Since this book is a joint effort between two authors, we have divided the labor as follows: chapters 1 and 2 and this introduction were cowritten by the authors together. Chapters 3 and 5 were conceived and drafted by Darrell Davis while Emilie Yueh-yu Yeh took charge of chapters 4 and 6. The postscript was also cowritten. This book is not meant to be a comprehensive study of major Taiwan directors; if it was, it would do an injustice to the rich body of work of each director-author. In fact, Hou Hsiao-hsien, King Hu, Ang Lee, Li Xing, Li Hanxiang, Tsai Ming-liang, Wan Ren, Wang Tong, Wu Nianzhen, Edward Yang, and Zhu Tianwan all deserve complete monographs of their own. We hope that this treasury will be just a beginning, opening a new chapter in Taiwan film studies in anticipation of engaging, in-depth books on Taiwan filmmakers.

Parallel Cinemas

ONE

POSTWAR HISTORY AND MAJOR DIRECTORS

*Taiwanese must dress, eat, and live as Japanese do, speak the Japanese tongue as their
own and guard our national spirit in the same way as do Japanese born in Japan.*

—GOVERNOR KAWAMURA TAKEJI, 1929[1]

*In its present form the KMT Government more closely resembles an Occupational Govern-
ment than a Government of the people.*

—LT. COMMANDER MAX BERMAN, R.N.V.R. FEBRUARY 5, 1946[2]

Background

As a colony of Japan, Taiwan was in a state of confusion at the end of World War II.
People's loyalties, their language, their very thoughts were up for radical revision.
Industry, institutions, and social organization had to be rebuilt. Taiwanese people
looked forward to rejoining the Chinese mainland. There were high expectations
among the island's elite for self-determination, but these were soon dashed. Taiwan's rule was handed over to the victorious Nationalist party (Kuomintang, or
KMT), though for several chaotic months after the surrender it was the Japanese
who continued to maintain order.[3]

Under colonial rule, film production in Taiwan was controlled by the Japanese, either through contracts with local filmmakers or by simply using Taiwan

as a colorful location, with Taiwanese aborigines as extras. With the exception of three films that were solely produced by the Taiwanese, most of the features shot in Taiwan between 1921 and 1943 were produced by Japanese studios, like Nikkatsu, Toho, and Shochiku.[4] The 1943 film *Bell of Sayon* (Shayuan zhi zhong / Sayon no kane) represents the colonial interest of filmmaking in Taiwan. This film was one of the "national policy" films (*kokusaku-eiga* or *guoce dianying* in Chinese) administered by the Japanese government.[5] Made for the Japanese audience at home, *Bell of Sayon* restages a real-life event about a young aboriginal, Sayon, who died for a patriotic cause. The film opens with a long documentary-like sequence introducing aboriginal life in Taiwan. Highlights include Japan's "enlightened" colonial governance that helps modernize and nationalize a primitive, aboriginal tribe. Sayon hence enters the diegetic story as a happy girl on a pig farm. Despite being an aborigine, Sayon is modern, diligent, and patriotic to the Japanese empire. Young men in Sayon's village are called to serve on the front. She helps with the ceremony to celebrate the conscription of the village youth. At the end of the ceremony, a rainstorm strikes the village, but Sayon insists on seeing off her friends. On the way she falls down into a roaring river and disappears. Her accidental death works as an emblem of colonial sacrifice and loyalty to encourage all Japanese subjects.

Shot on locations in Taiwan with the help of hundreds of aborigine extras, *Bell of Sayon* is a 100 percent Japanese film. It was produced by Shochiku, directed by Shimizu Hiroshi, featuring Japan's Manchurian star Li Xianglan, also known as Ri Koran or Yamaguchi Yoshiko.[6] Taiwan and its people were there to provide testimony to Japan's benevolent rule in Southeast Asia and around the empire.[7] Although the film was made on Taiwan, it was not conceived for the island's audiences. Instead, like every other resource Japan took from Taiwan, it was intended for the edifying entertainment of Japanese at home.

It is clear that cinema in Taiwan was treated by the Japanese as a typical captive market, one-sided, force-fed, and exploitative. Few, if any, opportunities existed for indigenous production on a commercial basis. The exhibition market bears this out, being dominated by imports controlled by colonial interests. Parallel to the lack of production, film exhibition relied on imports from all over the world, particularly Japan and Hollywood. Shanghai-produced Mandarin films were allowed before the outbreak of the Pacific War. Between 1941 and 1945, under strict wartime censorship, film exhibition was limited to those from Japan, Germany, and Italy. In 1945, film imports from the former colonizer stopped, and a vacuum developed on Taiwan's cinema screens.[8] Given the urgent needs of postwar reorganization, there were pressing tasks for the incoming KMT to complete, and film or cultural policy was not its immediate concern. Securing order and legitimacy was its top priority, and the party set about this with grim military efficiency. Ignoring the welcoming gestures of the Taiwanese, the incoming administration expropriated Japanese assets and seized the colonial reins. Within a few years, the party declared martial law, which amounted to dictatorship of the KMT for four decades.[9] The KMT's initial lack of interest in production, its neglect of film policy, and the corresponding importance of revolutionizing public consciousness all contrast markedly with the early Communist regimes in both the Soviet Union and China. Not until the 1960s do we see a full-fledged effort to establish a national cinema with pedagogical functions.

Parallel Cinemas

The gradual establishment of postcolonial Taiwan cinema can be viewed as a series of three parallels. "Parallel cinemas" offers a framework that captures the simultaneous linguistic, ideological, and commercial fractures in the 1950s and '60s.[10] The first is linguistic. The KMT was coming into an island society that had become acculturated, if not assimilated, to Japanese social organization. For local audiences, spoken Mandarin Chinese was a foreign language. In film production, pictures had to be made for distinct audiences in two different languages: in Mandarin or the "national language" (*guoyu*) for the post-1945 mainland transplants, then turning into a flood of refugees in 1949 with the Nationalist defeat. Pictures were also routinely made in the Taiwanese language for audiences who spoke southern Fujian dialect (*minnan yu* or Hokkien), a derivative of Fukkienese. As the KMT tightened its grip on Taiwan, Mandarin-language films were assiduously cultivated, and Taiwanese-language films were gradually eclipsed. The linguistic parallels of film production were not merely a segregation but also a form of intensifying opposition. It was not that Taiwanese-language films competed for the same audience as the Mandarin pictures. They were distributed and shown on different circuits. But because the ruling party came from the mainland and spoke the official "national language," its paternalistic objectives eventually took priority.

Another parallel can be seen in the type of films made: a highly commercial system of entertainment largely transplanted from Hong Kong, as opposed to a state-sponsored cinema of nation-building and propaganda. A further parallel is that of scale: between the major large studios and/or production companies—Central Motion Picture Corporation (CMPC, Zhongyang dianying gongsi), Grand Pictures (Guolian dianying), Union Pictures (Lianbang yingye), and First Film Enterprise (Diyi yingye), all making Mandarin feature films. In contrast to the large Mandarin studios, there were the small to mid-sized studios and production companies—Huaxing, Yufeng, Tailian, Jixing, and others—which turned out Taiwanese pictures on a smaller scale. Taken together these three parallels—linguistic, mode of address, and production scale—correspond to some of the deepest cultural differences and antagonisms which persist in Taiwan society to this day.

To describe the formation of Taiwan's major official studios, we must consider the filmmaking activities of the KMT while it was still based in China. The Central Film Studio (Zhongyang dianying zhipianchang, short for Zhongzhi), founded in 1934, was the KMT's earliest production house and consisted of propaganda and military film units.[11] When the Sino-Japanese War broke out in 1937, a film unit under the party's military commission was turned into the "China Film Studio" (Zhongdian, short for Zhongguo dianying zhipianchang). It made newsreels, documentaries, and anti-Japanese propaganda features during the eight-year war against Japan.[12] When the Nationalists fled to Taiwan in 1949, China Film Studio also moved and came under ownership of the Ministry of Defense.[13]

Eventually, the KMT would make films through CMPC to promote its vision of a healthy Chinese-Taiwan polity. In addition to China Film Studio, KMT consolidated two official Japanese film units into "Taiwan Provincial Film Studio" in 1945, called simply Taiwan Film Company (Taiying, short for Taiwan dianying gongsi).[14] Meanwhile, the party also took over an affiliation of distributors and theater chains that showed films during the Japanese period. Finally, another production unit was the Agriculture and Education Motion Picture Studio (Nongjiao, short for Nongye jiaoyu dianying gongsi), which made features up until the formation of CMPC in 1954.[15] These three—China, Taiwan, and the Agriculture studios—made a handful of films in the early years of Taiwan's postwar transition, but at this time there was a lack of facilities, film stock, and other resources.

In 1950 the Agriculture and China Film studio launched an official feature production in postcolonial Taiwan. *Awakening* (Emeng chuxing, dir. Zong You), an anti-Communist espionage story, was the first locally made Mandarin-language feature, and the inaugural film officially backed by the party in Taiwan. However, it was not the first feature produced in postwar Taiwan. *Turmoil on Mt. Ali* (Alishan fengyun) is the picture, a singing melodrama among the aborigines of the interior, marking Taiwan's initial entry into film production.[16] This 1949 commercial picture was directed by Zhang Che (Chang Cheh) for Wanxiang, a branch of a Shanghai / Hong Kong–based company called Guotai (not the same as the famous Hong Kong major Cathay). *Turmoil* was Zhang Che's first film. Thus, at nearly the same moment, two features were made and released in Taiwan: a nationalist piece of political indoctrination and a singing love story about an exotic, romantic indigenous tribe. Two parallel impulses, one political, the other commercial, complemented and often contested each other even within Mandarin-language production. These impulses—both transplanted from the mainland—dominated Mandarin production until the 1980s. Zhang's *Turmoil on Mt. Ali* is also an echo of the old Japanese appropriation of native tribal communities on behalf of colonial modernization, as in the *kokusaku* national policy film *Bell of Sayon*. The appropriation this time around, unlike the Japanese, was for entirely commercial ends.

It took some time for film output to steady and produce regular yields. At this stage it was the Agriculture studio that produced the most features, a total of nine films between 1950 and 1953.[17] On its initial formation through a merger of the Agriculture studio and the distribution / theater chains left behind by the Japanese, CMPC contributed just one feature, *Spring returns to Meigang* (Meigang chunhui, 1954; dir. Zong You).[18] Despite its quick start, CMPC was not to make films on a mass scale. Between 1954 and 1959, it made only thirteen fiction features, indicating the relative unimportance of film production for the KMT.[19] It was not until the mid-1960s, at a time of greater stability, that CMPC began a policy of explicit nation-building through film production. Meanwhile, Taiwan's screens were served by imports from Hong Kong, which produced films for the all-important Taiwan market in both Mandarin and *minnan* languages.[20] In addition, since there was so little domestic production, the KMT allowed imports from Hollywood, Europe, and even Japan, in spite of an initial ban on Japanese features.[21]

Taiyu pian

Before Mandarin-language production found its feet, a lively and productive Taiwanese-language film industry—*taiyu pian*—was established. *Taiyu pian* served the millions of *minnan*-speaking viewers, which made up a numerical, if not political, majority. Production of these films was robust enough to justify application of the term "Golden Age of Taiwanese film," or to be more precise, two distinct Golden Ages.[22] In the first, from 1956 to 1959, 176 Taiwanese films were made. The second Golden Age saw the production of at least 800 titles from 1962 to 1969. In 1962 alone, 120 films were released, while only seven Mandarin-language films were made.[23] It is noteworthy that long before Ang Lee's *Crouching Tiger, Hidden Dragon*, a *taiyu* martial arts picture, *Tiger Lo and Dragon Jen*, was directed by Liang Zhefu in 1959. Liang adapted his film from the same source as Lee.[24]

The large numbers alone might indicate something of the type of pictures *taiyu pian* were: Taiwanese opera, folklore, comedies, and popular serials based on well-known community events were turned out very quickly and cheaply. One of several factors in the success of *taiyu pian* was the unexpected popularity of *Xue Pinggui and Wang Baochuan*, an opera film made in 1956. Directed by He Jiming in collaboration with a big opera company, Gongyueshe, this film uncannily recaps the importance of opera in early Chinese film history. Initial attempts to film opera by mainland Chinese filmmakers in the teens were echoed in Taiwan four decades later. As a colonial filmmaker, He Jiming was trained in Japan and became an educational documentarist during the occupation period. Occasionally, He was a *rensageki* (linked drama) director, helping local opera troupes build up business by inserting segments of moving images between live acts.[25] After the war, he continued to work in the official sector. With the success of *Xue Pinggui and Wang Baochuan*, He established his own film studio, Huaxing, in central Taiwan.

However, He was not the first to adapt Taiwanese opera to film. In fact, before *Xue Pinggui* a local opera troupe called Duma had already made a 16mm feature shot in 1955, *Six scholars in the romance of the west chamber* (Liu caizi xixiangji). It was a commercial flop but, parallel to Mandarin production, it reveals the nascent *Taiwanese* production in the postcolonial period, branded and constrained by martial law. The prints have been lost but, according to secondary recollections, the film was not as polished as *Xue Pinggui* and suffered from many technical flaws.[26] This failed attempt indicates a cinema sought after by indigenous theatrical organizations to gain a foothold for traditional folk arts, similar to the Japanese *rensageki* of the silent era.[27] One year later, in 1956, Gongyueshe decided to film one of its popular shows. Unlike Duma, the company took no chances and asked an experienced *rensageki* director to get involved. Even though it is based on a popular opera, *Xue Pinggui and Wang Baochuan* was an experiment in incorporating cinematic elements into a traditional theatrical presentation in order to rejuvenate it. Tracking shots, irises, symbolic inserts, close-ups, and rack focus were used to give the familiar repertoire a new look.[28] Its huge popularity took the company by surprise, but it lost no time making other films in this vein. This opera film marks the beginning of the first Golden Age of Taiwanese production.

Some examples include opera films like *Pang Gu opens the sky* (Pang Gu kaitian, 1962; dir. Hong Xinde) and *Grandma Yang sheds her cocoon* (Yangling popo tuoke ji, 1962; dir. Li Quanxi). The former has a perceptive frame story in which little boys with bamboo poles harass a fortune-teller, claiming they want to open the sky, like Pang Gu. They show the man a picture book they have been studying. The fortune-teller explains the sky is too high for mortals to reach, even with long poles. Besides being a god, Pang Gu lived in the primordial mud a long, long time ago, and, by the way (he asks), would you like to hear the whole story? At this point the scene shifts from the spellbound children to the Xin nanguang (New southern light) opera troupe, which dramatizes a folklore version of the creation story. For the transition to heaven, the sound track has chimes playing the Christmas carol "It Came Upon a Midnight Clear." The film is less opera-on-film than a charming mix of songs, myths, monsters, and stylized fights, alternating between theatrical sets and mountain locations. On location, the story tells how prehistoric apelike humans learned to do all the things gods did: build houses, make fire, perform rituals, play tricks, fight, and drink.

Besides being a veritable local entertainment form, as *taiyu pian* quickly developed into a profitable venture they began to expand and diversify by drawing freely from all sorts of cinematic idioms. Far from being isolated or parochial, *taiyu pian* were highly imitative of Japanese, Hollywood, and Hong Kong genres, stories, and styles. This type of Taiwanese film was promiscuous and elaborate. *True rose, fake rose* (Zhenjia hong meigui, 1966; dir. Liang Zhefu) is a wartime spy story that takes place in Amoy (Xiamen), Tokyo, and Taiwan. Liang had made an earlier film that year called *Red rose spy*. Along with Japanese, Hong Kong, and Hollywood films, *taiyu pian* also copied the James Bond franchise. Liang was from Hong Kong and had already made over a hundred Cantonese-language films as assistant director before starting a career in Taiwan.[29] *True rose* has the requisite ingredients of intrigue, disguise, and agile, ninja-like spies, whose tight black gear almost conceals the fact they are attractive women (the film stars Bai Lan) (fig. 1.1). The women work at a pottery factory in the daytime and easily seduce bumbling Japanese sergeants looking for clues.

More typical is *Morning train from Taipei* (Taibei fa de zaoban che, 1962; dir. Liang Zhefu). This lurid melodrama, made for Jixing Company, is a cautionary tale about going to the big city and the difficulty of returning home. With a sick mother, innocent Xiulan (Bai Lan again) moves to Taipei to earn money as a taxi dancer. She is remade into a stylish city girl, but at the cost of her innocence and virginity. Her country boyfriend comes to the rescue but he is beaten by thugs and goes blind. Meanwhile, Xiulan can only escape bondage by killing her lascivious consort with a pair of scissors. During the struggle, her face is splashed with acid and she is badly disfigured. In addition, she is given a long sentence by the judge. But in the end she is briefly united with her boyfriend, who now cannot see her disfigured face and agrees to wait for her while she is imprisoned.

Morning train exemplifies several characteristics of Taiwanese-language film. First, the film ends on a blatant appeal to the audience: "What will happen to these unlucky lovers? Will they ever be reunited? Be sure to watch the next chapter of *Morning train!*" These concluding titles indicate the serial structure of this and many Taiwanese films, partly accounting for their large numbers. Actually, the second part of *Morning train* was never made. But this film follows another title by the same director called *Last train from Kaohsiung* (Gaoxiong fa de moban che, 1962). In a way, then, *Morning train* (Part One) is itself a follow-up of an earlier film, indicating narrative overlap and a serialized mode of production.

The film also has an integral flashback structure: in the opening scene a painter is working on an abstract and rather ugly portrait of a woman. This shifts to a scene in the country where the painter looks for picturesque subjects. He finds Xiulan, a beautiful peasant girl who is the film's protagonist. Xiulan then takes over the

1.1 Taiwanese-language film star, Bai Lan
(COURTESY TAIPEI FILM ARCHIVE)

story. Only late in the film is the painter brought back, motivating the portrait after Xiulan's horrible disfigurement is explained.

Finally, the film employs deft parallels between city and country, such as a sound match between a trumpet blaring in a Taipei nightclub and the soft sounds of the boyfriend's flute.[30] Not only is the contrast between city and country accentuated; the danger of the city's lure is underlined because the flute becomes a way for the blind man to survive on the cold city streets. In this film too, a wide range of popular soundtrack music is used, from a remix of a popular Mandarin song written by Hong Kong's eminent Mandarin pop songwriter Zhou Lanping, to an appropriation of Hollywood music such as the galley slave theme from *Ben-Hur*.

Why were *taiyu pian* so prolific? In the late 1950s and early '60s, foreign films and Hong Kong Mandarin films continued to dominate Taiwan's screens, even though *taiyu pian* were made in the hundreds. The imports provided an important template for low-budget *taiyu pian*. Small Taiwanese studios and distributors did not have sufficient clout to compete with major corporations so they were not as profitable. But *taiyu pian* continued to be made, and shown, in volume. Low-budget *taiyu pian* used a familiar idiom, well-known operas, and folk repertoires to attract loyal local audiences. These audiences were sufficient to sustain *taiyu pian* production through the late 1960s. Another factor that contributed to the flourishing of *taiyu pian* was the pragmatism of CMPC. Compared with the meager figure of local Mandarin-language film production, *taiyu pian* were far more numerous, thrifty, and popular. When CMPC was formed in 1954 to make Mandarin-language films, it averaged only two to three pictures per year for the first few years. CMPC was too big for its own production needs. Its people and its facilities were therefore utilized by the burgeoning Taiwanese-language film industry. CMPC was happy to lease its facilities and equipment to Taiwanese producers, and its staff was pleased to have work. For example, CMPC leased He Jiming its facilities to complete postproduction of *Xue Pinggui and Wang Baochuan*.[31] CMPC director Li Jia worked on a number of *taiyu pian* before he was given feature assignments by the company, which is discussed below.[32] In addition, a new foreign-currency control ordinance was passed that allowed more black-and-white film stock to be imported into Taiwan.

It is important to note that *taiyu pian* borrowed liberally from foreign sources even though its spoken language was distinctly local. There were many crossovers not only to foreign but also to Mandarin-language film. This free "mixing" of Taiwanese film is apparent in titles such as *Tarzan and treasure* (Taishan yu baozang, 1965), *Laurel and Hardy 007* (Wangge liuge linglingqi, 1967), *Drunken swordsman and Zatoichi* (Da zuixia yu mang jianke, 1967), *Arabian nights* (Tian fang ye tan, 1963), and *Alibaba and the forty thieves* (Alibaba yu cishi dadao, 1963). *Tarzan and treasure* depicts a Taiwanese Tarzan fighting off Macao triads in Malay jungles. *Laurel and Hardy 007* is a cocktail of Hollywood slapstick and spy clichés. With the success of King Hu's *Come Drink with Me* (Da zuixia) in 1966 and the long-running Japanese blind swordsman series, *Drunken swordsman and Zatoichi* pays tribute to popular martial arts films from both Hong Kong and Japan.

The bride from hell (Diyu xinniang, 1965) is an adaptation of *Jane Eyre*, by way of Hitchcock's *Rebecca*. This widescreen picture is an exception to the predominantly B-picture quality of *taiyu pian*. Made by the Japanese-trained Xin Qi, *Bride* is a stylish thriller that begins briskly, then becomes ghostly and melodramatic as a murder plot is gradually uncovered. It boasts many flashy visual touches, from an extreme long take of a "haunted" house to canted point-of-view shots to split screens and eerie low angles. The setting is generic idle rich on the coast, with nightly cocktails, white suits, convertibles, and jazz bands. The music is equally eclectic: Burt Bacharach, "Danny Boy," the James Bond theme, and Japanese folk songs are all sampled, giving the picture an "international" flavor. The film's stars, Jin Mei and Ke Junxiong, recall Audrey Hepburn and Cary Grant types. In narrative, visual style and sound, *Bride* could just as well have been made in Hong Kong, Tokyo, or Hollywood (fig. 1.2).

In many ways, *taiyu pian* shared traits with Cantonese film production in Hong Kong in the 1950s and the 1960s—low budget, volume production, makeshift, and utterly recycled. But unlike its Hong Kong counterparts, *taiyu pian* was never

1.2 *The Bride from Hell* (1965; dir. Xin Qi)   (COURTESY TAIPEI FILM ARCHIVE)

given a "second" life. After a short period of decline in the late 1960s, Cantonese film made a successful comeback by introducing comedies featuring new urban colloquial idioms.[33] Its resurrection depended on the fact that Cantonese, Hong Kong's majority Chinese language, was never usurped by English. This contrasted with the gradual ascendancy of Mandarin in Taiwan. Postwar baby-boomers in Hong Kong were able to use their mother tongue, Cantonese, to forge a strong local identity in the early 1970s. Cantonese film aided and abetted this development. But none of these conditions applied to *taiyu pian*. Instead, political and social institutions worked against the growth of the Taiwanese film industry. The KMT's language policy suppressed the use of *minnan* language in public institutions and the mass media. The arrival of television in 1960, broadcasting predominantly in Mandarin, precluded a younger generation of audience for Taiwanese film.[34]

Other changes in the industry contributed to the decline of *taiyu pian*. First, local Mandarin-language film, with its higher production values, got under way in earnest in the mid-1960s. These included not only CMPC's "healthy realist" genre but the combined products of Grand Pictures, Union, and the First Film Enterprise. Some *taiyu pian* directors, like Li Xing and Li Jia, decamped to Mandarin productions and began their second careers in healthy realism. Production of Mandarin films became truly full-fledged with the appearance of costume melodramas based on novels written by a young woman writer, Qiong Yao, the pen name of popular romance writer Chen Ping. Both CMPC and Li Hanxiang's Grand Pictures quickly signed up Qiong Yao for multipicture adaptations. Between 1965 and 1971, no fewer than twenty films were made from Qiong Yao's novels. The turn-of-the-century Republican period setting in many Qiong Yao stories suited

Li's production preferences at Grand: rich costumes, traditional Chinese architecture, and generational conflict. CMPC saw the potential for this women-centered melodrama as a sentimental but commercial offshoot of healthy realism.

Finally, color films became the norm by 1965 (the first film shot in color was in 1962), and color was simply too expensive and logistically complex for the small, artisanal Taiwanese-language film industry.* Nonetheless, *taiyu pian* continued to be made, in ever smaller numbers for a dwindling audience.[35] By this time the KMT had largely accomplished its mission to forge a new, Mandarin-speaking Taiwanese nation, though this project came at a high price. One of many such costs was the fading and disappearance of *taiyu pian* cinema. Taiwanese film directors like Li Xing, Li Jia, and actors like Ke Junxiong realized that *taiyu pian* was at its end and made the transition to Mandarin-language film. Other prominent directors like Xin Qi, Li Quanxi, and actors like Jin Mei simply switched to television.

"A Good Chinese Cinema": Central Motion Picture Corporation and the Rise of Healthy Realism

Commercial, ephemeral, and escapist, *taiyu pian* offered a form of entertainment that the KMT wanted to discourage. Since its founding, and especially after 1949, the party saw itself as the sole legitimate repository of Chinese polity. It therefore sought to promote a culture of civic unity based on mainland Han ethnicity and Mandarin anticommunism. This was a task to be undertaken by CMPC. As we have seen, CMPC's production output was relatively slow at first, but in the mid-1960s, when political and economic conditions stabilized, studio executives began to think seriously about the making of a Chinese "national cinema," incorporating in that term the Chinese mainland along with Taiwan. CMPC's mandate from the KMT was to make films that promoted a nationhood authorized and governed by the Nationalist party.

A new opportunity arose in 1961 when CMPC's studios were rebuilt in a suburb of Taipei; the old studio in Taichung was destroyed by fire in 1959. Under newly appointed manager Henry Gong Hong (Kung Hung), a task force was charged with creating a new, "good" Chinese cinema that would unify and uplift Taiwan's

---

*The year 1962 marks the use of color in a Taiwanese production and this was a *taiyu pian*. However, most histories do not count this as the first for two reasons: this was shot by Japanese technicians with Japanese equipment, so this is why Chinese-language histories only acknowledge *Oyster Girl* (1964) as the first locally made color film. The second reason is that before 1994, when Taipei Film Archive published the first oral histories of *taiyu pian*, the contributions to Taiwan film history of *taiyu pian* were overlooked and/or ignored. We also acknowledge the problematic status of "firsts" as if the earliest uses of color, sound, or other innovations provide any solid explanation of their importance.

audiences. Gong Hong proposed the concept of "healthy realism" (*jiankang xieshi zhuyi*) to undertake a new, aggressive orientation that served the party's mission to make a good Chinese national cinema. The first two projects were *Oyster Girl* (Ke nü, 1964; dir. Li Xing and Li Jia) and *Beautiful Duckling* (Yangya renjia, 1965; dir. Li Xing). As the new national cinema, these pictures had an influence out of proportion to their numbers and their political aims.

Gong Hong coined the term after being impressed by the neorealist pictures from Italy two decades before. Gong liked their realist approach, but did not want to follow their dark, sometimes pessimistic, themes of poverty and corruption. He proposed a modification of the Italian movement: adapting its technical style to local stories, which encouraged a more uplifting, healthy appeal to Taiwan's audiences.

There were three main elements—style, theme, ideology—in the constitution of healthy realism: in style, these films borrowed from Italian neorealism, emphasizing real locations over sets and countryside over city. Ordinary people were the heroes of healthy realist films, especially farm workers or fishermen. The style of healthy realism aimed to move away from bombastic, blatant propaganda. One sees government policy represented in these films, but it is integrated into characters and story. For instance, kind government officials offer help to peasants struggling to develop their agricultural practices or to contend with the elements.

In theme, these films were humanistic and what we would now call environmentally aware, extolling the beauty and harmony of nature, a premodern, pastoral lifestyle, and corresponding social relationships. Ideologically, healthy realism depicted stable, peaceful, and organic Chinese communities in which tensions and conflicts, whether individual, class, or ethnic, are eventually and naturally resolved. The main point of these films was to establish that malevolence does not really exist in Taiwan society: villainy, corruption, and violent conflict are banished in these films, in contrast to the Manichean dichotomies of propaganda films of the 1930s and '40s. This delicacy was certainly in stark contrast with realities of life in Taiwan under the KMT.

There is a shot in *Beautiful Duckling* that graphically sums this up. Director Li Xing uses a tracking shot to hint at discord, but pulls back to reveal a plenitude of natural delights. At the county fair, we see a small hand reach for a mango from a stand. The hand belongs to a little boy who surreptitiously rolls away the large fruit and walks off with it. One expects an angry vendor to come running, but as the shot moves back and upward, we see this is not a fruit stand at all, but a much larger exhibit made up of colorful fruit and vegetables. The mangos are piled high into a triangular patch and stand next to a section of green radishes, attractively cross-hatched, which contrast nicely with alternating piles of watermelons, carrots, and so on. The whole ornamental tower of produce stands nearly twenty feet high and signals the richness of rural Taiwan's agriculture. A little boy pinching one mango does not even dent the largesse of Taiwanese bounty. This image echoes a motif of nature stimulating artistic impressions. Watercolors of rural Taiwan and its picturesque ducks, painted by Lan Yinding, a celebrated artist known for his Chinese ink paintings, are introduced at the beginning of this film.

Oyster Girl and *Beautiful Duckling*

Oyster Girl was a propitious start to healthy realism. It was able to bear out Henry Gong Hong's hopes, being one of the top ten box office earners of the year 1964 and taking its place beside the big Hong Kong productions by Shaw Brothers and MP and GI (Motion Picture and General Investment). Boasting beautiful seascapes and filmed in Technicolor, the film was a triumph for its two directors, Li Xing and Li Jia, who in turn was also the cinematographer. In fact, the two shared director credit because the film was the first Taiwan-made widescreen color feature. (See note about color, p. 25.)

Oyster Girl is a sea pastoral about separated lovers. Together with other women workers, the eponymous heroine spends her days tending artificially cultivated oysters on Taiwan's west coast. Nature plays a major role in its beneficence and its dangers, such as typhoons. Village life also takes its toll in the form of petty rivalries, a local election, and addictions such as drinking and gambling. A memorable brawl in the oyster beds has rival girls scratching and biting each other through the muddy tidepools, heedless of their fragile mollusk crop. This racy scene reverses the central conceit of the film—impervious hard shell protecting sweet, soft flesh—to reveal female spite simmering beneath a harmonious setting. Though played partly for titillation, the brawl also depicts a primitive underbelly in Taiwan, a backward community in need of modernization. The next scene shows the girls being patched up in a clean, modern clinic whose charismatic doctor easily wins the village election.

Beautiful Duckling (fig. 1.3) centers on Xiao Yue, the dutiful daughter of a kindly duck farmer, Lin. Her secret, of which she is unaware, is that she is an orphan. An unscrupulous half-brother blackmails Lin, threatening to take Xiao Yue away to a decadent life in Taiwanese opera. She is also pursued by a fat neighbor boy (the same actor plays the village idiot in *Oyster Girl*). When she rejects him the boy lets fly: "Your ducks don't belong to your family and neither do you!" Xiao Yue is a character in thrall to various men, for whom she is chattel: potential wife, domestic helper, performer. Even her beloved father Lin keeps her identity a secret from her; like the ducklings she cares for, she has imprinted herself upon a stranger, while the man she despises turns out to be her own blood. Of course, when she discovers the truth she is shattered. Xiao Yue's fate parallels that of the old man's ducklings,

1.3 *Beautiful Duckling* (1965; dir. Li Xing): the beginning of healthy realism   (COURTESY CMPC)

which are crossbred and individually identified in a new genetic experiment. In contrast, Lin's neighbor and rival raises ducks the old-fashioned way, as a noisy flock of indistinguishable birds. Xiao Yue's future is dependent on her choice of identity and role. Though she is a peasant, Xiao Yue is called upon to outgrow her naïveté and exercise responsible judgments. This means balancing filial piety with self-awareness and active choice.

In the end she chooses to go with father, as does her foster brother, which seems to teach a Confucian lesson. But the emphasis is on her choice among several alternatives. Will she go with her blood brother and his grasping wife, who want to start up a new opera troupe? From a strict Confucian standpoint, this would be her most appropriate obligation. Or can she start her own family with a young rice farmer to whom she is attracted? This is what her father wants most for her. Xiao Yue's dilemma is the universal human one of growing up, which inevitably brings renunciation along with development. Here, Xiao Yue renounces blood ties and the promise of her own nuclear family to remain with her foster, but more familiar, kin (fig. 1.4).

Because of the success of these films, healthy realism became an artistically satisfactory and commercially viable subgenre. CMPC followed this successful formula with *Orchids and My Love* (Wo nü ruolan, 1966; dir. Li Jia) and *The Silent*

1.4 *Beautiful Duckling*: healthy farm girls   (COURTESY CMPC)

Wife (Ya nü qingshen, 1965; dir. Li Xing). The former, like *Beautiful Duckling*, is a blatantly Oedipal story of a beautiful little girl struck down by polio. She relies on the unconditional love of her father to get her through a terrible ordeal. The sentimentality dovetails nicely with conservative Confucian family values. But *Orchids and My Love* is more than a simple female Oedipal melodrama. Like its predecessors, it introduces agriculture and country life—in this case, an orchid farm—to integrate its healthy realist principles. The triumphant ending for the girl is her independence, not the ability to walk again, as she is transformed from a spoiled little ballerina into an orchid rancher. If *Oyster Girl* and *Beautiful Duckling* are the touchstone of healthy realism, *Orchids and My Love* is the prototype of ideal healthy realism. It shows that healthy realism is adaptable; it is not limited to policy films but is applicable to popular genres like women's films, historical epics, comedies, and even Chinese "noodle" westerns (outlaw stories set in China's far West).

Though it is fair to characterize these films as melodramatic, was healthy realism a movement or a genre? We might consider this question in comparison with Italian neorealism. Similarities with neorealism include a preoccupation with the working and peasant classes; an interest in locations, with a corresponding resistance to studio work; and in narrative form, simple stories and straightforward narrative styles. Healthy realist films are character-driven, using step-by-step cause-effect structures, and given to empathy and identification with sympathetic characters.

Unlike neorealism, healthy realism was uncritical of its chosen social millieux. Directors like Roberto Rossellini, Luchino Visconti, and Vittorio De Sica, at least in the beginning, shone a harsh light on Italian society, exposing its inhumane structures and practices. Their uses of melodrama centered on a defeated nation and depleted masculine energy, while healthy realism emphasizes women's suffering, victimization, and powerlessness. Women in healthy realism eventually find relief, or prevail over their circumstances, to achieve a happy ending with family and community. Thus, unlike neorealism, the "good" Chinese cinema of healthy realism was a cinema of closure, of resolution, and of reassurance. It was, like neorealism, a movement, but a calculated movement with an explicit policy of national uplift. Its characteristics were circulated to writers, directors, and stars as doctrines to be followed, rather than as organically derived from real historical events.

Healthy realism was meant to be a movement, but it behaved like a genre. It therefore represents an invented, indigenous, and unexpectedly fertile Taiwan genre. Its motivation was civic rather than commercial or even artistic. It nicely straddles the distinction between state-sponsored propaganda and commercially motivated mass entertainment. Proof of this can be seen in the way it evolved in different directions, such as straight melodramas, comedy, and musical comedies. Occasionally it became something very close to the opposite of healthy realism, both sensual and stylized. Two directors, Li Xing and Bai Jingrui, show the evolution from prototypical healthy realism into its various ramifications.

Li Xing, Jack-of-all-Trades

It will be recalled that Li Xing got his start in *taiyu pian*, the Taiwanese-language film industry. Unlike most *taiyu pian* directors who had difficulties in relocating to the Mandarin film industry, Li Xing made the transition smoothly. Born in 1930 and educated in Shanghai, Li followed his family to Taiwan in the postwar era. His first Mandarin film was *Our Neighbors* (Jietou xiangwei, 1963), a "realist" portrait of an impoverished Taipei neighborhood (fig. 1.5). Li also made, along with cinematographer Li Jia, the first and most influential healthy realist film, *Oyster Girl* (1964). Before this, Li had already made fourteen Taiwanese features and successfully created a Taiwan version of the Laurel and Hardy comedy serials. Films from this serial such as *Laurel and Hardy's grand Taiwan tour* (Wangge liuge you taiwan, 1958) and *Monkey King and Zhu Bajie* (Sun Wukong yu Zhu Bajie, 1959) were big hits.[36] This comic pair starred in seven of Li's own films, as well as many others. Li

1.5 *Our Neighbors* (1963; dir. Li Xing)

Xing is the most important director to understand Taiwan film history before the 1980s. This is because Li embodies the major structures and tensions—linguistic, commercial, ideological—we have identified so far.

Li made films on either side of the divide between Taiwanese and Mandarin-language production, but not at the same time. When he had the opportunity to make Mandarin films exclusively, starting with four pictures for CMPC, he never went back to *taiyu pian*. Despite this clean break, Li later acknowledged that *taiyu pian* was a valuable nurturing of his directing skills. Precisely because of its low budgets, Taiwanese film production was in urgent need of new directors, even if they had little or no experience. This was how Li got into directing in 1958. Due to tight budgets and schedules, Li Xing was learning to maximize a visualization of dramatic premises on shoestring resources.[37] However, different from most Taiwanese film directors who churned out an average of ten pictures a year, Li was working at a leisurely pace of only fourteen films in eight years. Li's relatively modest output continued for the rest of his career. Given this, we see a filmmaker who takes his time, taking his craft seriously, and who sees himself as a socially responsible artist/auteur.

Li's earliest auteur "signature" is more pronounced in his high moral purpose than in his technical skills. For instance in his first film, the semidocumentary *Laurel and Hardy's grand Taiwan tour*, Li places his critique of superstition above formal, stylistic concerns.[38] A combination of documentary style and silent gags is used to mask sloppy writing, rudimentary camera work, and a lack of production design. In his following films, Li does not hesitate to introduce modernity into his stories, balanced by the maintenance of traditional values. In *Our Neighbors*, produced by his family-owned company Independent (Zili), Li's didactic inclinations are revealed most obviously. The movie centers on a garbage man, Uncle Shi, and his poor neighbors in the slum area of Taipei. The film begins with location shots as Shi finishes his work, strolling back to his neighborhood. The camera then follows Shi through sleepy Taipei streets, in an amateur fashion, recording the city's premodern sights. This candid view of Taipei scenes is reminiscent of the urban imagery in the Shanghai realist films of the 1930s (which Li would have seen) and contrasts with the predominant studio setting in both Taiwanese and Mandarin films of this period. When the film cuts to an aerial shot overlooking the slum neighborhood, a series of subtitles begins: "This story takes place at one corner of the city. People who live there know no hatred but love—love between a mother and a daughter, between fellow citizens, between an orphan girl and her poor but loving friends. Only a society filled with love can make real progress, and have beautiful hope." When this prologue runs line by line across the screen, the fluid camera pans across from one neighbor to another, depicting a peaceful, cozy community atmosphere as everyone begins their day. At the end of the prologue, the camera tilts up and dollies back to give a concluding view of the neighborhood. Li shows an amazing self-consciousness in coordinating the visual presentation with the written prologue. This opening neatly summarizes Li's auteurism: a didactic cinema in sync with a documentary proclivity.

Li's moralizing signature in his pre-CMPC days is expressed in two effects: the lack of stars and a focus on filial love. Before *Oyster Girl*, Li rarely worked with major stars. *Taiyu pian*'s somewhat coarse, market-driven character led Li to work exclusively in two types of genres—opera and comedy. His *Laurel and Hardy* series was sufficient to make him a commercially worthy filmmaker. But when he made "serious" films, Li instantly switched to his favorite subject matter, filial love. *Our Neighbors* predates *Beautiful Duckling* in Li's lifelong interest in this implicitly "incestuous" subject matter. Uncle Shi adopts the neighbor girl Pearl when her mother dies. He even changes his job in order to save Pearl from being humiliated at school. But he soon falls ill from hard physical work and Pearl decides to skip school to help him. Two neighbors thus become loving father and daughter when both try their best to save each other. Eventually Pearl happily accepts being the daughter of a garbage man, and Uncle Shi goes back to his old job.

Perhaps this didactic tendency and the realist proximity to the Chinese mainland films of the 1930s is what brought him to the attention of CMPC, founded on the idea that cinema should teach lessons first and provide entertainment second. We see this clearly in *Oyster Girl*, in which modernity and democracy take the form of a clean, fair village council election, easily won by the dashing young physician. In *The Silent Wife* we see the recurrence of a didactic preface to provide a moral frame for the story. The film is about a fatal marriage set in the Republican period. A man (Ke Junxiong) marries his childhood fiancée even though she is born deaf. At first they live happily because she is beautiful and intelligent. Then tragedy hits. The couple's little girl is born as another deaf-mute. The husband can't bear to live with it and runs away. After years go by, the aging, silent wife dies from overwork and fruitless waiting. But her husband returns to unite with their daughter.

The Silent Wife, adapted from a short story by Qiong Yao, would have been a typical women's film if Li had followed the story faithfully. But with his healthy realist treatment, the film takes a different direction. It begins with the husband's voice-over plea of how we must not discriminate against anyone because of physical impairment. His handicapped wife is, in fact, better than any healthy person. This moral overtone runs throughout the film in specific pedagogical points. A special school is set up to help the little girl and children like her. The wife and the daughter communicate in sign language, and finally the husband runs away to avoid polygamy (since his parents are about to get him a concubine) and to stop the genetic reproduction of disabilities.

Li's didactic signature is also visible in his independent productions, which he continued intermittently throughout his later career. In 1965 he made *The Mount of Virtue* (Zhenjie paifang) in which a widow throws herself into the ocean to avoid making a choice between her desire and her obligation. An arch is being built to commemorate her pure loyalty while she is in love with a man in the village. Instead of putting an end to this Confucian tyranny, she resorts to the most destructive resolution. Here Li maintains his sympathetic attitude toward Confucian traditions by giving the widow no choice whatsoever.

Taiwan critics often attribute Li's conservatism to his family background, a convenient way to accept Li's persistent vision of traditional Chinese culture sandwiched within a modern/Westernized context.[39] Li is known for his filial piety. He openly acknowledged that parental love supersedes any other kind of relationship in his world. This explains the centrality of the father/son duo in many of his films. Criticism arises when Li's auteur signature becomes "backward," when his traditional values appear to obstruct any possibility for "social and cultural reform."[40] *The Road* (Lu, 1967; CMPC), considered the most ambitiously "serious" film by the director, provoked critics to question his (in)ability to envision true social progress.

The Road is about a rebellious son returning home and submitting to his father's will. This is a theme that Li revisits in his 1979 award-winning *Good Morning, Taipei*

(Zao'an taibei). A college man falls in love with an older married woman and decides to quit school. The father's tenacious love and need to see his son go straight impresses her. She leaves the young man for his own good and he returns to his father. Like *The Mount of Virtue*, every domestic disturbance or personal struggle will eventually be resolved, and order is temporarily restored. Reconciliation rests on the premise that romantic love and sexual relationships are inferior to filial love. But what is alarming about this line of argument is that a male-dominated, class-bound identity is represented as a free, individual choice. The woman's decision to relinquish her lover is, in fact, a self-defeating statement that age, class, and social status override free love. The triumph of patriarchy places *The Road* as another healthy realist milestone for CMPC, but the audience sent a warning to Li. On one occasion Li talked about his frustration when he saw a young audience, including his own son, flooding theaters to see Zhang Che's *One-Armed Swordsman* (1967). Meanwhile, his film couldn't attract an audience: "only older folks from mainland China, young intellectuals and a few college students went to see *The Road*."[41] After this film, Li turned to more lucrative genres.

Parallel to his lifelong relationship with CMPC, Li continued to make films for himself and for other small independent companies. For instance, Li also made films for Union Pictures and codirected an omnibus film with Li Hanxiang, King Hu, and Bai Jingrui for Grand Pictures in 1969. This film, in which each emotion is treated by a different director, is called *Four Moods* (Xi nu ai le) (fig. 1.6). In 1970, with Bai Jingrui, he founded his second production company called Dazhong (The People's) to enjoy more freedom—moving between commercial film and serious films without having to worry about aligning with official policy. Under Dazhong, Li directed several award-winning films such as *Autumn Execution* (Qiu jue, 1971), *He Never Gives Up* (Wongyang zhong de yi tiao chuan, 1978), and *Story of a Small Town* (Xiaocheng gushi, 1979). The latter two are heavily imbued with healthy realism.

Li never completely identified himself as a "national filmmaker," synonymous with the official agenda of CMPC, despite his commitment to making serious moral drama. Flexibility and relative independence permitted Li Xing to work in a wide variety of genres. In his early career, he made mostly comedies and folktales that could be made quickly and cheaply. In his healthy realist films with CMPC, he directed contemporary dramas about country life. Simultaneously, he would also direct costume melodramas set in the early twentieth-century Republican period (e.g., *The Mount of Virtue, The Silent Wife, Autumn Execution*). Flexibility also allowed him to enjoy an easy switch from a moral director to commercial romantic melodramas. When literary adaptations became a fashionable mode of packaging romantic melodrama, Li did not hesitate to capitalize on this profitable trend. Qiong Yao's novels provided the major resource for literary adaptations, which not only became the dominant genre in Taiwan but also created major stars for the industry. World-famous stars like Bri-

1.6 *Left to right:* Bai Jingrui, King Hu, Henry Gong Hong, Li Hanxiang, and Li Xing presenting the portmanteau film *Four Moods* (1969)

gitte Lin Qingxia got their start in Qiong Yao melodramas in the 1970s. Qiong Yao adaptations were important not only within Taiwan's film culture but also in their effectiveness in promoting Taiwan stars around the world.

Li was the first to direct a Qiong Yao adaptation, entitled *Four Loves* (Wanjun biaomei), a CMPC production in 1965. In the 1970s, Li Xing's career reached a high point with his sixth installment from Qiong Yao's novels. In 1973 and 1974, Li became the number one box office director in Taiwan and Hong Kong with his two hits, *The Young Ones* (Caiyun fei, 1973) and *Where the Seagull Flies* (Hai'ou fei chu, 1974). Both were based on Qiong Yao novels. These melodramas not only established him as a ruling commercial director, they also helped mark the peak of Taiwan film's so-called Golden Age (when Taiwan films were popular enough to get advance financing from around Southeast Asia). Romantic melodramas, dominated by Qiong Yao adaptations, comedies, and martial arts films made up the core that supported a flourishing industry.

Bai Jingrui, "Unhealthy" Realist

Like Li Xing, Bai Jingrui (1931–1997) was a director of contemporary drama, avoiding martial arts and period, costume epics. He also made pictures in a variety of genres: healthy realism, Qiong Yao melodrama, comedy. Like Li, Bai split his time between "official" pictures for CMPC and smaller, independent projects. If Li was the major figure in healthy realism and Qiong Yao adaptations, Bai Jingrui still provides a productive contrast. Instead of crossing over from *taiyu pian*, Bai began in the late 1960s, in Mandarin-language production.

Like Li Xing, Bai was born in China and came to Taiwan in 1949. Unlike Li, who stayed close to his family, Bai was a refugee student who was homeless most of the time. He saw *Open City* and *Bicycle Thief* as a college student and later went to Italy to study film. After he returned to Taiwan, as the first Chinese graduate from Rome's Centro Sperimentale di Cinematografia in 1963, he was hired by CMPC. Initially he proposed six projects to CMPC, which were all rejected because of their "sharp" social implications. Unable to direct, he was assigned to assist productions for the first healthy realist films such as *Oyster Girl, Beautiful Duckling,* and so on. Later he codirected with Li Xing and Li Jia a healthy realist propaganda film, *Fire bulls* (Huan wo heshan, 1966). In 1967 he was eventually given a chance to direct his first feature, *Lonely Seventeen,* starring Ke Junxiong and Tang Baoyun (from *Duckling*), provided that he smooth its sharp critical edges. The story is about a seventeen-year-old girl's sexual desire for her cousin. When the cousin dies in a car accident, the girl takes it as punishment for her transgressive desire and suffers from schizophrenia. Eventually she is cured when the truth dawns on her that his death has nothing to do with her.

Bai intended to criticize the stifling lives of youth in the industrialized towns of Taiwan, but CMPC insisted it be a "socially responsible" film and, hence, the happy ending. Bai had to apply a "romantic" treatment to mask his social critique. Here is his complaint about this interference:

> Teenagers in our times are under a lot of stress—from the lack of parental care and rigid training in schools as well. They have to resort to fantasy to seek paradise. Hence all sorts of twisted psychology and weird behaviors. I was going to directly tackle this serious phenomenon but CMPC was afraid that the Communists would use it to attack our government. As an artist, I should have insisted on my original intention, but as a CMPC director, I also needed to understand my responsibility. So I changed the story quite a bit and turned it into a romantic film. Anyone can see that this film has no business being a romance story! No matter how well it has been received, I am not happy with it at all.[42]

One may see how Bai would be upset about his decision. The film ends with the parents admitting their mistaken educational approach. In the last scene we see the girl join a skiing excursion organized by the KMT's Youth Corps in Taiwan's snowy mountains. *Lonely Seventeen* placed fifth in the country's Top Ten movie list in 1967.[43]

Still, Bai won the best director prize at the Golden Horse Film Awards that year, upsetting peers like King Hu for *Dragon Inn* and Li Xing for *The Road*. Following the acclaimed *Lonely Seventeen*, Bai dropped his trenchant topics and turned to comedy, a safer terrain for filmmakers working in an official studio. He directed *The Bride and I* (Xinniang yu wo) in 1968, and *Accidental Trio* (Jintian bu huijia) in 1969. The former is a comedy documenting the evolution of a Chinese wedding and its sociocultural contexts. He experimented with a few techniques such as the use of a reflexive, extradiegetic commentary to frame the story, an animated sequence for the conventional opening/closing credits, and a surrealist, subjective point of view. Bai's intention to use these "over-the-top" expressions was to emphasize a "healthier" gender politics in modern society. These innovative devices established Bai's caliber as a style-conscious director without sacrificing healthy realist principles. *Accidental Trio* (literally, "Nobody goes home tonight") is another example of Bai's satirical energy. In 1996 Sylvia Chang paid tribute to Bai by giving her family comedy *Tonight Nobody Goes Home* (written by Ang Lee's brother Lee Kang) the same Chinese title. Later he joined Li Xing, King Hu, and Li Hanxiang and directed the first part ("Joy") for Grand's omnibus *Four Moods* (1969; see fig. 1.6).

In addition to his experiments in form and narrative structure, Bai's ideological commitments were ambiguous and much less didactic than Li's. In a way, Bai's work could be considered "unhealthy" realism. In Li Xing we can see glimmers of dialectical developments whereby genres evolve in different, even opposite, directions. Bai took such developments much further than Li. One reason for this is Bai's directorial style, which contains not only technical experiments but may also delve into occasionally sordid aspects of contemporary Taiwan. Another factor, related to this, has to do with Bai's training in Italy, where he was exposed to neorealist techniques and narrative strategies. The result is a saturated, sweaty feel that is both stylized and true to the passions of Bai's working-class characters (cf. *Ossessione* [1942], Visconti's unauthorized treatment of James M. Cain's *The Postman Always Rings Twice*). Bai's work also points to the original Italian source for CMPC's conception of healthy realism. Still, depending on the funding source, Bai sometimes injects didactic messages into his stories, messages that sit uncomfortably with his sensual dramatic environments.

For example, Bai's *Goodbye Darling* (Zaijian Alang, 1971) has a number of moments that would have given Taiwan's censors plenty of worry (fig. 1.7). It was made for an independent company and takes place in Kaohsiung, southern Taiwan. An adaptation of a famous story, "A Race of Generals" (Jianjun zu), written by the leftist writer-critic Chen Yingzhen (Ch'en Ying-chen), it centers on a girl, Guizhi, working in a marching band. Marching bands in China are hired for weddings, funerals, and company ad campaigns and are often used as a variation on stories of itinerant players (cf. *Street Angel*, 1937; dir. Yuan Muzhi). In this story Guizhi

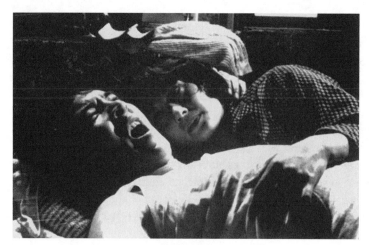

1.7 *Goodbye Darling* (1971; dir. Bai Jingrui)   (COURTESY TAIPEI FILM ARCHIVE)

negotiates advances from a much older musician, Lao Houzi (Old Monkey), who offers to pay her debts to the company if she marries him.

Bai's adaptation adds an additional character, Alang, to Chen's story and changes its focus. Alang is a specimen of traditional Taiwanese masculinity, unreconstructed by family duties, economic prospects, or modern codes of civility. Played by a well-known actor from *taiyu pian*, Ke Junxiong, Alang has the swagger of Elvis Presley and the raffish good looks of Ishihara Yujiro, the Japanese megastar from Nikkatsu. He sports a perm, wears loud shirts, and struts the neighborhood in wooden clogs (Japanese *geta*, much favored by gangsters). Alang also possesses a violent stubborn streak that works against the heroine's strenuous efforts to reform him.

Bai's handling of sexuality in this film is simple and exemplary: a series of big close-ups of Guizhi and Alang, faces sweating, as Alang deflowers her. There are repeated cutaways to a pair of hanging paper cranes, one resting on top of the other. The scene has no sound or music, not even that of the lovers breathing. Their faces radiate deep, ineffable pleasure, eyes closed and lips slightly parted. But it is their sweat that seems to catch the light most, along with flushed faces. Bai lingers on this, then the mood changes. Moments later, Guizhi delivers her postcoital demands that Alang marry her and become a responsible husband. Alang just laughs.

Narrative momentum comes from Guizhi's repeated attempts to domesticate Alang. He plays along, even once trying to make money as a street hawker. This fails, but Guizhi badgers and nags, even using her pregnancy and an offer of marriage from Houzi to ensnare Alang. He disappears, then returns in the nick of time to offer a fistful of money to Houzi. All would be well, but Guizhi demands to know where he got so much money. Alang reveals his new job as an all-night truck driver taking loads of live, well-fed pigs from Kaohsiung to markets in Taipei, 300 miles to the north. Mouth full, Alang happily explains, occasionally spitting bits of rice and spinach in his excitement. Because he drives so fast, overtaking other drivers on the dark roads, his pigs arrive in Taipei without yet having voided their bowels. Each pig is "two catties heavier!" Alang bellows. "Their shit turns into a shitload of extra money!"

Despite Alang's job satisfaction, Guizhi is alarmed. It is dangerous work; Alang has already crashed once. Guizhi puts her foot down. She will not allow this.

Here Bai sets up an unusual, flamboyant scene utilizing the wide screen. As the couple heatedly argue, he zooms madly into and back from their excited faces. They are approaching a standoff. This being a Scope film, the original effect must have been highly dizzying. He repeats the furious zooms three times. Then a new character enters the scene. It is Alang's boss and fellow driver. He moves in between the quarrelling couple. He tries to mediate, telling Guizhi he has two wives and six children, and all are happy. As he cajoles each in turn, Bai cuts in to close-ups of the boss's face. But he is facing the wrong direction, turning left to the wife, and right to Alang, who is ready to go back on the road. As a final flourish, the boss turns 180 degrees back around to face the camera, revealing a violation of the action's axis after the fact. Bai's shot setups and editing reverses the space and momentarily confuses spectators, but the overall effect of the scene is one of exacerbation, not relief. The boss's intervention does not mollify Guizhi, as intended. It makes things worse. She rebukes him, then gives Alang a final ultimatum: she announces she will return by train to her family in Taipei if he doesn't give up the job.

This escalating confrontation establishes the final, tragic collision between Guizhi and Alang. The film ends with a crash. In horror, Guizhi watches from the train as Alang tries to race his truck across the tracks. A coda shows her back in the marching band in a brand-new high-rise neighborhood. A voice-over informs us that there is no room in the new Taiwan for brutes like Alang, so prepare to say good-bye to all the Alangs of the world. The feeble attachment of a moral to this story of rich human fallibility is an example of the evolution of healthy realism into something ideologically unruly.

Another ambitious Bai Jingrui film combines a modernist style with an intricate narrative structure and some very traditional moral lessons. Made for CMPC, *Home Sweet Home* (Jia zai taibei, 1970; fig. 1.8) is an ensemble film with no less than fifteen major characters in three separate stories. It begins with a trans-Pacific flight approaching the Taipei airport. The screen splits into a number of Mondrian-

1.8 *Home Sweet Home* (1970; dir. Bai Jingrui)   (COURTESY TAIPEI FILM ARCHIVE)

like boxes, each containing different sets of characters talking about their plans in Taipei. As they meet their parties at the airport, these sets are juggled into three intersecting stories of alienation, crisis, and return. The film's structure is that of an omnibus film, in which each short story has a different look and feel. The first two use the split-screen montage-masking of the credit sequence, inviting viewers to make comparisons and judgments on characters.

One early scene is just as ostentatious as the one described above in *Goodbye Darling*. A foolish girl, Zhixia, has decided to marry a feckless waiter, Ho, because he promises to take her to America. As each member of her family—father, mother, brother, and sister-in-law—take turns scolding her, Bai zooms in and out of their shouting faces. Peeved, Zhixia turns and puts on a 45 rpm record. Suddenly, loud rockabilly music drowns out her relatives, but they keep on moving their mouths. As the music continues, Bai then splits up the screen using masking to isolate the heads of each remonstrating person. He plays with sound-image juxtapositions projected by Zhixia's heedlessness and indicates the paradigmatic quality of the family's objections. In other words, the friction between generations takes on an abstract quality, just as the masking and split screens seem to convey a sense of interchangeability to the stories being told.

Split screens are also used in more conventional ways. Zhixia meets her beau while he is trying unsuccessfully to romance a girl with whom he had been pen pals. While the waiter and Zhixia are courting, the jilted girl calls up her father back in town. Distraught, she appears in an iris on one side of the screen with her father on the other. In between we see Ho and Zhixia happily cavorting on the shores of Sun Moon Lake.

The first story is about a professional couple who decide to give up urban life in New York to help run the parents' ranch in the hills above Keelung. This decision is taken only after young Zhixia, the younger sister, has determined to marry, intending to leave her parents to go to America. It might seem fantastic that a professional Chinese couple returns from New York City to the wide-open range, livestock, and even a log house in Taiwan, but in fact the KMT initiated a rural homesteading scheme for veterans who otherwise would have been unemployed. Here the benefits of exercise and the outdoors—in contrast to the tense urban scrambles of New York—come together with a specific policy promoted by the government.

The second story deals with a somewhat louche woman, Lu, recently returned from the United States. She had been engaged to Wang, an artist, and now wants to restore the relationship and see how his career has progressed. Meanwhile, Wang is entranced by a beautiful teenager whom he employs as a model. A clash ensues between Lu, Wang, and the model, but all is tearfully resolved after the teenager confesses her innocence and admiration for Aunt Lu. Instead, she is joined by Lu to help run a nursery school—again, a new calling of nurture and honest living. The fascinating thing about this segment is the mise-en-scène. Most of it takes place in the artist's loft, which is decorated in the most garish, swinging-60s pastiche ever seen outside the films of Antonioni. In such a space, along with Bai's fragmentation of the story through more split screens, it is no surprise that the characters' mental health is precarious.

But it is the final story of *Home Sweet Home* that is most striking for its omissions. It is more-or-less straight melodrama about a man (Ke Junxiong again) returning from a ten-year stint in America to divorce his long-suffering Chinese wife. Immediately established is his possession of a Caucasian mistress waiting in America. Bai drops the split-screen device in this segment altogether; it never returns. It is almost as if he lost faith, or interest, in visual experiments when depicting such egregiously unfilial behavior. Against strenuous opposition from his own family, his adorable son, his old friends, and even the neighbors, the Ke Junxiong character doesn't have a chance. He holds out until the final minutes at the airport, though, agreeing only at the last moment to return to his Chinese wife and son. All happily climb into a moving truck to move house to a new high-rise apartment block. As in *Goodbye Darling*, the filial piety seems tacked on, a coda inconsistent with the narrative and stylistic excess that dominates the film.

Both *Home Sweet Home* and *Goodbye Darling* established Bai's "unhealthy" realist tendency with a critical and stylistic edge. *Goodbye Darling*, despite its acclaim at home and abroad, was a box office flop in Taiwan. Bai, under tremendous pressure and frustration, switched to romantic melodramas in the mid-1970s after he had failed to reinvent himself in two subsequent films—*Squire Hotel* (Laoye jiudian, 1971) and *Two ugly men* (Liangge choulou de nanren, 1973).[44]

Between 1974 and 1979, an unprecedented boom for Taiwan popular cinema, Bai made a total of eighteen films. Sixteen of these films are romantic melodramas. Among these sixteen films, *Love in a Cabin* (Baiwu zhi lian, 1974; CMPC), *Girlfriend* (Nü pengyou, 1975; First Film Enterprise; a Qiong Yao script), *Fantasies Behind the Pearly Curtain* (Yilian youmeng, 1976; First Film Enterprise; a Qiong Yao adaptation) were all box office hits. By the early 1980s, when romance could no longer sustain the industry, Bai Jingrui tried to reinvent his career with the support of Hong Kong–based First Film Enterprise. He made an anti-Communist film, *The Coldest Winter in Peking* (Huangtian houtu, 1981), which was banned, expectedly, by the Hong Kong government for endangering its "friendly relations with neighboring countries." In following years Bai appeared to run out of ideas and blindly followed the current fashions. Results include an exploitation social thriller, *Offend the law of God* (Nufan tiantiao) in 1982; a literary adaptation *The Last Night of Madam China* (Jin daban de zuihou yiye) in 1984 to reproduce the successful formula of the Taiwan New Cinema (see chapter 2); and a costume epic, *Forbidden Imperial Tales* (Jiadao gongli de nanren, 1989), plagiarizing Hong Kong director Jacob Cheung's *Last Eunuch in China* (1988). None of these exertions paid off in the redemption of his earlier reputation. *Lonely Seventeen, Home Sweet Home,* and *Goodbye Darling* remain Bai Jingrui's best films and signify his rather short period of directorial splendor. Bai died of a heart attack in 1997, a few months after King Hu's unexpected death.

Li Hanxiang and King Hu: Alternative Mandarin Production

With CMPC's production full-grown and healthy in the mid-1960s, Mandarin-language film gradually established its "national" trademark by pushing Taiwanese-language film to the margins and encouraging all small independent companies to follow suit. The decade saw a prosperous film industry sustained by directors who made popular genre films, mainly Qiong Yao romantic melodramas, and martial arts, or *wuxia*.

Note that CMPC was mostly outside this popular boom. At this time Taiwan was attracting runaways from Hong Kong's film industry, injecting new forces and pushing major changes in the production of Mandarin-language films. These figures saw no reason to leave the lucrative Taiwan market to the state-sponsored CMPC, especially since Mandarin-language pictures had worldwide distribution potential. Li Xing and Bai Jingrui were just two of many filmmakers to get involved in a flexible, post-Fordist mode of production. They formed their own companies to engage in contract work and make more personal films. But the major independent contribution to Mandarin film production came in 1963 when Shaw Brothers' leading director, Li Hanxiang, "defected" to Taiwan.

Li's founding of Grand Pictures was the product of struggles typical of a vertically integrated studio system, exemplified by Hong Kong's Shaw Brothers, as well as the official propaganda machine represented by Taiwan's CMPC. Struggles took place over directorial and artistic control as well as financial independence. Prominent Shaw Brothers directors Li Hanxiang (1926–1996) and King Hu (Hu Jinquan, 1932–1997) show how these difficulties and opportunities worked. Both came from a highly commercial system, and both chafed against its restrictions. Each in his own way, these directors sought greater independence, artistic control, and financial rewards. In the end, Li failed but Hu was able to gain limited self-sufficiency with painstaking effort. In their struggles against Fordist assembly-line, monarchical, and mercenary corporations, they enriched Taiwan film.

Shaws' main rival in Hong Kong was MP and GI. With the support of the Cathay Corporation, parent company of MP and GI, Li cut ties with the Shaws and started up a new company in 1963.[45] He entered a partnership with Union, the distributor of Shaw and Cathay films in Taiwan and founded Grand Pictures, whose Chinese name (Guolian) combined the first character of each partner: Cathay (Guotai) and Union (Lianban). Li's troubles with Shaw were not the only reason for his move to Taiwan. Authorities there were actively encouraging Hong Kong filmmakers with tax concessions, production assistance provided by KMT studios, cheap production costs, and beautiful locations. This was a time when shooting on the mainland was impossible for political reasons and, given the congested state of Hong Kong film production, Taiwan—the treasure island—looked like a golden opportunity.

Li's ideal was to set up a studio with management made up of practicing filmmakers whose decision-making was collaborative rather than dictatorial. Collaborative meant that Grand, a "director-as-producer" company, allowed directors to have more say in production. It also meant that Li himself would direct fewer films (he only made six and a quarter films), to give new directors more opportunities. Li's attention to collaborative management also shows in his training of new actors recruited in Taiwan. Li sternly reminded them that his purpose in setting up Grand's own acting school was to train capable actors, not glamorous stars. In Li's opinion, stars were the unwelcome result of vicious competition between big studios, hence, the star system must not be encouraged in his new establishment. The new practices that Li introduced at Grand were all lacking in existing studios like the Shaw Brothers and Cathay.

Contrary to his Shaw period, in which he was known as a "quick hand" (kuaishou), at Grand Li's working style changed to contrivance, precision, and meticulousness.

Considering he turned out the 1962 Shaw Brothers' blockbuster *The Love Eterne* (Liang Shanbo yu Zhu Yingtai) in fifteen days, his *Xi Si: Beauty of Beauties* (Xi Si, 1965) was a deliberative, slowly ripening piece, two years in the making. Instead of Shaws' incessant supervision, Grand opted for "quality control" rather than budget control. *Xi Si* overspent by 300 percent of the original budget, using more than 12,000 extras.[46] This extravagance paid off, and Grand was rewarded with three straight years of positive box office. *Trouble on the Wedding Night* (Zhuangyuan jidi, 1964) out-grossed all Shaw and Cathay films in 1964. The identical circumstance recurred in 1965 for *Xi Si,* and even the Qiong Yao adaptation *Many Enchanting Nights* (Ji du xiyang hong) took second place in the Top Ten movie list of 1966.[47] Grand is the place of Li Hanxiang's rebirth, and he was able to reclaim himself as his own director, not just one for hire.

Grand Pictures was set up much like Shaw Brothers in miniature—an integrated, self-contained production complex. It owned a studio with its own technical staff, laboratory facilities, actors, writers, and directors. But unlike Shaw, its production culture was more democratic and its pictures were more diversified. Li detested Shaws' centralized, authoritarian management and favored a collective and collaborative process. Productions were equally distributed among Hong Kong directors and scriptwriters whom he had brought from Shaws' and local filmmakers that Li recruited from the *taiyu pian*. Projects were assigned according to individual fortes instead of interpersonal relationships. Meetings were routinely held, and decisions were collectively made to oversee every step of the production.

In addition to continuing with Li's specialty, *huangmei diao* (yellow plum operas)—films such as *Seven Fairies* (Qi xian'nü, 1963), *Trouble on the Wedding Night,* and *Feng Yang Flower Drum* (Fengyang huagu, 1967)—and historical epics such as *Xi Si: Beauty of Beauties,* Grand branched out to psychological period films such as *The Dawn* (Poxiao shifen, 1968) and contemporary melodramas like *The Winter* (Dong nuan, 1969). This novelty is related to Grand's other initiative in the film industry. Beginning in 1965, Grand made twelve films based on literary properties. Eight of them were adapted from Qiong Yao's romantic work; four of them, such as *The Dawn* and *The Winter,* came from other contemporary writers of various specialties.

The Winter (fig. 1.9) was directed in 1967 but not released until 1969 because of Li's financial troubles at the end of Grand's operation. It is a sad, sweet story about a mainland émigré, Old Wu, and his Taiwanese friend Ajin. Old Wu is too shy to propose to Ajin even though both are attracted to each other. When Ajin's family marries her out, Old Wu becomes homeless because of urban redevelopment. Down-trodden, Old Wu sells noodles in the street. One cold winter night, Ajin shows up at the noodle stand with a baby. The couple finally reveals their feelings toward one another. This humble subject is rare for Li; however, he exhibits a stun-

1.9 *The Winter* (1969; dir. Li Hanxiang)   (COURTESY TAIPEI FILM ARCHIVE)

ning, fluid studio craftsmanship in his re-creation of a vernacular, parochial Taipei. Take the opening sequence for example.

Ajin jumps down from the bed of a truck into a lively, bustling Taipei night market. Briskly she winds her way through the narrow lanes, dodging noodle stands, signboards, hawkers, and shoppers. Paper lanterns, enormous steel pots, and clouds of steam fill every available space in the frame as Li smoothly dollies along with Ajin. Sound design is similarly intricate and fluid. Ajin calls out greetings to neighbors, is drowned out by the noisy scrape and whoosh of cooking fires, and strains to hear replies to her questions.

Li is fully in control of set design, direction of sounds and motion, and execution of crane and tracking movements. This film initially shows a brilliant coordination of all-round studio film techniques, reminiscent of Hollywood studio directors in the 1930s and the 1940s like George Stevens and William Wyler. The representation of Taipei in this film is so artificially beautiful and polished that a comparison with, say, Li Xing's homely, unostentatious cityscapes of the same period seems unfair. Nor does it follow CMPC's healthy realism as film-work within a larger political and cultural campaign of persuasion. Yet Li Hanxiang's ultra-aestheticization is not apolitical. The stunning mise-en-scène and complex camerawork represents a monumental stylization of everyday Chinese life. Eventually, this stylization finds apotheosis in Li's elaborate evocations of imperial China in his later work for the

Shaws, such as *The Empress Dowager* (Qingguo qingcheng, 1975). The hyperstylized ornaments of imperial privilege here signal a moral corruption so total that only the most brilliant of décor, costumes, and mannerisms can convey it. But at this stage in his career at Grand, Li is unable to sustain such intricate construction of style and meaning across the whole of his film. The second part of *The Winter* has the usual flaws of Li's hasty working style from Shaws (perhaps forecasting the upcoming bankruptcy of the company)—obvious plot holes, spatial ellipses, and many cheap shots. But Li's thoroughness in stuffing the scene with visual interest and his meticulous set design and composition is remarkable in the Taiwan cinema of the 1960s.

In 1965 Li lost his two major backers. Cathay's owner Lu Yuntao and Taiwan Studio's director Long Fang were both killed in a mysterious air crash. By 1966, Li had woefully overspent in the new company's first years, and Union refused to extend more credit. By 1967, Grand was in serious financial difficulties and broke off from Cathay and Union. Li quickly sought outside funding to maintain production and formed an alliance with another distribution company. Without Union's powerful distribution network, and lacking the mighty financial backup from Cathay, Li was not able to sustain his quality production. By 1970, Grand Pictures ceased operations. It had made a total of just twenty-two films.[48]

Although Li's ambition to build an independent studio comparable to Cathay and the Shaws failed, his Grand productions had a direct impact on the later development of Mandarin film in Taiwan. Actors from Grand ascended into mainstream Mandarin production in the late 1960s, and some of them became major stars in Taiwan and Hong Kong. Most of the Hong Kong crew who followed him to Grand stayed and were assimilated into Taiwan's film industry. Song Cunshou (*The Dawn*) moved to CMPC after Grand's closure and was soon recognized as a major director. In 2001, Taiwan's Golden Horse Film Awards honored Song with a lifetime achievement award. More significantly, Li's working methods, particularly his organization of period setups, battle scenes, costume design, and fluid camera work, were quickly picked up by Taiwan's major production houses such as CMPC and Union.

After breaking with Li, Union formed a production subsidiary called International (Guoji) and built a large studio in central Taiwan. Building on its experience with Li Hanxiang, it sought the talent of name directors. Using its Hong Kong connections, Union brought in another famous, but unhappy director from Shaw Brothers, King Hu. Hu had already made the hit *Come Drink with Me*, but his relationship with Shaw Brothers, especially Sir Run Run, was not completely cordial. Before *Come Drink with Me*, Run Run Shaw was not enthusiastic about King Hu. Hu's first effort was reshot by another director, and his second film, the anti-Japanese war film *Sons of the Good Earth*, went over budget and deadline and, when completed, suffered from being cut (about thirty minutes) to meet with political censorship in Singapore and Malaysia. Hu was even replaced in the middle of shooting his third film. Run Run Shaw was still finding fault with King Hu at the test screening of *Come Drink with Me*.[49] So when Union approached Hu with an attractive package, Hu moved to Taiwan in spite of unfinished contractual obligations to Shaw Brothers. Union hired Hu as the managing producer of its newly established studio. Hu was granted a partnership in building the studio, recruitment, and production. The first film from this new collaboration was *Dragon Inn*. *Dragon Inn* was the highest-grossing Chinese film of that year, outdoing many Hollywood releases and establishing Hu as a major director.[50] Furthermore, the film secured the *wuxia* martial arts genre as the dominant one in Taiwan and Hong Kong for many years to come.

Dragon Inn: Choreographing a New Genre

Dragon Inn (aka *Dragon Gate Inn*, Longmen kezhan, 1967), along with the seminal *Come Drink with Me*, represents the rehabilitation of a genre that neatly epitomized Chinese film itself. Though "martial arts" films (*wuxia pian*) had been a staple of Chinese cinema throughout its history, King Hu significantly changed its emphasis. As we will see, the martial arts genre label sat uncomfortably with the director, who thought that he was making something at once classic and modern.[51] This signals a gap between how the new genre was generally perceived and what Stephen Teo calls *cinema opera*, an apt description of what Hu was doing (fig. 1.10).[52] This in turn corresponds to a breach in the now-common understanding of martial arts as a regimen of athletic skill and discipline, versus the literal meaning of *wuxia pian*: stories of chivalrous knights. The impersonal, skill-centered connotation of the martial arts label diverts attention from characters motivated to employ fighting skills for specific reasons. And yet it was King Hu who brought a new focus on a stylized kind of action, even introducing the credited role of "martial arts director" or fight choreographer as an official job description.[53]

Before Hu's work on *Dragon Inn* and the previous *Come Drink with Me*, there were scores of costume and opera pictures employing martial arts. In the 1950s, the famous Huang Feihong (Wong Fei-hong) series was released from Hong Kong's Cantonese film industry.[54] The popularity of the series is usually taken as a signal breakthrough in vernacular Hong Kong popular culture, distinguishing it from its antecedents in Shanghai of the late 1920s and '30s. Analogous to this is the parallel cinemas of Taiwan in the same period, with official Mandarin and vernacular Taiwanese pictures coexisting in different market segments. In addition to these postwar martial-heroic tales, the folk legends in both *taiyu pian* and Chinese opera contained physical conflicts and combat. In the 1950s and '60s, actors such as

1.10 *Dragon Inn* (aka *Dragon Gate Inn*, 1967; dir. King Hu)   (COURTESY TAIPEI FILM ARCHIVE)

Guan Dexing (Kwan Tak-hing), who starred in the Huang Feihong series, not only performed kung fu (the Cantonese term for fighting techniques), swordplay, and other stunts for the camera, they also were real-life experts in the martial arts of southern China.[55] Guan Dexing and his contemporaries brought extra-cinematic expertise to their film roles. Yet martial arts in these films were shot differently from how the experts actually practiced them. Claims on the martial arts practitioner-athlete were different from claims made by the camera. In the films martial arts were played and shot "soft"—that is, attack and defense moves were stylized, dance-like exchanges of artificial slaps and blows that not only made no contact, they did not even appear to connect. Instead, they *signified* hand-to-hand combat, rather than forcefully simulating it. A number of reasons can be imagined for this suggestive, seemingly artificial convention. An analogy is with silent Japanese kabuki films, which employed *tachimawari* stage acrobatics as conventional signifiers of swordplay derived from the stage. These kabuki films of the teens opened the way to *chambara*, those films from the twenties that in the name of greater "realism," boasted kinetic, hyperbolic swordplay.[56] The "signifying" gestures of martial arts in earlier Chinese films could also be seen as heuristic, a tool to illustrate and teach various fighting techniques. Like a manual, emphasis was placed on the prowess of the expert, less for spectacular display than for pedagogical demonstration, requiring a more analytic, measured style of fighting, cinematography, and editing.

King Hu was from Beijing and incorporated many techniques from the capital's opera stage. He too was a teacher of sorts, being an avid scholar of Ming dynasty literature, history, and the arts. Drawing on this knowledge, he injected period accuracy but, unlike his friend and mentor Li Hanxiang, accelerated the pace of movement and editing in action sequences. He also used sound, particularly the distinctive wooden clappers from Beijing opera, to punctuate fights scenes. Close-ups of tense facial expressions, particularly eyelines, and coiled body language are used to lend a greater sense of expectation, impact, and intensity. Without giving up choreography, King Hu injected danger and menace into fighting sequences. Huang Feihong boasted choreography too, but not the poetry of King Hu, which approached an abstraction akin to "pure cinema."[57] Moving camera, mobile framing, and figure movement all put the stress on the unfolding of combat, not martial arts technique, even allowing it to go occasionally offscreen.

King Hu's martial arts style adds a large dose of athleticism in addition to grace. To make fight scenes *look* dynamic—fast, efficient, lethal—he used hidden springboards and trampolines to add power to combatants' leaps. In itself, this indicates a dramatic, not athletic, priority. On the other hand, in contrast to predecessors in the costume films, he avoided special effects like stop-motion, smoke-puffs, or lap dissolves. These were common in many low-budget action sequences of the period. (Hu did use some slow-motion sequences, but not usually in scenes of combat.) He devised complex fight sequences with more than two combatants, and a variety of setups and duration. Wide-angle shots, swish pans, and rapid tracking are employed to enhance involvement with the total action, lending panoramic views to the surrounding space as well as the combatants. These are mixed with close-ups of only a few seconds, inserted to suggest the blinding impact of a body blow. Another striking feature of King Hu's cinematography is his reliance on trees, cliffs, and other tall props. These allowed him to stage high-angle views on the combatants below, as well as an almost fetishistic repetition of figures gracefully jumping down from great heights. Many examples can be seen in *A Touch of Zen* (Xia'nü, 1970), *Raining in the Mountain* (Kongshan lingyu, 1979), and *Legend of the Mountain* (Shanzhong chuanqi, 1979).

Characters are not "individualized" in the sense of physical action motivated by interior states. It would be strange to say Hu's characters are well-rounded or dynamic personalities; instead, they fulfill certain types from traditional canons. They conform to "shells" already available and waiting to be inhabited. As Stephen Teo writes, "All the key players [in *The Valiant Ones*, 1975] are essentially shells of characters only because their human instincts and qualities are defined through action."[58] External types predominate over internal motivation. Examples are such figures as the literati, itinerant scholars who are physically weak, financially poor, but intelligent. They cannot fight, but they can distinguish good from bad, and they are cunning; they can write, calculate, and tell tales. The *xia'nü* woman warrior, Hu's major revitalization of the genre typology, has remarkable sangfroid to match her kung fu and sword-fighting skills, but she is often wooden, like actresses Shangguan Lingfeng *(Dragon Inn)*, Xu Feng *(A Touch of Zen)*, and Zheng Peipei *(Come Drink with Me)*. To speak of the evil eunuch (played by Bai Ying in *Dragon Inn*) is to be redundant, so identified with powers of darkness were the imperial eunuchs and their ruthless *dongchang* or palace guards. All these elements and more—the sumptuous design, the slightly wooden hero, the spectacular choreography by fellow northerner Han Yingjie— would be utilized as essential ingredients in martial arts films by Shaw Brothers, Cathay, and countless independents.[59]

King Hu is a formalist, immersed in the particular cultural forms and traditions of the Ming dynasty. The action sequences in his films are a tribute in performance to the concrete period details, along with classical literature, architecture, costumes, and calligraphy. King Hu is famous for his interest in archival authentication. With an academic preoccupation with details of costume, makeup, sets, and décor, Hu was very concerned with historical consistency.[60] One reason he got into trouble with Shaw was his insistence on documenting Ming dynasty footwear, hairstyles, or food, and slowly building up a society of spectacularly researched practices and mutual relations. This "thick production" took a great deal of time and money, and was an emphatic step away from Shaw Brothers' Fordist methods of historical filmmaking. The bookish King Hu was not content to merely suggest vague historical periods with conventional signals of historical mannerism; he wished to accentuate details, and revivify period dramas from the bottom up. His innovations in martial arts were a means to express this preoccupation with historical minutiae.

King Hu was not really interested in kung fu or swordplay except insofar as it illuminates practices of Ming dynasty intrigue. Themes are equally classical, rendering but not dwelling on conflicts of good and evil, or the rigors of acquiring knowledge, intelligence, and (occasionally) enlightenment. The transcendent epiphany of Zen Buddhism is powerfully expressed at the end of *A Touch of Zen*, but this is an anomaly; the later pictures have the mystical, specifically *Chinese* atmosphere of *Touch of Zen* but lack the explicit visualization of religious power.

King Hu's films elaborate a complete world in which physical action signifies a specific aesthetic-ethical arena. By retooling costume dramas, spectator involvement is solicited and sustained. Hu's stylization is essentially theatrical, but it is made dynamic through precision film techniques. The genre is romanticized by giving pride of place to the warriors (*xia*) over their skills (*wu*). Evocation of aesthetic-ethical horizons specific to Chinese tradition by way of the martial arts (*wuda*) is the objective in these pictures. So it is more accurate to call King Hu's films chivalric warrior pictures rather than martial arts because of his view that these arts were, like other arts, a means to an end.

What end is that? It is appropriate that we touch base with Japanese cinema and samurai swordplay films, especially those from Daiei featuring the blind swordsman Zatoichi. As we have seen, Zatoichi made an appearance in at least one *taiyu pian*, paired off against the Chinese drunken swordsman. In the 1960s, Japanese swordplay was very popular in Hong Kong and the whole region, to the gratification of Shaw Brothers, which distributed them. At the same time, Shaw characteristically used these Japanese *jidai geki* as models, seeking to upgrade production values in its own action pictures as well as boost quantity. The influence of Japanese films is one key distinction of the "new school" martial arts (see ch. 5, n. 13). Hollywood action, the James Bond series, and spaghetti westerns are others. *Come Drink with Me* was the film that made an important mark on the domination of martial arts by Japanese program pictures, and with *Dragon Inn*, King Hu confirmed the international appeal of Chinese martial arts, a genre that could hold its own with the Japanese. Therefore, one external factor in the rehabilitation of Chinese martial arts pictures was to recapture a lucrative market, competing economically and ideologically with a regional rival. Like Zhang Che, Chu Yuan (Chor Yun), and other directors, King Hu was influenced by the dynamic violence of *jidai geki*: Kurosawa Akira, Misumi Kenji, Uchida Tomu, and Okamoto Kihachi.[61] But of course Japan was an antagonist, as well as an inspiration. His directorial debut, *Sons of the Good Earth* (1965), was an anti-Japanese war film, starring King Hu himself. Its strident message attracted censorship problems in Southeast Asia and, rather sadly, was shot by the top-flight cinematographer from Japan, Nishimoto Tadashi (using a Chinese pseudonym He Lanshan).

Another factor in King Hu's success must be Hollywood, though James Bond is a figure that epitomizes generically Western, not just Hollywood, popular entertainment. King Hu's answer to James Bond espionage, suspense, and accoutrement testifies to 007's global popularity—and imitation—throughout the 1960s, as indicated in this statement:

Some people say I come from the kung fu genre; that's a mistake. I know nothing about kung fu. Action sequences in my films are neither kung fu nor martial arts, neither judo nor karate. In fact, they are just two fighters dueling, a form of dance. . . . Because I was exposed to Beijing opera when I was little, my action sequences are not real fights. They are "wuda," [stage combat] in Beijing opera. There's no such term as "kung fu" in the Beijing dialect. This is a Cantonese term used by Hong Kong people as a synonym for martial arts. In fact, *Dragon Inn* belongs to a kind of ancient Chinese espionage. It was made to respond to the prevalent James Bond 007 spy genre. The Ming dynasty is the era that has the strongest concentration of spies. They were controlled by eunuchs that were so powerful that they were immune from imperial authority. *Dragon Inn* is full of suspense and intrigue, and this is why it appealed to the audience.[62]

King Hu's commitment to the Chinese heritage manifests itself in the power of antiquity, expressed in the most vivid cinematic techniques. In addition, his distinctive execution of physical action moves beyond a simple response to Western templates to an exciting cinematic discourse of Asian labor power. Hu incorporates and surpasses the appeal of Japanese martial arts to counter a predominant Western formula for "high concept," spectacle-oriented mass cinema. If Bond was outfitted for his superhuman exploits by ever-greater capital expenditures of high technology, King Hu added value to his martial arts through tradition. This was manifested in concrete objects and the performance of Chinese period detail, including but not limited to the martial arts. The accumulation of archaic detail from the Ming dynasty answers, in a peculiar but powerful way, the outlandish, futuristic gadgetry of 007. The cultural armature of Chinese tradition, animated by ethical concerns of a bygone era, functions comparably to the Cold War mobilizations of technology and intelligence represented by the Bond franchise. Bond has a good body, and it sometimes goes on display, "but his main displays of energy consist of his ability to handle machinery" (including the bodies of women).[63] If Bond's intelligence ability comes from the amazing capacities of his cars, mobile phones, exploding pens, and so on, King Hu's heroes get theirs from devotion to ancient traditions, visible in the settings, props, and material objects surrounding them, as well as the specialized parries and thrusts of elite warriors. King Hu's contributions to martial arts and the action film come from his preoccupation with the past and, more exactly, attempting to externalize through action the authentic material culture of the Ming dynasty, filtered through conventions of Beijing opera. It is again a cultural patrimony that animates King Hu's rendition of martial arts, taking them into a realm of marvels through historical specificity.

In this connection, King Hu spans traditional and modern, theatrical and cinematic, lyrical and formidable excitement. He unites physical, mythical, and historical power. His is a twice-cooked procedure in that his material answer to Bond is archaic, not ultramodern, but also highly advanced, in the precision techniques of cinematic form. King Hu's staging, cutting, and scoring of his characteristic action sequences recall Beijing opera, but at a deeper level they appeal to contemporary cravings for kinetic display and the parade of virtuosity, whether in staccato sequencing or in single breathtaking shots. They are not antiquarian but arresting. Ultimately, despite King Hu's insistence on serving Chinese tradition, he is really displaying his mastery of cinematic form, in defiance of erstwhile superior filmmakers in Japan and the West, employing the riches of Chinese material as a potter does his clay. The variety of his professional experience in Hong Kong,

Taiwan, and even Korean film culture gave him perspective and great frustration at the limitations of the commercial system. This apparently motivated his desire to break from formulaic factory styles and give expression to a labor-intensive "hand-made" aesthetic.

With the phenomenal success of *Dragon Inn*, Union Pictures and Hu signed up to do *A Touch of Zen*, and though Hu continued to work with Union, relations were increasingly strained. Hu was working at an unprecedented scale and expense on what would become his mystical epic *A Touch of Zen*. Continuing interference and nagging from Union producers prompted Hu to move postproduction on the film back to Hong Kong. From there, he eventually sent a director's cut to Cannes, where he received a special award for technical achievement. The prestigious recognition—foreshadowed by Li Hanxiang's Cannes prize for his *Yang Kwei-fei* (1962)—allowed Hu to earn an international reputation no other Chinese directors enjoyed. By then, King Hu had severed ties with Union and moved his production base back to Hong Kong. When he did return to Taiwan in the early 1980s, the films he made—*The Juvenizer* (Zhongshen dashi, 1981), *All the King's Men* (Tianxia diyi, 1982), *The Wheel of Life* (Da lunhui, 1983)—no longer generated much impact or new sensations. King Hu's historical archaism yielded to a different historical authenticity coming from the New Cinema movement.

Challenges and Controversies
of the Taiwan New Cinema

After enjoying continuous expansion from the mid-1960s to the late 1970s, Taiwan cinema faced a series of impediments. Taiwan lost its most valuable overseas Southeast Asian market, following the success of Communist revolutions in Vietnam, Cambodia, and Laos, and sanctions were imposed on Chinese culture in Indonesia and Malaysia. The industry was hit by another problem in the 1980s: the decline of domestic Mandarin-speaking film audiences, who turned to exciting, tour de force Jackie Chan kung fu films and excruciating comedies from New Cinema City of Hong Kong. Furthermore, proliferation of VCRs let audiences stay home or patronize video parlors for better selection and flexible viewing. Video rental stores also received licenses from Hong Kong's two major TV networks—TVB and ATV—to distribute television dramas, some with better entertainment quality than local films.

This is the background from which Taiwan New Cinema arose. The New Cinema (*xin dianying*) is by far the most important development in Taiwan film history. Though it did not transform or rejuvenate the film industry, nor succeed in blocking invasions from Hong Kong or Hollywood, it nevertheless created the most vital cinema in Taiwan history and cultivated some of the finest filmmaking talent at the turn of the twentieth century.

The New Cinema in Taiwan was a distinct step away from the pedagogical orientation of healthy realism, the commercialism of studio genres, and the eclectic provincialism of *taiyu pian* (Taiwanese-language films). Beginning in 1983 with *Growing Up*, *The Sandwich Man*, *A Flower in the Rainy Night*, and *That Day, on the Beach*, the New Cinema represents major changes in style, theme, and audience. Styles and techniques became understated, yet called attention to their own quiet artifice. Themes incorporated elements of indigenous Taiwanese life, especially visible in language, literary adaptations, and rural subjects. Films of the New Cinema were made for a younger, more educated audience, specifically college students and young professionals. But questions remain. Was the New Cinema a movement, like Italian neorealism or the French New Wave? Was it a group style comprised by a number of like-minded directors, writers, and talent? Or, like healthy realism, was it a policy formulated by one or more authorities (e.g., the Central Motion Picture Corporation / CMPC, or the Government Information Office / GIO) charged with updating the film industry? Another possibility is the New Cinema as critical invention: influential critics and journalists who acquired cultural capital by defining characteristics of carefully chosen films and submitting these to scrutiny at international festivals. These various accounts are not mutually exclusive; Taiwan New Cinema in its formative stages was a combination of all these factors.

Today, a handful of Taiwan directors enjoy worldwide acclaim, and this stems partly from their initial public recognition in the New Cinema of the 1980s. However, the New Cinema's importance goes beyond its status as a training ground for Hou Hsiao-hsien, Edward Yang, or Tsai Ming-liang. Despite similarities to other "new wave" movements, it is a homegrown innovation that redefines and refines cinema in Taiwan. New Cinema advances the legacy of healthy realism toward a contemporary national art cinema. Paradoxically, it also impedes renewal of the commercial sector by pledging itself to international art cinema. Today the New Cinema is blamed for the total collapse of commercial cinema in Taiwan. Nevertheless, the New Cinema put Taiwan itself, not only Taiwan film, back on the world map. When we examine this history, we need to look at the organizing forces of the New Cinema as a whole—directors, producers, writers, technicians, and their sociopolitical conditions—that made the New Cinema viable. Directors such as Wang Tong (Wong Tung), Chen Kunhou, Wan Ren, Zhang Yi; novelist and screenwriters Zhu Tianwen (Chu T'ien-wen), Xiao Ye, and Wu Nianzhen (Wu Nien-chen); editor Liao Qingsong, cinematographer Mark Lee Pingbin, sound designer Du Duzhi: these may not be household names, but they formed the core of this small, genuine homegrown film culture. While space prevents us from discussing all these figures, the New Cinema could not have happened without their constant negotiations and struggle with unyielding, old practices. As a former cinematographer at CMPC, Chen Kunhou is a transitional figure between the old school and initial steps taken in the New Cinema. Zhang Yi's contributions to the New Cinema are found in his focus on women's film within familiar melodramatic forms, along with his novelist wife Xiao Sa. Like Chen Kunhou, Liao Qingsong came out of CMPC and remains the most important editor in Taiwan film, having cut all of Hou Hsiao-hsien's films. Hou's cinematographer Mark Lee Pingbin also began at CMPC and built a career from his work on New Cinema films. In 2000 he shared a prize at Cannes with another veteran of the New Cinema, Christopher Doyle (cinematographer for Yang's *That Day, on the Beach*), for his work on Wong Kar-wai's *In the Mood for Love*. Du Duzhi is responsible for the radical changes in synchronized sound in the New Cinema, at a time when dubbing was the norm. Du remains the most sought-after sound designer in Chinese-language cinema. This chapter portrays these figures within their rightful place in the New Cinema record. More importantly, by documenting their contributions to the New Cinema, this chapter outlines a selective historiography of the development of the Taiwan film industry in the 1980s.

"Newcomer Policy": Corporate Tactics and Ideological Constraints

New Cinema strikes a major shift from a cinema defined mostly by industrial terms to a pure "auteur cinema." Before the New Cinema, stars, genres, and audiences made up the preoccupations of Taiwan filmmakers. But the New Cinema seems to focus exclusively on directors. Existing accounts of the New Cinema rarely depart from that focus. From the official GIO publication *Free China Review* to festival catalogs and specialty magazines such as *Cinemaya*, directors are always the subject of cinema updates on Taiwan. This can be somewhat deceptive because directors did not simply walk onto the sound stages and begin dictating new ideas. Their way was paved by a variety of conditions and figures already in the film industry. These conditions were manifold: industrial pressures, changes in cultural spheres, calls for political liberalization, and younger voices in both the production and consumption of film discourse. Directors' entry into the film establishment was not smooth, or inevitable. Instead, young directors were brought in to serve specific purposes. Their presence was part of a larger strategy initiated by the establishment, and as such was subject to ideological and industrial priorities already in place. CMPC's "newcomer policy" (*xinren zhengce*) was one of these initiatives.

The newcomer policy came out of changing market circumstances, an attempt to literally rejuvenate the Taiwan film industry after twenty years of protectionism, conservatism, and repetition. Around 1982, CMPC, the flagship studio in Taiwan, proposed a flexible production model called "low capital, high production" (*xiao chengben, jing zhizuo*) to deal with several pressing problems.[1] These included the

2.1 The young New Cinema filmmakers (*from left*): Wu Nianzhen, Hou Hsiao-hsien, Edward Yang, Chen Kuo-fu, and Zhan Hongzhi (1987)   (COURTESY LIU ZHENXIANG)

increasing impact of Hong Kong commercial films; the lack of young, educated, and professional audiences for Taiwan films; and the failure to win a single prize at the 1982 Asia-Pacific Film Festival in Kuala Lumpur.[2] The "low capital, high production" model was supposed to address these problems through diversification and spreading risk. The newcomer policy was a low-cost initiative to attract new talent into the local film industry. Many of these fledgling directors, such as Edward Yang, Wan Ren, Ke Yizheng, and Zeng Zhuangxiang, boasted U.S. training.[3] Young directors already in the industry, such as Hou Hsiao-hsien, Chen Kunhou, and Wang Tong were also invited to work with CMPC in order to produce fresh, younger entertainment. (See fig. 2.1.)

The newcomer policy was not only a break extended to young directors; it was intended to create incentives for coproductions with independent producers as well as major Hong Kong studios such as New Cinema City and Golden Harvest.[4] Because it could not hope to compete with Hong Kong directly, CMPC tried to gather enough films from new directors to entice a new audience for Taiwan-made pictures. Students would never go see Taiwan pictures in the cinema, so the pictures were taken to them. The College Film Festival (xueyuan yingzhan) was a domestic minifestival circulated around the island in the early 1980s (1982–1984). The festival made the campus rounds annually, offering free screenings and arranging for directors, stars, and writers to talk face-to-face with students and teachers. Finally, there was an effort made to reclaim a share of the prizes at the Asia-Pacific Festival. Immediately after the 1982 festival the director of GIO, James Soong (Song Chuyu), established lucrative funds to reward films that could bring home prizes from the next year's festival, to be hosted in Taipei.[5]

It would be misleading to think that CMPC was boldly striving to promote the newcomer policy. In fact, in 1983 CMPC itself produced only one New Cinema film, *The Sandwich Man*. The other four made that year—*Growing Up, That Day, on the Beach, Kendo Kids* (Zhujian shaonian, dir. Zhang Yi), and *The boy with a sword* (Daijian de xiaohai, dir. Ke Yizheng)—were coproduced with either the independent Evergreen (Wannianqing) or Hong Kong's New Cinema City. The newcomer policy was an economy measure and limited diversification, not an aggressive product differentiation. Far from diving into uncharted waters, CMPC was spreading risk. It wanted to save money to spend on its traditional extravaganzas, like King Hu's *The Invincible Ones* (aka *All the King's Men*, Tianxia diyi, 1983) and *The Longest Night* (Zuichang de yiye, 1983), directed by the company veteran Jin Aoxun, who specialized in military genres.[6] Censorship within the company remained stringent, and KMT officials as well as studio executives subjected projects to ideological scrutiny.[7] Given this situation, it was two new production assistants, Xiao Ye and Wu Nianzhen, who understood the rules at CMPC and proposed projects in a way that helped the newcomer policy along.

However, within a sclerotic institution this took a certain amount of guile. To pass the studio's conservative line of ideology, these assistants would prepare "creative" proposals that disguised the real intent of the films. For instance, *Growing Up* is about a boy who turns to juvenile delinquency and drives his mother to suicide. He fails to live up to her ambition for him to go to college, and goes to military school instead. Xiao Ye wrote this up as a pitch that promotes the military academy as a place to straighten out wayward boys. *The Sandwich Man* was represented to CMPC as a picture celebrating the humanist philosophy of founding father Dr. Sun Yat-sen, from which was derived the basics of KMT nation-building. Each segment in this three-part omnibus supposedly depicted the long-suffering nobility of ordinary citizens of Taiwan.[8] In contrast to their proposals, the two films turned out much differently in the flesh.

An intriguing double-cross was secretly perpetrated by Xiao Ye and Wu Nianzhen. They were using CMPC as a base from which to push for objectives that were quite alien to CMPC's usual commitments. While they both wrote scripts for priority projects like *The Invincible Ones* and *The Longest Night*, they also joined newcomers such as Edward Yang (with whom Wu wrote *That Day, on the Beach*) and Zhang Yi (with whom Xiao Ye wrote *Kendo Kids*). On the one hand they worked "day jobs" as company employees, like Hollywood contract scriptwriters; on the other, they were allowed to promote a diversification of company output on a limited basis. At some level, CMPC must have been aware it was being "crossed" because this was consistent with its *xiao chengben* "low capital" policy. A good example of this double-cross and its unexpected consequences can be seen in "The Taste of Apples" segment of *The Sandwich Man*.

"Peeling the apple": *The Sandwich Man*

The Sandwich Man is a trio of short films based on Huang Chunming's stories of Taiwanese provincial life. It consists of "Son's Big Doll" (Erzi de da wanou, dir. Hou Hsiao-hsien), "Vicki's Hat" (Xiaoqi de na ding maozi, dir. Zeng Zhuangxiang), and "The Taste of Apples" (Pingguo de ziwei, dir. Wan Ren). Set in the 1960s, "Apples" is a highly satirical story about a man who is fantastically enriched when he is hit by an American officer's car.

"Apples" became something of a cause célèbre when it was exposed by conservative film critics. At the time, all films were vetted by GIO's film division. Until 1982 this process had been very strict, similar to the centralized precensorship that still prevails in the People's Republic of China (PRC). If a script was deemed unsuitable to pass the necessary ideological requirements, it could not be approved for production. However, in 1983 the rules were relaxed, and films could go into production without prior consultation with the government.[9] Under its newcomer policy CMPC had given the go-ahead to make *The Sandwich Man*, but once the film was completed there were internal doubts about whether it would be approved by GIO for release, especially since there were plans to send it abroad. It was not enough that films from Taiwan win awards at foreign festivals; they also needed to portray Taiwan in the correct light.

The film as a whole deals with issues of neocolonialism. "Apples" in particular portrays the dependency of Taiwan on American military and economic aid in the 1960s. Despite, or because of, its black humor, it was seen by conservative critics as a straightforward depiction of Taiwanese backwardness, in relation to both Chinese and American institutions. Americans were closely allied with the KMT throughout the Cold War and were intent on preserving a relationship that sustained U.S. hegemony in the Pacific. As a U.S. embassy junior secretary tells the officer who hit the victim, "Listen. This is an Asian country with which we have the closest cooperation and friendship. So I don't think there should be any problem. However, the President would be very unhappy if there was any trouble with any of the local people or the government." (See fig. 2.2.)

The KMT government looked down on native Taiwanese and systematically deprived them of rights and economic opportunities. Thus when a Taiwanese laborer is accidentally injured in a traffic accident with an American, the man fears the worst. Instead, he is whisked to an immaculate hospital for medical care, solicitation, and due compensation for his entire family, including an offer to send his daughter to the

2.2 The U.S. presence in "The Taste of Apples" (1983; dir. Wan Ren)
(COURTESY KWANG HWA INFORMATION AND CULTURE CENTER, HONG KONG)

United States for an education. As an extra treat they are offered apples, which at that time were an expensive, imported delicacy: "The silence of the room was broken by the crisp sound of apples being bitten into, gingerly, one after another. As they took their first bites they said nothing, although they felt that they weren't quite as sweet as they had imagined; rather they were a little sour and pulpy, and when they chewed they were frothy and not quite real."[10] The man and his family are pleased with their good fortune, but consider how their luck is entwined with injury and loss of limb. Why, the man wonders, is misfortune so lavishly rewarded by the powerful while daily toil on the street gets him nothing, or worse?

"Apples" was especially sensitive because it exposed potential rifts between the KMT government and its American overlords as well as Chinese-Taiwanese ethnic fissures. For instance, the Mandarin-speaking policeman who escorts the American to a poor neighborhood has difficulty communicating in what was seen as a dialect. When the family arrives at the hospital, they meet an American missionary nurse who speaks far better Taiwanese (*taiyu*) than the police officer.

The film got an advance screening for journalists, and an anonymous letter was sent to CMPC by a local critics' association to express its displeasure. The letter alerted the censors at CMPC. It even itemized offending sections of the film. The company decided to look closely at the film and hold it to the ideological fire. Some offending details were the following. When the victim's family arrives at the U.S. Naval hospital, they are amazed by the whiteness of the place: its walls, lights, sofa, and the white bandages of their wounded father. The whiteness extends even to the toilet, and the snow-white rolls of toilet paper, which the small boys delightedly strew across the room. Scolded by their mother, they run away to play with the duty officer's hat. Meanwhile, mother and daughter use the men's room, only to be surprised by a young soldier who walks in unannounced. Concerns were voiced about this picture of Taiwanese backwardness and ignorance. In the film, a local police officer comments on the accident, "lucky you hit Colonel Grey's car. Otherwise, you'd still be lying by the side of the road." Here too CMPC was uneasy about the implicit ridicule of Chinese morality and national identity. The company then decided to order a total of eight changes to "Apples," involving dialogue, tone, behavior, and the outright elimination of certain scenes.[11] CMPC's act of censorship was dubbed the "apple-peeling incident" (*xiao pingguo shijian*) by the press. This enraged Wan Ren, Huang Chunming, Xiao Ye, and Wu Nianzhen, who in turn used their connections with a sympathetic press to launch an attack against CMPC.[12] Embarrassed by the coverage in two major newspapers, the company withdrew its orders. Eventually, "Apples" was shown whole, thanks to the public intervention of the press, specifically Yang Shiqi, a *United Daily News* entertainment journalist who championed the New Cinema.[13]

This celebrated incident shows a number of important things. First, it clearly indicates that Taiwan film regulation was in flux. The film was made immediately after the relaxation of precensorship, and its producers tried with apparent difficulty to take advantage of the new rules. Second, one sees a struggle between an older, conservative establishment—critics who submitted an anonymous complaint—and the young critics who pushed this controversy into the public sphere. This corresponds to a third aspect of New Cinema, which was its effort to win a new, younger audience who had rejected Taiwan-made films in favor of Western and Hong Kong imports. Finally, and most important, the controversy engendered a sense of collective purpose among those who supported change in Taiwan's film culture. Far more than a successful but unthreatening film like *Growing Up*, *The Sandwich Man* ignited passions, both for and against its somewhat critical themes. The important thing was not so much the "peeling" of the apple, but a public stand against the idea of censorship altogether. This much larger insistence on cultural liberalization—and liberation—was the structure on which the New Cinema started to build.

Cultural Liberation and Taiwan Nativism

In the context of the New Cinema, cultural liberation can be understood as an urge for self-expression from a hitherto silenced group of people. For decades, Taiwanese cultures and languages had been marginalized. They were seen as provincial and rural, unsuitable for representation in major public forums. Control or sanctions on Taiwan's local expressions are particularly evident in audiovisual media because it has been assumed that cultures in Taiwan are extensions or branches of Chinese mainland culture.[14] The demise of *taiyu pian* discussed in the previous chapter is exemplary of such marginalization and hegemony. But beginning in the mid-1970s, through the work of nativist literature, Taiwan cultures and languages regained visibility. Nativist writers such as Huang Chunming (Huang Ch'unming), Wang Zhenhe (Wang Chen-ho), Yang Qingchu, and Chen Yingzhen (Ch'en Ying-chen) focused precisely on stories of provincial, rural, and "inconsequential" Taiwan people.[15] This "silenced" group includes those—writers as well as their subjects—whose languages and stories bear little relation to things that preoccupied Chinese émigrés and the KMT: developments on the mainland, anticommunism, or patriotism. Meanwhile, the sinocentric view of culture suffered a blow when Taiwan's position in the international community was gradually eclipsed by the PRC in the 1970s. If Taiwan was no longer recognized as China, then how could China function as cultural hegemony within Taiwan? With diplomatic setbacks and articulations by nativist writers, nativism began to sprout as an organizing ideology demanding a democratic civil society.

Taking cues from nativist literature, screenwriters and filmmakers pushed a return (or "regression") to daily practices of Taiwanese languages and behaviors, things that audiences for *taiyu pian* had lost, and that had never been seen onscreen by younger people. The concept of nativism, which literally means "root-land ideology" (*buntu zhuyi*), works as a narrative and psychological resource for these people. In fact, before the New Cinema, three mainstream filmmakers—Chen Kunhou, Hou Hsiao-hsien, and Lin Qingjie—had begun incorporating similar "homeland" sensibilities into their genre films. Lin started a new "student genre" (*xuesheng dianying*) by casting young, unfamiliar faces in a series of films about high school life and romance. His approach to the youth film is nothing if not low key. He emphasized a natural acting style, location shooting, and a plain, unadorned depiction of adolescents. Critics considered this a "refreshing" (*qingxin*) injection into a cinema that had been trapped in endless recycling and duplication. Audiences embraced it as an alternative to kung fu, gangsters, and Qiong Yao melodrama. There was even official appreciation for Lin's *My Classmates* (Tongban tongxue), which won the 1981 Golden Horse award for best original screenplay. The writer was Wu Nianzhen.

Another refreshing element could be seen in a series of romantic comedies made by Chen Kunhou and Hou Hsiao-hsien. Chen and Hou began their collaboration in 1978 when they both worked for the independent Young Sun (Yongsheng) production company. Young Sun was a midsized company established by a major distributor, Jiang Risheng, and a veteran director, Lai Chengying, uncle of Chen Kunhou. In the 1970s Young Sun produced a number of romantic melodramas when Taiwan-made romance was immensely popular in Southeast Asia. Hou and Chen were both Lai's protégés. They assisted Lai in scripts, directing, and cinematography. This situation lasted until 1980 when Chen was given his chance to direct. But the collaboration between them remained. Hou would write scripts for Chen to direct and shoot while Chen would serve as Hou's cinematographer when Hou directed. From 1980 to 1982, for a couple of small independents, Hou and Chen completed remarkably successful romantic comedies, including *Spring in Autumn* (Tian liang hao ge qiu, 1980; dir. Chen Kunhou), *I come with the wave* (Wo ta lang erlai, 1980; dir. Chen), *Bouncing sweetheart* (Beng beng yi chuan xin, 1981; dir. Chen), *Six Is Company* (Qia ru caidie fei fei fei, 1982; dir. Chen), *Cute Girl* (aka *Lovable You*, Jiushi liu liu de ta, 1980; dir. Hou), *Cheerful Wind* (Feng'er ti ta cai, 1981; dir. Hou Hsiao-hsien), and *The Green Green Grass of Home* (Zai na hepan qing cao qing, 1982; dir. Hou).

These films, like Lin's student fare, were low-budget romantic comedies casting fresh faces rather than aging and expensive stars like Brigitte Lin Qingxia (Lin Ch'ing-hsia). The other element that differentiates their films from other contemporary love stories is their visual style. Chen's wide shots of rural landscapes present a shift from the standardized *settings* of the Qiong Yao melodrama to concrete, refreshing *places*. His long takes incorporate specific locations into the narrative and, as a result, enrich the visual connotations of an expected romance story. Moreover, laconic humor and occasional sight and audio gags make their films appealing to working-class audiences and young students. To critics and young writers like Xiao Ye and, particularly, Wu Nianzhen, these films were more than light comedies; they dealt with conflicts between modern and traditional and differences between rural and urban life. The dual understanding of cinema as an entertainment with meaningful social critique brought Wu and Hou together, who began a long collaboration together.

Offscreen Heroes

The KMT's top-down political and social control finally faced a crisis in 1979 with the famous "Formosa incident" (*Meilidao shijian*). *Formosa* ("beautiful island," a name given to Taiwan by Portuguese traders in the sixteenth century) was a magazine published by leading political dissidents, most of whom identified themselves as ethnic Taiwanese, not Chinese. *Formosa* was founded as a direct means to spread oppositional views. The dissidents assembled a rally in Kaohsiung, Taiwan's second city, away from the political center of Taipei, to voice their demands for democracy. Political assembly was still prohibited at the time, but the Formosa group wished to use this rally to force the ruling KMT to relax its control. The rally ended with a brutal crackdown and the arrest of almost all the elite members of the opposition. Evidence of police brutality was quickly and neatly suppressed. The rally was officially characterized as a "political disturbance and subversion of national security." Yet the Formosa incident led intellectuals and middle-class cultural elites to reconsider issues of political and cultural legitimacy as represented by the KMT and its ideological foundations. Anachronistic sinocentrism was under pressure and Taiwan nativism was upheld as a new direction for cultural production in an increasingly modernized, open society. Government's brutal suppression of oppositional voices galvanized artists and writers to react in their own fields. If political liberation was premature and couldn't be tolerated by the ruling regime, then perhaps milder reforms could be achieved in less threatening areas such as art, culture, and the cinema. Xiao Ye was in New York City when he discovered the uncensored reports of the Formosa incident. He decided to drop everything and returned home, starting a "revolution" from within. Upon his return, he entered CMPC to "work on the cinema and within the institution that I despised the most."[16]

Xiao Ye

KMT thought they could still control the society and the media. They were wrong. I thought their days were soon to be over.

—XIAO YE (REFERRING TO THE "APPLE-PEELING INCIDENT"[17])

Xiao Ye (b. 1951) is the pen name for Li Yuan (fig. 2.3). Before joining CMPC, he had established himself as a prominent writer. When he was still a biology student at National Normal University, he published short stories and essays in the literary supplements of major newspapers. His work was very popular among college and high school students, and he remained one of the best-selling writers in the mid-1970s. The veteran director of youth stories, Bai Jingrui, took an interest in Xiao Ye's collection of stories, *Birth of a Moth* (Yong zhi sheng). In 1977, Xiao Ye adapted his story "The War of the Sexes" (Nanhai yu nühai de zhanzheng) into a script that was produced by Young Sun. Hou Hsiao-hsien served as the assistant director for this film. After graduation, Xiao Ye continued to work on the fringes of the film world by coordinating a column on film criticism for the *United Daily News*. He organized contributions by various literary and cultural figures on the state of Taiwan cinema. Since these pronouncements were invariably critical, film distributors took note of the low esteem in which Taiwan film was held by the intellectual establishment.[18]

2.3 Xiao Ye, writer and CMPC producer
(COURTESY TAIPEI FILM ARCHIVE)

After a year's stint in New York, Xiao Ye returned to Taiwan and entered CMPC as a scriptwriter and production manager in 1982, and immediately set to cowriting a script with another new production assistant, Wu Nianzhen, for an anti-Communist film, *Portrait of a Fanatic* (Kulian, 1982; dir. Wang Tong). But Xiao Ye was fortunate to enter a stodgy organization at its most vulnerable time. New ideas were being sought to respond to new policies and a weakening market. By the late 1970s, film censorship was under attack by the industry and critics as outmoded hindrances to domestic film development. The film censorship established in the 1930s by KMT's wartime cultural commissions was one of extreme propriety and almost fundamentalist proscription. Stipulations were enforced at the scriptwriting stage and included the following: no depictions of Chairman Mao, the PRC flag, or the PRC anthem, even within an anti-Communist story;[19] no more than 30 percent of dialogue could be in dialects or foreign languages; villains could not be killed off before they had a chance to repent; no ear waxing, nose-picking, or other backward behaviors; superstitious practices and the supernatural were to be discouraged; authorities had to be properly depicted, e. g., no policeman's wife could be licentious, and so on.[20] Brigitte Lin Qingxia's debut film, *The Window* (Chuangwai, 1973; dir. Song Cunshou) was banned outright because it was about a romance between a high school girl and her teacher. John Woo once remarked that if he had continued to work in Taiwan, he would never have been able to make his famous *A Better Tomorrow* films because suggestions of police proximity to criminal intent, let alone corruption, would never be tolerated.[21] The film censorship bureau would like to have sustained its strict pedagogical control of content for as long as possible; yet a civil society in the making and pragmatic considerations of market differentiation led the KMT government to gradually relax film censorship in the early 1980s.

Cultural liberalization enjoyed institutional support but it came gradually and incrementally. First, in early 1982 the GIO introduced a film law that reclassified cinema as a "cultural enterprise" rather than an "amusement enterprise" (comparable to bars, brothels, and dance halls).[22] This change immediately upgraded cinema to a different, higher tier within government administration. Reduction of taxes and tariffs on film, as well as subsidy programs and relaxation of censorship were to be implemented; government was now obliged to assist rather than simply regulate film development. In addition, a two-tier classification system (restricted and general) would be implemented for the first time.[23] This allowed a market differentiation in widening the scope of audience demographics in the hope of increasing film consumption. Second, the drop in preproduction censorship discussed above ("Peeling the apple") allowed a more efficient management of film production. Films could be made without submitting scripts to authorities; thereafter, production was made quicker and more responsive to themes and fads of public life.

It was within this changing context that Xiao Ye and Wu Nianzhen were assigned to undertake CMPC's newcomer policy. In an interview Xiao Ye acknowledges that it was difficult to wrestle the newcomer policy into place at CMPC.

> Our generation was reaching the age of 30 or more at a time when the society was becoming more open, mature and affluent. The market for film was very poor so we had to change. The tendency was for all things to change in directing. New directors, trained abroad in the U.S., came back with more open minds. Before the 1970s, it was difficult for them to go abroad.[24]

While representing the oldest studio to these newcomers, Xiao Ye and Wu Nianzhen soon became comrades with the new directors. This was not coincidental because, in addition to their common experiences under KMT rule, they shared similar ambitions of making works that went beyond the company line to express their personal visions. As Wan Ren commented on his work within the New Cinema, "common people's thoughts and feelings, the transition from agrarian to urban life, and the 'shadows of the directors'" can be seen.[25]

Xiao Ye's active involvement in the New Cinema expanded from writing proposals to writing scripts. After the initial success of his 1983 productions, Xiao Ye put forward more scripts: with director Wang Tong for his period drama *Run Away* (Ce ma ru lin, 1984), and with Ke Yizheng in *I Love Mary* (Wo ai mali, 1984), based on another Huang Chunming novel. Xiao Ye's most famous script is *The Terrorizers* (Kongbu fenzi, 1986), cowritten with Edward Yang. Xiao Ye's commitment to the newcomer policy continued through 1988 when CMPC signed contracts with yet another group of newcomers. In 1989 he quit CMPC, and so did his good friend Wu Nianzhen.

Wu Nianzhen

dou - san :
a borrowed life

> *Only when I went off to primary school, did I learn of the existence of China Central Broadcasting Station, and that Mandarin was the language everybody else spoke.*
>
> —WU NIANZHEN[26]

Wu Nianzhen (b. 1952), whose real name is Wu Wenqin, comes from a mining community north of Taipei. A local-born Taiwanese and son of a poor miner, Wu had to struggle harder than the postwar mainlander generation to which most literary, arts, and cultural elites belonged. Wu joined Taiwan's literary establishment in 1976 by winning awards in major competitions held by the Literary Supplement of *United Daily News*, a hotbed of literary discovery and talent. In 1978 he started writing scripts and was hired in CMPC's production unit in 1981. Best known as Hou Hsiao-hsien's screenwriter, Wu is the most prominent screenwriter in Taiwan. Now he has become an important director, commentator, and television personality in his own right (fig. 2.4). Wu is very prolific, drawing on his own memories and historical imagination of Taiwan's past. Dozens of his scripts have been produced, perhaps nearly one hundred, including films made in Hong Kong and China. Many of Hou Hsiao-hsien's most famous films, along with those of Edward Yang, Wang Tong, and Ann Hui, were scripted or coscripted by Wu. He prefers collaborative, improvisational composition, calling himself more of a "facilitator" than a scriptwriter, finding the actual writing stage to be mechanical and anticlimactic.[27] Wu also discovered that directors rarely made good storytellers, especially when sitting in pitch meetings with executives. As a charismatic raconteur, Wu performed as go-between, eliciting story ideas and striking images from young directors, and then enticing CMPC accountants into releasing funds to go into production. With a famously sharp wit, he acted as dialogue expert in story/scriptwriting conferences with Hou and Zhu Tianwen.[28]

Wu Nianzhen's affinity with nativism is connected to language, ethnicity, style, and gender. As a gifted writer, Wu incorporates Taiwanese dialects and expressions into his compositions. In his stories and scripts, he uses bits of slang and colonial residues (such as Japanese loan-words) that for some audiences would

2.4 Wu Nianzhen, scriptwriter and director

be considered gauche. The title of his first film as director is *Dou-san* (1994), the Japanese word for "Papa." The rest of the title (*A Borrowed Life*) is in English. In Hou's "Son's Big Doll," scripted by Wu, a Christian (Quaker) church is referred to as "Jesus temple" (*yesu miao*), a parochial expression that would be used only by local *minnan* speakers. Yet for these audiences such language would be refreshingly topical because it's taken from lived communities that hadn't been seen or heard in movies since the end of *taiyu pian* in the late 1960s. The presence of Taiwanese language in itself signifies certain ethnic and class backgrounds, in tension with the official Mandarin-language cultural policy. But it is not simply the presence of dialect that marks an irreverent attitude toward official standards. Taiwanese dialect is used liberally in a film like Bai Jingrui's *Goodbye Darling* (1971), in which dialect speakers sound loutish, backward, and doomed to reform (see chapter 1). Wu's use of the Taiwanese language relishes its cadences, its salty expressions, its non sequiturs and specificity in a way that normalizes it. In other words, Wu Nianzhen draws on the example of nativist writers before him in employing Taiwanese as a robust, living language rather than a dialect. Its subordinate connotations, which the KMT and mainlander community took pains to emphasize, are put aside.

Though Wu has written some of the most austere, challenging scripts for Hou Hsiao-hsien's films (such as *City of Sadness*), his work contains an earthy, sometimes vulgar sense of humor. A good example comes from *City of Sadness* (1989), when a raffish character named Old Wu—played by Wu himself—tells a story about changing to a new national flag. It is 1945, and after the war the Taiwanese people must replace the Japanese rising sun with the ROC (Republic of China, founded by the KMT party in 1911 and official name of Taiwan) national flag. The head of his village (in a remote mining town) has ordered everyone to get an ROC flag, but people are uncertain about which way it's supposed to hang:

> People argued: should the sun be on the top or on the bottom? They argued for ages. Someone told the District Head it was on top. He said with great authority that that was nonsense. When the sun comes out, the sky is all red. Some people were skeptical and the District Head was worried. People came back from Chiu-fen in the afternoon. They said this was ridiculous. The sun should be hung on top. You would be shot or jailed for this. The District Head was so nervous and broadcast the order for everyone to change. But it was already 5:00, time to lower the flag. And so the sky was full of red. What is funnier is that the Japanese flags were no use any more. Our women were so thrifty. They made them into clothes for the children. All the kids playing outside had red asses. Like monkeys.

"And not only the kids," pipes in a listener at the table. "Old Wu wore one too."[29]

This vignette deftly combines various themes about the Taiwanese postwar, postcolonial experience. Subtly, the arbitrariness of national iconography is exposed ("top or bottom?") along with sly references to socialism ("the sky was full of red"). The defeated Japanese are ridiculed, linking them to children, diapers, and monkeys, through the unbeatable practicality of Taiwanese women. The motif of "redness" continues when someone explains why Old Wu was wearing the pants: he has no children, so if he doesn't wear the pants, the rising sun will go to waste. Because he is a schoolteacher, further jokes about redness soon follow. "We don't want to give mainlanders the impression that all teachers here have red asses, do we?!" Here is an outrageous reference to the politics of educated locals, the very ones targeted for purges by the new mainland émigrés. These Taiwanese intellectuals happily drink and crack rude jokes about their prospects for political participation in the immediate postwar. Yet this rowdy, irreverent humor signals not only a characteristically Taiwanese boys' night out. It precisely contains the seeds of what the film *City of Sadness* is all about: Taiwanese expectations of a long-awaited reunion with the motherland, answered with a renewal of colonial domination.

Hou's staging and shooting of the scene enhances the stylish yet natural setup: a circular table, hotpot bubbling in the middle, people sitting in medium shot, drinking steadily, a dazzling stained-glass window in the background. It's the talk, however—specifically Old Wu's story—that occupies the center of attention. Wu's rapid-fire delivery, his expert timing, and salty Hokkien expressions show a master storyteller's art, as we are caught up in his tale along with the others around the table. The story is a political one, having to do with a succession of power and the common people who cope with it. Yet it is colorful, accessible, and very funny. Serious points are being made here, but they are couched in the easiest, most casual of rhetoric. Moreover, this is clearly Wu Nianzhen's métier, the kind of performance one sees in other Wu-scripted films centering on male camaraderie, earthy humor, and Taiwanese coming-of-age. There is a certain tone or signature here that could only be made by Wu, not by Hou, Zhu Tianwen, or anyone else.

An inventive sequence from *Dou-san* shows Wu's facility with memory and humor. The title character takes his boy to an old movie theater with a Japanese film and narrator (*bianshi,* or *benshi* in Japanese). As the weepy melodrama unspools, the benshi both narrates the tale and impersonates the voices of the Japanese characters in Taiwanese language. By this time (c. 1960), benshi were extinct in Japan because their role was to accompany silent films, which lasted in Japan and the colonies until the late 1930s. But benshi survived in rural Taiwan, Hawaii, Brazil, and other outposts. Here the images, the Japanese-language sound track, and the Taiwanese bianshi's performance overlap in a hypnotic mélange of sentimental nostalgia. A reverse shot shows the audience transfixed beneath the projector beam, thoughtfully chewing seeds and piercing the light with swirls of cigarette smoke. However, the lyrical atmosphere is suddenly interrupted. The bianshi excuses himself, saying (in Japanese), "Sumimasen." Then (in Taiwanese): "Mr. Seiga. Please go to the lobby for a phone call." Seiga, the boy's "Dou-san," gets up and tells the boy to stay put. The bianshi returns to the climactic moment in the story: "Matsuko-san!" (in voice-over). "Where are you?" Again, an interruption: "Ladies and gentlemen: another box of popsicles has arrived. Those who didn't get one before, don't miss out this time." The story continues, alternating between an account of the separated lovers and a ventriloquy of the heroine's tearful distress. On the screen, an overhead shot of the lovers embracing on a picturesque bridge. Seiga doesn't return to his seat, and the little boy sees someone he knows. Excited, he calls down, "Uncle!" The audience shushes him. He yells again. The bianshi stops his performance and asks, "Whose kid is that! Making such a racket. Please, would the parents attend to your child! He's disturbing the movie! Sorry about that, folks."

In this scene, we see several ingeniously intertwined elements: Japanese colonial residues, with which Dou-san is identified; the overlapping languages and diegetic worlds; the abrupt interruptions, which continue to this day in Taiwan's movie theaters;[30] the anxiety of a small boy's sense of abandonment to a dusky, disorienting environment not altogether friendly. Drawing on Wu's own memories of a primal event in his childhood, the moment incorporates palpable ruptures and incongruities. Discontinuities abound and testify to willful slices in the fabric of individual and collective memory. Discontinuities between screen diegesis, the bianshi's interpretation, and mode of exhibition; between Japanese colonial and

2.5 Theatre scene in *Dou-san* (1994; dir. Wu Nianzhen)   (COURTESY TAIPEI FILM ARCHIVE)

postcolonial, yet underdeveloped, Taiwan; and, finally, between a young boy and his throwback father; all these are skillfully layered in this key scene (fig. 2.5).

The discontinuities also hint at a transposition of historical modes of performance. Because of its ambiguous colonial status, native Taiwan works as a kind of time capsule. The rural movie house is at once a vessel of silent film, an example of colonial modernity, and a domestication of foreign cultural technology. This theater encloses an alien yet intimate and cherished performance. The sound track and diegesis are Japanese, yet the storyteller's art—including his interjections—enframes it for native purposes. No longer does a Japanese film work to propagate imperial values. Empire is extinguished yet its remnants are recycled, like the rising sun flag. The extinct Japanese benshi is in a way reincarnated, just as the melodramatic story is retold for a new audience in a new age. Storytelling practice and audience here invoke very old images of Asian popular art, even though the specific film pretext is only a few years old.[31] It isn't difficult to pick out the underlying features of silent film and, beneath that, traditions of the variety hall, itinerant entertainer, or sermon. It's significant that Dou-san leaves the theater to gamble and sing in a nearby brothel, where the boy is coddled and teased. In this sense Wu's film definitely represents the practice of "commingled media," Joseph Anderson's conception of the benshi institution.[32] From screen to voice, colony to homeland, boyhood traumas to stories of growing up, *Dou-san* signals a wide variety of transformations.

In the same film, Wu narrates in voice-over:

> All of a sudden, I recalled the time when I was a little kid and was abandoned by Dou-san, left alone in the movie theater. In a trance, I imagined that Dou-san has played his trick again and stood me up. I was again thrown into a void filled with subdued sobbing, and he went away to a place that was strange, mysterious, and beyond my understanding, to have good time with his old buddies.[33]

Here a sense of Taiwanese vulnerability is outlined, but it takes on a specifically gendered appearance. Wu sketches a concrete, downtrodden male identity that often appears in metaphors of injury: a debilitating lung disease in *Dou-san*; a wounded father and a friend who loses an arm in *Dust in the Wind* (1986); a brother whose finger is chopped off in *Buddha Bless America* (1996); a deaf-mute in *City of Sadness*, and so on. Such figures of debilitation signal a distinct sense of truncation from an organic, continuous past or patrimony. However, these images of downtrodden Taiwanese masculinity contrast with willful, intransigent women. They conspicuously overlook female experiences of Taiwanese postcoloniality and ethnic socialization, a highly visible element in many other New Cinema films, as in the work of writer Zhu Tianwen and the directors Wang Tong, Edward Yang, and Zhang Yi.

Wu's grassroots approach, his "facilitator" role rather than an auteur, is perhaps best seen in his contribution to lesser known but popular films of the 1980s. *Moonlight* (aka *Papa, Can You Hear Me Singing?* or *Da cuo che*, 1983; dir. Yu Kanping), *Old Mo's Second Spring* (*Laomo de dierge chuntian*, 1985; dir. Li Youning), and *People Between Two Chinas* (*Haixia liang'an*, 1988; dir. Yu Kanping) represent Wu's populist intent, to make films that "could actually reach audiences."[34] It was not through Hou Hsiao-hsien or Edward Yang that Wu could materialize his populist vision, but through his collaborations with other New Cinema directors who worked in popular formats. These filmmakers include Yu Kanping, Li Youning, Chen Kunhou, and Wang Tong. They are mostly unknown outside Taiwan because their films never won any major international awards. For New Cinema critics, they were often considered second-rate directors for their lack of "groundbreaking" work or evident auteur status. Perhaps because of their preference for "access" over "art," their films were able to attract audiences by simply exploiting old formulas such as melodrama. Perhaps because of the lack of auteurist preoccupations, their films were capable of directly tackling drastic sociopolitical change.

For instance, Yu Kanping and Wu first explored the issue of mainland émigrés in *Moonlight,* which centers on a deaf-mute KMT soldier and a baby whom he rescues from a garbage dump. He raises the girl by retrieving bottles, which he uses to decorate their home in the slum. The girl grows up and becomes a pop star. The deaf-mute papa, left behind, dies in emotional distress. This film has an overt melodramatic narrative with elaborate Las Vegas–style musical numbers, rarely seen in Taiwan cinema. Cross-cutting between a live concert in which the girl rises to her stardom and a bedridden father awaiting his little girl's return, the film reworks familiar grounds of pathos as seen in *The Jazz Singer* and *Imitation of Life*. Formerly a comedy director, Yu made *Moonlight* into a remarkable genre picture that deals with filial piety in a rapidly modernizing, capitalist Taiwan society. Within a year it was rereleased eight times in Taipei.[35] Wu Nianzhen cowrote the script and also wrote the lyrics for its soundtrack album, which was even more successful than the film.

Moonlight was very different from orthodox New Cinema films, compared to the scripts Wu wrote the same year, the genuinely nativist adaptation *The Sandwich Man* and the complex but rather cold *That Day, on the Beach*. *Moonlight*'s clear generic traits (musicals and excessive melodramatic sentiment) prompted critics to question its intention. Former Taiwan Film Archive director and eminent critic Huang Jianye described it as "sentimental and fantasy-driven."[36] But it opened a series of films depicting discharged KMT soldiers and their diaspora within Taiwan. When martial law was later lifted in 1987, Wu and Yu immediately worked on the reunion between KMT émigrés and their long-lost families in the compelling *People Between Two Chinas*. It tells the story of a retired KMT soldier who brings his Taiwan wife and son to meet his mainland wife, daughter, and granddaughter in Hong Kong. Through Wu's scathing treatment, a political change manifests itself in a melodrama of a family reunion reflected in shopping, feasting, sightseeing, clubbing, hair perms, and makeup. The reunion tour, though brief, brings up memories and old scars as well as differences of opinion, discontent, and conflict between peoples across the straits. Wu Nianzhen, once again, was able to realize his populist vision by reworking popular formats.

Long after Wu left CMPC, he gained wide acclaim for his television series on Taiwan's native cultures, *Wu Nianzhen's Taiwan* (Taiwan nianzhen qing, 1997–1999; TVBS network). In the mid-1990s Wu directed two films, *Dou-san: A Borrowed Life* (1994) and *Buddha Bless America* (Taiping tianguo, 1996). Both of these films explored aspects of colonial Taiwanese ethnicity, and the former, backed by Shochiku in Japan, was a modest success. A strong nativist tendency, derived partly from themes of the nativist writers of the 1970s, was brought out in the New Cinema largely through Wu Nianzhen's efforts.[37]

Return to History: Wang Tong

When I visited Japan, I stumbled on old Japanese books on Taiwan history. It was an eye-opening experience. Through these old books, I was able to get a closer look at the history of Taiwan.

—WANG TONG[38]

Before Hou Hsiao-hsien launched his famous "Taiwan trilogy" in 1989 (*City of Sadness, The Puppetmaster,* and *Good Men, Good Women*), Wang Tong had already begun his investigation into Taiwan history. Wang made his *Strawman* (Daocao ren) in 1987, the first installment of his "nativist trilogy" (*xiangtu sanbuqu*). *Strawman* is a black comedy set in the last stages of Japanese occupation. Like Hou Hsiao-hsien and Chen Kunhou in their apprenticeship, Wang Tong reworks popular genres to accommodate nativist themes, a pattern seen in his entry film to the New Cinema, *A Flower in the Rainy Night* (Kanhai de rizi, CMPC) in 1983.

Wang was already a veteran when he joined the New Cinema. Well before Edward Yang, Wan Ren, or other new directors entered the trade, Wang had already established himself as a known director. He had made two anti-Communist films, *If I Were for Real* (Jiaru woshi zhende, 1980; Young Sun) and *Portrait of a Fanatic* (1982), both of which were banned in Hong Kong. In addition, he directed two comedies, *Don't Look at the Moon Through the Window* (Chuangkou de yueliang buzhun toukan) and *One Hundred Point* (Baifen mandian) in 1981. Despite being helmed by a neophyte, *If I Were for Real* received three Golden Horse Awards, including best film.

Clearly, Wang Tong belongs to the old school and, as a result, critics have different views of his work as compared to younger directors. Upon graduation from the National College of Arts in the mid-1960s, Wang entered CMPC as a set designer, drawing models, props, and costumes. Since then, he has worked with almost every major director, across many different genres and different styles. He was involved in more than one hundred films, including healthy realism, propaganda policy films, war epics, martial arts, kung fu, comedies, and Qiong Yao romantic melodramas. Wang worked with famous directors of the 1960s and 1970s such as King Hu, Li Hanxiang, Li Jia, Bai Jingrui, and Li Xing.

Wang has a strong identification with nativism, despite his solid CMPC experience.[39] *A Flower in the Rainy Night,* a nativist classic by Huang Chunming, was Wang's entry into the New Cinema. *Flower* exemplifies Wang as an old school director in a new age, striving to balance the demands of studio affiliation and the emerging social consciousness of nativism. *Flower* was one of the most desired literary properties by many directors when the novel was first published in 1967.[40] But its subject matter was considered taboo according to the censorship rules of the time.[41] It tells the story of an aging prostitute and her will to begin a new life by becoming a mother. She picks a good-hearted fisherman as the chosen father and leaves her job when she becomes pregnant. Returning to her peasant family, she is determined to raise the child in a hard but honest life. Everyone in the village welcomes and respects her. When the baby is born, she takes the baby on a train ride to see schools of mackerel on the east coast. It is the harvest season for this virile fish; it is also the season of rebirth.

The prostitute theme proved to be an effective marketing device. *Flower* outperformed *Growing Up* and *The Sandwich Man* with a box office record of NT$ 23 million (US$ 600,000) in Taipei alone. It was a personal victory for Wang and a further endorsement for the New Cinema, considering that the standard figure for a hit was NT$ 10 million at the time and the fact that the average box office for locally made films had dropped.[42] *Flower* further proved nativist literature could be profitable and injected a great deal of confidence into producers and distributors, who would in the following years invest in many literary adaptations.

But the film received a lukewarm critical response. Chen Kuo-fu (Chen Guofu), for instance, indicated that the film was not worth considering despite belonging to the New Cinema. Zhan Hongzhi, a powerful opinion leader and a major backer of the New Cinema, called the film "relatively mediocre," compared to films by Hou Hsiao-hsien and Edward Yang.[43]

Flower is a beautifully shot film. Wang's treatment of character and meticulous organization of plot is also outstanding. The film features a delicate mesh of characterization. From the principal role (Bai Mei) to the supporting cast in the brothel, each character is efficiently sketched in order to convey and construct Bai Mei's story. Flashbacks are inserted to build motivation for Bai Mei's will to change her fate: "I don't believe a child with a mother like me can't have a future" are her final words in the film. According to Derek Elley, "Wang Tong's immaculate direction and visual sense unites the best of classic Chinese film-making with a realism drawn from the New Wave."[44] By scrupulously following classical narrative modes, Wang Tong delivers a nativist classic onto the screen in a modest but highly effective fashion. Why then was *Flower* dismissed by critical champions of the New Cinema as "mediocre"?

Perhaps they thought Wang's involvement in the New Cinema lacked credibility. Wang already had a liability because of his old school background. In addition, his ethnic and class background may have been another problem. For directors who want to work on nativist themes, their ethnicity and class matters. Born on the mainland, son of a KMT general, Wang had a comfortable, if not privileged, upbringing. This is well represented in Wang's 1999 autobiographical film, *The Red Persimmon* (Hong shizi, CMPC). He grew up principally under the influence of his mother, a Chinese ink painter. This specific kind of mainland, *Chinese* upbringing would cast doubt on Wang Tong's ability to sympathetically render local experience and expressions, essential to such a film as *Flower in the Rainy Night*. Critics of the time expected a personal investment as revealed in an authentic, authorial signature. This in turn would consolidate a reliable, sustainable aesthetic for the New Cinema to be recognized internationally. (See fig. 2.6.)

Instead of cultivating a more restrained auteur style, like most of his New Cinema counterparts, Wang returned to CMPC to make a film at the studio's bid-

2.6 *A Flower in the Rainy Night* (1983; dir. Wang Tong)   (COURTESY CMPC)

ding. After *Flower*, CMPC ordered him to make the neo-period, martial arts picture *Run Away* (1984), one step beyond what Wang wanted for his own career. He had already proposed the nativist comedy *Strawman*, but it was not approved.[45] *Run Away* was the company's attempt to revitalize one of the most persistent genres in Chinese-language cinema. It is an unusual, revisionist period picture about a group of bandits unwittingly civilized by a captive woman. But it has little in common with the aesthetic or social features of the New Cinema. As a journeyman filmmaker, Wang said that it was a necessary compromise if he were to make another nativist film.[46]

Wang got his wish. In 1987, CMPC allocated a smaller budget of under NT$ 8 million (cf. NT$ 20 million for *Run Away*) for Wang to make *Strawman*, number one in his "nativist trilogy." The story centers on peasants during the final days of World War II. Japanese military officers requisition all their valuables, crops, and animals. People are desperate for food as they watch the birds pick over their fields. From high above, B52s drop their ordnance on bridges and roads. Children play hide and seek among the ruins. An unexploded bomb seems to present an opportunity for two brothers and the village headman. Circumstances are so straitened that the villagers resort to wishful thinking. They decide to hand-carry the heavy

2.7 *Strawman* (1987; dir. Wang Tong) (COURTESY CMPC)

American bomb to district headquarters where they expect to be rewarded. The Japanese officer in command is terrified and orders them at gunpoint to toss it off a cliff into the sea. The bomb goes off. Hundreds of fish float to the surface. The peasants return without reward but loaded down with fresh fish (fig. 2.7).

Strawman is a comedy of the absurd against a background of wartime privation. Peasant life is communal, colorful, and childlike. Rural tics and idiosyncrasies, as well as outright blunders of village people, are lovingly depicted. Wang Tong is comparable in this regard to the Japanese director Imamura Shohei because both share an affection for the common people (usually portrayed onscreen as deprived or pathetic). Yet these are people whose appetite for life is the strongest. When Imamura went to Taiwan to film parts of his wartime prostitute story *Zegen* (1987), Wang was there to help as his art director.

Strawman, Banana Paradise (Xiangjiao tiantang, 1989), and *Hill of No Return* (Wuyan de shanqiu, 1992) completed Wang Tong's "nativist trilogy." Wang wanted to use these three films to document Taiwan's modern history, which begins with the Japanese occupation and ends with KMT's authoritarian rule until the late 1980s. Chronologically, *Hill of No Return* opens the trilogy by depicting Taiwanese and Japanese prospectors on the trail for gold during the Taisho period (1912–1923); *Strawman* stands in the middle by telling a comedy of hunger in the deprived countryside near the end of the Pacific war (the Showa period between 1924 and 1989); finally, *Banana Paradise* features the survival skills of bumbling KMT soldiers in postwar Taiwan. For forty years, these soldiers keep changing their names and forging identities to build a home in Taiwan while avoiding political purges.

Wang's investigation into Taiwan history is intertwined with the problems of identity. One may say that his nativist preference derives from the old school, with its benevolent gaze at Taiwanese country bumpkins, a trope connected to the healthy realist period. But Wang's nativist trilogy goes beyond a didactic ethnographic exposition, like his teachers Li Xing and Bai Jingrui; he puts a particular emphasis on the "incidental," the temporary uses of flexible identities, which permit clueless working-class folks to survive capricious politics. Identity politics was the dominant political issue in the late 1980s (and remains so today). Almost all New Cinema directors had to deal with this hot topic. Hou's trilogy focuses on extraordinary Taiwanese: artists, gangsters, leftist elites, and writers who were purged by right-wing regimes, both Japanese and KMT. Wang Tong, on the other hand, leans toward hungry farmers, disabled farmwives, foot soldiers, refugees, prostitutes, and deranged Japanese officers. Hou treats the issue of identity as a matter of conscience, of choosing sides; but in the final analysis he acknowledges the norm of Chinese nationality. Wang's view of identity politics is more pragmatic and contingent; it is no less than a matter of food and lodging. To these wretched people, identity is simply a mechanism for survival. For Wang Tong, origins of identity is a nonissue, given the layers and striations of colonial occupation. Wang's films try to get at the living, hybrid histories of Taiwan people rather than engaging in political debates. Wang has commented on this in an interview (fig. 2.8).

I think Taiwan is different from China. Taiwan is very interesting. Taiwan is Chinese, but it's also like Japan in the 1950s. It too accepts American aid. Its culture is very fresh. Even today, this continues. It's very complicated, but also rich and full. Taiwan has all kinds of cultures. Therefore, it changes fast. There's a deep influence from Japan. I used to love to watch Japanese films; we used to live in a Japanese house. Some of my friends spoke Japanese, our teachers spoke Japanese too. It's like living in Japan. But Taiwan is not Japan. I am a mainlander. Living in Taiwan is like living in a foreign country. It's very strange. When I arrived here, I felt like I was in Japan. But this place was full of Chinese people, Chinese temples, and so on. Later, American soldiers came onto this island. The complexity of this place makes it an excellent environment for filmmaking. There is no such country like Taiwan in the world. Unlike Korea, which hated and still hates Japan, Taiwan maintains a friendship with Japan. This country is very strange.[47]

Wang's preference for comedy may have prevented his trilogy from receiving sufficient critical attention. It is true that Wang's trilogy lacks the formal rigor of

2.8 Wang Tong in his Taipei office (2002).

Hou Hsiao-hsien's Taiwan trilogy. Furthermore, the use of comedy opens Wang to charges of primitivism, considering the gentle satire with which Taiwan's peasants are handled. Significantly, Wang has said that *Strawman* was partly inspired by the Botswanan comedy *The Gods Must Be Crazy* (1980; dir. Jamie Uys).[48] Although both Wang and Jamie Uys may claim they are making innocent fun with childlike natives, they cannot escape the colonial power differential endemic to the comic premise. At the same time, however, Wang's films are true to many native Taiwanese memories of the countryside. They have a sharp nostalgia that acknowledges the backwardness of provincial Taiwanese life, and do not sentimentalize it. Wang's film *Away We Go* (Ziyou menshen, 2001; CMPC) is characteristic of his regard for typical Taiwanese bumblers who somehow prevail through dumb luck. Wang's comedies are distinctive and acerbic, and they have an accessibility that captures the frequent incongruities of Taiwan's predicaments.

Invoking Taboos: Wan Ren

> With printing materials subject to strict censorship and television controlled by the government and the party, film was the only medium to express social criticism.[49]
>
> —WAN REN

Since the 1960s when KMT introduced healthy realism, Taiwan cinema has been defined as a cinema with two lives—popular as well as didactic—and with two missions—commercial success and artistic achievement. The cinema in Taiwan was able to sustain this duality for as long as two decades, thanks to a closed me-

2.9 Wan Ren

dia market characterized by complicated protection policies, draconian censorship, and strict broadcasting and publishing regulations. Taiwan-made films and television programs, though conformist and out-of-date, were guaranteed a large market share and were free from competition from imports. This warm bed for local media personnel became cold and threadbare in the 1980s with deregulation and a more open market. Hong Kong commercial videos carrying television programs with dazzling editing and fast-paced narratives captured the attention of the audience. New Cinema was thus an innovative corporate strategy to deal with this so-called "crisis." New Cinema not only was supposed to win back the audience, it was also expected to raise the overall standards of domestic production. The new directors, like directors in the 1960s, were expected to fulfill the dual objective—the clichéd balance of art and commerce, propaganda and entertainment. Wan Ren is yet another director who found himself trapped in this duality, something that turned out to be a schizophrenic demand.

Wan Ren (fig. 2.9) is perhaps the most explicitly political and the least auteurist of the New Cinema directors. Political, because Wan directly exposes social problems and, hence, has constantly run into trouble with censorship. Because Wan's work crosses a wide range of topics, genres, and styles, he cannot be easily accommodated within the auteur pattern. With only eight films by 2004 and a lack of repetition, it is difficult to judge his work according to familiar critical procedures.

Since the critical furor over *The Sandwich Man*, Wan has experienced even more intimate knowledge of the pressures of censorship. While we might suppose an artist like Wan would learn to negotiate censorship pitfalls, this never happened. Wan always seemed more concerned with his pressing topics than with institutional coping. After making the family melodrama *Ah Fei* (You ma cai zi, 1983), Wan, with his third film *Super Citizen* (Chaoji shimin, 1985), again faced state censorship. *Super Citizen* begins with a young man in search of his missing sister in the capital. In his relentless search, the man from the country encounters characters living on the fringes of the city—a con artist, a prostitute, a punk girl, and a lunatic bum. The film thus unfolds a decoupage of poverty, corruption, crime, and disillusionment with modern development and urban prosperity.

Motifs of "search" and "rescue" remind us of the famous captivity narratives in John Ford's *The Searchers* and Martin Scorsese's *Taxi Driver*. Both *The Searchers* and *Taxi Driver*, despite different settings and premises, place locales at the forefront of their concerns. To a large extent, the centrality of locale—the American West and New York City—overwhelms the characters. *Super Citizen* also personifies Taipei as a central character, the source of moral corruption. The brother never finds his sister, but he decides to stay in Taipei in the end. By following his sister's path, he, too, is engulfed by the metropolis's black, underground economy.

To depict the city in all its insidious and mystical allure, Wan Ren revisits the same slum locale he used in "The Taste of Apples," his short film for *The Sandwich Man*. Recall the opening shot of "Apples": the fade-in to a wide shot of an old, cluttered housing area surrounded by a few skyscrapers. Shot in black-and-white, this establishing view sets up the tone of the film, visually as well as thematically—an unpleasing past and a memory of underdevelopment. The slum thus functions as a visual motif, the "spectacle" of Taiwan's Third World privation in need of American aid. But he stepped on a censorship mine by making the mistake of anachronism. Censors asked, why was the Taipei of the 1980s being portrayed like the Taipei of the early 1970s (the setting of "The Taste of Apples")?

CMPC's political watchdogs had been alarmed by the strong reaction against "The Taste of Apples" by conservative journalists. In response, one of the stipulations CMPC required was to insert titles clearly marking the historical period in which the stories take place. Thus the film, in the segment by Hou Hsiao-hsien, opens with the words "1962. Zhuqi." Zhuqi is a small, south-central town near Mt. Ali (Ali Shan), in a forest reserve developed by the Japanese.[50] These titles mark a diegetic separation of the film from the realities of contemporary Taiwan in the 1980s. Wan Ren's segment is not specifically dated, but it is clear from the dialogue between American embassy staff and a colonel that it is set during the Vietnam War. And the color change in the opening sequence's final shot: first shot in monochrome, it then switches to color, with a zoom into a close-up of the chalk mark outlining the shape of a body run over by the American car. Colorization of the shot, like the expository title of Hou's beginning segment ("1962. Zhuqi."), works as a graphic temporal marker. It signifies the temporality specific to a historical past. This color transition functions as a safety bar, a kind of curtain that separates the impoverished past from the prosperous, progressive present.

In *Super Citizen*, however, Wan Ren does not simply revisit the same site; he also recasts the same disenfranchised citizens in his tale of modern Taipei. Unlike

"Apples," *Super Citizen* is not about the past, so it is unprotected by that safety bar. Its commentary on the contemporary cityscape and, more importantly, its "ethnoscape" provoked the censors. One of the major problems was the presence of a lunatic college professor who was based on a real person. Another was the use of a neighborhood known for abortion clinics in Taipei as the major location for the film. Two consultants invited by the GIO suggested banning the film outright, or else releasing it with major cuts. After hard negotiations between GIO and the film's production company, Long Shong (Longxiang), the film passed censorship with sixteen cuts.[51] But the resulting erasure of Wan's favorite character types renders the film a rather insipid exposé rather than a forceful social drama. Film critic Huang Jianye suggested that Wan had compromised too quickly to commercial pressure.[52]

Huang was somewhat correct in his criticism of Wan Ren. Like Wang Tong, Wan chose a "middle-way" approach in making his films palatable to local audiences. Other new directors failed the high expectations of producers and exhibitors in their second or third films. Hou Hsiao-hsien's *The Boys from Fengkuei* (1983) and *Summer at Grandpa's* (1984), Edward Yang's embarrassing 1984 box office flop *Taipei Story*, and Zeng Zhuangxiang's *Nature Is Quite Beautiful* (Wu li de disheng, 1984) were all major disappointments. In comparison, Wan's *Ah Fei* and *Super Citizen* both achieved modest commercial success. According to Wan, his approach in the New Cinema was different from the main paradigm. Beginning with "The Taste of Apples," he wanted to make films that were accessible to the audience but at the same time allowed him to make strong social commentary. Hence his preference for topical films, which he believed were viable formats for that purpose. These priorities appeared to meet the prerogatives of commercial cinema and enabled Wan Ren to collaborate with the major company Long Shong and even with ultracommercial Tsui Hark, who represented Hong Kong's New Cinema City at the time.

According to Wan Ren, other producers and distributors were as anxious and excited about the new directors as CMPC. Major players in the industry all attended the preview of *The Sandwich Man* to inspect the new directors. Immediately after the screening, a film investor, Lin Rongfeng (nicknamed Ebisu), took Wan to a coffee shop and offered him the chance to make a film of his own choice. Thus his next film—his first feature, *Ah Fei*—fell into his lap over a coffee break.[53] Ebisu also supported other young directors for their second installments in the New Cinema movement: Hou Hsiao-hsien's *The Boys from Fengkuei* and Yang's *Taipei Story*.[54] Apparently, during the early period of the New Cinema movement (1983 and 1984), each director had opportunities to engage with the more commercialized sector of the industry. But the experience of "co-optation" differed from director to director. Wang Tong, Edward Yang, and Hou Hsiao-hsien all returned to CMPC and made their best films in the 1980s. Yang finished his award-winning *The Ter-rorizers* (1986), which brought him wide international recognition. Hou Hsiao-hsien finished *The Time to Live and the Time to Die* (1985) and *Dust in the Wind* (1986), which established him as the most visible Taiwan director in the world. Wang Tong also had to rely on a reluctant CMPC to produce his nativist trilogy.

Wan Ren, however, was able to continue in the "nonofficial" sector of the film industry. Moreover, he ventured outside the national compound and joined trans-national corporations because of the success of *Ah Fei*. *Ah Fei* (aka *Rapeseed Girl*) is a family melodrama about the emotional growth of a woman named Hui during Taiwan's postwar transformations. As Hui's family fortune quickly declines, so does the existing patriarchal power. With the father no longer able to perform as breadwinner, the mother gradually reverses her lot, going from being a victim in an abusive patriarchal marriage to becoming an abusing matriarch. Hui's identi-fication with the suffering mother also changes to a sadistic relationship in which the daughter is caught between filial piety and self-autonomy. In this women's picture, Wan Ren presents an intriguing study of motherhood, which appears to be more damaging than anything else in furthering female subordination.

The centrality of female pathos seems to be key to the success of *Ah Fei*, espe-cially among female audiences. As a result, an offer came to Wan Ren from even bigger players to make, once again, a film of his own choice. *Super Citizen* was a joint production by Long Shong and New Cinema City's Taipei office, chaired by none other than John Woo. Woo was not only the film's executive producer, he also edited the trailer for the film.[55] Certainly this Hong Kong connection meant Wan no longer could stay on the middle ground. He was expected to follow suit behind the Hong Kong New Wave and transform elements of Taiwan New Cinema into more commercial ingredients. Wan Ren was not fully ready for this. Problems arose when Tsui Hark produced his next film, *The Farewell Coast* (Xibie hai'an, 1987). Wan intended to maintain his critical edge and, as a sequel to *Super Citizen*, wanted to make another topical film about youth crime. Meanwhile, Tsui wanted to push for a Taiwan version of *A Better Tomorrow*, an action thriller about the most wanted gunman on the island. Tsui hoped to add more gunfights to sensationalize Wan's cool depictions of the teenager-cum-fugitive. Wan refused to reshoot and insisted on making the film as a social exposé rather than a pure genre picture.[56] The film failed both at the box office and critically, and it was also the last film that Wan made in the 1980s. *The Farewell Coast* then became Wan's actual farewell to his unique collaboration with the commercial establishment, as well as his stand-ing as an auteur in the New Cinema.

Wan Ren's career in the 1980s, especially his attempt to be assimilated into the commercial establishment and his insistence on making socially relevant films, typifies problems of the New Cinema in relation to the realities of commercial production. It appears difficult to reconcile the main features of the New Cinema (nativism, low budgets, autobiographical elements, elliptical narratives, absence of stars) and the demands of popular cinema. There were plenty of opportunities to infiltrate commercial cinema by incorporating characteristics of the New Cinema, but not the other way around. New Cinema was too vulnerable to entertain "alien" ideas, ideas of popularizing its narrative style so as to become a mass entertainment vehicle. Filmmakers felt compelled to either commit to an author cinema or to "sell out" by making commercially viable films. There was simply no solution to this dilemma. Even Hou Hsiao-hsien experienced a failure to satisfy both ends in his *Daughter of the Nile* in 1987. Wan Ren's next film *Story of Taipei Women* (Yanzhi, 1991; CMPC) remained within this either-or dichotomy and dilemma.

Story of Taipei Women was one installment of CMPC's new production package of modern family melodramas initiated by the new managing producer Xu Ligong.[57] Others include Ang Lee's "father trilogy"—*Pushing Hands* (1992), *The Wedding Banquet* (1993), and *Eat Drink Man Woman* (1994). *Story of Taipei Women*, however, did not bring Wan back to the spotlight of critical attention nor vaunted commercial returns. This is because he was, again, caught in his own shadow. He wanted to make a more contemporary version of *Ah Fei*, with a completely different focus on ethnicity, language, class background, and lifestyle. Type-casting an aged Shanghainese socialite as the grandmother, an interior designer as the mother, and a spoiled pubescent as the daughter, Wan used these three women to depict a changing society in which women are always more adaptable to social transformation than men. This idea is a reiteration of *Ah Fei*, though Wan ambitiously attempts to recuperate an almost forgotten mainland diaspora, the core of founding Chinese communities in North America and Australia in the 1960s and 1970s. Here Wan shows his recurrent ambition of mapping postwar Taiwan society through different ethnic, social, and gender categories. Unlike *Ah Fei, Story of Taipei Women* represents the top tier of Taiwan's social structure, an elite class that continued to prosper in their exile to Taiwan. Cronyism and the Cold War enabled mainland transplants to enjoy the fruits of postwar economic domestic high growth at first and, later, transnational capitalism. This political awareness keeps Wan's depictions of these privileged women at a distance. It translates to a low-key narrative style with an icy visual design and awkward direction. This cool, distant tone clearly renders a disparity with a would-be melodrama of female reconciliation.

Entering the 1990s, with the dissolving of KMT's political hegemony, the island was permeated with pro-democratic, nativist movements. Unlike the days of "The Taste of Apples," a rapidly liberating and deregulating Taiwan allowed room for all sorts of historical reexaminations. Political dissidents from the past were gradually rehabilitated, especially those suffering persecution from the ultra-right-wing, anti-Communist campaigns known as the White Terror. Wan spent much time studying this history, and the result of years of research was his *Super Citizen Ko* in 1995.[58]

Despite the rehash of his earlier title, *Super Citizen Ko* (Chaoji da guomin) is nothing like the *Super Citizen* that Wan had made a decade before. Gone was the strong support from the core of the industry: 50 percent of the film's budget came from the GIO's film subsidy fund, and the other half came from Wan's own pocket. Here we see at least two ironies in New Cinema history: this, Wan's most politically sensitive film, was in fact coproduced by the government that remained under KMT rule. Without the GIO's funding, Wan could not have produced the film. The second irony: despite the lifting of severe political censorship, Wan had to confront a more serious impediment—a collapsing industry with a record low of just twenty-four films produced in 1994. At this lowest ebb for domestic film, few would risk their money on the movie business. Therefore, even with such a timely topic, Wan found no investors. Because the risk was so high for Wan personally, his director friend Ke Yizheng visited a fortune-teller to find an auspicious title for the film. Following the fortune-teller's advice, an additional word—"big" (*da*)—was added to its original Chinese title.[59]

Financial restraint does not necessarily thwart stylistic attainment, as many films have proven that money is not always invincible. In the absence of heavy commercial pressure, Wan was able to explore a different narrative and visual style. In this film about a former political dissident, Ko, Wan employs a restrained form to depict Ko's life after his release from decades of prison. The narrative consists mainly of voice-over monologues to convey the old man's thoughts. Through his recollections, Ko reveals his betrayal of comrades during the White Terror purges. Guilt and regret prevent Ko from reentering contemporary society, and also hamper his emotional reunification with his long-suffering family. The now-liberated society sheds little light on the darkness of Ko's guilt. It appears to be just another prison as Ko roams the city, not knowing where or how to begin his second life. Finally, Ko arrives at the graveyard of his old friends. In a long and poignant monologue, Ko confesses his guilt and lays bare the pain of being a survivor at the crossroads of a painful past and a confusing present. (See fig. 2.10.)

Ironically, the film's introspective narration and slow pace did not prevent it from receiving a welcome box office response. In Taipei alone, the film grossed nearly NT$ 5 million, outperforming Hou Hsiao-hsien's *Goodbye South, Goodbye* (NT$ 2.4 million), Wu Nianzhen's *Buddha Bless America* (NT$ 3.7 million), and Edward Yang's 1996 *Mahjong* (NT$ 0.65 million).[60] Corresponding to the strong box office, twenty-eight reviews of the film were published in major newspapers.[61] Not since *Ah Fei* in 1984 had a Wan Ren film received such ardent attention. Follow-

2.10 *Super Citizen Ko* (1995; dir. Wan Ren)   (COURTESY TAIPEI FILM ARCHIVE)

ing suit, Wan's next project, *Connection by Fate* (Chaoji gongmin, 1999), utilized a similar model. Supported by a government film subsidy fund, Wan pursued a post–New Cinema style focusing on the subject of political and social disillusion. This film completed Wan's "three citizen" trilogy.

Connection by Fate is a political ghost film. It centers on two ghosts—one political activist-cum-taxi driver, the other an aboriginal construction worker-turned-murderer. The aborigine kills his foreman out of resentment from long-standing racial abuse. Under the law, he must be executed, and he becomes a wandering ghost in the city. The ghost makes friends with the taxi driver, who is himself a walking dead man, unable to cope with the premature death of his son and his disillusion with political movements. The taxi driver has tried suicide several times. The encounter with the aborigine ghost helps him eventually to end his life and find peace.

In terms of narrative and style, both *Super Citizen Ko* and *Connection by Fate* signify a significant departure for Wan Ren. A previous oscillation between popular and art cinema disappears, and a pledge to ascetic narrative and a very controlled audiovisual style emerges. In respect to Wan Ren's work, these two films are the most important renditions of his favorite tropes—irony and sarcasm—since "The Taste of Apples." The Chinese titles of both films are called "super citizen" but with slight differences in meaning—one refers to a national attribute, the other its civic form. Still, the retention of "super" indicates Wan's enduring skepticism of the (pseudo-) nation-state, the capital city Taipei, and the collective endeavor to build a democratic, civil society. The "super" citizen of the metropolis and the modern state is a leftover from the time when there was a heroic collective determination to overcome dependency on authority. But once that authority was overthrown, the remaining space is devoid of orientation, and characters are marooned, suspended in a liminal state.

The New Cinema as a whole can be analyzed for its historicizing strategies, a way for Taiwanese artists and audiences to address events and issues that had been thoroughly suppressed. Yet Wan Ren is the most difficult to characterize in terms of style. He has made only eight films over twenty years, and one reason for his meager output is his commitment to difficult political themes. As these themes recede from contemporary public awareness, the style of Wan's films has attenuated, resulting in a greater aesthetic preoccupation or, more precisely, a relaxation of the impulse to persuade.

Conclusion

In its most ambitious films, the New Cinema entails an act of historical salvage, freely drawing materials from a local past that had been firmly off-limits. Up to around 1980 the issue of colonial history was virtually taboo. As an intensely political issue, colonialism and Japanese occupation could be addressed only in the context of Chinese nationalism and anti-Communist patriotism, under the banner of "Free China." Then, the abuses of the KMT, along with its Cold War collaboration with U.S. militarism, came under scrutiny by writers, artists, and intellectuals. This issue peaked with the release of Hou's *City of Sadness* in 1989. As the 1990s unfolded, the airing of historical revisions and grievances gradually found its way into social and political practice. Eventually the KMT became "just" another political party, albeit the world's wealthiest. In the unprecedented transition to an open, democratic, and fully capitalist economy reliant on multinational markets, the urgency of cultural liberation lost its edge. Somehow, Taiwan's film audiences became the most avid consumers of Hollywood films in the entire region. They are unlikely to watch the films of Taiwan directors, unless they claim as their own Ang Lee, an A-list Hollywood director. Hou Hsiao-hsien is the doyen of international film festivals; Tsai Ming-liang continues to make global art films financed by the French (e.g., 2001's *What Time Is It There?*). Meanwhile, the New Cinema celebrated its twentieth anniversary with a retrospective of films and panels at the 2002 Golden Horse Film Festival. New Cinema too has passed into history. The struggles depicted and engaged in by Taiwan New Cinema directors have been won, but at the cost of economic disarticulation within a global market organized somewhere over the horizon.

The New Cinema was a collective movement with a counter-hegemonic purpose. But it did not begin that way. It was supposed to be a homemade alternative to attract an audience already seduced by imports from Hong Kong and Hollywood. For a few years, it generated intense heat and melted away the backroom dealings that characterized film regulation. Wan Ren's "The Taste of Apples" was a flare in this highly public alliance between producers, critics, and audiences. The old, conservative practices of Taiwan's cultural patrimony were rattled but not completely overturned. Instead, market forces became the primary arbiters of production and consumption of film, especially with the unbridled explosion of cable television in the 1990s. Very much like Huang Chunming's description of the imported apples, the New Cinema turned out to be sour, not sweet, and its crisp promises, once tasted, were not quite fulfilled.

Navigating the House of Yang

Edward Yang (Yang Dechang) is *the* crucial figure in Taiwan cinema, along with Hou Hsiao-hsien. Together Yang and Hou represent a dialectical relationship to contemporary filmmaking, to the international critical reception of Taiwan films, and to each other. Though they are the same age (b. 1947), and are both mainland transplants and founders of the New Cinema, their films are radically different, along with their approaches to story structure and the profilmic. Both rely heavily on the help of regular collaborators, though Hou is more prolific. It would be safe to say Hou's approach is more intuitive while Yang is calculating, painstaking, a perfectionist. The two artists are both close friends and intense rivals. Yang's Western experience, along with his autodidact confidence, gives his films a distinctly cosmopolitan flavor, even when fashioning the urban historical in *A Brighter Summer Day*. This film boasts visual and narrative inventions we will call "tunnel visions," offering a rich phenomenology of historical-political nostalgia.

The Spiked Pyramid

At the beginning of Taiwan New Cinema, Yang was perceived as a "dark horse," an outsider and unlikely agent for a transformation of the film industry. Yang never finished film school; he was a self-taught filmmaker, an engineer-cum-comic book illustrator, not a director with an orthodox training in the craft.[1] He is a cinephile, with impeccable taste in European and American cinema. Inspired by the example of Werner Herzog, who used the money earned as a blacksmith to hand-make his own early features, Yang embarked on the same road.[2] But his commitment to film is part of a wide-ranging aesthetic sensibility that is more mathematical than expressive. Yang idolizes architects (I. M. Pei), musicians (Beethoven, Bob Dylan), and scientists (Einstein), not only artists and filmmakers.

At the risk of seeming pedantic, let's carve Yang's career into three parts: first, his early modern melodramas: "Expectations" (from *In Our Time*, 1982), *That Day, on the Beach* (1983), *Taipei Story* (1985), and *The Terrorizers* (1986). These are balanced a decade later by three postmodern comedies: two black and cynical, *A Confucius Confusion* (1994) and *Mahjong* (1996); and *A One and a Two* (*Yi Yi*, 2000), a lighter, humanist comedy. A single masterwork falls in between, the historical epic *A Brighter Summer Day* (1991). The whole oeuvre belongs firmly in the family of art cinema, although only the latter works, from *Brighter* onward, are truly independent, eschewing commercial talent and technicians. This artisanal working method, depending on young performers from Yang's drama classes, partly explains why the films take so long to finance and produce.

"The problem in Taiwan is that the business is so fragmented and run-down," explains Yang. "There isn't any longer a big pool of experienced actors to draw on, and if you have a very specific character-concept in mind it's not very likely that you'll find the person to match it. If you're aiming for authenticity, then it may very well be necessary to find and train actors."[3] Yang in fact had trouble negotiating the commercial practices of Taiwan's film industry from the beginning. From his first feature *That Day, on the Beach*, he found it hard to work with the crew assigned him by Central Motion Picture Corporation (CMPC), and this drove him away from commercial production.

The films of the first part are marked by emotional constriction, convoluted plots, and cold, glassy surfaces of the modernizing city. The films after *Brighter* are indeed brighter, moving from a dour European-flavored modernism to a carnivalesque but carnivorous global village. There is a strong sense that from *A Confucius Confusion* on, the world of Taipei—infested by hungry British, French, American, and Japanese expatriates entangled with Chinese yuppies, petty gangsters, students, and businessmen—is interchangeable with any other global city. Seen from this angle, Yang's career resembles a pyramid, but one whose apex soars high over the surrounding tapered structure like a steeple. Yang's early, serious work rises steadily, then spikes upward into *A Brighter Summer Day* before tapering down in a gradual descent to comedy, farce, and eventual postcinematic Web animation, Miluku.com.

Two questions immediately arise with this pyramid structure: why privilege *A Brighter Summer Day* by giving it the central, towering status, and why doesn't Yang's recent, highly acclaimed *Yi Yi* rate a similar appraisal?

A Brighter Summer Day is different from all the others. It is a period film set in the early 1960s, played out in an epic mode, at once departing from the restrained melodramas of *That Day, on the Beach*, *Taipei Story*, and *The Terrorizers*, and also responding to the international triumph of Hou Hsiao-hsien's *City of Sadness* (1989). *City of Sadness* threw the door open to reflections on the dark areas of Taiwan history that had been officially out-of-bounds during martial law, in force from 1947 to 1987. *A Brighter Summer Day* also has, unusually for Yang, a specific local reference, the Guling Street youth murder of 1961 which, except for the date, in fact is its Chinese title, *Gulingjie shaonian sharen zhijian*. There's a thickness in the texture of this film that demands perceptual immersion to properly appreciate it, let alone grasp its more subtle historical allusions. Yang has said he wanted the film to work as a background for discussions on Taiwan's future, whether it would become independent or reunify with China.[4] It's possible that this was an ironic comment on the film's designation as an American/Japanese coproduction at the 1991 Tokyo International Film Festival, an absurd attempt by the festival director to avoid upsetting the PRC.[5] The audiovisual complexities alone justify a separate study.[6] The film is thickened further by a personal, autobiographical element because it is an initiation story, a bildungsroman that explores the (de)formation of a boy growing up in the same period and circumstances as Yang himself.[7] In its historical specificity, the autobiographical aspects and visual strategies we call "tunnel visions," *A Brighter Summer Day* is not only Yang's own masterpiece; it epitomizes the New Cinema. Also, with this film we see a new emphasis on community and personal ethics, which finally reveals the humanist didacticism lurking beneath the modernism of Yang's early films.

This combination of factors does not hold for *Yi Yi*, though it too is a moral tale. Its gentle, contemporary family comedy appeals through its sympathetic characters and cyclical narrative. *Yi Yi* begins with a shotgun wedding and ends in a funeral. At 173 minutes, it is epic length but is no match for *Brighter Summer Day's* 240 minutes (director's cut). *Yi Yi* is a precisely focused film; its protagonists, goals, and lines of action are neatly laid out and resolved. *Yi Yi's* architecture, its storytelling as well as its dwellings and offices, is highly familiar and livable, comfortable especially for Western audiences. The film has a soothing design, especially its musical score, and its spaces comprise affluent surroundings: hotels, restaurants, concert halls, luxury flats. Clean, orderly locations, color schemes, balanced composition, acting, and mise-en-scéne evoke a sense of serenity, despite the inner emotional turmoil. The local spaces of Yang's previous films (night markets, back alleys, cramped quarters, criminal lairs) have all vanished. These observations are not criticisms, only differentiations that help justify the visionary, even monstrous quality of *A Brighter Summer Day*. If *Yi Yi* is Wordsworth, *A Brighter Summer Day* is Blake. A closer analogy might be made with Taiwan's cinematic legacy, with *Yi Yi* recalling healthy realism while *Brighter* burns with the obsessive-compulsive historical exactitude of Li Hanxiang.

Let us turn directly to *The Terrorizers*, reconsidering its achievements in itself, as well as its importance to Taiwan film's international reputation and to postmodern cultural criticism.

The Terrorizers

The whole arrangements of the nation, public as well as private, are based on a system of mutual responsibility, which of course involves a system of mutual surveillance. Even the Emperor, though nominally supreme, stands in awe of the Censorate, and of a popular revolution.

—ANDREW WILSON, *THE "EVER-VICTORIOUS ARMY"* (1868)[8]

Yang's third feature has been famously characterized as a postmodern film par excellence. Fredric Jameson argues its intersecting narrative constructs a peculiarly urban context epitomizing postmodern space, a series of boxlike packages that contain, separate, and isolate inhabitants.[9] Yet the grids and glass panels organizing social life in the city also allow chance encounters, forging unexpected connections. The narrative connections of *The Terrorizers* function as pretext, like an accident or collision, and almost always result in damage, recrimination, paranoia, and terror. The city is not so much a bad place as a kind of vacuum tube in which careening people sow infectious chaos in their wake. If Jameson identifies a general postindustrial urban space as facilitating the colliding narratives of *The Terrorizers*, another way of accounting for the film is through chance relations between humans. These simple contacts are compounded with reverberating consequences. In spite of this, *The Terrorizers* is actually one of Yang's more accessible films.

Our reorienting of the film around shifting human relations is consistent with Edward Yang's ideas about *The Terrorizers* as a kind of game or puzzle, and is a much simpler account than Jameson's geopolitical totality.[10] *The Terrorizers* (Kongbu fengzi), not "terrorists" (*kongbu zhuyi fengzi*), can also be seen as a film of nested genres. Its bookends are the crime thriller, with three or four middle-class melodramas sandwiched in between. The pleasure of the film comes in recognizing the intersections between different subplots, relationships, and genres. Negotiating the links between them makes the film an engrossing, satisfying experience, like the Sunday crossword, fully consonant with the coproduction backing of CMPC and Hong Kong's ultracommercial Golden Harvest. The film was cowritten by Xiao Ye (see chapter 2) and Edward Yang. It is yet another instance of the New Cinema combination of coproductions, new talent, and low budgets. But unlike previous efforts, this film paid off. *The Terrorizers* was a box office hit, which surprised Yang.[11] After this film, the New Cinema as a collective began to dissolve quickly. Evidence of the dissolution was a manifesto issued in 1987 by more than fifty film workers (including Yang himself) demanding more support from the government, producers, and distributors. In retrospect, *The Terrorizers* is the twilight of the New Cinema; it was also the last film Yang made in the commercial sector. After that, he became a true independent, sourcing talent and technicians through his own local network, and that of his executive producer Yu Weiyan.

Early morning: shots ring out; shots are taken. The film begins and ends with police emergencies, the Doppler of a siren rushing to a crime. More than anything else, a wailing police siren is a universal sign of urban apprehension—and a signal of genre. Both scenes involve what Jameson calls the White Chick, a Eurasian troublemaker. Her activities indirectly drive all the subplots of the film and catalyze various actions: crime photography, true-life serial fiction, two breakups, a robbery, killing spree, and suicide. The key to the story is that all these actions are by-products of the White Chick, and they are put in motion unintentionally. The enigmatic White Chick is a chance heroine, dispensing random acts of malice while convalescing from an injury sustained during the shootout. The accidental effects of her actions begin just before this when, unbeknownst to her, the photographer snaps dramatic shots of her escape.

But what matters is the photographer's and other characters' response to fateful brushes with her. They amplify the terror, enlarging small incidents of mischief, and, using her, take advantage of their own lovers and colleagues. Reactions to the White Chick are invariably egotistical; lonely, alienated city dwellers misapprehend her acts as personal communiqués rather than chance pranks played for the amusement of a bored teenager. Yang's pathetic, "mildly repulsive" characters (Jameson) are like inmates without all their wits, gabbling furiously at ambient noise taken for messages, random signs taken for wonders. In scenes between the girl and her mother, the latter behaves as if her child chooses to be delinquent just to spite her, but this only proves the mother's obliviousness. Mother's melodramatic feelings are of no concern to the White Chick; wrapped in a cocoon of nostalgia for an American bar culture, Mother is nothing more than a boozy jailer, and a rather incapable one at that. Other characters are also blinkered by boredom and loneliness. Photographer, novelist, doctor, policeman, they all expand and amplify the initial stings of fortune, in themselves nearly harmless but made incalculably worse by their reactions, reverberations, repetitions. Like expanding, contagious ripples of influence, these characters have a kind of allergy, sure to catch and capitalize on what they see as main chances, quickening the terror circulating in the urban network.[12]

The policeman is apparently in some superhero mode, as gunfire rings out above his head and fellow officers dive for cover. He keeps his head up, looking both bored and (he hopes) dauntless. Despite his posturing, he at least belongs in the same film as the White Chick. In the end, when rushing to the hotel to stop her, he smashes into a parked car before running in to arrest the villain, her accomplice, for a second time. Finally, what does it mean that Li, the cop's doctor friend, chooses to shoot himself in the old bathroom of a police dormitory? It is a tragic scene, but it also traffics in the absurd, partly because it undoes the terrible vengeance Li has just fantasized. As a place to blow one's head off, the bathroom is just inappropriate, out of place, unless Li wishes to hint that he holds the authorities somehow responsible for his bad luck. What would be the fallout for the policeman, having an old friend do this in such an intimate place?

Dr. Li Lizhong, husband and medical professional, is probably the saddest case because he believes he plays the game well. But he is hopelessly wrong, oblivious to his wife's frustration and affair, heedless of his supervisor's contempt for his clumsy attempt to smear a colleague. Li exemplifies the displacement of agency in this film, the sudden swing from contender to loser, but this appears also in Yang's other films as well. How many times do we see proactive, cocksure characters skillfully playing off friends and enemies to maximum advantage? Only to discover that they've been neatly played, taken in by smart, presentable people with such finesse that they maintain an ingenuous face, even to themselves.

Examples of these out-of-their-depth characters include Ah-Lon, played by a feckless Hou Hsiao-hsien in *Taipei Story*. He tires of his childish passivity and heroically intervenes on behalf of his girlfriend, only to meet a violent end on the street. His demise has a similar absurd theatricality as the death of Li. Xiao Si'er is another passive-aggressive antihero in *A Brighter Summer Day*, while wealthy bumbler Akeem, in *A Confucius Confusion*, turns the tables on his fiancée, Molly. There is a funny graphic match of Akeem, cradling a bruised jaw sustained from an enraged Molly. Just behind on the wall is a poster of Charlie Chaplin in an identical pose, pining for love and money (fig. 3.1). Both Akeem and Chaplin are naifs but survivors. Redfish, a rich kid frustrated by his inability to control things, turns to savagery at the end of *Mahjong*, proving that the upper-middle Chinese classes, not the career gangsters, are more likely to run amok. The effects of affluence and

3.1 Echoing Chaplin in *A Confucian Confusion* (1994)

privilege on a population raised on Confucian pieties are corrosive. More important to these narrative structures is the sudden swing from active to passive, from
doing to being-done-to: an upside-down world in which the pure of heart appear
like wolves because the rules of engagement are in such disarray. In such a world,
everyone is taken for a hypocrite, says Yang in the published screenplay of *A Confucian Confusion*.[13] Here, the name of Confucius is used to build up a mutual surveillance system, rather than a society of mutual benevolence.

Returning to *The Terrorizers*: the novelist and photographer are the most privileged—and therefore most empty—of those touched by the White Chick; both
are very well off, and the latter is some kind of scion from an elite family, killing
time until his national service comes up. Both have access to expressive means,
through writing and photography. Both lose their primary relationships—a love-
less marriage and a live-in lover—due to a creative surge occasioned by the White
Chick. Zhou Yufen the novelist, inspired by the fateful call, believes her husband
is having an affair and deals with it compositionally, rearranging events to make an
absorbing story. It is a story good enough to believe, and to rate a literary prize for
true-life fiction. For the novelist, the White Chick's call is two birds with a single
stone, a release from writer's block and escape from a blocked, barren marriage.
For the critic, this raises the art-versus-life theme that appears both anachronistic and postmodern. It reprises forms of reflexivity prevalent in early twenthieth-
century modernist fiction, but it also focuses attention on cinema as a representational option (compared to writing, photography, television) that unsurprisingly

prevails over these other contenders. Jameson calls this the "ontological primacy function," or more simply the Hansen-Bordwell hypothesis.[14]

For the photographer, another gift: a fetish object. For him his White Chick photos are objects of contemplation or, more exactly, sites of pure potentiality. Candid shots of a girl injured and desperately seeking escape have the dramatic immediacy of wildlife photography. He captures her instincts, of fight-or-flight impulses the more entrancing because of their exteriority, devoid of intention or deliberation. When the photographer rents her old flat, filling the interior with contact sheets of the White Chick's feral visage, it is an act of attempted domestication. He tries to fill in what had been just a criminal bivouac, shot from outside as a disembodied arm holding a gun. When she comes in and sees herself splayed like a trophy across the walls of her old room, she correctly recognizes it as entrapment. Then she collapses. Characteristically, she later makes an opportunity for herself, rejecting his advances and stealing his precious equipment. Uncharacteristically, she relents, deciding not to fleece the photographer the way he stole her image. For her trouble, the photographer retaliates. This response is weakly motivated, given Yang's study of atomization, indifference, and predatory behavior. Revenge is the only possible reason the photographer would inform Dr. Li that he had by chance discovered the false link between his wife and the White Chick. Yet revenge is a strange way to repay a favor.

To conclude this discussion of Yang's most canonized film, we can encapsulate the various human relations of *The Terrorizers* in terms of betrayal and "going behind one's back." This is a favorite Yang preoccupation, right up to his recent *Yi Yi*, and it does not always involve deviousness. In that film, the very young photographer Yangyang takes pictures of people's heads, from the back, so he can give them a record of their blind spot. Like Yangyang's subjects, images of the terrorizer White Chick are purloined; she in turn goes behind her mother's back to call out of her domestic cell, dispensing mischief; the recipient, Zhou Yufen, takes this misinformation as a chance to sleep with the publisher, behind her husband's back. He, in turn, betrays his colleague at the hospital, going behind his back to secure a promotion. The photographer allows his girlfriend to think he is cheating, which he is, but then the White Chick refuses to play along. In turn, he exposes the White Chick's trick and victimization of Zhou and Li.

This going behind one's back—the betrayal of friends, lovers, and the principle of forthright communication—leads to another sense of betrayal as *reflex*, the autonomic movement due either to a habitual response to outside aggression or because of a design flaw. Yang's film contains both notions of betrayal, as deliberate cheating and as systems glitch. His two-faced characters hoodwink each other for fun and profit, but these actions are then bounced back against the perpetrator. Though he tries to frame a colleague, Li is betrayed twice—once by his wife, and then by his boss. Li confronts Zhou with what he thinks is her mistake, asking her to return home with him. Her devastating response is "Fiction is fiction. *Don't you distinguish real from fiction at all?"* Completely thrown, Li responds with genuine shock, a reaction outstripping even his suicide. Similar emotional reaction repeats in the subsequent sequence when he realizes his career has suffered a severe blow. Generically, these melodramatic intersections are both framed and punctured by elements of a crime picture, as Li's thoughts turn to revenge. What starts and ends as police procedural detours into the twisting interiors of the indulgent middle classes.

There may be a deeper circulation of the political unconscious and allegorical representation at work: small shifts in a minor film from an insignificant Asian country. These may betray momentous fault lines for the whole world narrative system. For Dr. Li, it is a matter of complete self-delusion because even when he tries to rectify his victimhood, at home and at work, the scales are rigged. Under the weight of this implacable system, there is no going back, no restoring of agency once it has been lost. The system requires a cipher function. For this reason Li is allowed a precious revenge fantasy, a directorial trick that offers false compensation through genre. The microcosmic dual use of betrayal—the fertility of blind spots and false frames—becomes much clearer in Yang's second phase with the extraordinary *A Brighter Summer Day.*

Style, Unity, and Real-effects (an Interruption)

Style is almost always purposive. The way in which artworks appear to be made—a provisional definition of style—draws parallels with the work's thematic, narrative, or conceptual meanings. Traditional criticism assumes various forms of unity in the analysis of visual style, taking visual form as tied to propositions carried by the work. The unity of form and substance need not be organic; material form may disturb or block our apprehension of ideas, and even usurp the traditional priority of theme. Standard devices of modernism, such as the estrangement effects of direct address, reflexivity, distanciation, roughened or attenuated form, trade on this usurpation.[15] Even when "form and content" collide or compete, we want to attribute wholeness and purpose to artworks, even if the whole does not work organically. A disunified or disintegrative work still observes unity in the breach. Something like this operates in the Taiwan New Cinema, with narrative clarity displaced in favor of a wholeness related to perceptual activity.

In film history there is a critical tradition that prizes certain techniques for their holistic effect. André Bazin developed this line of thought most eloquently, arguing that long takes, long shots, and real locations sustained relations between screen and spectator that are perceptually closer to the phenomenological real. The realist foundation of this criticism is ultimately psychological, moral, even spiritual. It assumes phenomenological wholeness between spectator, filmmaker, and profilmic events. Another phenomenology, predating Bazin's, is more cognitive and revolutionary, indebted to the historical-materialist agitation of constructivism and Soviet montage. We might call this Vertov-Eisenstein tradition a haptic model, one that catalyzes disorientation as a form of action, sensation, and, ultimately, cognition.[16] Cinema may reveal aspects of psychological and socioeconomic life that usually go unnoticed, but it may also forcefully promote unexpected discovery through discomfort and dis-integrative experience. The commercial imperatives of controlled storytelling make it hard for filmmakers to employ the medium's potential. Spectators, in turn, habituated to the clarity, pace, and expository rhythms of classical narratives, must adjust their viewing practices to accommodate more holistic and haptic styles.

Taiwan directors like Yang, Hou Hsiao-hsien, and Tsai Ming-liang are masters of the long take–long shot aesthetic. All three challenge habitual viewing practices and at first are disorienting. The holistic experience of their films is both dense and seemingly unstructured. Though spatially diffused, the films seem opaque, hermetic—especially those of Tsai Ming-liang, whose films may produce claustrophobia. Tsai and Yang, the latter especially in *A Brighter Summer Day*, tend toward a haptic model of perception, while Hou's style seems more Bazinian. Their films' structuring principles seem at odds with the needs of efficient storytelling. They have a strong sense of contingency and chance, yet events unfold with a meticulous, fateful quality. Visual composition within the frame and the shot is similarly painstaking, yet indifferent to conventional plays of curiosity and suspense in commercial genres.

Distinctive Forms of Realism

For these filmmakers, composition frequently opposes the primacy of linear narratives. The holistic, non-anthropocentric narration models social experience as it is lived on a daily basis. This process is not just about ideas, but may be physical, leading to perceptual and cognitive shifts. Vagaries of geopolitical development (Jameson's "social totality") seem indifferent to everyday concerns of family life and survival, but still form a backdrop and a vessel for human predicaments. These framing, delimiting macrostructures are remote, perplexing, seemingly amorphous. The enormous gap between individual concerns and collective frameworks that are opaque to personal apprehension; the difficulty of making links between micro-experiences and macrostructures ... these existential predicaments are squarely faced and mapped out by these filmmakers, and their efforts carry great resonance not only within the diegesis, the world of the films, but may continue experientially in spectators long after the films are over. Aesthetic frameworks can, in the hands of certain artists, span or at least model perceptual experience of both work and world. The use of long take–long shot cinematography is only one avenue through which Taiwan directors negotiate this condition. In the long take, time comes forward in both its positive and negative aspects. Orchestrations within the shot, with or without camera movement, promote an impression of discovery and contingency (a sense of "could have been otherwise"), while an uncomfortable sense of pure waiting may translate into meditative states of detachment. The long take, in other words, may work as a painful training device.

Long (distance) shots, particularly in Yang and Hou, are used as an efficient synthesis of key settings and visual motifs that can be withdrawn for use during the course of a long film. While both filmmakers use painterly, recessional compositions with clear vanishing points, Yang tends toward cylindrical long shots that exaggerate depth with obstructing details and pools of darkness. Yang's long shots are concave, sucking angles and forms inward, while Hou's are convex, like an exhalation. Accumulation of concrete detail and meticulous plotting of event, sound, and image promotes the screen experience as a deep respiration or breathing. We might call these filmmakers realist, but of a distinct, special kind. One is tempted to call them modernist realists, connected to a tradition of ascetic realism. This puts them in the company of Dreyer, Ozu, Angelopolous, Tarkovsky, Sokurov, or Kiarostami, as well as the avant-garde school of Andy Warhol, Michael Snow, Yvonne Rainer, etc., all filmmakers of the interval, of waiting.[17] In addition to formal qualities, there are other, external factors behind the contemporary critical canonization of Taiwan directors.

These factors include the marginality of Taiwan itself in the world system, the refusal of official recognition as a nation among world bodies, and the pathos of attempts at self-assertion in the face of global indifference, derision, and outright hostility. For decades this hostility was external and bilateral, with skirmishes and arms bristling on both sides of the Taiwan Strait. But since the indigenization of once-mighty KMT—the Nationalist Party—political bitterness has taken an inward turn. Ethnic, historical, and linguistic differentiations split Taiwan's public into hyperpoliticized, paranoid, often acrimonious groups. Another factor is a heightened temporality of transience, what could be called the temporary full stop; in spite of economic stability, vigorous democracy, and deregulation of the media, long-term faith in Taiwan, let alone confidence, is tenuous, uncertain. Cautious provisionality remains the norm and the only condition people can count on, whether they are Taiwanese, Hakka, mainlanders, indigenous people, or foreigners. The artists, intellectuals, and cultural workers in the film establishment are mindful of this provisional, borrowed time, making the most of constantly changing government

TABLE 3.1 Ratio of Taiwan Films to Total Number of Chinese-language Films Released in Taiwan, 1982–1989

YEAR	CHINESE-LANGUAGE FILMS (TAIWAN/ HONG KONG)	TAIWAN FILMS	NEW CINEMA FILMS
1982	318	144	1
1983	311	79	10
1984	266	58	11
1985	248	65	10
1986	235	71	10
1987	252	86	7
1988	339	58	7
1989	303	101	3
Total	2,272	762	59

Source: The figures for Taiwan-made films and imported Hong Kong films shown in Taiwan are cited from Lu Feiyi, *Taiwan cinema, 1949–1994: politics, economy, and aesthetics* (Taiwan dianying: zhengzhi, jingji, meixue) (Taipei: Yuan-liou, 1998); table IIb: Taiwan and Hong Kong Film (1968–1992)

subsidies and policy support while simultaneously reaching for foreign finance and festival prizes. All the major directors including Hou Hsiao-hsien, Edward Yang, and Tsai Ming-liang have taken advantage of Japanese, Hong Kong, European, and American investment in their films.

A result of this is a consecration of visual and narrative styles that resonate abroad, especially in foreign film festivals, while alienating local viewers and many critics. The strategy has reaped rewards for international prestige for select auteurs and producers, for KMT-owned CMPC, and for Taiwan itself, but it also damaged the local industry. The interests of exhibitors and distributors, headed by small-minded entrepreneurs, run counter to the international ambitions of Taiwan producers. Exhibitors share the spoils of foreign (mostly Hollywood) imports, which have dominated 95 percent of the box office since 1997.[18] Table 3.1 shows the paltry numbers of New Cinema films screened since 1982.

While it is a mistake to blame the collapse of local production on a handful of award-winning films averaging less than one-tenth of Taiwan's output, it is understandable why there is a strong perception of an elite versus popular split, with government support going to the former at the expense of its own population. It can be argued that the "irregularity" of Taiwan's national cinema is located here: local consumers are fodder for international and regional flows of popular entertainment, while the richness of canonized Taiwan auteurs goes straight to export.

Among the richest and still underappreciated films of contemporary Taiwan cinema is *A Brighter Summer Day*.

Local Histories, Epic Narration   *a brighter summer day*

A Brighter Summer Day (*BSD*) is a complex, harrowing film, and it was made in difficult times. By 1991 the bottom had dropped out of the local market. Taiwan-made productions fell precipitously, numbering just forty-seven pictures, with audiences abandoning local films in favor of Hong Kong fare (releasing 168 films in 1991, many of which were coproduced by Taiwan companies).[19] The huge success of Hou's *City of Sadness* two years before, breaking box office records and enjoying festival acclaim, was a poignant memory accompanying a period of waiting and uncertainty. For Yang's audience, the waiting was longer yet, since it had been five years since the acclaimed *The Terrorizers*. Many wondered what was next for Taiwan New Cinema and whether the momentum of *City of Sadness*, particularly its role in the post–martial law period of liberalization, could be sustained. Was Yang capable of presenting another film event like *City*? As mainlander, Western-educated cultural elite, and self-taught filmmaker, how would he depict Taiwan's dark history? In the main, Yang's new film did not disappoint Taiwan's critics and, like *City*, it attracted prominent commentary by public figures who saw the importance of New Cinema's historical articulation of contemporary cultural politics.[20]

Showing for three weeks in Taipei, *BSD* grossed a respectable $9.93 million.[21] It also won a special jury prize at the 1991 Tokyo International Film Festival, though the festival tried to make it look like something other than a Taiwan film (see above, p. 93). Because a government-backed Japanese conglomerate, Mico, had put up money for international rights even before Yang started shooting, the film was entered as Japanese. The same arrangement was made for Hou's *The Puppetmaster* two years later. Despite the international profile, *BSD*'s factual subject matter, a sensational youth murder committed in 1961, is specific to local history. Like *City of Sadness*, *BSD* pours a localized, personal story into highly articulated structures of time and space.

As if in answer to Hou Hsiao-hsien, Yang's version of local history turns the lock on long-suppressed ideas. Historical specificity is the main difference between *BSD* and Yang's other films, and it grants access to multiple strands of family histories that crisscross generations and classes. Affiliations, obligations, and affinities stretch like tendrils between Taiwan, China, Japan, and the United States. To be schematic, we can identify mainland Chinese elements with a patriarchal ideological state apparatus; these try to smother Japanese colonial vestiges linked to a discreditable matriarchal legacy. The United States represents a popular youth culture offering escape into an endless summer of high economic growth and rampant consumption. Each of these four lines comes with historical and cultural tokens, and can be traced in the film's props: calendars, magazines, clothes, accessories, furniture, musical instruments, vehicles, records, songs, swords, hats, baseball bats, guns, movies, and even electrical power sources. In this geopolitical family game, the boys and their gangs loosely align themselves according to the gravitational attraction of these forces. The dynamics of Taiwan's film culture, torn between the siren of Elvis Presley and the prosaic routines of local genres, are played out in the competing loyalties dramatized in the film.

Questions of Composition

What of visual style? In *BSD*, compositional principles outline the contours of historical organization. Spatial articulations in depth are visual correlatives to Yang's ideas about regimentation and historical articulations. Perceptual negotiations of the image flow along with multiple narrative tributaries. Narrative diffusion is the basic norm, while visual strategies "stop down" the action to lend a concave focalization organized in depth.

What follows is an exploration of strategies taken to visualize these historical and geographical strands—in staging, framing, and editing patterns. Most of all, *BSD*'s visual style is distinctive for its chiaroscuro lighting. The film's basic premise is to superimpose school rituals—what passed for secondary education in Taipei, ca. 1960—onto the larger political repressions of the White Terror period. While it is tempting to call this allegory, it would be wrong because it implies the Guling street youth murder is just a device. But it is more than that. A better descriptive term would be telescoping—a large magnification of educational pressure and regimentation so that it expands, parallels, and occupies the screen of state-controlled regimes under martial law. Schoolyard politics are a microcosm; they authorize and stand in for a militarized, authoritarian civil society. Like a very slow zoom out, Yang gradually reveals what is happening in the larger world through the daily trials of a son, his schoolmates, siblings, parents, and neighbors.

Tunnel Visions

Tunnel vision is a characteristic figure of style in *A Brighter Summer Day*, composed of a long shot through arches, doorways, windows, and various other frames, promoting active exploration of a deep space. Recessional lines and staggered planes work like visual magnets, pulling the eye to "hot" places in the shot. In tunnel vision, darkness often surrounds and frames the space. Depth is enhanced through pools of light and shadow, which sometimes confuse priorities of distance. A light-

3.2 Colonial vestibule (*A Brighter Summer Day*, 1991)

ed window or bulb in the distance will immediately attract attention, overriding dark spaces in the foreground. We call these setups "tunnel visions" because they pierce a given space and thereby channel attention through a gauntlet of obstructing views, giving the shot a strong inward pull, as well as screening out larger social and political dimensions until just the right moment. Six examples of tunnel vision follow, organized from the simplest to the most elaborate.

Vestibule Much of the action at Si'er's night school happens in an arched passageway or vestibule between the street and the schoolyard itself. The school is usually framed from outside, at a high angle, on the colonial pillars and arches that suggest the neoclassical pretensions of empire found all over Asia. In this case, the connotations are imperial Japanese, by way of Victorian England. These elegant, flowing spaces promote motion as people criss-cross passageways, popping in and out of sight between columns. The main archway divides foreground from the schoolyard outside (fig. 3.2).

The vestibule space is introduced at the beginning of the film and becomes a familiar haunt. This space both connects and separates school from town. The Little Park Boys are loitering there, taunting a young woman with a searchlight, and Cat brings news of a fight at the grade school next door. Much later, Si'er, Cat, and two others are rushing down the long corridor after school and turn a corner, only to stop short in the vestibule. A fourth boy turns tail and runs. A reverse angle on their look shows the end of the passage, shrouded in darkness like the mouth

3.3 Interrogation in *A Brighter Summer Day*

of a cave. Nothing is there but menacing laughter. A basketball bounces out of the dark maw like a dribble of spit. In a previous scene Cat had attacked Tiger on the school's basketball court. Now the boys' enemies face them, but they cannot be seen—only voices taunting in the dark. The vestibule, despite its by-now-familiar confines, is hostile. Yang does not stage the subsequent beating, but skips to Si'er returning home with torn and bloody clothes.

Here we see the personification of an architectural detail. The vestibule works like a character, antagonizing Si'er in his quest to win Xiaoming, the girl caught between rival gangs. Using extreme contrast between light and darkness, the shot creates suspense, withholding details of an enemy presence and imminent confrontation. This is a 180-degree reverse-angle match, and like Si'er and Cat, our eyes strain to make out the numbers in the ambush. By skipping over the actual fight, Yang leaves intact the menace of the vestibule. At the same time, the shot tends to abstraction because it refocuses perception onto a momentary projection, a figuration of intense dread dragging the eyes into a (fearful) imaginary hole. This boring (drilling), tunneling effect is a major part of Yang's composition in this film but can also be found in other films by New Cinema directors, such as Hou Hsiao-hsien, Wu Nianzhen, and Xu Xiaoming.[22]

Interrogation We find another example of tunnel vision in the interrogation sequence. Yang provides an establishing shot of a long veranda running along the room where Mr. Zhang is being held. The building appears to be an abandoned boarding school, institutionally linking Zhang with his son. In the initial establishing shot, a man is in the far background with a pair of large blocks. Later, the direction is reversed and we can clearly see that these are huge blocks of ice. What are these? As Zhang walks past, he looks through a doorway to his right (screen left). He betrays a reaction of shock. Yang cuts on his look to show a man sitting with his back to the door, shivering on top of an ice block. Tunnel vision here turns into a T-shape, linked by Zhang's pause, eyeline, and object of his look. Glimpsing interrogation and torture, Zhang shudders. The primary veranda branches off into a terrible offscreen space. (See fig. 3.3.)

Pool Hall The 217 Boys' lair is a long room with two pool tables set end to end. Presiding over this narrow space is Shandong, the killer of Honey. Shandong sits calmly eating while his henchmen harass Lao Er (Si'er's brother) and some other characters. Shandong is attended by his gun moll, Shenjing (Crazy), giving him a sort of courtly gangster presence.[23] He is at one end, the pool tables are in the middle, along with various characters conducting the business of intimidation, and in the far background the room opens out on the street where people pass by. Blackouts periodically plunge this place into darkness, and then Shenjing lights candles, which further attenuates the space. The darkness and flickering candles give the room an eerie, even ritual air, but it also makes 217 vulnerable, letting a rival gang penetrate the space during a typhoon and take violent revenge for Honey's death.

Tunnel vision in the pool hall is anchored in the figure of Shandong, who as gang boss is the malevolent locus of the space, much like the darkness visible at the vestibule in Si'er's school. Grisly details of the attack on 217 are picked out by Si'er as he slowly moves through the space with his searchlight. Precision, low-light cinematography bounces keen flashes off the blades carried by Si'er and Shandong.

Streetwalking Another tunnel vision comes in a tracking shot down a dark Guling street after Si'er is expelled from school. He has assaulted the dean of the school with a baseball bat. The street is shot like the inside of a tunnel, cave, or shaft, whereas in the vestibule the staging recalls something like a proscenium, presenting the entrance to a dark, menacing aperture. The second example (Interrogation) places us alongside a long corridor, with wings leading to unspeakable horrors. Forking corridors and hallways, multiple doors opening to who knows where; such framings have a strong institutional association, like schools or prisons, in which extreme mental and physical discipline is enforced. Yang's compositional strategies find parallels with his paradigmatic narrative patterns.

On the street, the tracking camera slowly moves along with Si'er and his father as they walk their bikes and consider what just happened. Pools of light punctuate the dark street and elongate it. They walk by a street hawker, who calls out, mocking them in the dark. Puddles of light, sound, and shape outline a shadowy world negotiable by touch, or memory, groping along through obstacles. Successive patches of light, then sounds, and finally more amorphous forms or figures go by. Extreme deep focus is sustained through the dim light of the hawker's stand in the far background. Though highly organized, the space here is less charged or "magnetic" than the menacing vestibule at the school or the torture chamber at Zhang's interrogation. Nor does it have the strong vanishing points of the elongated pool hall. The eye is freer to roam. As the regular route between school and home, this tunnel vision is a repeat setup of an earlier walk down the same street, but in the daytime. Not only do Si'er and his father walk down this street, so do his mother and sister, as they discuss the family's fortunes after Zhang's interrogation. Here again is a pattern connecting Si'er's trouble at school with his father's questioning by the authorities. By the time Si'er and father walk the street at night, we have already taken that walk twice.

When Si'er saves the grocer, another tunnel vision opens up as he rides through the dark neighborhood. Here too the hawker plies his trade, piercing the warm night with his cries. As Si'er passes Uncle Fat (the grocer), the camera pauses with Fat as he drunkenly shambles down the street, swearing. Fat stops under a streetlight. As he moves out of frame, Yang holds on the light as Si'er appears, having doubled back on his bike. Thinking like a hoodlum, he apparently wants revenge for Fat's antagonism of the Zhangs. Cut to a reverse-angle long shot, with Fat chatting with Zhao the hawker, now urinating. Cut back to Si'er, who picks up a large rock. Mocking Fat, the hawker pedals away as Si'er moves into the long shot with his rock. The shopkeeper suddenly collapses, frightened of Si'er's approach, and warns him to stay away. Suffering a heart attack, Fat then disappears into a canal or ditch in the far background. Dropping the rock, Si'er runs to rescue him, calling Zhao for help. Fat's heart attack and his rescue lead to a major change in the family's fortunes, but the setup has prepared us to expect an act of aggression, not kindness.

These tracking shots lend a strong temporality to Yang's tunnel visions. In fact, any tracking shot forward or back forms an imaginary tunnel (recall the opening shot of Hou's 1986 *Dust in the Wind*, with a train emerging from a dark tunnel). Because these shots are repeated, a sense of routine and frequency comes forward. The circling hawker knows the people walking the street by name. The pattern also allows a more leisurely exploration of a dispersed space, but one that can be inferred, compared to more symmetrical, receding compositions. The time it takes to infer, to build up an imaginary three-dimensional construct, installs greater historical, as well as spatial, density. Like the vestibule at the school, Yang's tunnel vision is a connection with the past, linking the dimensions of the audience with the diegesis. Finally the camera itself is moving along with the characters' meandering trajectory through dark, close, but still familiar space.

3.4 An arboreal tunnel (*A Brighter Summer Day*)

The various ways Yang inscribes temporality—through graphic and spatial composition—distinguishes the figure of tunnel vision from the planimetric and trapezoidal playing spaces analyzed by David Bordwell.[24] Yang's film has many planimetric shots set up perpendicular to the lens, often using offscreen space or darkness to heighten curiosity, as in Si'er's confrontation with Ma in the rich boy's "genkan" or Japanese foyer. David Bordwell's able analysis of Hou Hsiao-hsien's precision staging, in affinity with European silent directors, also highlights temporal duration due to the time needed to decipher a carefully composed, changing picture plane full of important plot details. Bordwell attends most closely to the fixed long takes, analyzing the problems of continuity and attention management solved by resourceful directors like Hou. But tunnel vision as it works in Yang has a stronger centripetal force, drawing the eye into a deeper, concave composition through continuities of light, sound, shape, and color as well as through interruption and distraction. The perceptual movement in depth can be symmetrical and convergent (fig. 3.4) or asymetrical and divergent. Tunnel vision presents the image as a series of imaginary windows organized along a tubular or funnel-like space, whether in a single shot or sequence linked by eyelines or movement. Bordwell's conception of trapezoidal staging is flatter, more pictorial, and therefore synchronic. His analysis requires temporality in the duration of the take and in the director's adjustments within the frame through blocking.[25] But it does not account for the temporality of spectators' perceptual movement "down" inside the hole-space. As Zhang jokes to his son, "Remember, things with a hole in the middle bring headaches." Si'er is too young to understand.

Grade School The four-shot sequence of the grade school at the beginning is full of motion via figures and camera movement. The passage of figures running through this fight scene give it a sequential structure we can anticipate. A long shot of the grade school shows two levels linked by stairs. Yang tilts up as the 217 Boys run up, passing one lighted window, then another up above. The Little Park Boys run after them in pursuit. A long shot of the school pans back and forth along the arches as running bodies and flashing lights crisscross the halls inside. Shouts, motion, and lights emanate from the bank of dark windows. Moving inside the school, the two gangs clash within the dark halls and stairways.

A long, recessive shot straight down the corridor shows Si'er hesitating, then a light flashes on and off from one of the classrooms. Inside a classroom, Si'er gets a glimpse of Xiaoming, the girl with whom Sly betrays the leader of Little Park. But Si'er does not see clearly. Because of the darkness and flashing light, who can be sure who was there? In fact another girl, Jade, confesses she was with Sly that night. The exchange of girlfriends and alibis has important plot implications, since Si'er will be next in line for Xiaoming; but more important is the motif of darkness lit up by flashes which do not illuminate so much as blind.

Lights flashing in the grade school, like those in the pool hall, have much to do with the material conditions of Taiwan in the 1960s. Blackouts and brownouts were regular occurrences due to unreliable power grids, betraying a Third World infrastructure run by capricious, corrupt authority. Noteworthy is the nonchalance with which the 217 gang set to lighting candles and going on with their business. Lights blink off, then come back on; people are unfazed, even lulled. But the peculiar quality of Yang's lighting in *BSD* goes beyond verisimilitude, in favor of stronger, more basic expressive means. At the grade school, the on-off switching of the classroom light is unmotivated, though we receive a close-up of Si'er's hand flipping the toggle. At home, he does the same thing, then complains about his worsening eyesight. Si'er doesn't see well, and wants to determine where the problem is. Will an external light source help? The effect of the flashing classroom is like that of a beacon: bolts of luminosity shoot like a distress call far into the night. But this is no signal; it is a kid's idle guesswork, of troubleshooting. Si'er is hoodwinked, as is the whole neighborhood, if he thinks that more light means more understanding. In fact more light creates confusion, more disorientation: "the cognitive function of the conspiratorial plot must be able to flicker in and out, like some secondary or subliminal afterimage."[26] It actually multiplies the potential channels of interrogation, igniting explosive possibilities in what should be a murder story with a clear solution. The shadows of doubt appear when a hand reaches out for the switch.

Clinic: Articulated Tunnels In the clinic, Si'er waits for the nurse to come with an eye shot. Four shots beautifully articulate the rooms in which Si'er indulges his gangster fantasies:

1. Medium long shot: Bored, he tries on the doctor's hat. Military officer comes in, looking for nurse. Ignoring Si'er, he leaves, exiting right. Si'er points his finger after him and shoots. Steps to mirror on back wall, checks himself out. Turns around, then spins 180 degrees (fig. 3.5), shoots again into next room (match on action).

2. Medium shot of Si'er in front of window (archway outside). Spins again, shoots at camera. Sees someone (fig. 3.6).

3. Medium long shot: Xiaoming stands in doorway (fig. 3.7).

4. Medium shot (same as 2): Si'er takes off hat (fig. 3.8), Xiaoming comes into the shot. Both in profile, they face each other in front of window. They talk, and he puts hat on her (fig. 3.9). Smiling, she gives it back.

Doorways frame the two figures and limit the space visible to them and to us. This is why Si'er is surprised by the sudden appearance of Xiaoming. Since the ceilings are high and the backgrounds similar, the spaces feel less like tunnels than a kind of maze. Wherever he turns, Si'er seems to be in the same room, in the same position. White walls, regularly spaced doors and windows, make the rooms seem boxlike, interchangeable. But this is due partly to Yang's framing, which remains planimetric connected by 90-degree cuts. Once the nurse and doctor come in (shot 5), Yang changes the angle to 45 degrees and breaks the pattern. With this variation Yang signals the end of a visually rhyming, intimate moment between the two youths.

This engaging sequence is a simplified version of an earlier, more oblique exchange between Si'er and Xiaoming at the clinic. The first two shots in this sequence are falsely matched, as follows.

Image: Long shot of Xiaoming with the doctor through an open door.

Sound (over): Chat about Qingdao, China, and its German-designed drainage system ("It doesn't matter how hard it rains").

Yang plays a joke on the audience here because we see Xiaoming talking to the doctor, but we hear something else, something that jars. This play with lip-synching is a throwback to techniques that prevailed in Taiwan's sound production until the late 1980s. Only with a shot change do we understand the image-sound disjunction, seeing that the conversation belongs to the military officer, who sits with the nurse in a room next door. He is very interested in the school nurse and wants to impress her. As a mainlander, he may be looking for a bride, unfazed by the fact she is from a backwater like Hualien, a place on the east coast associated with aborigines. This is why he boasts about the modern amenities of Qingdao. The nurse looks up, offscreen left, and tells someone to come back later for shots. The sound-image mismatch is replaced by the nurse's eyeline, matching shot 2 to 3. Shot 3 is a medium shot of Si'er standing in the doorway, then reframed to

3.5–9 Clinic at the school

3.6

3.7

3.8

3.9

show him looking off left through another doorway, presumably at the scene of Xiaoming and the doctor talking. Then he turns, back to camera, walks slowly out the door past the mirror, pauses dramatically, and turns right. At left, the mirror reflects him twice as he goes out (fig. 3.10).

Shot 4, a complex, ostentatious reframing, has three parts. It begins in a doorway, empty of people. This is where Si'er was standing a moment before. Xiaoming walks through the doorway toward the camera (fig. 3.11), then moves out of frame left (fig. 3.12). As if to push her offscreen, the camera reframes right—*into a close-up of a white door.* Here it remains. Just visible in the shiny white paint is a faint reflection of the two young people, haloed by the brighter light of the window beyond (fig. 3.13). Offscreen, they talk quietly about Xiaoming's screen test: "Didn't you say you'd come to my screen test? Why didn't you show up?" This intimate exchange goes on for several sentences and indicates progress in the couple's surreptitious relationship. Then the camera reframes again, bringing the couple back into the shot, where their talk resumes, with a change of subject (fig. 3.14). Their voices come up, and the camera pans left to follow them downstairs.

The reframing of shot 4 is a flourish, pushing the couple offscreen to talk. It calls attention to itself, forcing spectators into a voyeuristic position that could be linked to the duties of the school's military officer.[27] His job is to see that students always comport themselves with discipline and decorum, though he himself is busy chatting up the nurse. The school is not coeducational, and boys and girls must be segregated. The shot could also be an authorial flourish, a small bit of business emphasizing the proficiency of director and cinematographer. If we continue with the tunnel vision idea, the reframing is a variation on the intersecting corridors and orderly institutional layouts that dominate the film. What might be called supervisory staging, motivated by the characters' need to conduct a secret romance, leads to Yang's overt direction of surveillance. Voyeurism and surveillance in *BSD* is not just institutional: one of Si'er's favorite hangouts is the soundstage next to the school where he and Cat peer down from high above.

This time, however, displacement of the action is highly obtrusive, unavoidable, and flashy. Our noses are rubbed in a setup that accentuates the *selection* of narrative detail, as if to say "as military officer [or film director], access to this exchange is restricted. You are allowed so much information and no more." Or perhaps the shot is meant to convey accident and contingency, a consequence of the officer's momentary lapse from supervisory duties. Despite its fastidious, even authoritarian, interference, the shot still has a certain distractedness. The distraction is dialectical, like a sound-image mismatch or the double-reflecting mirror, because it questions the centrality of the romance. Perhaps sweet nothings exchanged between young lovers are the distraction, and the "real" point of the scene is elsewhere, having to do with the door, the reframing, or an implied interruption, which may or may not signal point of view.

It doesn't matter how hard it rains.

3.10–14 An ostentatious reframing

3.11

3.12

3.13

3.14

Summary

Note how the examples above run a wide range of technical and dramatic features. Locations and sets, lighting, deep focus, offscreen spaces, figures and camera movement, editing patterns—all these have importance in tunnel visions. Overall functions of Yang's tunnel visions include elaborate funneling effects and associated dramatic focalization, intensification, a perceptual vortex pulling attention inward. Establishing shots down corridors or colonial hallways are not unique to Edward Yang, or even the New Cinema, but in *BSD* tunnel visions are highly concentrated, coming in complex, articulated forms. We also find compositional strategies (lighted windows, candles, etc.) that selectively spotlight "hot" areas to which the eye goes. The viewer is helpless to avoid looking at sources of light in a dark frame, but these are not so dark that space cannot still be palpable, especially in depth. Space comes forward as a kind of embrace, as we have seen in the Guling Street walk, but one that is alternately ominous and familiar (Streetwalking).

Tunnel vision involves complexities of depth, obstruction, and movement (by figures or camera) that guide attention centripetally, *within* a deep, articulated space, not just across a graphic plane. Centripetal motion into depth lends greater temporal resonance, as if traversing inward through an irregular space also meant burrowing through time. Thematically, there are strong institutional links with the orderly corridors, intersections, or other designs of officialdom (school, military, hospital, prison), and suggest framing as rigid impositions of control (even if it is fabricated) such as imprisonment, inspection, or at least surveillance. In a period film such as this, uses of tunnel vision mask as much as illuminate historical connections; tunnel visions actually obscure by separating figure from ground, eliminating relevant circumstances. The obscurities in turn suggest deliberate concealment, and potential unmasking. At any time, the beam could swing around to reveal some other clandestine violation. Tunnel visions invite a sense of incrimination: cylindrical structures pluck events out of context, not only inserting them into a cone of interrogation and iniquity but also blinding and immobilizing them with an implacable shaft.

The tunnel vision idea strongly affirms and is extended by the figure of the searchlight, the prop taken by Si'er from the office of the film studio. There is a strong *trajectory* to tunnel visions and the throw of light. Searchlights are a kind of projectile, they bore through the night with a keen cylindrical beam. They help illuminate in emergencies or navigation, but they cannot scan a broad expanse. Most often they are wielded by capricious figures of authority, blinding their intended perpetrators, like a uniformed man caught kissing a girl at the very beginning of the film. His response to Si'er's searchlight is typical: "Fuck you kid! I'll kill you!" Blinded by light, one is pinned like a moth to an incriminating hook. In *A Brighter*

Summer Day, Yang uses the searchlight-tunnel structure to bore into a local history that would rather remain in shadow.

The Later Films

Edward Yang is a moralist. His use of light and shadow is not just an exercise in style or even theme. He's interested in questions of enlightenment for Si'er, as for the other characters in every phase of his career. Characters fumble in literal and ethical darkness, lighting it up with feeble torches and candles. They lock themselves in offices, cars, bathhouses, and bedrooms as well as in relationships, roles, memories, ideologies, and scripts. In so doing, they negotiate the terms of urban survival and its consequences, the tradeoffs of security and fulfillment. All of Yang's characters are groping, they search for ethical frameworks that help explain and decipher their predicaments, seeking a way forward.

In the later films Yang's didacticism is still there, but the insistent sense of urgency is curtailed. Apparently he has relaxed his grip, seeking greater humor and lyricism. As a result, generic conventions come forward. There is a major difference in tone and style between *A Brighter Summer Day* and Yang's next film, *A Confucian Confusion* (Duli shidai, 1994; aka *Age of independence*). *BSD* was a culmination of Yang's existential melodramas, synthesizing the earnest, sometimes gloomy modernism of his first three features with the spectacular cinematography and period detail of serious political diagnosis. As mentioned before, maybe this was Yang's answer to Hou's monumental Taiwan trilogy. Perhaps because the world it projected was so close to Yang's own background, *BSD* was resolutely cinematic in both visual elaboration and narrative ambition. Yang's next two films step back into a more modest, if brighter, register. In particular, *A Confucian Confusion* (*CC*) shows the influence of Yang's activities as a drama teacher and director at the National Institute of Arts, where he started a second line of work around 1990.

Starting with *BSD,* Yang was able to draw on a new pool of people and ideas. On completing the film, he wrote and produced two short plays. *Likely Consequence* (Ruguo, 1992), a comedy based on a Japanese manga ("Death of a Salaryman") by Fukuyama Kenji, is about a young married couple inexplicably confronted with a dead body in their flat. *Period of Growth* (Chengzhang jijie, 1993) follows up on *Likely Consequence,* only this time there are two couples under the same roof, entangling themselves in each others' affairs. These plays show the kind of experiments in casting, genre, and structure out of which came the more elaborate feature-length *CC*. From this point on, Yang relied on young performers, colleagues, craft, and other talented people from the Institute of Arts, injecting new blood into Taiwan cinema and preserving his independence from the commercial industry.

On the other hand, this independence was bought with international hard currency and its attendant expectations. *A Confucian Confusion* was a Warner-Asia release, its first-ever Asian launch. It represents a distinct shift away from New Cinema aestheticism into entertainment, while preserving a satirical edge. In this regard it recalls the very beginnings of Taiwan New Cinema, whose deadpan adaptations of Huang Chunming were devastating (e.g., *The Sandwich Man*, 1983, discussed in chapter 2). But Yang's satire is chatty, broad, and quite cynical. Its address to spectators is very light, though also thought-provoking. According to Wu Xide, *Confucius* "launches a grand critique of emerging Taiwan consumer culture as well as its presentation for consumption on an international stage. This tendency is exemplified by Ang Lee's *Eat Drink Man Woman*, which appears to promote Chinese traditional culture. But the scope of Yang's film is much broader than any contemporary New Wave directors, going against the grain of exoticism, preferring to look for the essence of Chinese tradition in modern life."[28] The comparison with Lee (see chapter 5) is intriguing because both films stand before the bar of hypocrisy, at once exploiting and ridiculing choice morsels of contemporary society like haute cuisine or consumerism.

Confucian Comedy, Confucian Capital

Actually, *A Confucian Confusion* does not aspire to a grand critique; it is critical, but it also looks and feels like a highly intelligent, acerbic sitcom. Unlike all Yang's previous films, CC employs rapid-fire, witty dialogue. Some writers, including Yang himself, have likened the film's clever talk and revolving ensemble to the work of Woody Allen, though Robert Altman might be a closer match.[29] Ten major characters move in and out of the spotlight, sharing meals, friends, gossip, office politics, and lovers. The tone is immediately established with playwright Birdy, who delivers a flippant disquisition on the essential likeness of politics and entertainment. Politics is nothing more than a kind of theater, he says as he rollerblades around a group of journalists, and voting is no different than buying tickets. A journalist responds with the thought that he (Birdy) is just trying to get rich, under the guise of playful postmodern performance art. The sharp point about Birdy's sincerity signals the film's exploration of things that have always preoccupied Yang: betrayal, selling out, human bonds as forms of capital. Yet the visual presentation of this fluff is the opposite of Yang's tunnel visions in *BSD*. Instead of the vortex, there is a proscenium shot in wide angle, a long take staged with primary colors and little movement, save the merry-go-round Birdy skating rings around his puzzled audience. Above, tiny reflections on metal rafters add to the artificiality. The long takes in this film add to the emphasis on patter, performance, and overall theatricality.

3.15 NBA sports bar (*A Confucian Confusion*, 1994)

We soon discover this is Birdy's studio–living space–love nest, and this partly explains the campy, bright fantasy set piece.

Generically, this opening primes us for comedy, farce, or even a musical; we are also prepared for the importance of setting as expressive device.[30] The action in T.G.I.Fridays, sports bars, and clubs works not only to characterize by environment but also highlights the "hangout" itself as yet another conspicuous consumer item in the new global marketplace (fig. 3.15). In *BSD* the ice cream parlor, pool hall, and garage also express schoolboy-gangster fantasies, along with American pop music, but the difference is one between a corporate franchise and a fashion statement. The former is about consistency of quality, which diners at Fridays literally ingest; the latter, a gesture of differentiation, not uniformity, in defiance of parental tastes. As the red title introducing Birdy's press conference reads: "In this Utopia where everyone thinks alike."

So Yang is now working a different genre, the smart, sassy comedy about yuppies. It is interesting to consider whether this is due to student talents from his drama classes, the Warner-Asia backing, or simply a new direction. But let's step back into the film itself. What is the function of those title commentaries that occasionally interrupt the spoken performance? Whose voice(s) are they? They are words of Confucius, whose *Analects* are excerpted at the very top of the film in an epigraph:

CONFUCIUS: The city's too crowded!
DISCIPLE: What can we do about it?

CONFUCIUS: Make the people rich.
DISCIPLE: What comes after they are made rich?

This mock-Confucian commentary is sustained throughout. Occasional titles interpose an omniscient pre-view, i. e., characters saying words in a dramatic context that the audience has already read (in red for English and in yellow for Chinese) a few minutes before. But what is Confucius but a mouthpiece? Whose is it? It could be the trickster playwright since it is his voice-over initially heard over the title ("Taipei took just twenty years to end two millennia of poverty to become one of the wealthiest cities in the world"). Over these credits, Birdy prattles about his move into comedy; the titles then give way to a close-up of rollerblades, introducing us to Birdy's press conference. Another Confucius option is the writer, whose ideas Birdy apparently steals. Yang himself is the likelier candidate, using Birdy, the writer, and Confucius as puppets. The name of the unpublished novel Birdy picks up in Molly's office is . . . *A Confucius Confusion*. In his own press statements, Yang has repeatedly charged Confucian doctrine with irrelevance to contemporary Chinese realities. Confucianism turns people into drones, squeezing idiosyncrasy and irreverence out of us. Confucianism, Yang says, does not tolerate a spirit of inquiry:

Wealth was never really intended for the people in Confucian doctrines, which enforced more than anything else the central authority's legitimacy with rigid social structures coated with moral justifications to stress conformism, discipline and personal sacrifices for social harmony and group security. Ironically, this conformism and discipline bore fruit to all these countries in their economic miracles and double-digit annual growths of the past two decades.[31]

Such statements throw the antics of *CC* into high relief, because the target is not just amusing vignettes but the whole social dynamic of the "culture company," a world of PR spruiking peculiar to Taiwan's urban hypercapitalism. Birdy, Molly, Qiqi, Akeem, and the rest are busily making moves of upward mobility, but the periodic titles show underlying rules of the game, interrupting, forecasting, and mocking their plotlines, like the portents of a fortune-teller. Because the unpublished novel in Molly's culture company shares the title of the film we are watching, Yang includes his own work in the shell game of entertainment culture. These titles, both the name(s) of the film/novel and the red pre-view titles, also signal the scripting process, implying the presence of a scriptwriter. Characters deliver preprogrammed lines and only we can see the operating system. A Brechtian sitcom? Perhaps, though the phrase has a sour taste, like that of Yang's comedies themselves. These pseudo-Confucian interruptions raise questions about "human resources," or the value of personal relationships: friendship (Molly, Larry, Liren), kinship (the elder sister), and marriage (Akeem, Ming, and the writer).

A cunning speech by the lawyer Larry, a lecherous rascal who tries to seduce Molly, exemplifies "human resources." With the title card, "Few Chinese don't understand this reasoning," Larry extols the central Chinese value of *qing* (emotion). According to Larry, *qing* is at the heart of the whole culture business. *Qing* will always sell, it's the reason people buy culture, *qing* is what they need in life, cultivating it, just like their assets. The emotional bonds of family are long-term assets; friendship can be a long- or short-term investment. Romance, on the other hand, is high risk, but potentially high yield. All human relations are instruments of *qing* and need to be managed. Few Chinese don't understand this reasoning. Molly's company is a mess, and so is her *qing*. Perhaps Molly is missing something; she is different and . . . she must be very lonely. By the way, Larry asks, what are you doing tonight? Larry's entire spiel has been a pass. Only a phone call from Akeem, Larry's boss, interrupts what might have been a brilliant score. But the point has been made: the shrewd uses of people, including the self in a variety of guises, to manage and maximize *qing*, emotional assets. All other wealth indicators rise along with it.

As mentioned, the titles bear the conceit of late-twentieth-century Taipei people somehow chained by the ethics of a second-century B.C. philosopher. We see not only the simple device of forecasting the lines about to be uttered but also the historical misfit of Confucius and yuppies, as if Yang was playing with a vulgar setup ("Confucius say . . ."). The very idea of flashy young things in places like TGIFridays, watching NBA finals, flagrantly cheating on their fiancés . . . such people ruled willy-nilly by Confucian mores is ludicrous, if not grotesque. Except for the writer, characters pay no heed to Confucian thought, though their inherited, ancestral world is suffused with it. In any case, the Confucian theme is more prominent for Western viewers, who may not register Yang's Chinese-language title, *Age of independence* (Duli shidai), a reference not only to personal ambitions, especially those of women, but also to Taiwan's political status. The Japanese release title is *Age of Falling in Love*. The shifts in meaning through different titles, though, are not as far-reaching as the basic anachronism, the skewed picture of ultramodern consumer culture cradled awkwardly in Confucian piety. This oxymoronic comedy of mistimed social mores reappears in our discussion of Ang Lee (chapter 5).

(Sur)Faces of Women and Their Meanings

In the late films, the departure from *BSD* consists not only in genre but in the importance of female roles. This is a return to women's issues, a perennial subject in Yang's earlier work: "Expectations" (1982), *That Day, on the Beach* (1983), and *Tai-*

pei Story (1985). There is a familiar ring to the kind of roles on offer in Yang's films: the ingénue/virgin Qiqi, an Audrey Hepburn lookalike; the career woman, like Molly and her sister; and the tempting actress/vamp Feng. These women desire independence but also crave emotional security; they perform their roles because they wish to be players in control, on top of the career/family/romance game.

These are prototypes for all Yang's female characters. The ingénue appears first in Yang's short "Expectations" (*In Our Time*, 1982), about a schoolgirl befriended by a midget; *That Day, on the Beach* concerns two ingénues who turn careerists. Tan Weiqing and Lin Jiali's intertwined romantic disappointments are sublimated into professional achievement in the arts and business. The moody Chin in *Taipei Story* and the neurotic writer Zhou Yufen in *The Terrorizers* are careerists, gambling on greater rewards by giving up marriage for exciting but risky prospects. Chin's ruthless boss, Ms. Mei, eventually becomes *Mahjong*'s predatory American, Ginger, the "working woman." In *BSD*, the ingénue-turned-actress is the enigmatic figure of Xiaoming, while the gun-moll, Shenjing-Crazy, betrays a genuine love for the fallen hoodlum Shandong. Xiaoming's screen test, the one missed by Si'er, is an unexpectedly emotional toggle switch. A close-up of her tears suddenly yields to the neutral street face she uses for everyday wear. Jade, cast as Xiaoming's double, is clearly a temptress but, unlike Xiaoming, she is genuine and even scolds Si'er for his naïveté. Of all Yang's films, *Mahjong* (1996) is probably the hardest on women. Recall the trio of lupine forty-somethings who offer takeaway seafood to playboy Hong Kong, only to sexually humiliate him. Aptly named Hong Kong is played by grown-up Zhang Zhen, who had the role of Si'er in *BSD* and Lo in *Crouching Tiger, Hidden Dragon*. In *Yi Yi* there is a parallel between the sweet ingénue Tingting and her neighbor, the troubled cellist next door. Yang's women characters, like the terrorizer White Chick, will drive stories forward, but they also fulfill types, like vamp and virgin.

From virgin to vamp, from innocence to experience, Yang's women are emblems for socioeconomic transformations, the exchange of *qing* for economic gain and rapid replacement of old with new. The intertwined stories of two women in *That Day, on the Beach* masks the consequences of the economic boom in postwar Taiwan—selling out *qing* for money. Yang uses the two women to suggest that women are adaptable, and men are more vulnerable, to change. Men appear to be socioeconomic achievers, but they are the ones to bear the costs of competitive pressure. Traditional Chinese society uses marriage as a respite, but also to secure economic and social capital. This causes the betrayal of Tan Weiqing, and it is also what transforms her into a career woman, an acclaimed pianist. Lin Jiali's missing husband is not untypical of businessmen who disappear in the swift currents of high-stakes capital games. Similarly, in the *The Terrorizers*, Zhou Yufen's writer's block may be a ploy; thanks to a prank call, her burden shifts to her husband Dr.

Li and eventually results in his emotional blockage and suicide. Like an alchemist, Zhou manages to turn depression into a bestseller while Li drains his with a bullet. At the end of *Taipei Story*, with the help of role model Ms. Mei, Chin resumes her cold urbanity after a temporary lapse in confidence. But her fiancé Ah-Lon assumes the role of the missing "silent partner" when helping her sort out an affair. On the surface, Ah-Lon is killed in a petty street fight, but in the larger scheme he fails to cope with new orders of social and sexual relations. Then he expires. The French ingénue Marthe short-circuits Redfish's schemes, and the ending of *Mahjong* is a domino effect of failed Taipei masculinity. The economic miracle is real, but its beneficiaries are not those who flaunt wealth, intelligence, or sexual prowess.

The women in Yang's films cast about for a suitable feminine role to play, often wracked by indecision. Their angst and neurosis is nothing, though, next to the profound identity crises of males, particularly those negotiating rites of manhood. Perhaps this is why the virgin, ingénue, and vamp are such stable vessels for Edward Yang's dramatic imagination, since they are regulars on his animated Web site, Miluku.com. The feminine is hardly a sanctuary; even within women's relations we find intense rivalry. In *CC*, there is a hint of lesbian attraction between Molly and Qiqi, particularly Molly's possessiveness toward her adorable assistant. Qiqi needs to carve out her own space from Molly as much as from her fiancé, Ming. The close friendship of the young women contains seeds of claustrophobia and exploitation—not only by the pushy Molly but also through the information and influence carefully dispensed by Qiqi. Because of her irresistible charms, ingenuous Qiqi comes to be distrusted by all. Friendship and romance jockey for position in the characters' priorities, and the opportunity costs of loyalty are calculated. Over coffee at Fridays, Molly accuses Qiqi of avoiding her calls. Qiqi fiddles with her mobile phone, wondering if she should replace it. Molly retorts, maybe it is her boyfriend that needs replacing.

Money and the Missing Person 一一

Yang's ironic, metropolitan sensibility places him as a world cinema director comfortable within postmodern narrative and thematic idioms of filmmaking today. Clearly, *The Terrorizers*, with its intersecting narratives based on both chance and fate, was ahead of its time. Yet the social and cultural specificity of his films still identifies him as a Taiwan director whose creativity is entwined with the island's fortunes. This Taiwan specificity is clearest in his Web site, Miluku.com. In fact, Yang's preoccupation with a cartoon Web site, relegating further film projects to secondary status, signals his belief in the future direction of moving-image media, for financial as well as creative prospects. What Web sites allow, at least for now, is access to an enormous audience where middlemen are primarily technological rather than corporate. In cinema, Yang must raise cash, bonds, contracts, and agreements with all kinds of entrenched interests whose participation comes with too many strings. In current configurations of production, distribution, and exhibition, the role of a director lacks authority, too much like a switch in a vast capital network. It is ironic that with the triumph of *Yi Yi*, Yang is in the strongest position yet to not only make more films but to make them his way. Moving on to Web animation, though, must be a kind of homecoming because of his talent for cartooning and graphic design, as well as a higher degree and professional experience in computer engineering.

With *Yi Yi* there is a noticeable synthesis, or solution, to many of the problems in Yang's earlier films. In the early phase we find weak dialogue and acting, even as we admire the audaciousness of stories that jump between causal lines and temporalities. A pretentious effect results when characters speak in formal, noncolloquial language, such as a long speech in *That Day, on the Beach* delivered by Tan Weiqing's ex-boyfriend Jiasen just before his death. Similar dialogue exchanged between Ah-Lon and Chin formally discusses the prospects of their future together. The very awkward pauses in *Taipei Story* may have more to do with weak scriptwriting, for which Hou Hsiao-hsien and Zhu Tianwen share blame, than suggestions of contemporary urban angst.

Recall the long delivery of inner thoughts by Honey in *A Brighter Summer Day* and the writer in *A Confucian Confusion*. *That Day, on the Beach* has obvious flaws of casting, performance, and costuming. Sylvia Chang played a 17-year-old girl when the actress was almost thirty. The wig she wears looks just like a wig. The character of Tan Weiqing is an accomplished pianist but no effort is made to simulate her playing, and the actress Hu Yinmeng obviously doesn't play. The interaction between father and son, daughter and mother in the traditional, ethnic Taiwanese family is far too restrained, as if Yang (a mainlander) is walking on unfamiliar territory. Though their house is supposed to be Japanese, they do not remove their shoes. This is *after* Edward Yang had written and assisted on a film, *The Winter of 1905* (1981, dir. Yu Weizheng), shot on location in Japan.

But Yang's craftsmanship is impeccable in *Yi Yi*, combining the warm colors of his black comedies with the nested narrative structures of the early melodramas. There is a newfound, natural lyricism that gracefully balances generations, dramatic conundrums, and narrative parallels. Acting and dialogue are unforced and utterly convincing, thanks to the combined efforts of the Arts Institute talent and Wu Nianzhen, the most gifted writer in Taiwan cinema. The boomtown mentality of *CC* and *Mahjong* has given way to a mature, elegiac awareness of global interconnections. *Yi Yi* still has remnants of con artistry, scams, and shell games, but they seem puerile and atavistic, because flim-flam enterprises fail to see there is nowhere to hide in an utterly interdependent world. Instead, there is nostalgia for faded youth, idealism, and romance. Middle-aged N. J. (Wu) and his wife (Elaine Jin Yanling) are lost, as are the protagonists of Yang's other films. But the discoveries of their children compensate for the parents' limitations, balanced by Grandmother's dress rehearsal for death: she spends most of the film lying in a coma. Yet she is the missing element who creates an imbalance and a need for accounting in the whole community.

Missing persons are a common thread in all Yang's films, and their absence is connected to a loss of capital and confidence, both financial and emotional (*qing*). Yang's narratives are all based on the resolution of a puzzle. Each story begins with a misplaced piece, nearly always taking the form of the missing. *That Day, on the Beach* opens with the search for the disappeared husband; the vanishing Ms. Mei in *Taipei Story* uncovers the deficits of the major characters Chin and Ah-Lon. Nobody actually goes missing in *The Terrorizers*, but the whole film is based on deferral, displacement, and waiting. Honey is the missing person in *A Brighter Summer Day*, hiding somewhere in the South. During his absence, struggles for power and women break out in the gangs of Guling Street. But when he returns, he is murdered instead of restoring order. In *Mahjong*, a kidnapping is used to locate the missing father of Redfish, who returns, only to kill himself and his mistress. Similarly, the grandmother in *Yi Yi* returns to life after her long coma, then dies, bringing the family together again.

Like the faces of women, missing pieces play narrative and ideological roles in Yang's film structures. The missing illuminates a whole systemic pattern of relations. But when put back to rights, a new pattern emerges, rather than the comfort of a former state. Yang's films are pointed observations of swiftly changing ensembles of contemporary life, but they also stage abstract dialectics of elimination and restoration. In all his films, a piece is missing, removed to activate a plot. The ensemble reacts, frantically trying to restore balance, but when the piece actually is reinstated, the whole structure collapses. Retroactively, the notion that equilibrium depends on the missing piece is exposed as a sham; the puzzle doesn't suffer gaps in the whole but closes over them, automatically evolving into another figuration, despite efforts at restoration. Traces of the missing are left only in the minds of survivors, struggling always to restore patterns several steps removed. Yang's stories offer subversive deferrals of "restoration," at least those believed to have some redemptive capacity. In Yang's world, design flaws are endemic to the system and cannot be repaired by replacing a part. The social machinery changes faster than our ability to renegotiate it, but because of the perceived salience of the missing, there's nothing for it but to try. Like the railroads that used to structure Taipei's urban spaces and replaced by elevated highways, only to be reconfigured by a new subway system, social relations are constantly under renovation, shot through with missing persons and anticipated needs. Yang navigates and now "netvigates" a design of elimination, limitation, and adaptation.

With *Yi Yi*, Yang drops his earlier incredulity at the callousness of contemporary culture commerce. He reconciles with the vacillations of urbanites who don't know what they want, but miss what they have lost. There's a quiet resignation to the way the world works, particularly the competitive demands of capitalism. The solution to flaws and opportunities of human existence is simple acceptance.

Coda: Remapping Jameson

In his groundbreaking essay, "Remapping Taipei," Fredric Jameson writes, "like the punctum in the fatal photographs in Antonioni's *Blow-up*, . . . this one does not look back at you. Here the wind that blows through the great trees in Antonioni's park only mildly lifts and ruffles the segments of the portrait."[32] Jameson here refers to the mosaic-like enlargements of the terrorizer's face pinned on the photographer's wall. More arresting than this is the visual citation, Jameson's own half-page blowup of *Blow-up*, following the first mention of Antonioni's famous film.

Jameson signals his esteem for Edward Yang's film by putting him in elite European company.[33] Lately, the "Chinese Antonioni" idea continues to linger, with Tsai Ming-liang now regularly painted with the same Italian modernist brush.[34] In the English-language literature, Jameson's "Remapping Taipei" is inescapable. The famous essay has made Yang and Taiwan cinema somewhat forbidding, if only because we must read (and reread) Jameson to study Yang. Jameson's groundbreaking has remained that, at least in English-language criticism, without sufficient further cultivation on Yang or other directors. His reference to Antonioni, though, originated with Tony Rayns.[35] Further scholarly canonization of Taiwan cinema has had to wait, with major conferences at Wisconsin (2002), Yale, and Taipei (both 2003).[36] But canonization is subject to struggles between local critics and outsiders, between China-centric and Taiwanese emphases, even between European and American analytical methods and vocabularies.

As philosopher of capitalist postmodernity, Jameson is keen to decipher cultural formations, like cinema and architecture, with thoroughgoing capitalist foundations. Discovery of reflexive, modernist aesthetics at play in marginal places like Taiwan or the Philippines provides a key place for these in the world system, coeval with Euro-American economic hegemony. Coeval means contemporaneity in time, so Jameson is denying the developmental assumptions of modernization theory. He also brings aesthetics into parity with economic determinations, "*transcoding the dominant mode of production*."[37] Hence the gesture of remapping: Edward Yang's or Kidlat Tahimik's films have textures that hold for the whole world system, despite their marginality.[38] Yang's context is adjustable; his Taipei-set films may be taken to address key forms of the world system in general, like urbanization, bureaucracy, surveillance, spatiotemporal disorientation, personal malaise, and collective paralysis. Formal, systemic manifestations like these cannot be limited to just Taipei, but inscriptions specific to Taipei in turn reveal the world system.

These features of the world system invest major cultural forms in the West, like cinema. For Jameson, films like *Videodrome* (1983; dir. David Cronenberg), *All the President's Men* (1976; dir. Alan J. Pakula), *The Conversation* (1974; dir. Francis Ford Coppola), and other conspiracy films of the 1970s demonstrate problems of representation in dominant Western narrative forms. The main problem is the impossibility of imagining plausible relations between individual and collective, psychological and socioeconomic realms, text and context without recourse to obsolete models, like base-superstructure, modernization theory, and conspiracy. Representation lags behind accelerating late-capitalist formations, incapable of keeping pace with postmodernity and globalization. Postmodernity can be taken as something that perpetually outruns or overtakes its cultural representations. Lacking credible candidates to stand for contemporary, postmodern capitalist social forms, Jameson proposes that these forms must take shape allegorically, slipping back into representational modes of earlier eras. Curiously, he calls the above titles "post-generic" genre films.[39] Cold War staples like conspiracy do not adequately express postmodern anxieties, but rather flag an absence of postmodernist manifestations in significant, representative forms—by default more than design. If there is design, it is of an impersonal, implacable sort immanent to the world system itself, automatically written into its visible structure or signatures.

As the third, late stage of capitalism, postmodernity circles back, assimilating what by rights should be its opposite, the Third World. Particular, local elements in a "marginal" Taiwanese film testify to a universal or global condition in a particularly forceful way: "its 'diagnosis' a kind of globality, if not a universality, which is evidently what has made Yang's critics uncomfortable."[40] Late capitalism encompasses all, in time as well as space. Its recursive circuitry means that center-periphery topographies, correlated with assumptions of progress-retardation, do not hold.

The Terrorizers comes in here. Jameson's exegesis is part of a larger thesis, the essential univocality of the world system and its "dedifferentiation of social levels . . . so that the new post-generic genre films are allegories of each other, and of the impossible representation of the social totality itself."[41] The "dedifferentiation" is not just social, but also geographical, the same world system speaking allegorically through a modernist Taiwan film like *The Terrorizers*. For Jameson, *The Terrorizers* is also post-generic because of its Third World provenance, its remove from classifications of Hollywood commercial pictures. This position is one we have rebutted, showing how uses of the crime picture and other genres assist the film's modernist narrative. For Jameson, *The Terrorizers* certifies postmodern representation more forcefully, by necessity, than narratives from the so-called center.[42] It does so *necessarily* due to its position: in space, as a small, relatively marginal film from an ex-Japanese colony, now an Asian client state (of the United States), whose initiation into global capitalism was recent and abrupt. And in time, because its narrative and thematic patterns recall high-modernist styles of earlier masters (Gide, Renoir, Antonioni, Fassbinder, Vertov, et al.), Yang's film cannot help but betray its postmodernity—but this denies agency to the film's local production factors, including the director's consciousness, as can be seen in this passage from Jameson's introduction: "all thinking today is *also*, whatever else it is, an attempt to think the world system as such. . . . [*The Terrorizers* is an] example of the way in which narrative today . . . conflates ontology with geography and endlessly processes images of the unmappable system" (his emphasis).[43]

Of course, Edward Yang had no idea he was conflating ontology with geography, and this need not make any critical difference at all. But we suspect that this Taipei geography—Yang's geography—as well as the geometry of this particular film, occupies a completely different order from that of Jameson's world system. By what lights does Yang's film belong in this world system, rather than some other, more immediate world (industrial, authorial, generic)? Does the film do the work Jameson assigns to it? Is the allegory of space in the world system the best way to understand Yang's work? Maybe there are simpler ways to understand and enjoy Yang's film than the Jamesonian system. There is much to gain by putting it aside for a moment, with its allegorical inscriptions in obscure films, and viewing *The Terrorizers* straightforwardly. *The Terrorizers'* obscurity, its marginality, is an important part of its use-value for Jameson's model, but it is now fully canonized. Further, it is a high-handed, magisterial critical procedure that minimizes, if not overrides, the primary material conditions of an artist's work.

In fixing *The Terrorizers* so tightly in its allegorical spot in the geopolitical totality ("*all* thinking today") at the expense of what Edward Said calls the text's "worldliness," Jameson forecloses a host of interesting and essential connections on the ground.[44] Jameson is not saying "residues of the modern" make Yang's film backward by Western standards.[45] Its seeming datedness, rather, signals affinities with the most contemporary qualities of postmodern culture, like the anachronistic conspiracies lingering vestigially over 1970s American thrillers. A *dislocation* or *misfit* between modernist textual strategies and context, "*a kind of* modernism" *inappropriate* to *The Terrorizers'* geopolitical circumstances, makes it quintessentially postmodern, hovering in an interstitial state:

> this mutually reinforcing suspension [between the modern and the postmodern, subjectivity and textuality] may owe something to the situation of Third World cinema itself, in traditions in which neither modernist nor postmodernist impulses are internally

generated, so that both arrive . . . with a certain chronological simultaneity in full post-war modernization. *Terrorizer [sic]* thereby enjoys the freedom of a certain distance from both.[46]

Jameson believes that modernism cannot be endogenous in Third World cinema, and therefore modernist style in *The Terrorizers* necessarily refers to something outside its own geopolitical position.

At both ends, this rhetorical structure is framed by questions of urban social organization posed by Western philosophical paradigms. It weaves film criticism with reflections on the history of narrative form, considered in relation to benchmarks in the West. It is a zig-zag argument that builds up an evocative, poetic, but fragmented case, in which the links only gradually emerge. Like Yang's film, Jameson's piece rewards reviewing and tends to call forth insights specific to different occasions.

Reprise

Space awaits the event, just as the landscape of Taiwan awaits nationhood, the marginality of province and colony about to become a center.

—FREDRIC JAMESON (OCTOBER 31, 2003)

What about Jameson's more recent thoughts on Taiwan cinema? Has he changed his mind? Not in the least. In fact, events since "Remapping Taipei" seem to have borne out his original thesis. In a keynote address given in late 2003, Jameson ratcheted up his argument to incorporate other Taiwan filmmakers—Ang Lee, and Tsai Ming-liang. He also integrates Taiwan New Cinema into the even more general, comparative rubric of International New Waves, like the French, Polish, and American varieties. Taiwan New Cinema continues Jameson's activity of "mapping a collectivity in space," a collectivity signaled by crowd scenes, multiple actions, and other devices that allegorically inscribe even larger collectivities that perhaps may stand in for the nation.[47]

On this occasion Jameson did not stray from his earlier cartography, illustrating the inescapability of "Remapping Taipei," perhaps even for its author. The references to Antonioni are still there; Hou's network of small suburban trains, with a clip from the wistful beginning of *Dust in the Wind*, remains; Yang's multiple plotlines ("simultaneous monadic synchronicity" or SMS) are there, now tied in with references to *Short Cuts* (1993; dir. Robert Altman) and *Pulp Fiction* (1994; dir. Quentin Tarantino); *The Terrorizers*, now "the supreme achievement of the New Cinema," represents a form of spatial colonization through varieties of simultaneity, and the logic of "meanwhile." Jameson cites Benedict Anderson, who provided one of the most acute diagnoses of nationalism in its need for Benjamin's empty, homogeneous time ("meanwhile"), underwritten in turn by such "machineries of representation" as the newspaper and nineteenth-century novel.[48]

The citation of Anderson is curious for an argument that would rather sidestep the quagmire of nationalism, preferring the more generic term "collectivities." The reference to Anderson also seems dated. But taken together with the mention of Altman's and Tarentino's films, this is a shrewd gesture of retrojection. Jameson pronounces a self-benediction for outlining, before Anderson, the concept of simultaneity-through-multiplicity. Meanwhile, though Jameson's SMS lacked the wide impact of *Imagined Communities*, it's striking how artists, filmmakers, and theorists have cottoned onto temporal superimpositions and overlapping plotlines as a key narrative principle, even in the most mainstream pictures.[49] Jameson's original essay was all about space and its cinematic mapping; the reprise is also about space, but now space has a kind of prescience, if not providentiality: "Space, this particular form of it—interlocking apartments, juxtaposed, superimposed in rectangular or in deep focus boxes—is part and parcel of what the Taiwan New Cinema wants to convey," Jameson says. Then he claims that "filming such space becomes a historiographic interpretation in its own right," and gives an example from *A Brighter Summer Day*. Yang has described the difficulty of finding old Japanese settings and objects from the 1950s, spaces that overlapped and coexisted with the Americanized military space of the Vietnam era.[50] Yang's activity of historical salvage and collage, hunting for a particular kind of electric fan or bicycle from the period, is taken now as the New Cinema's historiographic intent. Again, Yang is made to unintentionally conflate ontology with geography or, more exactly, archaeology with ontogeny. Creation of the overlapping historical spaces of *A Brighter Summer Day* becomes a solution to the generalized, generic globality of urbanization in *The Terrorizers*. Whereas the narrative dispersals of Yang's early films find visual expression in the "obsessive selection of rectangles" (Jameson), now Yang's preproduction spadework stands for retrospective adjustments made by the critic, positing a conceptual-formal prediction borne out in the intervening years.

"Little by little space is marked as with a stain, or symptom," Jameson says. Spatial articulations work as a form of index, bearing witness or betraying a presence no longer there. But can the "no longer there," as in a stain, also indicate a "not yet there"? If "space awaits the event," Jameson seems to hint at an a-chronological tense or state of affairs in Yang's films that he, Jameson, now elaborates as a kind of prophetic indexicality. For Jameson the prophetic impulse, retroactively installed, is not just predictive, but transformative, a call for collective renewal, and a "new transfigured present."[51]

Trisecting Taiwan Cinema with Hou Hsiao-hsien

In many ways Hou Hsiao-hsien has become a synonym for Taiwan cinema of the 1990s. Among his peers Hou enjoys by far the most extensive and intensive examination within and outside Taiwan.[1] On top of the long list of Hou Hsiao-hsien literature is Olivier Assayas' documentary film on Hou Hsiao-hsien, *HHH: Portraits de Hou Hsiao-hsien* (1996), the only documentary film ever made about a Taiwan director by a French filmmaker. Following the film is a string of critical accounts, scholarly essays, dissertations, and books contributing to the hermeneutics on Hou Hsiao-hsien.[2]

Two prevalent discourses have been identified in the written work on Hou Hsiao-hsien. One is the East-West binary, of cataloging Hou Hsiao-hsien as an Oriental director, along with Ozu Yasujiro, Satyajit Ray, and, more recently, Abbas Kiarostami, Kitano Takeshi, and Wong Kar-wai; another is the usefulness of Hou Hsiao-hsien as a "critical sphere" for debates on representation and politics within Taiwan.

Hou's long-take aesthetics, characterized by contemplative, distant photography, temporal ellipsis and loose causality, and additionally his observing, sympathetic attitude toward life, are frequently explained as manifestations of an Oriental detachment and have firmly positioned Hou as a director of the East par excellence. The East-West divide is a classic colonialist tool giving ample scope for comparisons that are, nevertheless, sometimes valid. French and French-inspired Japanese criticism on Hou have fashioned a *chinoiserie* by fixating on Oriental cosmology and epistemology in their interpretation of Hou's work.[3] A patently Oriental discourse is perpetuated to render Hou's films comprehensible to Western, Japanese, and even Chinese critics and audiences.[4]

Hou himself and his writer Zhu Tianwen even found the East-West binary profitable in making an impression on the history of film art. As early as 1986, Zhu Tianwen had attempted to situate Hou within so-called Eastern film practices, characterized by subtlety, humor, and a coherent set of options between European modernist insurgence and the American craft of entertainment.[5] When *The Puppetmaster* competed at the 1994 Cannes festival, Hou came out openly about his propensity for Eastern / Oriental aesthetics, particularly in his use of *liubai* as a key narrative strategy in *The Puppetmaster*. *Liubai*, leaving space blank, is a common compositional device in traditional Chinese ink painting to prompt emotional contemplation. In cinema, *liubai* entails inviting audiences into a cinematic space, not to understand, connecting cause and effect, but to experience: in other words, an aesthetic of deliberation. Thus, spatiality is emphasized to privilege aura, ambiance, and mood, leaving temporal markers as mere footnotes.[6] Ellipses, elimination of a significant portion of plot, are likened to the traditional compositional principle in which a small section is believed to be more revealing than a totality.[7]

Compared to the singularly smooth international reception, on the home front Hou and his films worked like a volatile spark, rapidly enflaming Taiwan's pluralistic cultural scene. During a short-lived but crucial moment of film studies in Taiwan, Hou Hsiao-hsien was read in the mid-1980s as a symptom of contemporary cultural politics. Hou's stylistic turn toward an abstemious or ascetic realism (see chapter 3) and his incorporation of nativist sensibilities aroused unprecedented deliberation among critics. Debates on which direction Taiwan cinema should take, toward art or commerce, brought the insularity and factionalism of Taiwan's film institutions to light.[8]

In the lead article of the 1987 cinema yearbook published by Taiwan's Motion Picture Development Foundation, Hou was called the "cultural ambassador" for his high exposure in European and North American film festivals.[9] But Hou was also called "box office poison" at this time because of his declining popularity with mass audiences. Hou's rising international reputation and decreasing commercial value divided critics into two distinctive camps: the pro-Hou and anti-Hou factions. Critics representing different tastes, generations, and interest groups such as the Government Information Office (GIO), Central Motion Picture Corporation (CMPC), film distributors, and publishing firms all weighed in on the controversy, centering on Hou the renegade from commercial cinema. The debate, focusing on questions of accountability to both public and industry, was so tense that Hou wanted to make *Dust in the Wind* (1986) a commercially viable film. In addition,

Hou's writer Zhu Tianwen published the screenplay and shooting script of *Dust in the Wind* with a string of short essays explaining Hou's aesthetic choices.[10] Though Zhu hoped to mollify anti-Hou critics, her efforts did not pay off because the film itself did not fulfill Hou's promises. On the contrary, *Dust in the Wind* augments Hou's trademark asceticism.

Later Hou instigated another, even bigger, cultural debate with the first film of his Taiwan trilogy. The criticism of *City of Sadness* (1989) culminated in the 1991 anthology *Death of the New Cinema* (Xin dianying zhi si). Contributors from various disciplines and backgrounds were not happy with Hou's distant photography and obscure storytelling in his depiction of the regime's brutality toward Taiwanese in the February 28 Incident, a major uprising against the Nationalists' neocolonial rule. As the most horrific incident in Taiwan's modern history, the February 28 Incident was then a collective trauma and has become a national scar. People were waiting to see some justice done in the film. But they did not. As a result, Hou was seen as a complacent, conservative artist who had yet to see the political light. The troubled local reception of Hou's *City of Sadness* manifests the difficulty of coming to terms with history and historical representation of Taiwan's scarred past.[11]

Between these two ends—Oriental aesthetics and Taiwan cultural politics—a third approach began to exert influence. Since 2000, studies on Hou reached a breakthrough with precise, illuminating formal analyses by film scholars who choose to work on the poetics of Hou and delineate various cinematic strategies that Hou has developed throughout his career. Hou's ingenious compositional approach, particularly his strategies of blocking and framing, is compared with the precision techniques of silent film masters such as Victor Sjöström, Louis Feuillade, and Lev Kuleshov's mentor, Yevgenii Bauer.[12] In addition, Hou's poetics cannot be divorced from its material basis, the very conditions of Taiwanese filmmaking. Hou's stylistic changes are in fact adjustments, conditioned by constraints and opportunities provided by a local industry characterized by meager capital, outdated equipment, and flexible techniques.[13]

With such a wide range of discourses, in Asia, Europe, and the United States, what then is left to be said about Hou Hsiao-hsien? What can we offer that goes beyond the obvious, the commonplace? In what ways can our analysis add a significant chapter to Hou Hsiao-hsien studies? A synthesis? A synergy? Or something apart? In the following we propose to use a bookend approach to Hou Hsiao-hsien. One side is a macro perspective, a long view juxtaposing Hou's career with the wax and wane of Taiwan cinema. The other is a micro, close analysis of Hou in relation to cultural patrimony. We consider Hou's uses of autobiography as a narrative device and repatriation to Chinese and Taiwanese cultural heritage.

Hou Hsiao-hsien and the Triptych Taiwan Cinema

Hou's cinema can be divided into three episodes: the commercial past (1975–1982), the New Cinema (1983–1988), and the international auteur (1989 to the present). Dividing Hou's oeuvre into a triptych provides a lucid chronological framework to understand Hou's poetics and politics. It corresponds with the development of Hou's mastery, from apprenticeship in a genre-dominated industry, to an increasingly famous auteur, and finally his more speculative experiments with narrative and historicity. We could speculate that these phases correspond with sources of funding: Taiwan's independent commercial sector, then the CMPC, followed by coproductions between Taiwanese media conglomerates and Japanese (and later French) companies. What is important to note, however, is that this triptych frame also covers the dominant structures of collective film practice, rather than just a singular reflection of Hou's own work. In many ways, this division accounts for Taiwan's film history from the 1970s through the New Cinema to the new millennium. Like the movement of Hou's career in the past two decades, Taiwan cinema evolved from a state propaganda and commercial system to a self-conscious artistic virtuosity, which then stalled with the reintroduction of commercial priorities and Hollywood domination.

In this chapter, we will study Hou's developing repertoire within this connected but clearly divided triptych. We emphasize the transitions and joins between the three parts, recognizing the hinges and erasures that testify to the indivisibility of past and present, and indicating the retrospective creation of periods and stages. The crucial debt to literature, especially Hou's muse Zhu Tianwen, must also be explored since Hou's preoccupations are not limited to cinema and do not evolve in a vacuum. It was novelist Zhu Tianwen who introduced Hou to the value of autobiographical techniques of representation. Our operating assumption is to set aside a cardinal doctrine of auteurism, which is the singularity of artistic sensibility, and propose instead Hou's representativeness, if not typicality. Like a lightning rod or chameleon, Hou's vision and techniques evolved along with that of a community of artists and cultural workers. Breaking from methodological individualism, we may expand the triptych framework to accommodate contemporary Taiwan film history. In other words, we aim to merge institutional historiography with auteurism and vice versa.

Apprentice

When Hou Hsiao-hsien began to appear as the most important auteur of contemporary Taiwan cinema in the mid-to-late 1980s, little was said about his early days as a successful commercial director. The deliberate forgetting or overlooking of the past is an understandable tactic because the connection with the past may be a problem or even a prohibition, like an embarrassing uncle from the country, to legitimizing Hou as a budding auteur. Acknowledging the relation makes it even harder to sustain the unique place that the New Cinema created for itself at home and in the eyes of international critics, so the connection was suppressed.[14] Only recently were Hou's early films recuperated as part of the scholarly endeavor to build a more comprehensive study of Hou Hsiao-hsien. Bit by bit, Hou's deep involvement with the old establishment was uncovered.

Hou entered the industry in 1972 as the apprentice of Lai Chengying, a long-time cinematographer for Li Xing. "Lai san" (Japanese meaning "Mr. Lai," as Hou respectfully addressed his master) was a prolific cinematographer in the 1960s and '70s. Lai was responsible for the photography of many Taiwan classics, including the 1965 healthy realist *Beautiful Duckling* and a number of famous Qiong Yao romantic melodramas. Hou was brought in to work as a continuity keeper on Li Xing's 1973 romantic melodrama, *Heart with a Million Knots* (Xin you qianqian jie), a Hong Kong and Taiwan coproduction meant to cash in on the huge success of Li's earlier hits. As an apprentice to the film industry, Hou's major task in his formative period was to learn various genre conventions in order to assist his teachers and seniors.

In 1975, Hou was promoted to assistant director and followed his teacher Lai Chengying to Young Sun (Yongsheng), a distribution and producing company. Hou continued to work as Lai's assistant director and scriptwriter. It was during this period that Hou established a collaborative relationship with Chen Kunhou, Lai's nephew and Young Sun's in-house cinematographer. In the next five years, Hou worked on ten films directed by Lai and collaborated with Chen on several romantic comedies.

Entering the 1980s, Hou's apprenticeship came to an end. He was credited as the scriptwriter for Li Xing's award-winning healthy realist *Good Morning, Taipei* (Best Picture in the 1980 Golden Horse Awards). Then he was given an opportunity to direct and write, with Chen Kunhou as cinematographer, three films in the following two years. The first two films, *Cute Girl* (aka *Lovable You*, Jiushi liu liu de ta, 1980) and *Cheerful Wind* (aka *Play While You Play*, Feng'er ti ta cai, 1981), are somewhat like "package films" in terms of making them as double bills based on one premise, one idea. *Cute Girl* and *Cheerful Wind* share identical casting; their stories are comparable; their narrative structure and visual-audio style and even comic gags are almost indistinguishable. Both films cast Canto pop singer Kenny Bee (Zhong Zhentao) and Taiwan pop icon Feng Feifei. The surplus value of casting pop idols is to fill the soundtrack with many popular songs by the two leads. This was a standard practice in romantic melodrama in the 1970s, a symbiotic, cross-media cooperation between the recording and film industries. Pop singers plus comic features granted Hou a hot ticket to the rather closed film distribution network. These two films were released for consecutive Chinese New Year holidays, traditionally the most profitable period of the year for the movie business. With these two films, Hou was able to establish himself as an A-list commercial director. In 1982, Hou directed *The Green, Green Grass of Home*, the film believed to have been a spark for the commercial director to defect to art cinema in the approaching New Cinema movement.

Despite being commercially calculating, Hou's early films represent new attempts by young filmmakers to modify the standardization of romantic melodrama. By the mid-1970s, romantic melodrama had become the representative genre for Taiwan films in domestic and overseas markets although martial arts and kung fu took up more than 40 percent of annual film production. Action films from Taiwan were usually perceived as shoddy imitations of higher-quality Hong Kong fare because most of them were "quickies" lacking imaginative action choreography or credible kung fu as practiced by masters like Bruce Lee and Lau Kar-leung (Gordon Liu). But romantic melodrama was different. With its moving stories, fantasy surroundings, love songs, and moral messages, romantic melodrama was able to appeal to female audiences across the Asia-Pacific region. The heartbreaking, tear-jerking narrative is partly related to the genre's literary genealogy, which also has a significant bearing on healthy realist pictures.[15] Romance novels by Qiong Yao and other, younger woman writers provided vast resources for screen adaptation during the Golden Age of Taiwan film production. We can safely assume that the literary feature helped create a distinction for Taiwan cinema abroad.

The prominence of melodrama allowed the émigré Taiwan-based directors like Li Xing and Bai Jingrui to continue to work throughout the 1970s by enjoying dual positions, a second career in their working life, unlike their friends Li Hanxiang and King Hu, whose careers took singular though quite divergent directions. By the early 1970s, Li Hanxiang had returned to Shaw Brothers and reinvented himself in soft-porn period pictures and Republican warlord comedies; King Hu had become an internationally acclaimed art director pursuing costume films with an astute historical sense and philosophical sensibility (see chapter 1). But Li Xing and Bai Jingrui were able to work comfortably in Taiwan because of the high demand for melodramas. They remained useful to the industry by continuously churning out profitable romance pictures. On the other hand, they were able to retain their reputations as serious directors by incorporating the imperatives of healthy realism (the exercise of ethical and, sometimes, aesthetic sensibility) into popular entertainment.

Like most established genre pictures, the mode of production for romantic melodrama was dominated by standardization and repetition. Stories of one kind

4.1 *The Young Ones* (1973; dir. Li Xing)

(COURTESY TAIWAN CINEMA NOTES, COUNCIL FOR CULTURAL AFFAIRS, AND TAIPEI FILM ARCHIVE)

would be repeated in a number of films, with three pairs of first-tier actors and a couple of bit players alternating roles for each of these similar productions. The well-known pictures were written and/or adapted from romance novels by the same scriptwriter (Zhang Yongxiang), the same songwriters (Luo Mingdao and Zuo Hongyuan), and the same technical crews in sound recording, makeup, costume, and art design. This factory-like process guaranteed quantity production of romantic melodramas to ensure Taiwan cinema's market share in the region, despite familiar production design and formulaic plot arrangements. With very few exceptions, such as Jimmy Wang Yu (who quit Shaws and moved to Taiwan to become an independent producer and director), or military film director Ding Shanxi, everyone in the business was compelled to make romantic melodramas. Romantic melodrama was the definitive Taiwanese genre, in the sense that it was lucrative and simultaneously distinguished itself as a *Taiwanese* genre. In 1973, Li Xing's *The Young Ones* (fig. 4.1) even out-grossed Bruce Lee's *The Big Boss* (aka *Fists of Fury*, 1971) and *Return of the Dragon* (aka *Way of the Dragon*, 1972) in the Southeast Asian market.[16]

This "A picture" production formula eventually went to its inevitable doom. At the beginning of the 1980s, romantic melodrama ceased to bring high returns to the film establishment and was thus seen as a problem, even a crisis. Qiong Yao films could no longer sustain their popularity, even with new faces and new stories. Various attempts were made to tackle this problem. One of them was to repeat an old trick—introducing pop singers to the big screen.

Nativist Sensibility in Pre–New Cinema

In the 1970s there was perhaps only one singer in Taiwan whose popularity across a wide range of age groups could topple that of the perennial Teresa Teng (Deng Lijun). She was Feng Feifei. A "native girl," Feng was also a top television host in variety shows produced by China Television Network (owned and operated by the KMT). Her television appearances helped build her up as the neighborly girl-next-door type, but laced with glamour. Although her songs were not entirely different from those of Teresa Teng, her public image was nothing like Teng's gracious, classy image as a mainland descendant and a talent trained in Japan. Compared with Teresa, Feng Feifei was comical, sometimes feisty and vulgar, and, most of all, local. It is safe to say that her distinct Taiwanese appeal accounts for her popularity despite rarely using Taiwanese dialect in her shows, public appearances, and songs.

Few companies made an effort to capitalize on her crossover capacity, and when they did they cast her in period melodramas with typical female pathos such as *Winter chill* (Chun han, 1979) and *Autumn lotus* (Qiulian, 1979). The latter was written by Hou Hsiao-hsien and directed by Hou's mentor Lai san. Both films feature Feng Feifei as an afflicted character, playing against her popular image as a cheerful, funny, fashionable, and down-to-earth modern woman. Feng Feifei's image in Taiwan pop music and television was eventually projected to the big screen in Hou Hsiao-hsien's first two films, *Cute Girl* and *Cheerful Wind*.

Feng's affable, native star persona meshes perfectly with the refreshing new feeling and approach brought by these young, but experienced craftsmen of the film establishment. Her huge popularity with children in her television shows encouraged Hou to place children around her. Feng's natural fit with the local soil and an earthy temperament puts her at ease in the rural landscape of offshore islands (*Cheerful Wind*). Her fun-loving, wry jokes and misdemeanors were perfect for humor that was essential to renovate stagnant, melodramatic formulas. In *Cute Girl*, Feng Feifei is a runaway bride, escaping an arranged marriage. She finds peace and freedom in the countryside, which also provides an opportunity for a lovely romance and a solution. In *Cheerful Wind*, she's an outsider again in a small village where she finds inspiration for her photography and lots of fun just being an observer. Even though *Cheerful Wind* returns to the city after the first thirty minutes, Hou avoids standard settings from melodrama such as living rooms, disco pubs, coffee shops, and the empty beach, and moves the scenes to a park, a zoo, and night markets.

Cute Girl (or Lovable You, 1980)

Hou's first feature exemplifies seizure of opportunities for renewal, as well as maintaining continuity with a popular tradition. Youth subject matter, family ethics, the Taiwanese countryside, popular music, and low humor commingle in an appealing mixture of romance and comedy. Hou capitalizes on the "Taiwanese" quality of Feng Feifei, a Taiwan girl popular with Taiwan natives through her songs and television work. Using popular music and television, Hou took previous forms in a new direction away from the sentimental, literary quality of the film melodramas of the 1970s. Audiences appreciated the new emphasis, at once lighter and more topical.

Cute Girl (fig. 4.2) was made for an independent production house, Dayou. It follows the adventures of Wenwen, whose wealthy family is intent on marrying her off. To escape the pressure, she disappears for a few days to visit relatives in the country. There she enjoys the natural life and appears to forget her urban worries. She observes a dispute between the villagers and a survey crew who want to cut a road straight through her neighbor's yard. The workmen try to make the villagers understand by repeating phrases like "development," "progress," and "life will be better," but the country people remain unconvinced. A standoff ensues. One young surveyor has his leg bitten by a snake and the villagers allow him to believe it was a viper. Wenwen is worried and insists her neighbors help him. They do so, begrudgingly, then reveal to her that the snake wasn't poisonous and the bitter antibody—administered in triple dosage—was only a laxative. The workman, Daming (Kenny Bee) spends the next few hours in the outhouse.

Charmed by the misunderstanding, Wenwen falls in love with the young surveyor. For the next few days they cavort in the sunshine and play at courtship as if they were in a classic pastoral romance. Reality intervenes, and they must return to their city lives. Wenwen's betrothed, the chemistry student Ma Qian, returns from France and she is thrown into a classic love triangle. Hou handles this in comic fashion, with the two men seemingly oblivious of their competition. At first Wenwen appears to be sidelined by the sudden friendship between the two suitors.

In the end things resolve for Wenwen, Daming, and Ma Qian, but not before more misunderstandings and absurd situations involving friends, family, and animals in the zoo. The lighthearted sight gags and non sequiturs are reminiscent of Ozu's early silent comedies (which used to be known as "nonsense pictures"). The snakebite trick is followed up in a famous Taipei snake restaurant, where Daming introduces Ma Qian to the medicinal properties of cobra organs. Here Kenny Bee's

4.2 Feng Feifei, Chen Kunhou, and Hou Hsiao-hsien on set, *Cute Girl* (1980)

(COURTESY HOU HSIAO-HSIEN)

Taipei native has fun with the returnee, who plays the straight role, the man-in-the-dark, in contrast with the unfilial and unfaithful Ke Junxiong, who plays the foreign returnee in Bai Jingrui's 1970 *Home Sweet Home* (see chapter 1). The film is also full of sound gags and songs, boasting an infectious score, especially the title song by Kenny Bee, "Lovable You." *Cute Girl* may seem a long way from Hou's mature works. However, two themes reappear later in different forms. They are the contrast between competitive city and communal countryside, and an important aspect of the modern Taiwanese family, namely, that a seemingly rigid kinship can actually be malleable, with some ingenuity, sincerity, and good humor.

Cheerful Wind (or Play While You Play, 1981)

Hou's second film is a clever romantic comedy released for the Lunar New Year. Like *Cute Girl*, its charm is so effortless that the artfulness is easily overlooked. If it seems like commercial fluff, *Cheerful Wind* has much unexpected richness. The opening scenes that take place on the P'eng-hu Islands (Pescadores) take great liberties with generic and thematic expectations. When the story moves to Taipei after the first thirty minutes, it settles into a more conventional moralistic musical comedy.

On location in a village on the Pescadores is a film shoot. A gang of mischievous boys explodes firecrackers in cowpats and receives faces full of ordure. In this nasty, but funny business, Hou immediately shifts gears by revealing the setup—a commercial shoot for laundry detergent. But the crew fails to get the shot. A prop man is dispatched to scout for more manure. He confronts an unhappy cow, and urges her to produce more props. A musical cue prompts another sudden shift in tone. A guitar solo turns the scene into a face-off between man and beast, à la a Spanish bullfight but with the prop man increasingly on the defensive. Meanwhile the protagonist, a photographer named Xinhui (Feng Feifei) delightedly snaps photos of this scenario, revealing her professional expertise and a gift for seeing humor in odd situations. Her job is not only to shoot stills for the ad agency but also to provoke real-life comedy for the camera. Sometimes photogenic moments just arrive unannounced, like a serene young man playing harmonica in a slow-moving oxcart. Later, on the beach (the standard location for Taiwan melodramas), she steals a look at the young man.

With the introduction of Jintai (Kenny Bee), there is a tour-de-force of visuality gone awry. The filmmakers are shooting candid shots of an actual street hawker ("Made-in-Japan parts!") and the harmonica player Jintai is in the crowd. The director wants a hidden-camera effect. An optical point-of-view shot from the viewfinder picks up Jintai's face, but he gazes back into the lens, directly at us! This completely spoils the candid effect sought by the commercial director because it blatantly betrays the presence of the camera. The crew shouts at Jintai, telling him not to look at the camera. Then we see, as the surrounding villagers tell the crew, that Jintai is blind. Discovering this, the director recruits Jintai for the commercial, filming him walking along the breakwater. As soon as he calls "cut," Jintai falls off the edge. On screening the rushes, the director tries out different slogans for the laundry soap: "Pure as a blind man's heart."

The handsome star Kenny Bee as blind protagonist? This is indeed what Hou Hsiao-hsien has devised. Is it going too far to anticipate Lin Wenqing, the deaf-mute played by commercial heartthrob Tony Leung Chiu-wai in *City of Sadness*? In that film the elimination of speech enables a rich discourse of written narration. In many ways this is a superior approach to the shock of the February 28 incident and its attendant sociopolitical and ethnic traumas. In *Cheerful Wind*, Hou contrives various comic and dramatic possibilities based on the conceit of sight, oversight, and blindness. When Xinhui decides to have her rural elementary students repaint a school mural, it creates a bureaucratic fuss; she also uses Jintai as a setup for taking candid photographs outside a city park, but is chastened when her car, meanwhile, is towed away. In this scene Jintai explains to some curious children what it's like not to see, using an analogy to hands, which do not miss the faculty of sight but are content with the sense of touch. Interestingly, the name Lin Wenqing appears in Hou's next film, *The Green, Green Grass of Home*, as one of the mischievous Three Musketeers in Kenny Bee's class. As noted, the presence of children is appropriate to a film starring Feng Feifei. And children, especially when used in rural or outdoor settings, underscore Hou's realist tendency. Some writers also link the prominence of children to Hou's documentary impulse.[17]

Due to her appreciation of his insight and courage, photographer Xinhui secretly falls in love with Jintai, initiating a break with her ad agency boyfriend where she works. Unlike the love triangle in *Cute Girl*, Hou allows some hard feelings into the characterization, which are not resolved until the very end. Midway through the picture, however, Jintai gets a corneal transplant. *Cheerful Wind* still continues the gags and motifs related to sight, visual prosthetics, photography, and art classes. Xinhui's first postoperative appearance to Jintai is a slightly cruel joke when she sends an impersonator. Xinhui volunteers to read aloud at a Braille class, a sequence with remarkable sound technique. As she reads, the clattering Braille machines lend staccato accompaniment with an incongruous comic effect. She soon becomes restless, skipping pages from the hefty novel before her. After a short while she apologetically excuses herself. Hou cuts to the book she was reading: *The Brothers Karamazov*. The blind class is indifferent to the foreign provenance and heft of this dark Russian work, but Xinhui is intimidated.

Cheerful Wind's healthy realist moral is to have faith in youth, for their resilience is as refreshing as the "Breath of Spring," one of many songs sung by Kenny Bee. The obstacles to love may be daunting, but solutions are never too far away. This sunny optimism and sense of fun is very remote from the heavy melodrama of Hou's cinematic forebears. The patrimony of Qiong Yao (despite its feminine origin) and her derivatives furnished a base from which to depart for sunnier places. Would-be profundity and emotionally turgid situations have little place in this story, unless it furnishes a joke, as in the Braille class. This doesn't just target Xinhui's awkwardness but the perceptual interest of the audiovisual juxtaposition of literary and acoustic modes. Hou's apprentice cheerfulness also becomes muted in the films he made in the next phase, the New Cinema proper.

The Green, Green Grass of Home (1982)

The Boys from Fengkuei (1983) and *Dust in the Wind* (1986) are about the migration from the country to the city, representing prominent themes in Hou's New Cinema period. Before the New Cinema, however, Hou deals with the relief and delight of escaping the city to the countryside in such films as *Cute Girl* and *Cheerful Wind*. The last film in this period, *The Green, Green Grass of Home*, follows this leitmotif. Despite their lightheartedness, it is fair to say that as an auteur Hou has already started to emerge in these early films.[18]

Especially when we place *Green* in the evolution of Taiwan film style, this film marks a rapport with the genres of healthy realism and romantic melodrama. There is a certain leniency with which it takes the issues of the law and human foibles, which follows the ideology of healthy realism. A man, apparently an ex-KMT soldier, marries an aboriginal girl, who soon runs away. In frustration, he electrifies fish in the river, then collects them to take to market. A trio of naughty village boys starts to imitate him. This depredation of the environment was actually a common problem in mountain areas of Taiwan, but the film uses an emotional pretext to give it pathos. Emotional imbalance, the loneliness of a mainland father and his son, is therefore linked with ecological imbalance. This eventually leads to a local environmental campaign, whose slogan is "Love your river home, protect our fish." To further encourage embrace of the lesson, the film uses pop musical interludes in the tradition of romantic melodrama. The lyrics, with one exception, seldom deal directly with love and romance, but instead focus on nature, friendship, and communal life, the central concerns of healthy realism. Children's songs are liberally used as well. An exception is a classroom exercise in which the attractive teacher (Jiang Ling) goes over the lyrics of a love song line by line. The song, "I take another sip of Coke, as I tightly hold your hand," could just as well be about friendship and trust, and therefore works for instruction as for personal affection.

All this takes place before Kenny Bee's arrival in the village to start as a substitute teacher. He comes from Taipei with a good degree and is welcomed by the whole community. But he has much learn about country people, their close-knit community and sense of pride. Confronting the electrical fisherman in the river, he is soundly beaten and must appear in the classroom bruised and bandaged. Yet this humiliation is what initiates his efforts to protect the river and unify the community behind the conservation program.

Such features seem to contradict the formation of a New Cinema auteur. But in following the dominant genres of the time, Hou had already started to inject his own vision, transforming a would-be melodramatic propaganda film into a fertile, early exercise in thematic flexibility and stylistic experimentation. For example, *Green, Green Grass* doesn't employ a very rigid or unifying perspective to construct the contrast between the city and the countryside. It presents moments when contradictions can be overcome as well as places where they are irreconcilable. At first the countryside seems utopian, with happy, energetic children dutifully doing their lessons. Kenny Bee appears to be an instinctive country bumpkin, eating and playing with gusto, but later his city girlfriend comes looking for him. She is immediately demonized through her clothing, her automobile, and her behavior, and she means to take him back to civilization. This causes a great scandal in the village, as Kenny had already started a romance with his fellow teacher. In addition, the propaganda slogan "Love your river home, protect our fish" is transformed into a genuine love for nature and a rousing environmental statement. Hou's privileging of the profilmic through cinematography and editing ensures that the stunning natural beauty of Taiwan's countryside is spotlighted. In these early works there are clear signs of a budding master, with experiments in tone as well as audiovisual contrivances, well before Hou begins working in the New Cinema with its dramatic changes of style.

At this point Hou was a flexible maverick capable of taking what was available locally, in subject matter, genre, and style, and mixing it with new elements without upsetting the system. With a light but local sensibility, Hou's romantic comedies proved to be a feasible middle approach. Compared to the 1982 picture *In Our Time*, a four-part film conceived as a breakthrough voice for the Taiwan film industry, it is evident that Hou remained loyal to the old school: the star system, the generic conventions, musical numbers, and close ties to the distribution establishment. But it is important to argue that these earlier efforts by Hou, Chen Kunhou, and Wang Tong (see chapter 2) helped create an environment conducive for the New Cinema to flourish—within two years.

Auto/biographical Acts: From Personal to National

When Hou's *The Sandwich Man* (1983) was released, a sharp contrast was evident between the film's melancholic tone and the lovable, cheerful mood that dominated his early, commercial works. By way of nativist literature, Hou had stumbled onto unfamiliar but fertile ground, new raw materials, and a different style. With double-digit economic growth in the 1960s, the emotional strain on masculine/patriarchal identity seems to have started an introspective turn, provoking Hou to explore the past via close examination of personal history and memory. Beginning with *The Boys from Fengkuei*, Hou's entire body of work in the 1980s and 1990s is patently auto/biographical, with a few exceptions (*Daughter of the Nile*, Niluohe de nü'er, 1987; *Goodbye South, Goodbye*, Zaijian nanguo zaijian, 1996; and *Millennium Mambo*, Qianxi manbo, 2001).

Why Autobiography?

Autobiography is a major form of storytelling in the rise and development of the various new wave movements, including the French, German, Japanese, and Chinese new waves. These new wave films, despite cultural, industrial, stylistic, and historical differences, share a similar Oedipal complex in terms of their revolt against both cultural and cinematic patrimony. We see in these various new waves a general rejection of conventional genres. In replacing old forms set up by their forebears, most new wave directors choose autobiography to suit a new identity as prodigal sons and daughters. Autobiographical films can almost be treated as an important "generic" distinction between the new wave and their objects of rebellion. These autobiographical texts tend to center on a troubled childhood, youthful defiance, and memories of political or social upheaval. Examples are numerous: François Truffaut's *The Four Hundred Blows* (Les quatre cents coups, 1959), Wim Wenders' *Kings of the Road* (Im Lauf der Zeit, 1976), Oshima Nagisa's *Cruel Story of Youth* (Seishun zankoku monogatari, 1960), and Tian Zhuangzhuang's *The Blue Kite* (Lan fengzheng, 1993). By telling stories of their own and those of their parents, new wave filmmakers are able to enter the symbolic realm to compete with and eventually usurp the speaking power of their fathers.

Similarly, Taiwan New Cinema begins with a cycle of self-exploration and self-disclosure, eventually culminating in an assumption of the narrating position, to tell the story of the fathers, including the ambiguous origins of Taiwan itself. We can assume that personal memories of social and political changes are keys to understanding the tangible autobiographical acts in the New Cinema. But at the same time, many films in this category are not just autobiographical but biographical too. In telling one's own story or stories, filmmakers and writers tend to cross-reference the stories of other people. For example, the character of Lin Wenqing, the photographer in *City of Sadness*, is based on a real person named Hou Conghui (with whom Hou Hsiao-hsien discussed the events of February-March 1947), whose recollections form a key strand in the narrative of clan, city, and nation. *Good Men, Good Women* is the story of a real-life couple whose experiences are framed in a complex structure of fiction, memory, performance, and historical documentation. Autobiography and biography are a mixed mode in the hands of Hou Hsiao-hsien and a dominant mode in the New Cinema as a whole. They are so amalgamated that it is difficult and probably hopeless to try to disentangle or separate them. Why is it not enough for Edward Yang, Wu Nianzhen, or Zhu Tianwen to simply and faithfully relate their own stories? Instead, they impose autobiographical forms onto well-known public figures or people close to them. Examples include the protagonist Mao Wu (Xiao Si'er) of the Guling Street murder incident in Yang's *A Brighter Summer Day* (1991), the "Dou-san" (father) of the narrator in Wu's *A Borrowed Life* (1994), and neighbor Xiaobi in Zhu's *Growing Up* (1983), directed by Hou. Edward Yang even claimed that the characters in all his late films are based on stories of his friends. It seems, then, that autobiography developed into a generic form that was not only capable but preferred by New Cinema filmmakers as a vessel for narrative structure, in common with other prominent new waves around the world.

This conscious, intertextual writing, shuttling between stories of self and those of others, prompts scrutiny of autobiographical films on two levels: the forms of writing about oneself (what can be termed the "poetics of autobiography"), and the functions of autobiography ("autobiographical acts"), probing the what and why of autobiography, and how the poetics of autobiography relates to depictions of the nation-state.

Autobiography has long been an established literary genre. Criticism of auto-biography, like literary criticism itself, has undergone major development in the past few decades. New criticism, structuralism, poststructuralism, postmodern-ism, and postcolonialism have defined and reshaped studies on autobiography at various stages. In the 1970s, Elizabeth Bruss wrote about the "changing situation of a literary genre," employing Barthesian concepts of text and author to study autobiographical acts.[19] Taking the increasingly unstable notion of the "I" in auto-biography as a formal device, recent writing on autobiography proposes a poetic approach to examine autobiography. The autobiographical act, according to John Paul Eakin, is a synthesis of memory and imagination in order to "serve the needs of present consciousness."[20] Autobiography as literary or filmic text is no longer treated by critics as a "faithful and unmediated reconstruction of a historically veri-fiable past," but as an "imaginative art" based on both psychological and cultural sources.[21] As an imaginative art, not just recollection, the truth of autobiography is "an evolving content in an intricate process of self-discovery and self-creation."[22] This is where poetics comes into play in analyses of the changing form and func-tions of autobiography. Fiction, invention, and the process of making things up are central constituents of the truth of any life, personal or collective. A poetics of auto-biography urges us to look at the dialectical interplay between memory and imagi-nation, between the autobiographer's impulse to self-invention and the received selfhood of his acts in the surrounding culture.[23] In other words, autobiographical invention takes place as negotiation between memory and fiction-making tech-niques, and further between the textual and contextual, or social consequence of the autobiographical assertion. The poetics of autobiography allows us to examine autobiographical acts in multiple frames and to see them as fluid and flexible texts, or texts-in-process.[24]

The poetics of autobiography are especially prominent in the work of Hou Hsiao-hsien. We argue that the theory of autobiography helps in providing a new conceptualization of Hou Hsiao-hsien's work and a framework for thinking about Taiwan film historiography. In many ways, the developing career of Hou marks the changes in Taiwan cinema's history during the past three decades. These changes, however, are not always in tandem. There are of course sharp divergences between the personal history of a professional filmmaker and the evolving history of a small (and shrinking) national film industry. As Hou ascended, the film industry precipitously declined. The overall picture is somewhat schizophrenic, with Hou presiding over an increasingly embattled industry as a symbol of cinematic quality and leadership.

Hou's work in the early 1980s tried to synthesize commercial genres with nativist sensibilities. When he moved decisively to an autobiographical narrative mode during the New Cinema movement, Hou's auteur status was secured. This status was won due to the relevance of autobiography to a rapid social and political transformation, and to the literary devices introduced from the nativist tradition. Hou's autobiographical acts culminated in the 1990s with his "national biography" in the Taiwan trilogy. Hou managed to transpose his autobiographical acts onto the biographical materials of Taiwan itself, and through these national-biographical films, onto people who could stand in for the island: Lin Wenqing in *City of Sadness*, Li Tianlu in *The Puppetmaster*, and Zhong Haodong and Jiang Biyu, the protagonists of *Good Men, Good Women*. With these films Hou became the leading director in Taiwan and consolidated his international reputation. The more recent works (*Flowers of Shanghai, Millennium Mambo*) continue to employ autobiographical acts. Written by Zhu Tianwen, these films play strange, sensuous games with time, uncoupling the links between personal memory and empirical history. Even in his 2004 *Café Lumíere* (Kafei shiguang), Hou deftly blends the story of Jiang Wenye, a gifted Taiwanese composer of the 1930s, into a drifting life of a modern Tokyo woman. Today, the film industry of Taiwan looks to Hou as an apprentice looks to his master, for guidance, craft secrets, and inspiration. Concepts of autobiography and methods of analyzing autobiography illuminate an intricate, entangled relation between filmmakers and the cinema network in Taiwan. More important, autobiography allows a different approach to the problem areas of Hou's work, such as national identity, femininity/masculinity, the criminal, and the provincial. All four of these problem areas are opened to view by the scalpel of autobiography.

Following is a three-part catalog of film work constituting the autobiographical acts of Hou Hsiao-hsien. We may treat these acts as poetics by attending to the processual dialectic between self-invention and the evolving frames—industrial and cultural—within which Hou is understood.

I. Films Directed by Hou Hsiao-hsien

1. Hou's own autobiographical film, *The Time to Live and the Time to Die* (1985). His autobiographical inserts in *The Boys from Fengkuei* (1983).
2. Scriptwriter and filmmaker Wu Nianzhen contributes his autobiography to Hou's *Dust In the Wind* (1986).
3. Taiwan's leading woman writer, Zhu Tianwen, contributes her autobiography to *Summer at Grandpa's* (1984).

4. *The Puppetmaster* (1993), Li Tianlu's auto/biography.
5. *Good Men, Good Women* (1995), biography of a political dissident couple of the 1940s and 1950s (Zhong Haodong and Jiang Biyu), framed within an actress's rehearsals.
6. *Flowers of Shanghai* (1998), Han Ziyun's recollections of living in Shanghai's pleasure quarters (published in 1894).

II. Autobiographical Films Directed by Other New Cinema Filmmakers

A Brighter Summer Day (1991) by Edward Yang (see chapter 3)
Dou-san: A Borrowed Life (1994) by Wu Nianzhen (see chapter 2)
The Red Persimmon (1999) by Wang Tong (see chapter 2)

III. Films Based on Novels with Strong Autobiographical Acts

Ah fei (aka *Rapeseed Girl*, 1983; dir. Wan Ren), based on Liao Huiying's 1983 award-winning novel under the same Chinese title.
Jade Love (Yuqing sao, 1984; dir. Zhang Yi), based on Bai Xianyong's famous novel, *Madam Yuqing*, published in 1960, an account of his childhood memory.

The films by Hou do not exhaust the repository of autobiographical acts in the New Cinema. Autobiographical acts and poetics in Taiwan New Cinema are far from being individual, personal indulgence; they take place within institutions and communities, with gestures of self-invention transmitted between artists, writers, and critics. They are always intertextual, cross-referential, and recurrently allegorical. Eventually they become hallmarks of a group style or a movement, called into being from the outside (as in foreign festivals) as much as by endogenous expression.

Having established the centrality of autobiography to the New Cinema, we want to trace Hou's autobiographical acts to a moment in which he received a splendid gift from a new friend. Unlike his peers, who eventually would create their own stories and direct their own screenplays, Hou never went solo. Research, brainstorming, writing, and finalizing screenplay and script treatments—all these important parts of Hou's creative process involved close collaboration with his two most important muses, Zhu Tianwen and Wu Nianzhen.

Encountering Zhu Tianwen: Nativism as a Meeting Point *growing up*

The "primal scene" of the New Cinema can be dated back to the day when Zhu Tianwen met with Hou Hsiao-hsien and Chen Kunhou, two old hands that de-

4.3 Zhu Tianwen

fected to the newcomer camp. Zhu Tianwen (b. 1956) comes from "the most noted literary family" in Taiwanese literature (see fig. 4.3);[25] her father Zhu Xi'ning (1926–1998), a Christian mainlander, is a celebrated novelist and a cultural officer, and her Hakka mother, Liu Musha, is a respected translator of Japanese fiction. Growing up in a congenial literary circle and raised in Confucianism, Christianity, Chinese and Japanese literature, Zhu Tianwen began to publish in various newspapers' literary supplements when she was still in high school. When Zhu entered college, she and her two sisters and close friends cofounded the Three-Three Society (*Sansan shufang*), captivated by Sun Yat-sen's "Three Principles of the People" (*sanmin zhuyi*) and the Christian concept of the Holy Trinity (*sanyi*). Sun's Three Principles of the People are nationalism, democracy, and livelihood (*minzu, minzhu, minsheng*). These formed the backbone of Sun's project of national rebuilding in the early twentieth century, when China was facing disintegration by corrupt dynastic rule and foreign imperialist aggression. With Sun himself a Christian (who had an Anglican education when he was young), his ideas of Chinese national salvation appear to perfectly match the Christian doctrines of faith, hope, and charity. Following the conviction of the May Fourth movement, that literature can liberate mind and social practice, Zhu and her Three-Three group firmly grounded their literary practice in traditional literati paradigms.

According to Hwei-cheng Cho, author of a doctoral thesis on Zhu Tianwen, Zhu and her Three-Three romantic, nationalist idealism was soon to disintegrate because of the changing political conditions in Taiwan. The once solid national identity began to fracture with the U.S. government's normalization of diplomatic relations with China. In 1978 the United States snubbed Taiwan in order to reestablish formal relations with China. This was a national shock, but it prompted people like Zhu to reconsider the long-standing KMT doctrine of national salvation and recovery of the mainland. By the early 1980s, society at large was moving toward a Taiwanese sensibility, as nativist literature had always hoped. And it was during this period, through her involvement in the New Cinema, that Zhu came into contact with a Taiwan previously unknown to her.[26]

Zhu Tianwen came into the film industry as a result of publishing a prize-winning piece, "Growing Up" (Xiaobi de gushi, "The story of little Bi," published in the *United Daily News*, 1982). Hou Hsiao-hsien and Chen Kunhou were interested in the story of Xiaobi and arranged to meet Zhu in a coffee shop. Thus began a rich creative partnership that continues to this day.[27]

Zhu Tianwen was not entirely a stranger to the film industry. Back in the 1960s, when Grand Pictures launched its production in Taiwan to compete with commercial fare from Cathay and Shaws, Zhu Xi'ning's period short story, "The Dawn" (Poxiao shifen, 1963), was adapted to film by Li Hanxiang and Song Cunshou (see chapter 1). Although Zhu Xi'ning was generally known as an anti-Communist writer, he spent most of the 1960s writing stories about country life in northern China and has since been recognized as a "native-soil writer" (*xiangtu zuojia*). *The Dawn* (1968) remains until now the key text that identifies the artistic ambitions of Grand Pictures' production strategy. This film served as a sign of Grand's intention to raise the quality of Taiwan cinema by absorbing nutrients from serious contemporary fiction in Taiwan.

Two decades later, when the industry needed new ingredients to renew itself, contemporary fiction was again seen as a profitable resource. And this time, Zhu Xi'ning's daughter was recruited. Two decades was a huge temporal, cognitive, and political disjuncture. New Cinema shared little with the independent art cinema of the 1960s (like *The Dawn*) concerning its relationship with China. Art films of the 1960s, organized by Taiwan's mainland émigrés, remain manifestations of spatial and cultural dislocation. This explains why a large number of costume and historical dramas were produced during this period, because they often function as evocations of the "authentic" cultural China, an imagined homeland for the Chinese diaspora. The New Cinema, on the contrary, is more interested in private selfhood and in its articulation entwined within the social and cultural history of postwar

Taiwan. This self-articulation is also a break; it comes at the expense of maintaining ancestral links with the Chinese film tradition established in Shanghai and Hong Kong. It is less concerned with renovating established genre pictures, as with Grand Pictures' production two decades before. Instead, Taiwan New Cinema was preoccupied with a more immediate, highly fraught, and contested past.

We may see the strong presence of autobiography as something of a reflex in the early stage of the New Cinema. Autobiography is an act to make a new identity in a context where patrimony is at stake and cultural genealogy must be reexamined or rewritten. Autobiography is thus an act of self-disclosure, using forms of first-person narration, regardless of whether the narrated self is an individual, personal one. Memory and history are examined in order to come to terms with the present. This is why many of these autobiographical films are told from the vantage of the present tense. Take Zhu Tianwen's first screenplay, *Growing Up*, as an example. Zhu's title of the source, "The Story of Little Bi," suggests a strong biographical and autobiographical inclination. Here Zhu was interested in documenting the true life of an ordinary boy growing up in a small township with a stepfather old enough to be his grandfather. The boy is sensitive and energetic, but the fact that he was born a bastard and adopted as a stepson of a military man predestines his troubled childhood. As the title indicates, it is a "story," the fictionalization of an ordinary life that makes it extraordinary.

If Zhu were a regular biographer, she might have taken the precaution of observing the codes of biographical writing to keep her story objective, true to the life of her real-life subjects. But in the poetics of auto/biography, the story is written in the first-person point of view of a grown woman remembering *her* childhood. This textual device repeats itself in the film. On many occasions, the otherwise omniscient narration is accompanied by the voice-over of the neighbor girl, to inform the spectator of her own reflections on the troubled boy next door.

When the story was adapted to the screen, Chen and Hou kept the original narrative devices intact, in deference to Zhu's credit as the main writer of the screenplay. But the heavy-handed use of first-person voice-over narration in the film creates textual inconsistencies with an objective cinematography. These inconsistencies, or narrative ruptures, can each be seen as an entry to the narrative's double-fictive structure. These voice-overs not only indicate the presence of a second narrator (who is herself active in the story) but in addition suggest a strong sense of an autobiographical act. By telling the story of another person, the narrator is also coming to terms with her own growth in similar, adjacent social and cultural conditions. Observing and writing the other, the author invents herself.

Zhu invents herself in the sense that she consciously resorted to a childhood experience that was always there but latent since they were not suitable for her Three-

Three imperatives. However, by reconsidering the question of identity instilled in her by KMT ideology, Zhu began to recognize herself not just as Chinese but as a Taiwanese as well. Zhu might have realized that when she was a privileged girl growing up in various veterans' villages (*juancun*), she was also a granddaughter enjoying rural life in a provincial Hakka town. One is a distinctly KMT upbringing and the other Taiwanese, blended with remnants of colonial Japanese life. These two identities, once totally antithetical, began gradually to converge as Zhu came to be in touch with nativist views. In an essay about her family, Zhu makes a remark about her father's obstinate, anachronistic refusal to put down roots in Taiwan: "Father never thought of buying a house, after we had lived in *juancun* for fourteen years, moving from village to village. He gave me a reason that surprised me: 'Why a house? How are we supposed to return if we set up home here?' " Zhu's response to this reply was, "Return, meaning going back to the mainland. Even to me a reason like this is too naively loyal."[28]

The *Juancun* Pathos As an autobiographical act, *Growing Up* is historically specific in terms of the practice of intermarriage between mainland sojourners and local Taiwanese. The film's setting, the veteran's village, also exemplifies a specific locality in autobiographical accounts by the second generation of mainland immigrants such as Zhu Tianwen (see fig. 4.4).

Veterans' villages were communities planned by the KMT immediately after the Chiang Kai-shek government had relocated in Taiwan. These communities were built all over the island in the early 1950s to house and protect the vast population of mainland military personnel and their families. After the February 28 incident in 1947, the KMT government particularly felt the need to segregate mainlanders from the locals. But it does not mean that locals were excluded from these villages. In fact, many wives in these villages were Taiwanese with distinct regional and ethnic identities: Hokkien, Hakka, and the various aboriginal tribes.

It was a common social phenomenon for local, "damaged" women of lower status to marry out of their own ethnic, clan, and class surroundings in order to obtain a proper social identity for themselves and/or their children. To some extent, that social history is nothing less than autobiographical, a part of the author's own family and community history. Zhu's family background is part of the changing ethnoscape of postwar Taiwan. Due to barriers political (the KMT regime) and cultural (language, customs, and outright xenophobia), most Taiwanese families resisted any close relations with mainlanders. Marriage was the institution most guarded of assimilation, not to mention that of a local family with a distinctly genteel identity, such as the one in which Zhu's mother was raised—the most prestigious doctor in a small (at the time) town, Hsin-chu. Since it was not normal practice for a good Taiwanese family to marry the daughter to a mainlander, Zhu's mother, Liu

4.4 A melodramatic *juancun* scene in *Growing Up* (1983)   (COURTESY CMPC)

Musha, eloped to marry her father. Zhu's maternal grandparents later accepted and honored the marriage, acknowledging an increasing mobility in the young generation who crossed linguistic, cultural, political, and regional boundaries.

But the Zhus' happy ending might just be an exception. Many intermarriages in veterans' villages were initiated with compromises and ended up with cuts and burns. In *Growing Up,* Xiaobi is born out of wedlock. In order to give him a proper name, Xiaobi's mother marries Laobi (Old Bi). This matrimony typifies unions of convenience between aging mainland servicemen and young local outcasts. When Xiaobi rejects his stepfather's discipline, the stepfather admits to Xiaobi's illegitimate birth. Realizing the stain on her past is indelible, Xiaobi's mother commits suicide.

Although *Growing Up* can be seen as typical family melodrama with an Oedipal struggle and victimized motherhood, there are also the contradictions of age difference, language, and cultural barriers, and imbalances of power in marriages where an older man manipulates the plight of a single mother. As the narrator notes, Xiaobi's mother was silent, reserved, and submissive. She was more like a maid than a companion to her husband.

Growing Up, to the surprise of the filmmakers (including the scriptwriter herself), was a commercial success. This triumph pointed the way to *the use* of the autobiographical act as a viable new form for the New Cinema to create a niche for itself. Even though relating the past is supplemented by subjective, autobiographical reflection on the present, this narrative displacement proves to have accomplished multiple functions. Regarding reception, the departure from the star system to a focus on ordinary people shows a certain appeal to audiences. While it is easy to imagine movie stars playing the lives of famous figures in history, the New Cinema cast unknowns to represent anonymous, historical subjects. Capitalizing at the same time on greater authenticity, this decision also saved enormous production costs. This leads to a formal, aesthetic implication: the casting of ordinary people—either nonprofessionals or character actors—enabled Hou Hsiao-hsien and Chen Kunhou to develop and refine their long take–long shot aesthetic (see chapter 3) at the expense of zooms, intimate conversations, and close-ups. The long take–long shot aesthetic later flourished as one of the defining traits of the New Cinema. More importantly, the autobiographical act facilitates a critical identity for the New Cinema, permitting critics to define the New Cinema in terms like generational difference, introverted, self-reflexive and, most of all, *historical.*

Depictions of life in the close community of the veterans' village give a rare sense of history in retrospect as well as history as it happens. Given the fact that most village communities were quickly disintegrating, the once-crowded, lively *juancun* had by this time become ghostly ruins of anti-Communist ideologues. *Juancun* as a synonym for mainlanders, however, survives as an auxiliary ethnicity underscoring the unsettled and contested nature of Taiwan identity.[29] *Juancun* themselves embody the open question of what is Taiwanese? They challenge an underlying assumption of originary Taiwan people (*Taiwanren*) as exclusive to Hokkien, Hakka, or anything besides patriotic Chinese mainlanders. A decade later, Zhu Tianxin, Tianwen's younger sister, published yet another award-winning piece called "Recalling my brothers in the *juancun*" ("Xiang wo juancun de xiongdimen," 1992), a nostalgic essay with poignant political impact, laying bare the mainlanders' schizophrenic anxiety and reaction in the midst of burning Taiwanese nativism.

Zhu Tianwen's autobiographical writing let Hou and Chen move from a typical Taiwanese rural setting to that of *juancun,* the provincial mainland compound. This was a clear break from the carefree, playful, albeit realist, romantic comedy characteristic of the Hou/Chen partnership. By incorporating an eyewitness account of life in an intimate community, they address a vivid Taiwan ethnoscape as mixed, troubled, and politically problematic. By choosing to end the story with a mother's suicide, they entered a new perspective and approach. With Xiaobi's story, the New Cinema opened itself to trauma, pain, and the difficulty of reconciliation. The healthy realist world of popular songs, innocent children, comic gags, farce, Kenny Bee, and Feng Feifei has retired into the background.

By means of autobiographical acts, Zhu unveils the raging libido of youth and subsequent punishment and discipline inside the *juancun*. This darker picture of the mainland community is far removed from her earlier autobiographical reflections of the congenial, peaceful *juancun* life. A first-person account adds weight to a sense of historical authenticity, entailing revelation of the veterans' village pathos. In sum, we see two unrelated terrains meet and converge—the Taiwan Hakka pastoral and the KMT *juancun* community—each moving from its formerly innocent, superficial views of Taiwan society toward an engaged and reflective nativism. Perhaps nativism needed the contact with its opposite number in order to flourish as a cultural and political force. The nativism of Hou's earliest films, still recycling the wholesome messages of healthy realism, was not worthy of the name. Once he found the mainland-oriented Zhu Tianwen, a distinctive and aesthetically challenging nativism emerged. In the following years, several other films would follow suit by turning *juancun* stories into tear-jerking melodramas. But by then, Zhu and Hou had long moved on to explore new frontiers.

Encounter with Shen Congwen: Romancing the Provincial

Zhu Tianwen entered her partnership with Hou by means of her poetic ways of associating autobiography with biography. Their partnership was furthered through yet another autobiographical crossing. Zhu introduced Hou to the autobiography of Shen Congwen, a soldier-cum-writer in the early twentieth century.

Whatever one may think of the trustworthiness or relevance of authorial commentary, Hou made the following statement on his solution to problems of narrative form, specifically in response to Western models brought home by directors like Edward Yang and Wan Ren. In an interview, Hou talked about his stylistic turn:

Before making *Fengkuei* my ideas about cinema were rather simple: narrative, to tell the story in the script. Later on I met some filmmakers who had returned to Taiwan from abroad. They had a lot of theories about cinema, which got me all confused. I was puzzled; the script was ready but I didn't know how to give it form. After listening to me, my scriptwriter Zhu Tianwen showed me a book called *Autobiography of Shen Congwen*. After reading the book I discovered Shen's point of view was somewhat like looking down from above. Like natural laws, it has no joy and no sorrow. That I found to be very close to me. It doesn't matter if he's describing a brutal military crackdown or various kinds of death; life to him is a river, which flows and flows but is without sorrow or joy. The result is a certain breadth of mind, or a certain perspective that is very moving. Because of this, it produces a generosity of viewpoint. I decided to adopt this angle. The problem was how to transplant it to film. I didn't really have a solution but I discovered a simple device, and that was to constantly tell the cinematographer to "keep a distance, and be cooler." It allowed certain real situations to naturally unfold themselves. The camera just stayed at a distance and quietly watched over them.[30]

By encountering Taiwan filmmakers with Western training, Hou experienced cultural shock and a loss of confidence. But by reading an autobiography of the 1930s, Hou discovered a new language, a new form for articulating his ideas of life, his own and others.

For several years in the 1980s, Shen Congwen (1902–1988) was very close to being awarded a Nobel Prize in Literature. Originally called Yuehuan, Shen changed his name to "Congwen'' (meaning "following literature'') when he traveled to Beijing and decided to go back to school at age twenty. One of China's foremost modern writers, Shen was virtually self-taught. Born in western Hunan province to a soldier family, Shen joined a warlord army at age twelve and began his long years of roaming the countryside, encountering all sorts of exotic sights. In the late 1920s, he acquainted himself with prominent liberal leaders of the New Literature such as Hu Shizhi, Ye Gongchao, Xu Zimo, and Chen Xiying and became a professional writer and editor. In 1934 he published his autobiography, *Congwen's Autobiography* (Congwen zizhuan). After the revolution, Shen's writing came to a full stop since he was classified as a right-wing author who used to produce pornographic, *taohong* (pink red) literature. He tried but failed to kill himself. Then Shen was assigned to work as a clerk in a history museum. During the Cultural Revolution, he was downgraded to the post of janitor. Although he was later allowed to conduct research on ancient costumes later in the 1970s, he never wrote another major work of fiction. In the 1980s he was rediscovered and enjoyed massive popularity when Taiwan lifted its ban on mainland writers in 1987.

Shen's writing has had great influence on many modern Chinese fiction writers, including Zhu Tianwen's father, Zhu Xi'ning, who also was a soldier-cum-writer.[31] Shen identifies himself as a bumpkin with a bumpkin mentality from a bumpkin land.[32] But according to Jeffrey Kinkley, who wrote Shen's biography, Shen's literary achievement is no less than that of Lu Xun, acclaimed as the greatest author in modern Chinese literature.[33] Most critics associate Shen with "native-soil fiction" for the glaring regionalism in his work. But David Der-wei Wang goes further by situating Shen as a writer of "critical lyricism" in his poetic, idyllic treatment of the most "ghastly human contingencies" such as decapitation and massacre.[34] The incongruity between Shen's subject and his language, according to Wang, is where Shen's fiction can be understood afresh. Shen is by no means a reflective realist of his homeland, western Hunan. He writes about his beloved provincial, barbarous Miao country in a highly mediated, poetic style. Shen is aware of the paradox of writing about a place as a lost paradise and a source of creation. Thus his lyrical portrait of a manifold life in the provinces can be seen as a recollection of history *and* the making of a mythical utopia.[35] Shen's lyrical discourse enables him to sketch the inevitable loss as mythical *and* realist and thus creates a space between the enunciator and his people, landscape, and sounds. In Shen's eyes, peasants and soldiers can hardly be judged by urban rules.[36] Rather than pass judgment on them, Shen *observes* them, in Hou Hsiao-hsien's words, with a certain "breadth of mind," a "generosity of viewpoint."

Shen's "imaginative nostalgia," in Wang's terms, struck a chord with Hou. The accepting attitude toward caprice and catastrophe exemplifies a poetic conciliation to trauma and shock. What might have been dreadful atrocities like those massacres Shen witnessed as a boy were treated as basic life experience, as if to say, no big deal. Or in Hou's own words, it illustrates a respect for "natural laws," which are "without joy and sorrow."

In his autobiography, Shen (fig. 4.5) reminisces about his carefree childhood and how he habitually skipped classes in order to play in the wild and the streets, and how nature and the township served as the best teachers for him. A mischievous childhood, curiosity, enthusiasm, loose family ties, male bonding, and disdain toward schooling are traits in common between Shen's autobiography and Hou's films. Shen became a soldier out of his own choice, not from family poverty. To him traditional private tutoring was inhibiting. But the world outside was full of interesting things to learn.[37] " 'Seeing' is the only thing that I will never get tired of."[38] Observing and watching underlie Shen's adventurous childhood and youth. Shen's love of seeing is invested by a tremendous inquisitiveness.[39] There's an ethnographic curiosity in Shen's displacement of his excessive libido—enhanced by growing up in a border military base, surrounded by a mixed ethnoscape of Han and Miao nationals, with witchcraft, rich natural surroundings, and a lively, exotic commerce typical of a forgotten place in a remote corner of China. The visual allure of ethnographic spectacle in a border town lies precisely in its remoteness and provinciality, far away from the metropolitanism burgeoning at that time in Shanghai or Beijing. This visual allure without judgment must have been quite exciting to Hou when he was confused and perhaps even threatened by those neophyte filmmakers without hands-on experience but full of *Western* knowledge and theories of the cinema.

Instead of chasing his shadows and thus acknowledging his lack, Hou went the other way. He reverted to the 1930s and found his métier in modern Chinese literature. Unlike many famous writers and intellectuals of the same era, Shen never went abroad to study nor did he learn any foreign languages.[40] In the Chinese colloquial, Shen never "drinks Western ink" (*he yang moshui*). This too is in common with Hou Hsiao-hsien. The 1930s was an era filled with confusion and urgent attempts to find new directions for Chinese language, literature, and the arts. A comparable

4.5 Shen Congwen in the 1930s

explorative mindset might have made the 1930s a useful referent for struggling artists like Hou in the midst of debates over the New Cinema. By discovering Shen Congwen and recognizing the affinities between them, Hou was able to connect himself to the pantheon of Chinese literature. If Shen's commitment to the provinciality of China fulfills his mission in modern Chinese literature, Hou's rendition of provincial Taiwan might bear similar fruit.

Through Zhu Tianwen, Hou found a new identity, which enabled him to rediscover a viable position and a method—a poetics of autobiography—to rearticulate a worldview still in fashion. Shen's lyrical storytelling entails a spirit of evanescence, where nothing much happens. This view enables Hou to treat life, human relationships, and incidental encounters with subtlety and sensitivity. Ironically, it is Chinese literature, *not* Taiwan or Chinese cinema, that became Hou's new shrine. What is crucial is that though Hou wanted to turn his back on his mentors (Lai san and Li Xing) and his stock-in-trade (romantic comedy), he would remain within the cultural patrimony of modern China. It is as if he was compelled to choose a genealogy. What could be more completely historical and nativist—as well as national—than Shen Congwen? Ten years later, Hou would face another, similar situation, and it would be Li Tianlu, the puppetmaster and national treasure, who was recruited to legitimize Hou's Taiwan trilogy.

With Shen's autobiographical trope firmly in mind, Hou's self-referential imprint began to emerge in *The Boys from Fengkuei* (1983) and *Summer at Grandpa's* (1984), culminating in *The Time to Live and the Time to Die* (1985) and *Dust in the Wind* (1986). In these films, Hou actively employs a telescopic view on his provincial subjects, photographing picturesque country scenes, rural boredom, work, crime, and play in the provincial towns of Taiwan ("Like natural laws, . . . no joy and no sorrow"). The opening of *Fengkuei*, shot by Chen Kunhou, shows the filmmakers' fascination with and desire to capture the village's ethnic rhythm: inside a makeshift pool hall, a match is in progress and a rugged old man uses chalk to keep score on a decrepit blackboard. The focus here is plainly the old man, much like Shen Congwen's description in his autobiography about his fascination with strange-looking folks in the provinces. The interest is not storytelling so much as opening an *exposure* with sensitivity, a kind of visual anthropology, seeking out striking faces and scenes without being intrusive. Like the city photographer played by Feng Feifei in *Cheerful Wind*, Hou's crew cannot resist the photogenic qualities of this offshore fishing village, stuck in a time capsule. But Hou is aware of this ethnographical curiosity. He even makes a sight gag out of it: when a Japanese tourist asks one of the boys to take snapshots of them against the scenery, the boy mischievously reframes the picture to move the subjects out of the shot.

Observers in Hou's autobiographical films are also protagonists, who see but do not judge. By witnessing, these observers initiate their rite of passage, and by not judging they develop empathy and sensitivity. By way of reading and learning about Shen Congwen, Hou Hsiao-hsien pours his story content into a "form" of empathetic observation, of "respecting the object" (*zunzhong keti*). Furthermore, by finding this form, Hou is capable of linking his documentary-like photography with his silent observers and establishing his stylistic signature of detached long take–long shot aesthetics.

Detached cinematography connotes the silent observer at a psychological distance, a space to breathe and to contemplate ("keep a distance, and be cooler"). Oblique storytelling signifies the sensitive observer's own reserve and perhaps repression. Aqing, the feisty, energetic boy in *Fengkuei*, turns silent when he becomes an observer in the city. In a rented house in Kaohsiung, he is in love with the girl next door, but he remains quiet. What might be judged a deficiency in the provincial mindset becomes a virtue in Hou's work because it allows the observer to see, without getting involved and offsetting the equilibrium, "the law of nature."

This equilibrium need not be cold, as can be seen in *Summer at Grandpa's*. For Hou's second autobiographical account of Zhu Tianwen's childhood spent in the house of her grandparents (the film is actually shot in the same house), we remain with the silent observers. These are the two grandkids from Taipei, Dong Dong and his sister Ting Ting. They are apprehensive, puzzled, then charmed by provincial life in a small town. The film is structured by the dichotomy of the world of adulthood and that of children. Children see things that go normally unseen by adults. They are capable of witnessing but slow to interpret, so they too become quiet onlookers of extraordinary things happening on a daily basis. Because they are both children and outsiders, they do not clearly distinguish between extraordinary and routine events. Dong Dong would witness the murder of sleeping truck drivers by local hoodlums in the quiet summer afternoon. Ting Ting would connect with the local madwoman who, in the nick of time, saves her life on the railroad tracks.

The Time to Live and the Time to Die pushes the autobiographical act to a different level of thematic unity and stylistic maturity. It begins with an establishing shot and the director's voice-over: "This film is the memory of my childhood, especially those of my father." Following this opening sentence, Hou goes on for over three minutes, describing the family's move from Guangdong province to Taiwan as part of China's massive migration due to postwar political changes. It is worth noting that this opening is the only occasion in Hou's work in which he is heard speaking in a subjective voice. The direct address apparently contradicts the device of the silent witness; nonetheless, the film is still dominated overall by quiet but sympathetic bystanders. This is largely related to the fact that Hou's father suffered from chronic illness and remained mostly quiet and inactive. Hou's autobiography unfolds itself with memories of migration, instability, and illness brought on by these shifting, transitional activities. A foreboding omen, the family's history is destined to proceed to several deaths and an ultimate, inevitable disintegration.

In this autobiographical film, Hou occupies two images. In contrast to the retiring father, Aha (Hou's childhood name in Hakka) is willful, mischievous, and full of life. But when Aha returns to the domestic sphere, he resumes the position of a quiet boy, a sensitive observer. The boy Aha and the teenage Aha are frequently depicted as mute when they witness these traumatic moments in the family's history: the sudden deaths of his invalid father, his cancer-ridden mother, and his elderly grandmother. In these sequences, Hou-as-boy remains mostly astounded and wordless, watching the parents' suffering, feeling their pain but having no way of helping them. A dialectical relation is at work in the speechless passion of the boy. On one hand, the wrenching, seemingly endless series of illness and death in the family forces Aha to face the inevitable course of life at this early stage of his youth. On the other, the young Hou is a hoodlum, indulging in all manner of petty crimes and misdemeanors. It seems the latter actions form a compensatory economy for the difficulty of handling grief and the impending separation with his parents and grandmother.

dust in the wind

Encountering Wu Nianzhen: The Wretched Taiwanese Story

Besides Zhu Tianwen and Shen Congwen, Wu Nianzhen has often played an important role in Hou's creative process. In addition to his skill as a scriptwriter and pitchman (see chapter 2), Wu also offered his life as source material, volunteering service for Hou's autobiographical repertoire.

Dust in the Wind is known in Hou's oeuvre as Wu Nianzhen's autobiography, but the discrepancy between the story and the finished film was so stark that the scriptwriter himself was utterly disappointed in the film.[41] Hou's treatment of Wu's own story actually imposes his Shen-inflected autobiographical acts—namely, the peculiar vision of rewriting the past, of detachment through self-narrativization. Hou mixed Wu's memories with his own contemplative depiction of landscape to suggest a metaphysical view of a precarious order, of "changes" in life.[42] These changes, however, are anything but capricious. In Hou's film, the metaphysics of Taiwan history emerges through Taoist folk superstitions, a sense that the vicissitudes of life are the consequence of some foreordained order. These metaphysical connotations are consistent with the ethnographic, visual allure Hou received from reading Shen Congwen.

However, this is not how Wu envisioned *his* autobiography. He wanted to represent his circumstances from the inside, as it were, including all the emotional turmoil and struggles of responsibility that suffering always brings. The transfer of autobiographical act over to another's life may be problematic if a subject's memories are being overwritten or substantially changed. In the story of Wu Nianzhen, the writer wanted a more straightforward display of emotions—joy, agony, grief, and anger. This is particularly apposite, at least to Wu, for a life of struggle, the rites of passage balancing exploitative work, illness, military service, and a failed romance—all in the absence of supportive family. This is very dramatic material, and Wu wanted his project realized with strong commercial appeal. The script's working title was "Romantic city of the wind," possibly a reference to the windy climate of Jiufen,[43] Wu's home district. It's also crucial that Wu's background is working class, coming from a poverty-stricken miner's family up in the hills, cut off from bourgeois comforts. But Hou mostly suppresses these privations and emotional discharges because he regarded them as contrived expressions, as excess, not in accordance with the natural path of life, seeing the past as memory-sediments, as flashbacks from a distance.

Shards of memory can strike like epiphany, however, in *Dust in the Wind*. This is sometimes represented in quite startling imagery. After a series of setbacks, the protagonist has been caught in the rain and receives shelter in a military base. Ayuan sits with a bowl of noodles, shivering, staring at a black-and-white television screen. There is a news program about mining, and as he focuses on the screen Hou cuts to a close-up of the TV. The flickering image depicts a tracking shot, sliding through the tunnels of the mine and the cramped conditions of the coalface. The forward motion on television suddenly gives way to a reverse tracking shot inside the dark mine. This is a visual rhyme with the many railroad tunnels that connect Wu's mountain village with the world outside. Apparently, Hou has cut "inside" the TV to the actual scene of the accident. Inside the carriage,

4.6 Mining accident in *Dust in the Wind* (1986).　　　　(COURTESY LIU ZHENXIANG)

injured workers are being pulled back up to the surface. As they reach the top the sky opens up. The sudden flash of light makes them squint. Then a reverse-angle cut to figures, faces, the wife and children anxiously running into the mouth of the shaft to see if father has survived. These are the figures of the mother, Ayuan, and his sister from about a decade before. We realize we are inside Ayuan's mind, having flashed back to a memory of his father surviving one of the periodic explosions deep inside the mine. Hou has taken us inside Wu's memory using the small screen as a transition (fig. 4.6). When the family catches sight of father and husband, carrying an injured comrade on his back, we come out of the flashback to young Ayuan, who topples off his seat to the floor. This is vivid, dramatic, and traumatic, literally staging the repressed memories of Wu Nianzhen through the television device. The excitement is brief but compares with the suspense of mining accidents in other films like Wu's *Dou-san* (1994) and Wang Tong's *Hill of No Return* (1992).

What happens next, however, is characteristic of Hou's detached style. Ayuan is now seriously ill due to the cold drenching received at the beach. He lies in bed, delirious with fever. A voice-over leads into another flashback, or could it be only crosscutting back to the sick boy's hometown? We move into a long take of Li Tianlu, the grandpa, who calmly tells Ayuan's father why the boy is sickly. He notes that he was born healthy, but by age three has developed an illness that neither Chinese nor Western medicine can heal. The reason is that he failed to give the boy his mother's name, as agreed when the father married into his wife's family. Until he keeps his promise, the boy and the family will be subject to illness and misfortune of every sort. What befalls Ayuan is the result of a foreordained cosmic structure and unless it is respected, life remains out of balance. The agency in Ayuan's life is not Ayuan or even chance but the fates, as deciphered by the elders. By extension, the events that materialize in Hou's film are attributed less to the active recovery of autobiographical material than to a transcendental perspective rising far above individual memory.

Nearly ten years later, Wu Nianzhen made his own autobiographical film, *Dou-san: A Borrowed Life*, in which he is not evasive about laying bare his emotions on camera. Whereas Ayuan's father is a shadowy, reticent figure, the focus in *Dou-san* is much more on the eponymous father, one of the strongest, most intransigent characters in Taiwan cinema. Dou-san, played by the singer Cai Zhennan, dominates the film and the family with his willful idolization of the Japanese colonial era.[44] Certain sequences excluded in the final cut of *Dust in the Wind* are resurrected in Wu's second film, *Buddha Bless America* (1996).[45]

In his sickbed, when Ayuan is recovering from illness, he hears his roommate relating a long story about the war games conducted in Hengchun, a small fishing town on the tip of southern Taiwan. Although Hou shot the scene, it was excised in the final cut. Wu staged and shot his own black comedy about the joint war games between Nationalist and American military units stationed in Taiwan, with impoverished Taiwanese villagers caught in the middle, in order to restore these memories to the record.[46] Other significant scenes removed from Hou's final cut include more explicit scenes of affection between Ayuan and Ayun, Ayuan's discovery of modernist classics such as those by Camus and Kafka, and the infamous whorehouses set up around offshore military bases called Eight-Three-One (*ba san yao*).[47]

According to Zhu Tianwen, who documented the creative process and changes made during the postproduction stage, these adjustments were made not out of disloyalty to Wu's story but rather from an antipathy to generic and emotional contrivance.[48] In addition, there were problems with the casting of the main character played by Wang Jingwen, who, to Hou, lacked sufficient naiveté for the role.[49] Though *Dust in the Wind* set out to have a more commercial appeal by focusing on the romance between two poor youngsters working as migrant laborers in the city, Hou felt the need to articulate autobiographical acts that respected the natural ebb and flow of Taiwanese life. Travails of individual experience, like declarations of affection, criminal acts, and the wickedness of employers, all detailed in Wu and Zhu's script, were diluted.

The Puppetmaster: (Auto)biographical Epic in Post–Martial Law Liberation

The epic modes on display in Hou Hsiao-hsien's celebrated Taiwan trilogy—*City of Sadness* (1989), *The Puppetmaster* (1993), and *Good Men, Good Women* (1995)—do not rule out the intimacies of autobiographical disclosure. In fact, autobiographical acts become ever more evident in Hou's attempts to outline a national biography, although they may not appear as the main narrative line, as in *City of Sadness*.

City of Sadness, cowritten by Wu Nianzhen and Zhu Tianwen, is the first film in which Hou and his collaborators started doing extensive historical research at the preproduction stage.[50] In the late 1980s, there were not yet any reliable sources published on the February 28 Incident.[51] Rather than relying on the official report, the team followed its own historiography for this sensitive period. They read government documents, interviewed survivors or victims' families, reviewed diaries and personal letters, conducted field trips to infamous sites. The purpose was not just to collect stories and check historical facts but also to grasp the overall "structure of feeling" of the period.[52] From the excitement over reunion with the motherland to the excruciating sadness toward the brutality of the military crackdown, Taiwan experienced yet another truncation from China. Hou's interest lies in seeking out the origins of that fault line. Autobiography, in this regard, is reconfigured in the present tense, where we see characters keeping a diary of personal activities implicated within surrounding political turmoil.[53] But *City of Sadness* is far from being interested solely in the individual suffering of Taiwanese. The film tries to strike a balance and suggest that it was a collective trauma for both Taiwanese and mainlanders, a result of the tug-of-war between the three main writers: Taiwan native Wu Nianzhen, the mainland transplant Zhu Tianwen, and Hou Hsiao-hsien himself, who stood between the two poles.[54] This attempted balance was problematic after the film's release because the film was considered by many to be detached and uninvolved. But it opened up a whole new area of writing history about and for Taiwan, a new approach to the Janus-like, multivalent Taiwanese. *Taiwanren* ("the Taiwanese") consist of mainlanders and locals, all immigrants, and in fact, also incorporates Japanese remnants and Chinese exiles, rightwingers and progressives, patriotic intellectuals and collaborating artists.

If *City of Sadness* was seen to fail the victims of the February 28 Incident, it did prove one thing: the difficulty of rubbing out Japanese colonialism. And it seemed natural for Hou to take the next step to explore entanglements between Japan and Taiwan, after having addressed the primary taboo—the February 28 Incident—in modern Taiwan history. If the KMT is usually the major villain in the New Cinema, the next target is Japan, Taiwan's adopted "father" for half a century. Within that period, Hou located Li Tianlu, the most respected godfather of Taiwan's folk puppetry. As the subject of *The Puppetmaster*, winner of the Grand Jury Prize at Cannes in 1994, Li became internationally famous. Already he was a well-known figure in the New Cinema for appearing as the perennial grandpa in several of Hou's films, including *Dust in the Wind* and *Daughter of the Nile*. In *City of Sadness*, he plays a strong patriarch, surviving both the Japanese and KMT rule. In real life, Li was enjoying a late career revival after being "discovered" by French sinologists who were rigorously preserving the dying art of Chinese puppetry. Students from Europe and Asia came to study with Li and returned home, establishing branches of Li's puppet troupe to carry on his artistic lineage. Li became not just Taiwan's venerable old folk artist but a puppet master of the world.[55] Hou Hsiao-hsien himself was still enjoying international acclaim with the Golden Lion at Venice in 1989. Within Hou's film and outside of it, the world of Li Tianlu ends up containing the period of Japanese administration by means of "an order beyond the visible."[56] This immensity, the long view far outstripping the half-century of occupation, is in line with the "critical lyricism" of Shen Congwen.[57]

To enter the field of auto/biographical intervention, let's begin with an anomaly, an atypical moment. *The Puppetmaster* is a film that spans the period of Japanese occupation, from 1895 to 1945. Midway through the film, during the war, there is a striking employment of the puppets for imperialist propaganda. Though all forms of outdoor amusement in the provinces had been suspended, there were exceptions for patriotic occasions. In a rural setting, circa 1944, a puppet show honors the death of a local conscript. Douki-san, a radio operator on a dangerous mission, has been killed in the line of duty. Unlike the film's other puppet sequences, this one is a contemporary reenactment of the events leading to Douki's death in New Guinea. It is a commemoration of valor as part of the funeral rites honoring the war dead.

Several things distinguish these puppets from the others seen so far. First, the language of the narration is in Japanese, except for the nonsense words issuing from the mouth of the enemy who shoots the hero down. (Although the subtitles say "Douki-san," the narrator calls him "Douki-kun," a more familiar diminutive of his name.) It is colloquial, unlike the ceremonial narration heard in the formal, operatic style of Taiwanese puppetry. Sound effects are similarly casual, with crude explosions and vocalized gunfire ("bang, bang!"). Second, the costume and wartime setting in New Guinea contrast radically with the elaborate classical myths and folktales that dominate the *budai xi* (pocket play) or *zhang zhong xi* (palm play) of Li Tianlu. The visual presentation of Douki and his cohorts is very rudimentary, crude, even childish (fig. 4.7). It is a specific, recent event in the South Pacific, while *budai xi* presents a remote, fantastic world of gods, demons, and operatic aristocracy. Its connections to the everyday are far more tenuous than the facts of Douki's exploits. It contrasts markedly with the high style and lavish costumes of the *budai xi* tradition.

4.7 Douki-san in the propaganda puppet show, *The Puppetmaster* (1993)

Despite the simplicity of his vocabulary, the narrator's inflated rhetoric drives home the message: "Douki-san's death is like the falling of cherry blossoms in the morning sun. A valued citizen of the Japanese Empire, his name lives with the glory of the Japanese Empire forever and ever. May you rest in peace now, Douki-san." (Bugles, drum roll.) When the events themselves are dramatized with a question of the volunteers' apprehension, Douki-san replies, "How can I be afraid?! Taiwan is part of the New Japan. We are now citizens of the Japanese Empire. To ensure victory for Japan, even if I die, I die as a Japanese spirit. It is such a joy. . . . [As he dies, he continues:] I have fulfilled my mission to die for the glory of the Emperor. Now I truly am a Japanese spirit. Long live the Emperor!" The scene ends at dusk, with a plaintive rendition of "Kimigayo," the Japanese national anthem. ("Long live the Emperor! *Tenno heika, Banzai!*" Three times.)

This puppet show is an example of what Homi Bhabha calls a "pedagogical" expression of nationality: "The scraps, patches and rags of daily life must be repeatedly turned into the signs of a national culture."[58] Its intention is to give an object lesson in Japanese patriotism. It does not seek to entertain the villagers but rather to impress on them the apotheosis of a native son. To die for the emperor is an honor and privilege. It exemplifies the Japanese policy of *kominka* (imperialization), the campaign to transform Taiwanese colonials into imperial subjects. That the transformation is at the cost of Douki's life indicates not only the Japanese reverence for military sacrifice but also demonstrates the worthiness, even sacredness, of their cause against the West.

The Japanese imperialization policy was carried out in language, name changes, custom, religious indoctrination, and so forth. But its most successful implementation was the military volunteer program, directed not only at conscript soldiers but women (field nurses), children (civil defense drills), and, also, artists like Li Tianlu.[59] There was good reason for the intensifying campaign of "Japanization," as it is translated in the subtitles. Without it, it was impossible for Japan to prosecute its campaigns in China and the Pacific. There just weren't enough soldiers from the Home Islands alone, hence the urgent need for honorary imperial subjects—Taiwanese, Korean, and even aboriginal people. Douki was not a Han Taiwanese, but an aboriginal boy whose story was set down by his Japanese officer and given to Li Tianlu to draft a propaganda puppet play (*xuanchuan ju*).[60] Shimizu Hiroshi's 1943 pastoral romance, *Bell of Sayon*, also incorporates the aboriginal girl into the sacrificial scheme. She drowns in a raging torrent on the night her beloved goes off to war and, like Douki-san, inspires all with her bravery (see chapter 1).

This puppet play, staged by the "Taipei Propaganda Troupe for the Defeat of America and England," is suspended, like the lovely footbridge slowly crossed to arrive in the village. What does it have to do with Li Tianlu? Hou does not allow a clear view of the men manipulating the little khaki-clad soldiers. The sequence seems to hang there as an interlude, following as it does Li's strange tale of the mistress whose illness was cured by a bucket of frogs. When they first appear, without preamble, the *kominka* puppets seem out of place. This does not mean that they are "not taken seriously," only that their importance is deferred to a larger, cosmic frame.[61] After the national anthem has given way to a landscape do we hear, and then see, Li (in his fourth appearance) come to explain how he joined the "New Nationalism Reformed Puppet Troupe."

But this is not the troupe we see presenting the tale of Douki-san, just as the *kominka* message of assimilation—godhood via military sacrifice—is not the ultimate point of this puppet show. Within the immediate diegesis, the soldier puppets are supposed to inspire belief in the empire's triumph. But there is a secondary diegesis, the autobiographical recollection of Li Tianlu that "trumps" the proximate wartime meaning. If the work of the Taipei Propaganda Troupe is too grossly topical, embodying a particular message of patriotism, then the messages of traditional *budai xi* are universal, cosmic, incantatory.

The Puppetmaster ends with the surrender of the Japanese army. Li recalls how busy he was immediately after the good news. This was because the Taiwanese believed that it was the local gods that ended the war and freed Taiwan from occupation. Every neighborhood wanted to commission puppet shows to show gratitude for answers to prayer. Although Li was suffering from malaria at the time, he had to perform day and night. This account emphasizes the puppet shows' ritual, occasional function, which elaborates a repertoire whose significance lies in the performance, not in a pragmatic message or homily. Hence the centrality of the puppet masters and opera actors. What the folk puppets "mean" in theme or story is less important than what they are, their role as a continuing craft practice. This is in contrast to the staging of the propaganda puppets, whose instrumentality sets off in high relief the performative richness of Taiwanese folk arts organically tied to the community.

The Shifting Meanings of Puppets Now we return to the key element of autobiography for Li and Hou. Though the aesthetic impoverishment of the propaganda puppets is all too plain, its placement in Li's life story is crucial. Despite its rudeness, the propaganda troupe allows Li to return to his craft. Stuck doing opera at the Happy Stage Theater in Taichung, Li met his jealous mistress Leitzu. She clings to him, but Li returns to Taipei, his family, and the beloved puppets. Here, he finds himself invited to join the New Nationalism Reformed Puppet Troupe.

Some background can be filled in from Li's memoir: with the onset of war, puppet shows were largely suspended. Only politically approved *gezai xi,* or *gua'ahi* in Hokkien (Taiwanese opera), were allowed. So Li had to dissolve his just-formed troupe and went into selling raw oysters with his father-in-law. Losing money, he decided that he couldn't work as a merchant. He accepted an offer and moved alone to Taichung to work as an assistant director for the Happy Stage opera. Later, two puppet troupes were permitted after they "reformed" their shows into "new age puppet show" (*xin shidai budai xi*), a mixed form of semi-Japanese, semi-Taiwanese hand puppets. Inspired somewhat by *jidai geki* swordplays, all puppets were to be dressed in Japanese costumes, wearing Japanese swords, choreographed in samurai action, dubbed in Japanese, and accompanied by Western music.[62] Li was asked at this point to join the New Nationalism Reformed Puppet Troupe.

Almost immediately, however, he is hired away to lead the Taipei Propaganda Troupe for the Defeat of America and England, because a police chief took an interest and made him an offer he could not refuse: Japanese protection, privileges, and rations. This is the company that stages the story of Douki-san. Joining it meant Li's entire family would be well looked after in senior police quarters. *Kominka,* the dreaded Japanization of colonial subjects, provided a chance to maintain the Taiwanese cultural tradition and make a good living during the hardest part of the war.

What looks initially like crass exploitation of the puppets is revealed by Li to be a providential break. Two consequences follow from this: that the true meaning of performing arts (puppets, opera, music) comes not in their intended message but elsewhere, in a context not immediately apparent. The imperialist message and even the progress of the Pacific War is superintended by something more cosmic: the need for skilled craftsmen to return to work. So what if the empire they are working for is doomed, or politically obnoxious? As one character remarks, it is a "sign of things to come" that the Japanese chief takes such care to protect Li and his family, even against Japanese soldiers. The Japanese too seem aware of the transcendent value of Li's talent and offer patronage. The second consequence is the status of the cosmic order in which traditional craftsmen and artists are in tune. We might call this order providential, but what Jameson calls "the providential plot" means that Li is unaware of the connections and near misses that govern his life (see chapter 3). This is plainly not the case, as he is mindful of how "man's fortunes are unchangeable." Granting that there is a gap between levels or registers of significance, how does the cosmic order of things reveal itself? "Drama, dream, life" is *The Puppetmaster*'s Chinese title, and this offers a clue to the structure of Li's divination.[63]

First, showing the drama: by representing events such as the memorial of Douki-san or fight with the drunken Japanese soldier, shot so far away as to be almost illegible. Second, telling the dreams: using stories in voice-over accompanied by landscapes or other ambient scenes. Examples are Li's recounting the circumstances of his birth, grandmother's illness, the deaths of grandfather and other relatives, and so on. Eight times Li's voice comes up, commenting on things we are about to see, may have seen but not registered, or do not see at all. These voice-overs usually lead to Li's onscreen appearance, which is presented six times. These sequences present the life, inextricably rooted with the drama and dreams. The life stories are sometimes riveting, like the mistress's frog poultice or the irony of a mob scene. Li tells us Japanese soldiers were savagely beaten for burning rationed rice—but which was no longer edible. His anecdotes may also be tedious, like the detail about the Shirasaki cigarettes smoked by Leitzu. The mob scene is never dramatized, remaining a reminiscence, but after the Shirasaki story the courtship of Leitzu and Li is staged in a teahouse, where they sensuously light cigarettes by brushing their lips together.

The cosmic order also emerges in the way drama–dream–life is sequenced in time, as well as the overall causal structure. This is illustrated in a single remarkable long take of over seven minutes, punctuated only by slight reframings. Within this single shot, the ordering of drama–dream–life gradually unfolds.

Drama: Li is at the Cherry Garden teahouse in Taichung, waiting for Leitzu to return from Taipei. Under a single orange bulb he reads and sips tea. Gimying, a

4.8 Leitzu and Li Tianlu

(COURTESY HOU HSIAO-HSIEN)

girl at the brothel, calls to him from behind the door. He refuses to let her in, despite her repeated entreaties. Leitzu suddenly arrives, confessing she had set him up. The lovers jokingly accuse each other, then discuss money and Li's travel to Boli. She is warned not to follow. Three more girls arrive with food. They begin to celebrate Li's loyalty (fig. 4.8).

Dream: Li's voice-over breaks in about five minutes into the shot, "To speak of wandering . . . " Over the warm teahouse image Li continues the lovers' story into the next stage of their romance. He relates Leitzu's unwanted arrival in Boli and their return to Taichung. Still in voice-over: the embarrassment of apologizing for the appearance of having eloped. This drives a wedge between the teahouse image—the drama time of representation—and that of the voice, belonging to Li's reminiscence-dream. The contentment of the teahouse image opposes the recalled chagrin of making the rounds, smoothing ruffled feathers. Between the image and the story, Li appears as something like a "kept man," which may explain his imminent departure from Leitzu.

Life (straight cut): Li appears, bundled against the cold with a cigarette in hand. Then he recounts the sudden onset of Leitzu's illness and the frog poultice, which cures her.

The overlapping progress of drama(tization), dream (voice-over), and life (personal testimony) reveals the symbiotic relation between reenactment and memory. Memory is dependent on reenactment, which in turn is indifferent to questions of accuracy. The dream, that mixed mode combining depiction and narration, is double-sided. It mediates showing and telling. Hou Hsiao-hsien's deft movement from mimesis to diegesis and then to actual oral history is all based on the same narrative material, even within the same shot. This truly exemplifies the name of Li's troupe, *yi wan ran*, "Also Like Life" referring to the statement of a wise man: "Puppets in performance are like people. So puppet plays are also like life." Li Tianlu's plans to start Also Like Life were derailed by the clouds of war. But the war clouds provided other materials for practice, and life eventually discloses itself as a well-made play.

When looking at *The Puppetmaster*'s intricate structure—drama, dream, life— its artful arrangement of fact and confabulation is exquisite. According to Zhu Tianwen, in order to realize Hou's vision of Li's life within a historical course, he developed a new editing pattern for *The Puppetmaster*. Calling it "cloud patch" editing, Hou's intention was to simulate the concordant movement of clouds, accumulating and overlapping, generating a thick and heavy sky. Likewise, the drifting wisps of drama, dream, and life help create a history dense with "magical causes" and unfathomable motives.[64]

In Search of the "Roots" As a national cultural treasure,[65] Li Tianlu lent his story and his presence to a film exploring the history of Taiwan under the localization policies of another Li, president-to-be Lee Teng-hui (Li Denghui). In the aftermath of the lifting of martial law, demands arose to redefine Taiwan as a nation-state independent of China. Despite being chairman of the ruling KMT, Lee was the major driving force behind the project of nation-building. Hence the need to trace the "roots," the planting of a new Taiwan identity through recuperation of a history that was often talked about but yet to be documented in Taiwan film.

In this, *City of Sadness* was a milestone, and with *The Puppetmaster* Hou Hsiao-hsien continued his documentation. Only this time he enlists documentary footage to create a historical agent that is still alive, a living theater on which to reenact the history of Taiwan. Li's life is used to illustrate the vagaries of Taiwanese existence under the Japanese but, curiously, the personal seems to drive the political. As we've seen with the puppet show, Li Tianlu belongs to some cosmic order beyond the Japanese occupation. Though he works with them, accepting Japanese patronage and even friendship, he also sees them off the stage. By collapsing the life of Li with that of Taiwan, both personal and national identities can be mutually affirmed. This, however, is a process fraught with problems, beginning with Li's birthday:

My mother gave birth to me on the lunar calendar of November 23, two years before the Republic, which was also the fourteenth year of the Japanese occupation. For a trans-dynastic Taiwanese like me, there were four ways of telling a year. The year I was born, you could call it Pre-Republican 2; Qing Xuntong (Emperor Pu Yi) 2; (Japanese Emperor) Meiji 43; or 1910. Like many children caught in the historical gap, I was taught classical Chinese first, then with *kominka* I learned "ah yi ooh eh oh," and after restoration I learned "bu pu mu fe." Now I have to know a little bit of "A B C D." As for my name, my father wanted me to have his name, Xu. But my grandfather reminded him he had married into the wife's family, as a "yoshi," and so I had to be named after my mother. My father thought he was young enough to have more boys so he agreed. Who would have thought I would be his only son?[66]

Li's memoir here raises problems of periodization, of era designations, dynasties, and the delineation of time frames. Which frames? Whose nation? Whose history? By what name? In what language? And whose genealogy? Li's birth straddles the complicated nexus of Sino-Japanese, Sino-Taiwan history but also the imperial frames of Qing and Meiji (thus the prominent vignette of cutting the Qing dynasty pigtails), feudal and modern (dynastic versus Republican), as well as struggles between patrilineal and matrilineal institutions. As a result, throughout Li's whole life he is caught between two parents and two names. A Japanese district chief says his name is like a composition with the wrong title. Still, within the family, it is as if Taiwan-as-Li were given up for adoption to Japan by a China who never thought it would one day want to renege. Li also speaks of the more recent history of occupation by the United States (learning his ABC's: the "A B C D"). It is as if the occupation never quite ended. Taiwan's ambivalent identity, its seeming tolerance of interlopers and dissonant voices—at least since the 1980s—cannot hide the pathos with which these struggles are cataloged.

The very idea of "roots" must therefore be questioned and demythologized. In Taiwan, the roots are there but they appear in a tangled mass, difficult to count and even harder to recount. For Li, as for Shen Congwen, narration partakes of the divine: it "is not only a ritual of exorcism but also a form of incantation, ushering one again and again into the cavern of memory, throwing different lights on that cavern's dark passages."[67] Like Li's multiple grandparents, and the many names of family, regimes, and faces of himself, the remarkably lifelike puppets in his troupe take over the speaking parts.

The fact that Taiwan's modern history begins with identity confusion presents a challenge for Hou who, at this post–*City of Sadness* time, was anxious to showcase Taiwan and the problem of cultural Taiwan. Taiwan was a backward colony for centuries. But it is also a treasure island, not just through the efforts of Hou and Yang, specializing in modern Western forms such as cinema, but also because of Li Tianlu, a traditional folk artist. Through Li, Hou again finds the cultural patrimony he needs (fig. 4.9), boasting a unique appeal, if not always authentic. Traditional

4.9 Hou Hsiao-hsien
and the master, Li Tianlu
(COURTESY HOU HSIAO-HSIEN)

theater/opera/puppetry is one of Taiwan's unique cultural sites, an intertwined heritage of Chinese nation and Taiwanese provinciality, traditional and modern, pillaged by Japanese and KMT propaganda, but flexible, possessing endurance, perseverance, and longevity, like Li himself. On the other hand, this specific theater and its tradition is not high art, far above the level of ordinary folks. It is a provincial art, originating from southern Fujian, far from the Court. In his memoir, Li spends time talking about different schools of *budai xi* and how pleasurable it is to visit masters on the mainland to discover different skills in the craft of set-building and the puppets, and how to handle them. Puppets often have lives longer than people, although their aliveness depends on the people who play them. To puppeteers, puppets are not just their actors, their props, but also their best friends. This explains the only caring moment between Li and his father, when the father passes his puppets to the son. Over the protests of Li's abusive stepmother, the father (also a puppeteer) gave Li all his treasures before his death. Puppetry is an art of tradition and of immortality, outlasting various political regimes.

Perhaps this is also Hou's ambition, to film Li Tianlu, albeit in a very different, more fleeting medium. Recall Hou's self-proclaimed connection of the film's aesthetic to classical Chinese ink painting: "Leaving the empty space" (*liubai*). This is

Hou's explanation of the fragmented documentation of Li's life and his puppet art. In his seventies Li Tianlu was given the opportunity to leave a name in the history of folk art and world cinema. Hou's distinguished craft can very well characterize him as another vernacular master from Taiwan, even allowing for a certain distance between outdoor puppet shows, the story of Douki-san in the South Pacific, and a distinguished film honored at Cannes.

Conclusion

I used to film movies about Taiwan's history, with solemn stories and characters, because people were facing enormous upheaval—family, country, separation from relatives—but contemporary subjects are not so heavy. They are basically about subtle, interpersonal involvement, "the unbearable lightness of being," grievances, instincts, your sensory capability. This kind of self-centered desire, where the self is like an animal, the world of passions and desires, is a topic toward which I am moving, inevitably.

—HOU HSIAO-HSIEN, SPEAKING ON THE DOCUMENTARY *THE TAIWAN NEW CINEMA*[68]

There is no doubt that Hou Hsiao-hsien marks the development and changes in Taiwan cinema's history in the past three decades. Quoting novels by Milan Kundera, Hou has moved into a cosmopolitan space. We see the transition from genre pictures in the 1970s and early 1980s, to the autobiographical New Cinema films, followed by "national biography" in the Taiwan trilogy, to his millennial concern with evocations of concrete spaces in abstract times. These three posthistorical films are *Goodbye South, Goodbye* (1996), *Flowers of Shanghai* (1998), and *Millennium Mambo* (2001). Hou's films are milestones not only for him but for Taiwan film culture as well. What accounts for this movement is a combination of changes in the film culture of Taiwan, a succession of creative collaborations, and a creative restlessness that continues to roam widely over new problems and challenges. Hou Hsiao-hsien and his films do not stand alone as individual achievements but may be seen as a microcosm of contemporary Taiwan cinema. From box office darling to international auteur; from box office pariah to the godfather of Taiwan cinema—Hou's winding path shares the same route as the cinema that first nourished, then thwarted, then pushed him out of his home territory. Trisecting Hou Hsiao-hsien's career gives a clear overview of the development of contemporary Taiwan cinema. Describing Hou's work this way maps a contemporary Taiwan film historiography that is always codependent upon the activities of auteurs.

Confucianizing Hollywood

━━━━━━━━━━━━━━━━━━━━━━━━━━━━━ **FIVE**

FILMS OF ANG LEE

Ang Lee (Li An) is one of many non-American directors to have negotiated Hollywood production and found success (fig. 5.1). But he differs from most in coming to the table not from a foreign commercial career, like John Woo, for instance. Lee's route to Hollywood was circuitous, from the American independent sector and a Taiwan-made coproduction to a couple of English-language literary adaptations, a Civil War epic, and finally a pan-Chinese prestige picture. Though personally Lee always felt like an outsider, even in Taiwan, his director training was firmly mainstream. Trained first in theater at Illinois, then at New York University film school, his storytelling skills were recognized very early in New York. This initiated a long, frustrating period of writing and development meetings with prospective producers.

The outsider role is practically mandatory for fledgling—especially non-American—directors knocking on Hollywood doors. Another in-between-cultures director is Wayne Wang, an Asian-American who, like Lee, has a background in alternative, low-budget production. Wang also tells stories about family, Asian values, and confused cultural identities, and he alternates between big-budget star vehicles and more personal, independent fare. But Wang's way does not touch the range of transnational production, financing, and distribution instruments utilized by Lee.[1] Though Lee's professional training was similar to Wang's, he has taken advantage of

Ang Lee
Lessons
learned on
the road to
Success

5.1 Ang Lee on the cover
of *Reader's Digest* (June 2003)

opportunities from Asia proper. Almost by chance, Lee has become adept at bringing Asian money, organization, talent, and working methods into profitable accommodation with American film and Hollywood. Lee's thoroughness and attention to detail at every level of the process shows a seriousness of purpose uncommon in Hollywood, one that, at the risk of sounding ingenuous, we could call Confucian.

By "Confucianizing," imagine reintroducing Hollywood to virtues of discipline, diligence, and old-fashioned economy, in both its financial and narrative senses. Confucianizing Hollywood means attempting to renew a culture of courtesy, fairness, and sincerity in a notoriously cutthroat industry. Given that such a culture's existence is and always has been highly dubious, is this even a remote possibility? How can Ang Lee represent or reconstitute such ideals in Hollywood? And what use are they to industry discourse? Are Confucian practices handy in the day-to-day of pitch meetings and location scouting? Chinese filmmakers like Jackie Chan, John Woo, Sammo Hung, Jet Li, Chow Yun-fat, and Michelle Yeoh are famous for their work ethic and modesty. But Confucianizing means more than a Chinese director who just happens to make movies in Hollywood; it is an injection of righteousness into the production process itself, upholding merits of patience, decency, and concern for the entire community and the whole process, not just oneself. A Confucian workplace would inoculate all against cynicism and exploitation. It is the polar opposite of every-man-for-him-selfishness and the kind of savage, Hobbesian excess thought to characterize the conducting of show business and especially that of Hollywood movies.[2]

Confucian Affiliation and Power

Edward Yang has made an incisive statement on Confucianism in the book published with his screenplay for *A Confucian Confusion* (see chapter 3). In this pithy declaration, Yang accounts for the (mis)placement of Confucian values in contemporary Chinese societies:

> Confucian dogma—including the values of conformity, discipline, obedience, diligence, sacrifice, etc.—was employed as a way to question universal standards of value set by Western powers. But these Confucian "virtues" also deny imagination, creativity, and critical thinking. What are the consequences of this denial? Interpersonal suspicion and cynicism. The resurgence of Confucianism in Asian society in the late-twentieth century is not without questions. Contradictions precipitated by Confucianism's utility—conformity and homogeneity—are the keys to Asian wealth and success but, at the same time, prevent Asians from creating new terms of reference for a new era of choice. "What should I do? What is a good person? How should we live?" are questions my characters are constantly asking, because they now have the luxury to ask them.[3]

To this list of questions we could add, "Where do I belong?" Belonging, especially within family, is to assume the proper place, an act of affiliation, submission, and assent to a Confucian hierarchy. Parent-child bonds are not just biologically given; they are idealized, especially those of father-son. In addition, the major Confucian loyalties governing human relations are husband-wife; elder-younger siblings; friend-friend; and ruler-subject. As can be seen in the last two pairs, family bonds can be abstracted and may be used to organize sociopolitical relations in the wider community. According to Yang, this is important for rulers who forge (or exploit) a conviction of righteous benevolence over a large, subordinate population. Their subordination is sustained under authority of the sovereign but also differentially, by means of international and intercultural competition for resources, power, and prestige. And the community within which Confucian ethics are supposed to hold is no less than the whole East Asian framework, its history and structure, norms and deviations. This Confucian framework is defined, and politicized, partly by its perceived difference from the West. In Confucian terms, the cardinal virtue is *li*, usually translated as ritual or decorum, and carrying notions of respect and ethical rectitude. Lee is perceived to embody *li* in his films, as in his personal demeanor.

Whatever the genre, Ang Lee's films all explore personal aspects of the difference between the outspoken West and Eastern *li*, the conflicting ways of belonging to family communities, both intimate and distant. His films are especially sharp on the tradeoffs and compromises of family affiliation and individual fulfillment. His narratives are made to speak to all audiences; however Confucian Lee is in preproduction or on the set, the most crucial move is a diffusing into what we might call ecumenical Confucianism. Lee entices American viewers, famous for disdaining subtitles and everything foreign, to drink deeply at a Chinese movie well. Confucianizing Hollywood therefore entails adjustments in film culture, not just the novelty of a Chinese at the helm on a Hollywood picture.

Given this, we must ask, is Ang Lee a Taiwan director? Lee is Taiwan-born and raised, and the more prominent he becomes, the more aware he is of his accomplishments for millions of compatriots in cultural China, including overseas Chinese communities. He is claimed for cultural China, not just Taiwan, because of his hard-won immigrant success and original mainland connections. These connections were at one time impeccable, steeped in both Confucianism and Chinese nationalism. Lee gives the impression that there was little place in such a world for movies. With an exacting school principal for a father and KMT general for a grandfather, Ang Lee's Chinese background was very proper. In interviews and memoirs, he stresses that his family, especially his father Lee Sheng, was embarrassed at his choice of profession.[4]

The fact that Ang Lee makes Hollywood films accentuates his status as Taiwan filmmaker. He has thoroughly assimilated Hollywood narratives, and journalists enjoy finding thematic links between his Chinese and Western pictures. Confucianizing Hollywood means a convincing proficiency in mainstream Western genres that, nonetheless, make way for typical Ang Lee motifs. But he also makes films in Taiwan, and in China. These are not the same as Taiwanese or Chinese films; they are "Ang Lee" films and they appeal to audiences worldwide. Thus, a wider, more interesting sense of Confucianizing emerges. Lee's "Chinese" films reach non-Chinese audiences, helping these viewers acquire "good" taste, and opening a market for more Chinese films, genres, and popular culture. Lee's delivery of well-crafted Chinese films to an appreciative Western audience works reciprocally, mirrored by the fact of a *Taiwan* director making English-language films to worldwide critical and commercial profit. Though he has the least identifiable style of all Taiwan directors, Lee's status is all the more pronounced because of his sense of mission toward the craft. He is deeply committed to both dramatic integrity and the state of the art in all its digital, financial, and multinational complexity. Besides, there is something archetypal about Lee's place in American cinema, coming into a long line of émigré directors, mostly from Europe, who shaped American cinema from its inception.

Foreign, but famous names: Charlie Chaplin, F. W. Murnau, Alfred Hitchcock, Josef von Sternberg, Jean Renoir, Michael Curtiz, Ernst Lubitsch, Fritz Lang,

Greta Garbo, Marlene Dietrich, Errol Flynn, Sean Connery; presently Wolfgang Petersen, Roland Emmerich, Mathieu Kassovitz, Alejandro Amenábar, Alfonso Cuarón, Takashi Shimizu, and a recent vogue for talent from Hong Kong. Hollywood film is inextricable from its exotic transplants. The Hollywood colony beckons as a melting pot of accents, fashions, and flourishes. But this is not unique to Hollywood; the lineage stretches further back into the nineteenth century. Figures like Charles Dickens (*American Notes*, 1847) pronounced some of their sharpest, most English opinions while observing American customs, while Alexis de Toqueville's French proclivities and prejudices are displayed in his seminal work on America (*Democracy in America*, 1835–1840). Similarly, Lee's tackling of key American genres reveals a certain self-consciousness of history and cross-cultural curiosity. He has a taste for thorough research and discovery; through this, a Taiwanese sensibility comes through. This sensibility sits on the fence between the expatriate directors assimilating into Hollywood studios and the bemused intelligence of a foreign writer intrigued by American life.[5]

Epistolary Confucianism

Though we are about to explore Lee's Chinese-themed work, we propose that, in all his films, Confucianizing Hollywood is a type of epistolary activity. Lee composes letters to the world on *wuxia pian* stationery. These letters are made of antique but popular materials. They are precious but humble, not rare or expensive. "I wanted [martial arts films] to be admitted to the hall of respectability, but retain their irrepressible impertinence," he says.[6] This sounds like something Griffith, Zukor, or Fox might propose, but it jars with another statement Lee made about *Crouching Tiger, Hidden Dragon* (*CTHD*). He describes its aesthetic as "an abstract form of filmmaking, where the images and editing are like a dance and music."[7] And this: "The greatest appeal of the kung-fu world lies in its abstractions. It is a conceptual world based upon 'imaginary China.' This world does not exist in reality and is therefore free from its constraints."[8] With this flowing tension—impertinence, respectability, fantasy, abstraction—comes a rewrite of American canonical practices from outside their usual contexts, throwing them into relief. But before the rewriting, there is much reading, watching, sifting. Despite disappointing his headmaster father, Lee has the impulse of a student, and a moralist. There is a strong sense in Lee's work that he has much to learn from American film, perhaps more than he has to teach. This is not humility but practice, leading to mastery, perfection; Lee painstakingly lays out particular genres, conventions, narratives from widely disparate traditions and brings them into contact. Nowhere is this apprenticeship in translation clearer than in *Crouching Tiger, Hidden Dragon*.

In this film Lee explores the key Confucian ethic of friendship, and where it spills over into romantic and parental commitments. In the Civil War story *Ride with the Devil* (1999), young Missouri bushwackers align with the Confederates, in defiance of cautious immigrant parents. The film is about patriotism and civil loyalties (ruler-subject) across family and race lines. *The Ice Storm* (1997) is a more intimate story about a single family, but its central concern is between a husband and wife, and both are drawn to unfamiliar temptations in the American counterculture. Here Lee's Confucian predilections lend an unwonted harshness. *The Ice Storm* may be one of the creepiest movies ever made about the counterculture. Every drop of tawdriness is wrung from the swingers' party. For a moralist, everything is subordinated to a unified, patriarchal, authoritarian theme. Very strong judgment descends on the ineffectual father, who shows no sense of propriety in the swinging, suburban '70s (*li*, again). *Sense and Sensibility* (1995) is on more familiar ground, a comedy of manners centering on three sisters, which explores conflicting sibling relationships, also found in *Eat Drink Man Woman*. Of course Lee's Chinese trilogy, *Pushing Hands* (1991), *The Wedding Banquet* (1993), and *Eat Drink Man Woman* (1994), are all about the dilemmas of fatherhood, despite their increasing complexity and polish. *The Hulk* (2003), too, is a "father-knows-best" film, only this time father is insane and needs to be banished forever to oblivion. The film's genre is a license to do breathtaking battle with the father, but its Confucian core remains inviolate and surprisingly overt.

Crouching Tiger, Lee's most important film, rehabilitates the reputation of a whole genre and renders it a beacon of cultural China. The film goes a long way to redeeming or at least making "respectable" the pleasure of martial arts films in general. Not only was this film a stunning critical and commercial triumph, it signals Lee's stated goal of elevating the standards of Asian cinema. Lee wants to revamp a tradition, and an entire genre of popular culture, not only aesthetically but also through innovative financing. This will be discussed below ("Hollywood Investment? Not at all"). The film's importance for the international film industry can hardly be overstated. *How* the film was made and marketed is probably more important even than sensational box office and its many awards: four Academy Awards, including Best Foreign Film, out of ten nominations, one of which was Best Picture. It is a benchmark film.

Consider a brief aside on the idea of the benchmark. This is a film that sets standards other filmmakers and companies try to surpass. Zhang Yimou's *Hero* (2002), for instance, is regularly measured by the aesthetic, critical, and economic pattern set by *CTHD*. Other films that have tried to follow the tiger's trail include *The Touch* (2002, with Michelle Yeoh, directed by Peter Pau, Lee's cinematographer on *CTHD*), the Jackie Chan vehicle *The Medallion* (2003), and the Stephen Chow film *Kung Fu Hustle* (2004, another Columbia pickup) as well as the blind swordsman story *House of Flying Daggers* (2004, directed by Zhang Yimou, produced by Bill Kong, Lee's coproducer on *CTHD*).[9] Benchmark is a useful concept for various films in the region, such as Hou's *City of Sadness* (1989); Chen Kuo-fu's *Double Vision* (Shuan tong, 2002); Nakata Hideo's *The Ring* (1998, remade in the United States in 2002); Kang Je-gyu's Korean blockbuster *Shiri* (1999); and, before that, Im Kwon-taek's *Sopyonje* (1993). Setting a benchmark means not just popularity but influence: the establishing of a new template, a genre, or even a franchise potential.

With the idea of benchmark, we return to issues of cultural power, differentiation, and subordination. The recent success of Hong Kong expatriates in Hollywood—John Woo, Jackie Chan, Yuen Wo Ping, Chow Yun-fat, Jet Li, Sammo Hung, and others—validated their talent and Hong Kong style generally. American film is enriched but, as mentioned, absorption of foreign expertise is a familiar pattern going back to the silent period.[10] Hollywood cinema is rejuvenated by the injection of *wuxia* and kung fu, but these elements, no matter how big the budget or star, have vestiges of a subculture. Cross-cultural and historical transposition revalidates on Hollywood terms what are regarded as essentially B pictures. Going back to an earlier generation, Zhang Yingjin argues there is "a haunting sense of rootlessness" in the most famous martial arts filmmakers like Bruce Lee, King Hu, and Zhang Che.[11] This permeates what Stephen Teo calls cultural nationalism, a vague, parapolitical ideal, and rootlessness allows it to sidestep specific claims on audiences of any given party line.[12] This political evasiveness enables martial arts films to travel, well beyond the Chinese-language market. Martial arts films have been embraced by audiences and filmmakers worldwide. Viewers of every political stripe found in "new school" martial arts an anti-imperialist aesthetic of defiance and soon turned Bruce Lee into the most famous star in the world.[13] Similarly, Ang Lee updates the floating Chinese signifiers of a bygone genre, as well as bringing their quality standards "up to code"—technical, dramatic, cultural, and commercial codes—of the international art film. The aesthetic of defiance and assertive cultural nationalism is gone, but a vague wistfulness and longing for cultural China remains.

The most recent wave of Asian film talent—John Woo, Jackie Chan, Jet Li, and so on—have stuck with the old product differentiations. They did not have ambitions of transforming Hong Kong or Chinese cinema by using Hollywood. Ang Lee does. Rather than exploiting the stereotypes of martial arts, their "coarseness," as he says, Lee seeks to elevate *wuxia pian*, to give them substance, a dignity proper to an international form. Has this happened? Did it work?

Crouching Tiger, Hidden Dragon

" 'We Kicked Jackie Chan's Ass!' " is the gleeful title of an interview James Schamus did with Stephen Teo about *CTHD*.[14] Schamus was chortling about the film's box office, which far outperformed Chan's film *Accidental Spy* (about $21 million world-wide). Besides box office, Schamus and Lee gave the Jackie Chan brand a thrashing. With *Crouching Tiger*, Chinese action pictures were radically differentiated. *Wuxia pian* was no longer synonymous with puerile, cult-driven, shoddy entertainment. Lee's work is a benchmark in altering perceptions, giving *wuxia pian* and classical Chinese culture a romantic Hollywood gloss. Additionally, its industrial operation successfully "modernizes" Chinese filmmaking. Immediately after *CTHD*, Columbia-Asia produced Chen Kuo-fu's *Double Vision*. Money from Columbia meant that "advanced" capitalist, Hollywood protocols were followed by the crew from Hollywood, Hong Kong, and Australia. *Double Vision* performed well above expectations of Columbia's executives in Los Angeles, despite friction between local crew and foreign experts (for more on this film, see the postscript). On the other side of the Taiwan Strait, Chinese director Zhang Yimou followed suit with his *Hero*, boasting an almost identical production format: Hollywood distributor, *wuxia* genre, transnational crew and casting, location shooting in China. Although *Hero* succeeded in the domestic market thanks to the PRC government's full participation, it was kept on the shelf at Miramax for two years before it was released (with great success) in the United States in 2004. Thematically, its blunt imperialism made Chinese critics very uncomfortable, especially at a time when the concept of a unified China is still contested.[15]

Ang Lee is not making an American film or a Chinese film; he's making a Hollywood/Chinese film, creating a new, not-quite-seamless blend. It is not surprising that Lee was accused of catering to the West, of perpetuating Orientalism. Because of the calculation with which Chinese materials were packaged in Hollywood wrapping, he was accused of self-Orientalizing. But such critiques do not help in understanding the intermingled layers of genre and national cinema, its transnational operation and cross-cultural apparatus. Particularly, they cannot explain some of the more interesting issues of filmmakers who are caught in conflicting frameworks of cultural and identity politics. The question is, if Ang Lee represents a recent fulfillment of the American dream, do we need to see in his achievement a successful assimilation? Where is Ang Lee in relation to Chinese cinema and where is Ang Lee as a Taiwanese/Chinese making it (up) in Hollywood?

Alter-nations and Alternatives

A Chinese film that becomes a global hit is inevitably thought to be Orientalist. That was the line taken by *Variety*'s Derek Elley, who did not think the film was "really Asian," and called it a cultural shotgun wedding.[16] Lee concedes that, from the start, he wanted to make *CTHD* agreeable to a global audience. But this claim is implicated with the dual citizenship of Ang Lee as a Chinese and Hollywood director, and his attempt to alter two things: the stubborn, "feudal" ways of making movies within China proper and the stereotypes of Chinese film in the West. What better genre than *wuxian pian* as a place for Lee to hit these two birds with a single stone.

Addressing a global audience for *wuxia pian* requires generic and cultural differentiation from trappings of so-called Chinese film, which to Lee are constructed by popular film traditions established in the 1960s. To him, Chinese film history is marked by costume genres, action films, and family melodramas by studio directors such as Li Hanxiang, King Hu, Zhang Che, Li Xing, and Bai Jingrui (see chapter 1). Lee suggests that our understanding of Chinese history and culture is largely shaped by the mise-en-scènes of these genre pictures. These diasporic directors not only staked out Chinese cultural imagination in the postwar period; they also standardized modes of narrative, expression, and production for Chinese films in Taiwan and Hong Kong.[17] Lee's overview of Chinese film history outlines a clear defense against charges of the "inauthentic" China pictured in *CTHD*.

Lee's critique of the perceived deficiencies of Chinese film is twofold. In terms of production, Lee used *CTHD* to introduce "quality" to Chinese industry practice—"quality" in the sense of organizing a crew that can work coindependently with the director. This means a clear division of labor as well as expertise in every technical area. Rather than treating the crew and actors as laborers carrying out instructions, Lee worked intensively with them in order to allow them to comprehend the intended thrust of the project. Subsequently, the crew must have the ability to solve problems rather than await creative lightning to strike the director. Lee's Western method would be foreign to Chinese and Taiwanese crews used to taking orders and following standard procedures. But Lee believes that "quality" production lies in teamwork of shared efficiency, professionalism, and cooperation.

With respect to stereotypes of Chinese cinema, Lee used *CTHD* to challenge standard views of *wuxia pian* and to provide an alternative to the images of Chinese film in the West. Again, this required deviating from standard production methods. Lee wanted to separate not only from the 1980s action films from Hong Kong but also from the heavy costumers of the Fifth Generation.

The first problem Lee encountered in his making of a modern martial arts film was action direction. Lee had serious differences with Yuen Wo Ping, a master *wuxia* action director from the Hong Kong school, because Lee wanted to change decades-old methods and rules. This school, dominating Chinese production from the time of Bruce Lee and Zhang Che, is all kicks, blows, and blocks. The impression is of blinding speed and deadly force, which is one of the keys to Jackie Chan's, Jet Li's, and Yuen Wo Ping's lucrative work in recent Hollywood films. But to Lee, this old school also created a stereotype of Chinese film being "superhuman" (Bruce Lee and Jackie Chan) or camp-heroic and artificial (Zhang Che and Tsui Hark).

Instead of reproducing the hard-impact action as seen in Yuen's signature work *The Matrix*, Lee sought combat scenes of ethereality, disorientation, and abstraction, qualities clearly seen in the bamboo grove sequence. Asked to design this kind of floating encounter, Yuen dismissed it as wishful thinking.[18] Lee insisted on a "mesmerizing, dazzling" presentation instead of arborial combat.[19] More important, it was Lee's intended alternative to the neutral mise-en-scène of martial arts films that privilege action over atmosphere. Lee emphasized that in "regressing" to the martial arts genre, he wanted to return to martial arts fiction, a major source of Chinese vernacular narrative that offers both Confucian teaching and Taoist mysticism. Lee believes that the latter has been greatly neglected in the cinema, and he wanted to use *CTHD* to introduce this utopian imagination of martial arts fiction. In order to simulate the fantastic, Taoist-inspired ambiance, it was crucial to stage soft and airy combat scenes with light touches of nature, like water, leaves, and wind.

CTHD's evocation of Chinese film history creates a new, mainstream market for Chinese-language films. After this film, there are excellent reasons to make and rerelease Chinese films—and not just for festival awards.[20] This is especially important because of the film's allusions to earlier works, which opens the way to an archive of unseen and unfamiliar pleasures. The genre itself has been revamped, and steps taken toward the normalization or mainstreaming of Chinese-language period films. The way to make *wuxia pian* globally palatable was often bumpy, however, with Chinese viewers and connoisseurs sometimes laughing at the film's concessions. One of these is language. As a subtitled film, it matters not to non-Chinese audiences what dialect or accent was heard. What matters most is what characters say, and do. Yet their speech carries a thousand nuances, sometimes unintended.

"This is the way we Chinese talk," was Lee's reply to Schamus when he questioned the stilted, wooden language of Yu Xiulian, the swordswoman played by Michelle Yeoh. Schamus's retort was that the film was doomed from the start because the character's speech would make her a laughingstock. To Lee, Xiulian is a repressed spinster, a professional bodyguard who sublimates romantic desire into the sword, in deference to the Confucian order. Speech, as well as deportment, dress, movement, and attitude are all supposed to be governed by the Confucian ideal of *li*. Yu also believes that the pampered aristocrat Jen should know her place and follow her elders. "Chinese have no trouble understanding and accepting such traditional values," Lee says. However, Yu Xiulian ought not sound like a right-wing extremist, as Lee was afraid would happen unless she got new lines.

Eventually Lee asked Schamus to rewrite all her dialogue to make it sound more natural to Western viewers, utilizing devices from American detective films and melodramas.[21]

Schamus also got the task of writing the love scenes in the desert, complete with shooting stars and an exotic landscape. This time it was the bandit Lo's language that was problematic. Viewers in Asia complained that the character of Lo (Zhang Zhen) sounded too contemporary, his diction and unmistakable Taiwanese accent inappropriate to the period and the far western setting. Here, too, a mythical, fantastic quality accompanies the romance of Jen and Lo, a passionate affair defined against the Confucian propriety of Jen's city life. Some viewers took this dreamlike interlude as a betrayal of the Chinese martial arts spirit. But the change in tone is consistent with Jen's yearning, derived in part from her reading of martial arts tales. In general, Lee decided early on to adjust some conventions of martial arts stories if they did not suit the requirements of a foreign-language film epic. Some Chinese critics and audiences thought the alterations were ruthless, jettisoning the stylized, archaic qualities they felt were essential to *wuxia pian*.[22]

Lee's manipulation of the sound track was guided by dramatic and emotional impact. Traditional Chinese martial arts films' dubious reputation is due partly to the almost universal practice of dubbing. The lack of language nuance and sound design contributes to the genre's vulgarity. This feature can be attributed to Zhang Che, who persuaded Shaw Brothers in the early 1960s that action scenes could be enhanced by not shooting in synchronized sound. It allowed greater flexibility of action and casting of Cantonese-speaking actors in Mandarin-language films, which was Shaws' major product. Seeing a chance to economize, Shaws responded to Zhang's idea and put him in charge of the now obligatory dubbing department.[23] Since then, dubbing and subtitling has become a mainstay of Chinese-language cinema and television.[24] It extends market range, but it also makes an artificial, occasionally shoddy impression that now has cult movie connotations—at least in the West.

Unwilling to reproduce a Shaws/Golden Harvest-flavored cult cinema, Lee refuses to use actors as live mannequins who are spoken for by standard voices. Lee also declines dubbing the actors for linguistically correct reasons:

From the start . . . I made up my mind to make an all-Mandarin-speaking film, knowing full well that Chow and Yeoh can speak only Cantonese Mandarin. Honestly speaking, the Mandarin spoken by Chow in the film is better than that of Chen Shui-bian, Tung Chee-hwa, and even Jiang Zemin. I think 90 percent of it is no problem at all. There are problems though, with Michelle Yeoh's pronunciation and intonation. But I think the quality of the voice which is capable of carrying emotions is more touching than listening to dubbed standard Mandarin. Therefore I kept their voices.[25]

Lee's priority goes to "realism" in the sense of carrying out convincing character-ization, which may not be familiar to Chinese ears. What is more telling about this blunt statement is his multicultural interpretation of language politics. Lee sees language as a realist reflection of diversified Chineseness, from all corners of China rather than from some exalted center, be it Beijing or Taipei. Compared to Zhang Yimou's caution in dubbing Cantonese-speaking Hong Kong stars Maggie Cheung and Tony Leung into standard Mandarin for *Hero*, Lee's language politics demonstrates his rejection of a univocal Chinese-language practice.

Lee's view of the Chinese language parallels his ambition of incorporating a foreign, Chinese genre into the global entertainment factory. But this is not simply an East-West alchemy or hybridization. It is a larger vision that goes beyond "give and take" (in Ang Lee's words) and includes a remaking of Chinese cinema and the reception of Chinese cinema. In his memoir, *My ten-year dream as a filmmaker*, Lee questions the dichotomy between Hollywood as popular entertainment and Chinese film as art house, festival-boutique cinema. Lee argues that it is true Hol-lywood must keep circulating globally popular culture, if only to sustain its enor-mous distribution-marketing network. However, this does not mean Hollywood producers must be confined to throwaway popular entertainment, while non-Hol-lywood films are barred from entering the global market. But Asian producers be-have as if this were so. As a result, national film industries and filmmakers outside the Hollywood system abdicate from popular filmmaking and dedicate themselves to festival and art house circuits. The best they allow themselves to hope for is a golden palm, bear, or horse from a major festival.

Lee believes this distinction has become calcified and, furthermore, dictates the terms of many national film production policies, like the two Chinese new waves of the past two decades: PRC's Fifth Generation and Taiwan New Cinema. Direc-tors who do not produce for American markets think they are *ineligible* to aspire to popular genre filmmaking and are obliged to make art films for festivals. Two consequences follow: the proliferation of formula Hollywood movies—and their imitations—in the global network; and a diminishing of distinctive voices and new material within the American film industry. And so the chasm between art and entertainment widens.

The diagnosis comes in Lee's conviction of his independence, as only someone who knows the diversity of film cultures can have. He declares his independence not only from the Hollywood mode of production but also by unshackling him-self from any single genre, style, subject, or even language. Unlike directors like Wayne Wang, who alternate Hollywood projects with small, independent work, Lee would like to cross-fertilize, making provocative, artful blockbusters (*The Hulk*) and adrenaline-pumping art films (*CTHD*) where it's acceptable to eat popcorn. Lee's outsider status is something he jealously guards, though in the past it was a great burden. He assiduously maintains his Chinese roots, never having applied for American citizenship. He wants to prop open a space from which to reconsider and twist popular American forms. Like many other reflective and ambitious directors, Lee is anxious not to be swallowed by the Hollywood system and is equally anxious not to squander opportunities to work. One way of doing this is to harness the power of Hollywood distribution in order to make "really Asian" movies.

"Hollywood Investment? Not at all."

This phrase, from a section of Lee's memoir (381 ff.), proposes that *CTHD* is a textbook case of how production and distribution are confused. Even now the belief persists that the film is a coproduction, hybrid or, in a reversal of Asian movie piracy, a Hollywood version of classic *wuxia pian*.[26] Its polish, digital effects, awards, and above all its popularity with Western viewers are taken as signs of American provenance. But this confuses the message with its marketing. Besides impeccable production values and careful scriptwriting, the film comes stamped with trademarks like Columbia Pictures–Asia and Sony Classics. Posters, soundtracks, and other promotional materials prominently display logos of Columbia and other Hollywood brand names. In Australia, Columbia launched its Asian push as part of a series called "Silk Screen," including Zhang Yimou's *Not One Less* and *The Road Home* (both 1999), Tsui Hark's *Time and Tide* (2000), and *CTHD*. Despite their various origins, these were all distributed as Hollywood films.

Therefore, it was easy for people to suppose that *CTHD* was a Hollywood-produced film. But film promotion and marketing are not the same as production and preproduction film financing. These mistaken assumptions testify not only to Hollywood's monopoly on the public imagination of popular forms. They also betray a lack of confidence in how Chinese films can look and sound.

It must be conceded that *CTHD* is no ordinary Chinese film. But as far as its capital was concerned, this is indeed a Chinese project. Its production budget was exceedingly small: $15 million (one-tenth the cost of Lee's next film) with several million more invested in marketing by Sony Classics.[27] The project was conceived, initiated, financed, and insured through efforts of those outside of Hollywood, and America. All the financial risk on this film was borne by Ang Lee, Xu Ligong (Zoom Hunt International in Taipei), and Bill Kong (Edko Films in Hong Kong). These core figures represented their own belief in the project along with the major markets of Hong Kong / PRC, Taiwan, and North America. Two things allowed production to commence: Bill Kong's arrangement of a completion bond, which guaranteed returns on credit in case of project interruption; and bank loans issued on the basis of the bond. Completion bonds are a recent innovation in Asian production, and one was issued to *CTHD* because of Lee's track record and agreements made with distribution arms of the studios. In this regard the project had credibility with Hollywood—but not outright approval, because Hollywood was the buyer, not the seller initiating the project. CTHD was a Sony-Columbia acquisition, not production. These distributors promised an after-completion "negative pickup"—agreement to distribute following submission of a satisfactory negative. The buyers were semiautonomous subsidiaries of the majors: Sony Classics for North American markets; Columbia-Asia for Asia, and Warner in France for Europe.

The whole process exemplifies domination of international distribution by Hollywood players, yet the fact remains that these players will acquire promising non-Hollywood fare. They may not risk preproduction cash, but a promise to distribute is almost as valuable, considering the millions poured into prints, advertising/promotion, and lobbying for Oscars. This is a reminder of the distinction between popular Hollywood production and popularity itself. It is too easy to confuse the categories of Hollywood film and popular film entertainment, imagining Hollywood has a lock on popularity. Hollywood distributors, furthermore, do everything possible to encourage this slippage. They would like consumers to believe only Hollywood has the know-how for mass popularity. Even in large regional cinemas like Hong Kong or Bombay (Mumbai), equivocation persists between the very idea of popularity and Hollywood movies. Sony Classics and others' decision to pick up this project was amply rewarded: a U.S. box office gross of $128 million, plus $85.4 million overseas.[28] In the United States the film spent thirteen out of its fifteen theatrical weeks in the top ten.[29] CTHD became the most profitable foreign-language film ever made. So much for the notion that only Hollywood-made pictures may be popular, and therefore commercial.

Narrative Structure

Another persistent view of the film concerns its narrative concessions, that it follows a Hollywood pattern of pacing and motivation. If we take the norms of international action films, CTHD does not follow them closely. It starts and closes very quietly, in defiance of the action film's opening explosion of action, usually before the credit sequence. Lee's film makes us wait sixteen minutes until an exciting pursuit of the black-clad thief (scene no. 3 in segmentation, p. 216). The first fifteen minutes is verbal exposition, which, in the hands of a journeyman *wuxiapianiste*, could easily be supplied after a flashy opening set piece. This soft opening, a quiet talk between Yu Xiulian and Li Mubai, signals the film's basic style. Similarly, the conclusion of CTHD is curiously flat. Jade Fox is attacked and killed within a few seconds. This revenge killing, which motivates Li Mubai throughout, is anticlimactic, lacking the "overwhelming denouement" that is almost invariable in Hong Kong films.[30] It is the now shattered friendship of Yu and Jen, and the death of Li, that take center stage. Both beginning and ending are very attenuated by the standards of martial arts and action film generally.

This is not to say that Lee neglects pacing. He is no King Hu, taking an hour in *A Touch of Zen* before allowing any significant narrative incident. But *CTHD* is experienced—and criticized—as being fairly slow for a *wuxia pian*, a quality it shares with its literary source. Compared to the frenetic pace of Hong Kong action films, *CTHD* is almost funereal. A second battle occurs in scene 9 (36m) when the police detective Tsai is killed after a bloody fight with Jade Fox. Her exposure surprises because Fox was part of Governor Yu's household, working as Jen's governess. Zheng Peipei's ferocious appearance is a shock, particularly to those who recall her from King Hu's *Come Drink with Me* and other Shaw Brothers pictures of the 1960s. As the actress typifying the righteous *xianü* of an earlier generation of *wuxia pian*, Zheng Peipei was inspired casting. Actress fuses with character, as both represent a venerable, still formidable tradition that is doomed to grow old. Following this clash and major turning point, there is an action lull of nearly an hour. An important scene is no. 12, however, a brief, nocturnal encounter between Li and Jen. After teaching her a lesson, he proposes to accept her as a disciple. The parental parallel between Li Mubai and Jade Fox is installed here, and in the next scene. We find an erotics of submission to the master; note how Jen kneels before Fox (no. 13) even as she speaks of surpassing her in skill. But when humiliated by Li, who holds only a stick, Jen rebels and insults his school. Li and Fox both play on the meaning of "lesson" (no. 12), which can be either enlightenment or a painful punishment.

The flashback in the desert (no. 16) is full of action, but its purpose is less a display of martial arts than a form of courtship. The flashback motivates Jen and Lo's passionate affair and it literally eroticizes *wuda* (close combat) as foreplay. It also motivates Jen's abiding fascination with the skills of wandering swordsmen and their code of honor, the world of *jianghu*. Lo also tells the legend of the filial son who sacrifices himself for his father's life: "a faithful heart makes wishes come true." But the sexual element transforms Jen's experience of the *jianghu* and makes it unorthodox. For genre purists, eroticization of martial arts may be objectionable. It might also be this (impure) dimension of Jen's martial arts that fascinates Li Mubai.

The most striking thing about the placement of fight sequences is the accelerating triptych in scenes 23–24–25. The succession of these fights has a wonderful cumulative effect even with completely different moods. The first is cheeky and takes liberties with typical characteristics of *wuxia pian*: the mock formality, the long-winded names, and the pedantic recital of different techniques as they are executed. One strong man in the background carries a plastic barbell that he waves around like a baton. The scene directly cites King Hu's showdowns in Chinese inns (e.g., *Come Drink with Me* and *Dragon Inn*). Specific props (hurled wine barrels, coins, umbrellas) and set design (beams, hanging lamps, railings, stairways) are used to demonstrate superior agility and technique. The back-and-forth of challenge and response resembles a card game. Touches of lightness and sly humor derive from comic business in the Peking opera. But unlike Zheng Peipei or Xu Feng's self-control, Dragon Jen indulges herself in a spectacular display of martial skill. After she leaves, the lighthearted tenor gets a fillip when Yu reveals why a poor thug named Gou received especially harsh punishment. Gou is the name of Jen's betrothed.

After a break and change of scene, the main duel between Yu and Jen begins. This earnest, all-out clash between two *nüxia* (swordswomen) is animated by hard feelings. Betrayal is the subtext of their battle in Yu's headquarters. Recall Jen acknowledges Yu as an amiable elder sister on their first meeting. But this friendship sours. The "spoiled dragon" Jiaolong (her Chinese name) deliberately violates the customs of family propriety and the rules of the *jianghu* underworld. Yu Xiulian will exact payment. Unlike the fat man with fake barbell, Yu desperately tries to lift an enormous halberd that is too heavy. Swords crash down on stone with pulverizing force. The music, dominated by Tan Dun's drums, marks a complete change of mood from the demonstration at the inn. Finally, Li Mubai intervenes and still another fight ensues. The music shifts again. Li Mubai's engagement with Jen goes into a mystical realm of water and bamboo that is just as suggestive as the desert flashbacks (fig. 5.2). Li's purpose in taking on Jen is not only to subdue, but to seduce. He says he wants to teach her, but when he pacifies with a pointed finger between her eyes, sexual tensions overflow. Discipleship shades into the quicksand of courtship, an idea stated bitterly by Jen: "Wudang is a whorehouse! Keep your lessons!" (no. 12).

The quick succession of the three set pieces gives them great power. The 1–2–3 acceleration provides a preconclusion climax. It does not yet resolve the story, but it varies the pace and clarifies the true stylistic importance of *wuxia*: expressive movement uncovering human relations, not just a lethal weapon or tool of revenge. The presentation of these three fights represents *wuxia* of the 1960s, the '70s, and a timeless, mystical Tao. Within the story, these martial arts successively reveal hubris, recrimination, and longing. This is why the dispatching of Jade Fox seems almost an afterthought. The succession of fights is compensation for the long wait since the last conflict, and prepares for an extended, romantic denouement. It also bears out Lee's description of his perennial dramatic rhythm: "repression—release. Repression—acceleration."[31] Lee says the martial arts form "externalizes the elements of restraint and exhilaration." [32] The pattern works for a Jane Austen adaptation, a Civil War story, and for a Connecticut family melodrama set in the 1970s. When employed in a *wuxia pian,* it does not compromise but rather illuminates structural and generic possibilities that have traditionally been overlooked.

5.2 Li Mubai and Jen in the bamboo grove, *Crouching Tiger, Hidden Dragon* (2000)

The End: A Leap of Faith

The ending of *CTHD* opens out to multiple interpretations. In the end, does Jen go her own way in a liberating, if tragic, release from Confucian fetters of obligation? If so, this is an affirmative version, which views her final leap as a triumph for individual, feminine, and, particularly, youthful self-assertion. Perhaps it is similar to the "happy" ending of *Thelma and Louise,* another film whose conclusion many women and feminist viewers enjoyed.

A variation on this is an affirmative national allegory. Taiwan separatists found pleasure in a political reading in which Jen refused to submit to the larger Chinese community. In this view Jen would rather obliterate herself than rejoin the motherland, to marry in Peking or stay on Wudang Mountain, sustaining tradition. In any case, her leap is seen as a rebuff to the call of any patriarchal or patriotic duty.

The affirmative version, however, neglects the palpable sorrow Jen shows when she returns too late to save Li Mubai. She bows her head to Yu, ready for ultimate punishment. There may be a weakness in the script because Jen's repentance is inadequately motivated, unless it is Jade Fox's deathbed confession that she wanted to kill Jen out of envy: "You know what poison is? An eight-year-old girl, full of deceit.

193

5.3 Jen's leap (*Crouching Tiger, Hidden Dragon*)

That's poison! Jen! My only family . . . my only enemy. . . . " (see p. 216, no. 28). The poison metaphor, used earlier by Li Mubai himself, captures the spell Jen casts on everyone around her ("Is it me or the sword you want?" she asks). Both Fox and Li have otherworldly powers, but both failed to win Jen over. She has powerful magic, too, a willful passion none can domesticate, wildness both destructive and highly attractive. Whether this quality survives in her at the end of the film is ambiguous.

Jen's final act can also be viewed as thoroughly sacrificial, Confucian: Jen atones for wrongs she has caused Li, Yu, and her own family. To Yu she says, "Trust me. As you have helped me, let me help him [Li]." How does this figure in terms of a happy ending, i.e., what we usually expect of an entertainment picture? Clearly she tries to do what is just in rushing for an antidote to Fox's poison. Does it matter, in the larger economy of iniquity and redemption, that Jen fails to deliver in time? A "just in time" rescue is a staple of Hollywood narratives. But a happy outcome, not just heroic effort, is indispensable. It seems Lee offers this possibility, then snatches it away, as if to say "we all know the forms here, don't we, but shall we try something different?" Also, there is a cycle of generational repetition: Fox killed Yu's fiancé and Li's master; Li kills Fox in revenge; then Jen "kills" Li by returning too late. The Fox-Jen poison has deprived Yu of her lovers, not once or twice, but thrice: 1. fiancé; 2. Fox's dart in Li's neck; 3. Jen's lateness. Jen has something to make up for, at least if she recognizes her implication in this web of responsibility.

The issue of submission, in both its Confucian and narrative senses, appears again. An ethical reckoning accompanies Jen's leap, as sacrifice to the Confucian gods of order, authority, and obligation. Considering the havoc caused by her recklessness, Jen's death balances things out. For a Confucian reading, it would be felicitous if her leap were a form of filial piety that worships the ancestors, like the original legend. Jen learned her lesson: this is how some other, more skeptical feminists understood Lee's conclusion as yet another example of patriarchal film-maker eliminating uppity, headstrong woman.

But there is an imbalance if we take as Confucian the unyielding norms of popular storytelling. We have already seen evoked the just-in-time rescue, only to be denied. Will there be a second chance, maybe the prospect of young lovers eloping? This does not happen, so what do viewers do with Jen's leap (fig. 5.3)? If we think she dies, then it is at best a bittersweet ending. If her act is suicidal, it can be recuperated by the affirmative version outlined above. Or perhaps it is sacrificial and represents payment of a debt to a Confucian obligation, atonement, and forgiveness. Alternatively, the most far-fetched view is that Jen's leap is simply not a fall, but a kind of flight; throughout the film, Jen tends to float upward in her martial arts. She miraculously doesn't die, and literally fulfills the legend told earlier by Lo. "He jumped. He didn't die. He wasn't even hurt. He floated away, far away, never to return."

This is what we actually see on screen. The mise-en-scène is painterly, mythical, dreamlike, and the falling figure has a lyricism that matches the incantation: "A faithful heart makes wishes come true." There is a moral here, and nothing is more Confucian than a moral lesson. Believe what we are told, the moralist says, and accept what we are shown. We have been promised an apotheosis and this is available, if we accept it. Taking flight, Dragon Jen pursues a course known only to herself. The ending of *CTHD* is tragic, or sacrificial, only if viewers suppose that gravity sucks her down and there are rocks waiting beneath the clouds through which she falls. As we will see next, Wang Dulu's original story does not allow this inference, and instead takes readers on a different path. But in Lee's film, as in the *wuxia* genre, gravity can be defied and rocks may part, or yield to softer places. Most important, the film suggests a historical leap as well, because it casts back to the *wuxia shenguai pian* (martial arts–magic spirit pictures) of the 1920s. An account of Yungu, "maiden of the clouds," from the silent film *Red Heroine* (1929), could describe Ang Lee's Dragon just as well: "The leap into a new dimension, or a cinematic space . . . endows her with the sartorial attributes of an androgynous angel [and] also considerably alters her social and gender identity."[33] *CTHD* ends on a miraculous note, a fantastical combination of romance, martial ferocity, and human fallability.

Sourcing Wang Dulu

Wang Dulu is a northern Chinese writer of the 1930s and the 1940s. Wang made a reputation in his twenties as a writer of "Mandarin Ducks and Butterflies," gaining proficiency in romance fiction.[34] According to martial arts historians, in the 1930s Wang made a "sudden switch" to martial arts fiction, injecting into this traditionally masculine, hard-boiled genre romance, emotion, and tragic flaws. Thus in the history of martial arts fiction, Wang invented a subgenre called "tragic warrior romance" (*beiju xiaqing*).[35]

Wang's writing style, however, is full of contradictions and concessions. His structure is often lengthy and meandering, typical of peripatetic martial arts heroes. He tends to insert large chunks of flashback, interrupting the smooth flow of storytelling and convoluting narrative structure. But the language is simple and concise, complemented with crisp local Beijing colloquialisms.[36] This makes the work easy to read and comprehend, appropriate to a highly commercial, serialized format published in daily newspapers. Wang is also known for rich characterization, lending psychological depth to his heroes and heroines. He romanticizes landscapes, using mythical imagery as setting and correlative to the intrigues of the *jianghu*, "rivers and lakes" of the moral frontier.[37] Unlike his contemporaries, Wang sticks with an older type of pulp fiction called "court case tales" (*gong'an xiaoshuo*) and as a result, his martial arts stories are not particularly concerned with the martial arts themselves as a display of physical prowess or supernatural power. An ethical dimension comes forward. Heroes are defined as those who use martial arts to defend and protect, not to compete or show off. And that hero is often a chief bodyguard, like Yu Xiulian in *CTHD*. Wang uses terms like *jianghu* (the vicissitudes of wandering warriors) and *lülin* (banditry and hooligan exploits), instead of *wulin* (realm of martial arts), indicating his preference for lawless drifters over structured martial arts competition. Wang's is an introspective style of martial arts storytelling. There are many scenes of discussion, like we see in *CTHD*, on the cost-benefits of the wandering warrior life. These are self-reflective because swordsmen question and probe their roles as sometimes reluctant heroes and, by extension, the value of martial arts storytelling. Another Wang Dulu adaptation, Zhang Che's *Trail of the Broken Blade* (1967), also contains discursive interludes on the *jianghu* life. In addition, Wang's novels include comic figures derived from Peking opera to provide humor and entertainment in his tragedy-driven pulp fiction.[38]

Dragon Jen and Tiger Lo are main characters in volume four of Wang's sprawling, five-part epic (serialized ca. 1935). Its narrator throughout is the guard Bo (Liu Taibao), who makes only token appearances in the film. The depiction of Tiger is significantly reduced as well, which may account in part for some viewers' criticism of his role in the film. Two minor characters in the book, the swordsman Li Mubai and chief bodyguard Yu Xiulian, are elevated to the level of protagonists (Li and Yu are major characters in earlier volumes). This major adjustment has much to do with casting decisions. For the film to be marketable globally, particularly in the United States, catalyst of the world box office, filmmakers must cast familiar faces. By this time Chow had appeared in three major American titles (*The Replacement Killers* [1998], *The Corruptor* [1999], and *Anna and the King* [1999]), and Yeoh was known for her turn as a formidable Bond girl in *Tomorrow Never Dies* (1997). Certainly these two actors were already more than familiar to Chinese viewers. Schamus and Lee relate how Beijing airport had to be shut down for forty-five minutes to allow immigration enough time to welcome Chow and get his autograph.[39]

On the other hand, Lee economized by doubling pairs of characters and organizing them into binaries—middle-age versus young; reserve versus passion; traditional versus modern; reflective versus impetuous—and this simplifies the characters' predicaments, making the film's thematic structure comprehensible to world audiences. These themes are connected with ideologies of individualism, obligation to society and family, and hierarchy/social norms. They point toward Lee's Confucian motifs, especially the issue of submission to authority, and the use of formula required by a global media commodity. The binarization and structural simplicity is implicit, but not clear from Wang's epic story. The commodity formula is familiar to readers of martial arts fiction: character traits and goals (involving romance in Wang Dulu's case) are established early and clearly, and reinforced in the course of the story. This is combined with a character "arc," some kind of character change in response to trials undergone in pursuit of the goal(s).

Wang Dulu uses many flashbacks to fill in the history of his many characters. This complexity must be reduced to bring clear focus to a screen adaptation. Regarding the Dragon character, Wang repeatedly describes her inner struggles and emphasizes contradictions in her personality. But in the movie, Dragon's psychological dimension is reduced, with one exception: her confession of fear to Jade Fox when she realizes her own power. In most of the film, Dragon seems impetuous, unreflective. This too was a necessary virtue in the casting of Zhang Ziyi, whose appeal is primarily physical, even superficial, unlike the subtlety of her elders. In Wang's book, Dragon is trapped in a dilemma, caught in the class difference between herself and her lover Tiger: her pursuit of martial arts–romance clashes with filial obligations to her parents. Thus in the novel Dragon has a lively interior dialogue with herself, bordering on neurosis. This subtle difference may explain the change of emphasis Lee makes at the end of his film.

The ending of the novel is as follows: Dragon fakes her suicide in order to reunite temporarily with her lover, Tiger. After a night of enjoyment in a mountain cottage, she does not go off with him in a happy ending, but disappears by herself, away from any obligations whatsoever.[40] To her parents, she is dead, and to her lover she has fulfilled a promise of reunification, if only for a night. Wang describes this; then, true to the martial arts form, he adds an expository coda addressed directly to readers. Wang writes:

This is where the author should put down his pen. Intelligent readers should know the couple who spent a dreamlike night together in the cottage. Readers should also know why they separated. Since then, living in the same cottage, Tiger spent most of his time thinking about that night. He became reclusive and retiring, eventually becoming a "crouching" hermit. As for Dragon, she could not stop thinking of Tiger's devotion, but she was bound by promises to her parents. In sum, though she stepped out of her high rank, she cannot change who she was; though Tiger has quit banditry, he is still a bandit by birth. So Dragon could never be his wife. Thus, she came to sleep with him, but dared not linger. And she left him the next day, without hesitation, like the tail of a celestial dragon slipping away, always "hidden," never to be found.[41]

At the very end, Wang fully reveals the truth of the events previously described using a restricted point of view. This is a device typical of Chinese martial arts stories, which, as a popular form, shuttles between description/action and discussion/exposition. It is also endemic to the martial arts genre, such as Shaw Brothers' swordsman films of the 1970s. Background and characters are always formally introduced at the beginning, usually in expository titles along with an authorial voice-over reading the prologue to ensure audiences are informed.

Ang Lee considers this narrative structure flawed, archaic, and possibly intolerable to audiences of modern art films. He dispenses with such redundancy and alternation in the original story. Instead, Jen finds a level of self-awareness and (perhaps) sacrifice, which had eluded her throughout the film. In throwing herself from a cliff, she shows a newfound maturity that befits her skills as a true martial artist. Whether she dies or not, she sacrifices herself, but also finds fulfillment in sacrifice—a curious re-Confucianization of an original story with many more twists, turns, digressions, and qualifications.

Despite or because of its ambiguous ending, the film fulfills the expectations of an art film audience. Ambiguity and open endings are a hallmark of art film narration, but there is emotional closure because the protagonist comes to an understanding and resolution of psychological dilemmas. This is a didactic ending, more so than the Wang Dulu source. An irony is that Wang's book presents Dragon as far more aware of her dilemma than the willful troublemaker played by Zhang Ziyi.

Abstraction and Confucianization

CTHD boasts an elegant classicism, hovering between tradition and innovation; it balances spectacle and psychology, an unexpectedly smooth fusion of martial and dramatic arts, of action and emotion. The bamboo forest scene is exemplary in citing King Hu's classic A Touch of Zen, updating Hu's jagged editing in favor of a spellbinding duel in the treetops. There may also be indirect allusions to the bobbing and weaving camerawork of Miyagawa Kazuo in Kurosawa's *Rashomon*. Throughout Lee's film Jen constantly levitates upward, with both Yu and Li grasping her heels to pull the Dragon earthward ("Get down here!" says Yu in the first combat scene). As a whole the film has a powerful upward thrust, culminating in the bamboo grove and again in the apotheosis of Jen.

The Confucian question connects to our apprehension of a moral. Like Dragon, perhaps Lee is reaching too high; his mind is in the clouds, as Yuen Wo Ping remarked. Lee wants transcendence, he needs epiphany, but Lee the moralist lacks an identifiable style. His passions tend to be muted, hemmed in by the formidable engineering of social constraints and narrative structure. Criticized for shortchanging heroism, many of Lee's characters are bland ("humourless and pedestrian"); there's little humor and when found it is very dry.[42] Lee's funniest film is a droll English costume drama written by Emma Thompson. Forces of anarchy are always personified in women, or girls. The shrewish wife in *Pushing Hands* is a true monster; Weiwei, the precious source of an heir in *The Wedding Banquet*, is an interloper, breaking into the happy gay couple. The homesick mother-next-door in *Eat Drink Man Woman* is as obnoxious in her prattle as her filthy chain-smoking habit. Despite this latent misogyny, Lee always seems sincere, eager, perhaps desperate. At worst, he can be dour, and even depressing. Unlike Dragon Jen, Lee appears domesticated, pat, square. He broke out in *The Hulk*, indulging in wild experiments with editing, multiple panels, and very dark themes. But Lee is still a message filmmaker, audience-centered and constantly calibrating the effects of shot selection and dialogue. With the possible exception of *The Hulk*, Lee may not be sufficiently challenging compared with stylists like King Hu, Wong Kar-wai (*Ashes of Time*, 1999; *In the Mood for Love*, 2000), or even Zhang Yimou, if we recall the audacious narrative loops in *Hero*. But these filmmakers do not have even a fraction of Lee's audience. Could this commercial utility be explained by Lee's U.S. training—short on experimentation and long on functional mainstream narrative? More generally, Lee tapped into an escalating global interest in martial arts, and Asian film generally, but can he also be credited with the contemporary explosion of interest in martial arts?

Ang Lee seems to be an introverted person, but an extroverted filmmaker. He is a director of great ambition, wanting to vault over all competition and surpass even himself. He is a director who attempts to reinvent himself with every new picture. It is no wonder he needs at least a year to recover from his last project. This is something to appreciate, to be celebrated, because it indicates Lee's belief in the medium as something transformative, for himself as for his expanding audience.

To conclude this line of abstraction, we may attribute to Jen's leap a synthesis of two kinds of immortality. In popular culture, heroes squeak by hazards that annihilate villains or ordinary characters, in order to live to see another adventure. In other kinds of stories, the hero dies for a cause that outlives him or her, attaining apotheosis in the minds of those who hear the tale. Death works here as a gospel, bringing the good news that death can be transcended, meaningful, and even beautiful. Asian popular storytelling is full of such romantic conclusions (Japanese love suicides are exemplary) while Western narratives generally confine death to more tragic registers. Sacramental qualities accompany such images, although in folktales—like westerns, epics, or martial arts stories—explicitly religious doctrines are not normally found.

Jen's leap, as we have seen, may be a sacrifice, an escape, or a purely aesthetic invocation of transformation. Consider comparing the final image of *CTHD* with two other signature images of flight. At the end of the opening sequence of *Die Another Day* (2002), James Bond throws himself from the top of a massive dam in North Korea. He goes into freefall for a long, long interval before finally pulling out and saving himself. Nonetheless, he is captured and tortured. "A hero never dies" is the moral here even when the hero is tortured, between trademark 007 credits of gyrating females and priapic scorpions, an adage that serves as touchstone for the everlasting appeal of the Bond franchise. Apotheosis here means ensuring that the whole series, not just a character or premise, is immortal, surviving as long as global capitalism can sustain spectacularly fetishized regimes of visual consumption.

Another flight over the edge is the final image in Roland Joffé's *The Mission* (1986). This slow-motion process shot depicts a Jesuit missionary strapped to a cross going over massive falls in eighteenth-century South America. Transcendental apotheosis is quite literal, in that the missionary finds his reward in heaven for earthly labors on behalf of Indian savages. The magic of this scene comes not from popular culture's recyclable commodity fetishism, but the sacrificial economy of reward in heaven. The cycle does not pull back from death, but takes off from it as an otherworldly compensation.

Returning now to earth, we savor the dramatic and culinary delicacies of Ang Lee's Taipei feast *Eat Drink Man Woman* (1994).

Eat Drink Man Woman

A widower shares a big old house with his three unmarried daughters. As a famous chef, he insists on preparing large banquets for his family every Sunday. But these are not joyous occasions. The three sisters dread the rituals because they have other, more pressing plans: jobs, romance, and the church. They are worried about their father and hope that he will remarry. Awkwardness and guilt pervade the household because everyone tries to conceal their yearnings and desires for independence. The title *Eat Drink Man Woman* refers to a well-known Chinese maxim that means sex, like eating, is only natural.

Eat Drink Man Woman (*EDMW*) is a type of preview; it looks forward to Lee's later work and in this sense is a transitional film. Though it belongs to the "father-knows-best" trilogy, it is also a departure and anomaly. The previous two films, *Pushing Hands* (1991) and *The Wedding Banquet* (1993) were in large part English, but here all dialogue is in Mandarin. New York gives way to Taipei; and stories of unsettled immigrants shift to those of prosperous Taipei people. From fathers and sons, Lee moves over to father-daughter relationships. In contrast to the multi-cultural hybridity in the first two films, an emphatically Chinese feast suggests a solid national and class setting. More importantly, the film is a distinct step away from independent production to a more polished commercial style; its production values far surpass the basic functionality of Lee's first two films, due partly to the unexpected financial success of *The Wedding Banquet*, the single most profitable film of the year.[43]

In returning to a Chinese setting in Taipei, Lee assimilates his New York stories within an older, more intimate background. He has said that it was important at this stage to establish himself as a *Chinese* filmmaker.[44] This makes *EDMW* a preliminary or dry run for the grand synthesis of *Crouching Tiger, Hidden Dragon*. The film is crucial to Lee's early work because it marks a bold move into familiar Chinese terrain. At the same time, this terrain is shaped, scored, and directed at a worldwide audience, culminating in a Best Foreign Language Film nomination at the 1994 Academy Awards. Lee's previous films had the jostling languages, cultures, nationalities, and sexualities in transition, the exercise of acculturation. Now he was back on home territory, culturally and linguistically, except for mode and scale of production, which was suddenly bigger, more ambitious, and therefore not so familiar. It looks as if Lee himself had emerged from an immigrant niche, while his choice of subject matter returns to an unequivocal "foreign" domain, at least for his intended audience. This is not so much a paradox as a rite of passage.

EDMW is a forerunner of bigger things to come; it looks ahead toward the spectacular balancing act Lee eventually achieves in 2000, several years later with *CTHD*. The two films show intricate weaving of multiple storylines and ensemble acting. Action and emotion are skillfully blended, folding together dramatic and martial-culinary arts. And like *Crouching Tiger*, *EDMW* also transposes model films from the past, specifically the 1950s. In retrospect, we might say that *EDMW* is transitional/looking forward but also transpositional/retrospective, recasting a mid-1950s vintage family melodrama for contemporary use.

As forerunner, *EDMW* is intent on breaking out of the small, independent sector that was the filmmakers' original métier. According to Lee, the first two films were made for mainly Chinese audiences, a smallish niche market.[45] But *EDMW* was meant for a worldwide audience, coming from a U.S.-based Taiwan-Chinese director of an American project. The film had a shooting schedule of forty-seven days, while *Wedding Banquet* had twenty-six. *Pushing Hands* had just twenty-four.[46] *Wedding Banquet*'s huge returns paved the way for smooth presales of *EDMW*, which allowed it to break even before starting production. On the other hand, Lee's breakout from his New York immigrant setting is a crucial differentiating move; what appears risky actually removes some pressure after a big success. Rather than remain with the dynamics of *Wedding* and accompanying high expectations, Lee switched from cross-cultural issues of race/language to an intracultural world of gender and generation.

EDMW is the first film not based on an original script. It is Lee's first film to be shot in Taiwan, and is also the first screenplay where the Lee-Schamus partnership admitted a woman writer, Wang Huiling, from Taiwan. According to television writer Wang, "Eating is about what you put on the table. Desire and gender is about what lies beneath it, which is never available for discussion. This explains the absurd behavior of the characters."[47] Splicing cuisine and sex, traditional and cosmopolitan, Confucian patriarchy with modern individualism, and commercial polish with independent snap, *EDMW* is an intricate, heady blend. Extreme contrasts and incongruities abound and encourage unlikely parallels. In *Eat Drink Man Woman*, there is a mischievous reprisal taken against authority figures in the "father-knows-best" trilogy. This is connected to the film's standing as a form of martial arts. Links open up with *Crouching Tiger*, along with historical sources in Hong Kong films of the 1950s. Here, consider how food is used in the film's targets.

Ritual, Food, and Father-knows-best

The Japanese film *Tampopo* (1987; dir. Itami Juzo) was touted as the first "noodle Western." In this film food is an aphrodisiac, used not only as a prelude to sex (oysters) but also as sex toy (the egg yolk). It mixes genres like its cuisines: Continental and Asian, raw and cooked, street stands with one-night stands. *Tampopo* is a good example of a "food film," perhaps even "food porn."[48] In *Eat Drink Man Woman* food is used instrumentally, but also as a metaphor, a "kitchen confidential." Cooking and working with food is a means to both express and suppress basic human needs. "Most films are about sex," Lee says, "and get an instinctive reaction. They try to arouse, but why not arouse audiences with food, make them salivate, get them drooling? In movies we overuse sex, and don't use food enough. If food is sex, then one is to sustain life, the other is to multiply life."[49]

In production, Lee used four simple words as his working title. Eventually the working title stuck, and its import is seen in the Chinese character design: "eat drink" 食 飲 is formal, classical, with clear graphics that represent civilization. The "man woman" characters 男 女 are smaller, with a cursive font, a more fluid graphic representing the heat of desire. Together these four words represent life at its most basic: the civilized and uncivilized parts coexist, but somewhat awkwardly. These two parts are mediated by ritual, and ritual is central to the preparation and serving of food.

Ritual works as a kind of hinge between the physical and social body. Intensely interested in this, Lee presents key contrasts involving both food and ritual. He depicts a gulf between elaborate gourmet food and the cold feelings of people supposed to be enjoying it, but weighed down by rules. "Sometimes the things children need to hear most are the things parents find hardest to say, and vice versa. When that happens, we resort to rituals."[50] This is an irony that represents the absurdity of things and the rich, often incongruous feelings of Lee's characters. Rituals serve as masks and vessels for awkward emotions and situations. Here we find a version of Confucian *li* that is excessive, lacking in humanity. Chef Zhu's commitment to *li* prevents real closeness with his closest kin, and the mechanical devotion to rites and rituals is manifested in the chef's loss of taste.

Central to the film is Chef Zhu's character arc, his transition from constricted old man to unconventional romantic, with a taste for food and life ultimately returning to him. Zhu eventually breaks out of a Confucian cycle and pursues a lost but cardinal desire for life. This signals an Ang Lee maxim: "*The greater the repression, the greater the outburst of appetite and energy.*"[51] John Lahr's detailed profile of Lee reveals this in terms both culturally specific and psychologically universal: "In my culture, you're part of the group. You have to find harmony, so you repress, repress, repress. So far, repression has been my biggest source of creativity. Repression—release. Repression—acceleration. That's a good story."[52]

Repression in *EDMW* is literal, for good reason. Zhu's dealings with his daughters are strained due to an assumption and expectation that *they* need escape and fulfillment. Meanwhile father is left holding the reins, knowing what's best for them but dissatisfied with and for himself. The beautiful daughters arouse Zhu; they excite his appetites but he cannot even acknowledge, let alone act, on them. Hence his discomfort, a pressing need for surrogates and displacements. This is graphically illustrated with a shock cut early in the film from a torrid, mid-coital kiss to a shot of Chef Zhu blowing hard down the gullet of a plucked goose.

This is a black comic transition comparable to Luis Buñuel. Like Buñuel, Lee is drawn to human rituals as a way to hide embarrassing truths. One of these is the role of sexuality within the family and especially patriarchal sexuality. In proper Chinese families this is an oxymoron, if not a contradiction in terms. The very notion of father enjoying himself, let alone taking carnal satisfaction, is discomfiting. In *Eat Drink Man Woman*, there is an element of mischievous reprisal taken against authority figures in the "father-knows-best" trilogy.

As a nationally recognized chef, Zhu retires and trades in his authority for a domestic, conjugal life. He is conflicted, not knowing how to be with his adult daughters and enduring an excruciating intimacy with them, even when they are his own kin. Though he behaves woodenly, he is not made of wood. He cannot be both father exercising patrimony and sexual being who acts on his desires. These two roles are incompatible and one must be eliminated. As his daughters grow up, and into their own sexuality, they are supposed to fly away. As compensation, they expect father to connect with a lonely widow. She is annoying and a little grotesque, a caricature of the homesick, grumpy mother. But there is a surprise, and a reversal. Rather than stepping aside and watching his daughters blossom, Zhu preempts their prerogatives and their imminent homebuilding.

Consider the trilogy as a whole, and the father's position at the end of each film: a Tai Chi master gets an independent but lonely life in New York's Chinatown (*Pushing Hands*); the father uneasily accepts an alternative, interracial family, even if it is homosexual (*Wedding Banquet*); and finally, Chef Zhu's abdication of fatherhood and the dissolution of the family in *EDMW*. Plainly father does not know best, and additionally, his power is gradually leached away with every succeeding film. Some writers have characterized the trilogy as "resuscitated patriarchy," but it is hard to deny that with each film the father's special power is attenuated.[53]

Lee then may not be the conservative director he sometimes seems because he is willing to "kill" the father, not out of resentment but just by letting him go. He allows father to jettison the father-principle in favor of human release and indulgence.

Lee encourages autobiographical interpretations of his work and actively reads his own autobiography into the films. As first-born son, he speaks of his guilt at abandoning his family in Taiwan in order to pursue film in the United States, a dubious career prospect in a conservative Chinese family. He also worries about becoming too Westernized, an irredeemable betrayal of one's parents.[54] As Lee's own consolation, what could be better than simply letting father live for himself; in effect, to cease being father, to abdicate the throne and disappear? The father begins again, starting his own nuclear family and restarting his libido at an advanced age. In Chinese families, people are expected to be sacrificial. "Family ethics revolving around a patriarchal figure is, after all, the foundation of Confucian cosmology," writes Sheng-mei Ma.[55] But the question is, what do fathers want? Even to ask such questions attributes needs to patriarchy and opens a seam in the fabric of filial piety. In this final installment of the trilogy, father not only identifies what he wants, he also seizes it, and in effect exchanges fatherhood for basic human need. In *EDMW*, Lee suggests a complete dissolution of the family in favor of personal contentment. The radical resolution comes not in the daughters leaving home—this is only natural—but in the regenerated, resexualized father. In the first two films we have merely a separation between father-son, and parent-child, a temporary gulf that is potentially bridgeable. But this once solid Taipei family literally dissolves in the end.

Culinary Martial Arts

What is patriotism but the love of the good things we ate in our childhood.

—LIN YUTANG[56]

In *EDMW* father not only knows best, he *is* the best. Like the father in *Pushing Hands*, he is a true artist and master. The credit sequence of *EDMW* is a tutorial on high Chinese cuisine. On display is the masculine, even brutal, expertise of a professional assassin. Like an impassive martial artist, Chef Zhu dispatches fish, fowl, and frogs with surgical, military precision. The efficiency of killing, disembowelment, dismembering, and slicing are a tour de force, accented by crisp editing. Even the vegetables are shaken mercilessly. Close-ups of food preparation briskly alternate with shots of Zhu's face, frowning in concentration. A quick tilt reveals an entire wall of knives, choppers, and other sharp tools of the trade. With the exception of a phone call to give advice and a long shot of rhythmic chopping with twin cleavers, Zhu is a grim, hard-nosed specialist.

There is a short break in the chicken coop as Zhu chooses another victim. The carnage proceeds in a series of tight close-ups of increasingly intricate dishes shot with hand doubles (like porn), using three of the top chefs in Taiwan as stand-ins. The doubling partially explains the proliferation of close-ups, as well as the rapid-fire alternation of shots. Lee insists that to get the correct response—drooling—proper procedures must be followed exactly. Every new setup required cooking a fresh set of dishes, as Lee wanted to capture textures and colors, swirls of steam, the aroma of piping hot food. This necessitated repeating a whole new round of preparations. When actors were unable to deliver their lines, the food went cold. Ingredients would run out. Assistants prepared seven orders, but this was insufficient. Lee threw tantrums when this happened.

The script calls for original recipes for smoked fish and chicken. All kinds of seafood, meat, vegetables, and varieties of starch are prepared the traditional way. Imperial Beijing style, Sichuan, Yangzhou, Chaozhou, and Zhejiang (Shanghainese) cuisines are all represented. Zhu's colleague Old Wen asks him when he will finish his book of food. His recipes require raw sugar cane, rice bran, a woven straw colander, and pine tree branches to make fire for smoking. These are unobtainable at the supermarket. A whole duck is lifted out of an outdoor smoke barrel.

5.4 Home-made pots of sauce and condiments, *Eat Drink Man Woman* (1994)

Zhu raises his own chickens and fish; the signature image is a buffalo fish hauled out of a ceramic bowl and impaled down its gullet with a long chopstick. In Zhu's kitchen no refrigerator or modern conveniences are visible anywhere; ingredients are all fresh or made by hand and traditionally stored (fig. 5.4)—no store-bought bottles whatsoever. Zhu even makes his own soy sauce.

Another reason for the shooting and editing pattern is an affinity between Zhu's proficiency and that of a virtuoso filmmaker. In the kitchen, Zhu is like a general or chief surgeon. He is the master with the hauteur appropriate to his status. The opening sequence has a seamless fusion of "beauty and brutality."[57] In different circumstances such as cooking lunch boxes for the little neighbor girl, Zhu is an indulgent pushover. Similarly, Lee has spoken many times of a repressed, unconscious yen for tyranny when he is in the director's chair, something diametrically opposed to his meek personality.[58] In either case there is a Jekyll-and-Hyde, Banner-and-Hulk doppelgänger at work.

Here, we connect the technical challenges of *Chinese* culinary and cinematic arts: Ang Lee as master chef and artist. Culinary art begins in the home, but it is suddenly interrupted, switching to a public event for the political elite. What is appropriate at the Grand Hotel is overkill at home. This *gustatio interruptus* is integrated with the story of three lovely, unmarried daughters. With Zhu, we are tantalized with beauty and appetite, but this way is blocked and leads instead to Lee's real interest, repression and control.

In Zhu's culinary "war room" the camera pans across a series of photos on the wall. Here Zhu poses for shots taken with KMT's top leaders from the postwar period to the 1990s: former president Chiang Kai-shek, his son/successor Chiang Ching-kuo, the current president Lee Teng-hui, premier and ex-chief commander Hao Bochun (Lee Teng-hui's archrival). The last picture shows Chef Zhu with Zhang Daqian, the leading Chinese painter of the twentieth century.[59] The snapshots clearly show Zhu's ethnic affiliation as first-generation mainlander, as well as his stature. The panning motion across these trophy photographs parallels the virtuoso Steadycam movements through a series of large, spotless kitchens at the hotel. Lee said this was a composite of three different kitchens to elaborate and make Zhu's entrance more dramatic.[60] Zhu has been called in to handle some counterfeit shark fins at an important function. Later, in the hall of the Grand Hotel, there is a shot of another actual KMT boss, Wu Boxiong, the minister of home affairs. All of these photos, political cameos, and the Grand Hotel itself function as "certificates" that authenticate Zhu's identity and rank as the "National Chef." Endorsement from three generations of KMT leaders indicates Zhu's pedigree, authority, and unimpeachable skill.

In his professional capacity, Chef Zhu embodies a national tradition. He is called in to officiate in the salvage of an imminent culinary disaster threatening the fortunes of a famous political family. On this occasion—the wedding of a famous general's son—everything must be perfect. The sign of approval comes in the tasting of Zhu's signature dish, "dragon and phoenix bestowing good fortune" (*longfeng chengxiang*). The sequence abruptly juxtaposes the political with the personal, and practices of cooking for sustenance versus public performance. Clearly, Lee intends to score points about the discrepancies between domestic contentment and traditional ideas of "face," of saving reputations, proper place, and prestige.

Cooking, Sublimation, Foreplay

Confucianism lies implicit in the utility of food and of sexuality, an idea of sex/cooking as both personal fulfillment and consolation within an anachronistic, calcified society. Middle daughter Jiaqian (Wu Qianlian) uses sex to compensate for the thwarting of her ambition to cook, while Zhu cooks as sublimation not only for sexual inhibition but for suppressed parental love as well. In the course of the film he and Jiaqian move toward one another and exchange qualities. He begins to look after his own needs while she becomes more sacrificial. The other two daughters, a religious virgin (Yang Guimei) and romantic teenager (Wang Yuwen), solve their problems by themselves.

The introductory shot of the house brings us through the kitchen. This kitchen is like a time capsule, a throwback to another age. It is a Japanese-style house. For

Lee himself, the most important rooms of any house are the kitchen and dining room.[61] These areas are like an old stage, they conjure a lost China, already extinct through dispersion but for a few lonely old men. Diaspora extends also to food, carried by fleeing KMT soldiers in 1949. They set up restaurants and stands selling the flavors of their youth: the classic, authentic tastes of Sichuan, Yangzhou, Chaozhou, and so on. As they grow old and die, the homeland tastes and cooking methods also vanish. Younger chefs with little firsthand knowledge of China train in Hong Kong, Europe, and America. They cater to new, international expectations of Chinese and Asian food. Ingredients, seasonings get mixed up in novel "fusion" cuisines. Cantonese food is the de facto Chinese cuisine—even in Taiwan—partly due to its impressive presentation, and also for its delectable sweets. By its very nature, Cantonese cooking is creolizing, the original fusion cuisine. But traditionally, Cantonese was never officially recognized in the culinary pantheon of China; it was always too adulterated with concessions to the West, with recipes calling for foreign ingredients like ketchup, canned pineapples, and *mayonnaise*.

Late in the film the manager of the Grand Hotel asks Zhu to return to work. He compliments him, telling him he's not only an expert chef but he is also the only remaining specialist in the major Chinese styles. Zhu replies that specialty or not, it doesn't matter, after forty years all the different regions are now jumbled and adrift in a culinary ocean. Complaining about the carelessness of culinary preservation, Zhu hints at the high cost of globalization. What may appear to be cosmopolitan cross-fertilization is really just an insipid mishmash. Chef Zhu is a trove, an archive of old Chinese culture. His cooking represents a lost world, not only in Taiwan but also on the mainland. No one maintains the old recipes anymore because there is no market for them; the required tastes simply do not exist. This explains Zhu's attraction to Jinrong (Sylvia Chang) and her daughter because they, unlike his own family, are good eaters; they appreciate his cooking innocently, finding its value as sustenance and affection, rather than ritual.

Jiaqian eagerly cooks for her boyfriend, but his response is not innocent. She cooks for love, not ritual, but something is not quite right. Her devotion to the correct taste is not properly received. She tells her lover the dish requires a big bamboo steamer. So it is not authentic, but try it anyway. She loves cooking what she calls "kung fu cuisine" (*gongfu cai*), which presents a parallel between Chinese cooking and martial arts. This calls to mind quasi-martial feats of technical skill, like the film's opening sequence. But the term has another connotation. *Gongfu cai* is an analogy of elaborate preparation, not warfare. It requires a surfeit of chopping, cutting, carving, and prep work. In using the term Jiaqian really refers to the time, effort, and patience needed to make such elaborate concoctions. There are too many steps, too many special tools to be compatible with a modern, convenient lifestyle. She knows how to practice the old arts, but lacks the time, the kitchen, and an appropriate guest. There is a mismatch with her shifty boyfriend, just as the weekly banquets at home are inappropriate, excessive, a form of "torture." The fussy, overbearing richness is not the comfort food Zhu's daughters crave; besides, the dishes don't even taste right!

Fattening a Story for Market

In Taipei, Lee met with Wang Huiling and reached agreement with her on the basic story, centering on a father's empty life built on lies and an ideology of sacrifice. James Schamus was then brought to the table, and he suggested the device of lost taste buds as a symbol of declining vitality. Schamus also suggested a subplot about the competition between airlines for international routes.[62] As a New York–based producer, Schamus reimagined the Taipei setting within transnational business competition, bringing a global aura to the story. It is not just any company Jiaqian works for. She is with a specifically national corporation, the KMT-owned China Airlines. Her character is underlined by the compelling, assertive way in which she deals with international negotiations. Because she belongs to a national corporation, actively competing with the West, her profession is closely paralleled with that of her father.

Significantly, this Taipei-based Chinese language film was the filmmakers' first serious tilt at an international market, targeting all audiences. The crew's newly won professionalism, with unaccustomed, appetizing choices in cinematography, production design, food consultants, and location, augured a move to Hollywood. Despite fielding offers, Lee did just the opposite. Rather than moving up to "the major league" from a modest New York apprenticeship, his next project took the crew far from its "destiny," back to Lee's birthplace. Wasn't this a big risk, to reach a world audience with an ensemble film about a Taipei family? Actually, the film was carefully designed to capitalize on the burgeoning popularity of Chinese-language art film (fig. 5.5).

As a foreign-language film studded with exotic locations, stylish protagonists, and mouthwatering cuisine, *EDMW* falls easily into a market segment made viable by the mid-1990s: the colorful bittersweet-comedy genre of Asian art film. Other popular Chinese titles, *"the* hot ticket item of the international festival circuit in the late 1980s and early 1990s," were *Judou* (1990), *Raise the Red Lantern* (1991), *Farewell My Concubine* (1993), *The Story of Qiu Jiu* (1992), *Vive l'amour* (1994), John Woo's last Hong Kong films, and nearly all of Wong Kar-wai's films.[63] The visible success of these, indicating a rising tide of appreciation for Asian themes, could not have escaped Lee's notice. Like his Chinese counterparts, Lee's film raised issues of exoticism, commodification, and complicity, leading to charges of pandering to Western tastes, as was the case with many Fifth Generation directors.[64]

5.5 *Eat Drink Man Woman* cover design (COURTESY MGM HOME ENTERTAINMENT)

According to Chinese critic Dai Jinhua, "Chen Kaige had succumbed to the gaze of the West by following the recipe of film festivals and cooking up a dish palatable to such circuits."[65] Lee, unlike Chen, could not really sell out a background he had only vaguely known. His version of Taipei is highly idealized, romantic, even mythical, like *Crouching Tiger*. Here, too, there are premonitions of controversies that dogged the success of *CTHD*. A more important parallel between the two films is that between a rising wave of worldwide appetite and Lee's timely release of a high-quality "Eastern" that satisfies and refines that taste. Though *EDMW* was not as big a hit as *The Wedding Banquet*, and in fact goaded Lee to reconsider the international prospects for Chinese films, it works as a draft of elements similar to those of *CTHD*. Those elements include a Chinese-language script, Chinese setting, famous performing arts (like martial arts and cooking), and a revisiting of classic literary-cinematic properties.

Transposition: Recasting a Hong Kong Classic

In the development of Lee's work, *EDMW* plays a transitional role, leading eventually to the classic status of *CTHD*. A more specific transposition is historical. Both *EDMW* and *CTHD* are loosely based on classics in Chinese film and literary history. The idea for both films came from the astute Taiwan producer Xu Ligong, who launched a hit television series about four daughters and their widowed father, called *Four Daughters* (Si qianjin, "four thousand gold"). Xu was production manager of Central Motion Picture Corporation, which had backed Lee's script in 1990 and offered $400,000 toward the production of *Pushing Hands*. Under Xu, Central's policy changed from the support of New Cinema auteurs to promoting more audience-friendly material that would win back local viewers. During Xu's term CMPC not only produced newcomer Tsai Ming-liang's first two art-house films, *Rebels of the Neon God* (1992) and *Vivre l'amour* (1994), but also Ang Lee's "father-knows-best" trilogy. Xu left CMPC in 1997 due to health problems, but he immediately formed Zoom Hunt, a small production company focusing on developing literary adaptations for film and television. Xu asked Wang Huiling, an established television writer, to develop a script based on the series she had written earlier, *Four Daughters*. This was in turn based on a classic Hong Kong urban comedy, *Our Sister Hedy* (1957, dir. Tao Qin; MP&GI/Cathay). *Our Sister Hedy*, like Lee's film, is emphatically modern, urban, and feminine, if not feminist.

There are many parallels between Ang Lee's feminizing of patriarchal self-discovery and Tao Qin's more forthright display of father-daughter relations. While *Our Sister Hedy* is set in a cosmopolitan, rather glamorous Hong Kong, Lee uses Taipei as a backdrop for a love story of a father and his three daughters. In Hong Kong, father and daughters dwell in the same socioeconomic world, but Taiwan is layered with different, clashing temporalities.[66] The two settings mark a difference between a breezy colonial modernity—characteristic of Cathay's finest films—and a negotiated modernity-in-transition—appropriate to the didactic, nationalist history of KMT-owned CMPC. In both films the daughters occupy various types, from spinster schoolteacher to professional woman to blossoming teenager. Although it is ultimately another father film, *EDMW*'s feminine permutations—girls, tomboys, ingénues, hearty sensualists, spinsters, sisters, divorcées, and widows—are central, and derive from *Our Sister Hedy*. The basic problem in both stories is which daughter will be married off, in what order, and in what circumstances. And what will become of father, a widower? This is an embarrassment because sex is a taboo in Chinese families. Parents, let alone a widower, can never discuss romance and sex with their children. For Lee, "awkwardness" is the main emotion that binds all his stories of filial relations, and this comes partially from Lee's own family experience.

This awkwardness is not just interpersonal, but historical. It comes from Chinese films' long engagement with the problem of filial piety in changing times. If *EDMW* is a forerunner of bigger things, it is also an echo of key films from the past. It appropriates, interrogates, and updates landmark films and cycles of film history. *EDMW* can be seen as a belated remake of Asian—and specifically Confucian—film motifs, not just a sequel to Lee's first films of the early 1990s. It revisits and negotiates ethical conundrums of family, modernity, and the impact of popular culture, a force threatening to scatter carefully maintained norms of behavior. These norms, so powerful in Lee's personal and creative constitution, may have interfered with the reception of *EDWM*. The world according to Chef Zhu was already archaic, the stuff of myth, by the time the film was made. To viewers in Taiwan, Zhu may have appeared merely as a device, an old-fashioned foil instead of a convincingly contemporary Taiwan father. This could help explain why it was received enthusiastically abroad, but coolly in Taiwan.

Xu Ligong had asked Wang Huiling to write a script based on *Hedy* and its later incarnation as a televison serial. Wang changed it to three sisters and, instead of a salary man, made the father a *qipao* dressmaker (traditional Manchu style) who works on women's bodies all year. A *qipao* tailor has the right nuance of anachronism and sensuality but lacks patriarchal heft. Lee, considering what would be cinematic, decided to change the father's profession to that of a nationally known chef. Both professionally and libidinally he is the center that links the sisters' predicaments.

Our Sister Hedy, on the other hand, presents its four sisters as a group, literally putting them on stage for a beaming Papa. Their quarrels are primarily with each other, not with him. *Hedy* begins with a charming musical pantomime on an abstract set, framed like a picture window (fig. 5.6). In the credits each daughter has subtitles sketching her character and outlining story conflicts. The lyrics are transcribed and each sister is musically differentiated. The opening scene similarly sets up inside a small tobacco shop, looking out on windows facing the street. The camera is in roughly the same position of the shopkeepers behind the counter. Each daughter comes in, and asks to buy the same birthday gift for father—a pipe. One by one, four pipes are sold. The scene works like an audition, displaying individual style and character, and encouraging a comparative, and competitive, scrutiny within a restricted play of roles.

The most striking presentation of the daughters in *Hedy* comes in the next scene. The four sisters gather round the father, who decides to give each one a gift even

5.6 Four daughters framed in a picture window, *Our Sister Hedy* (1957, dir. Tao Qin)

(COURTESY HONG KONG FILM ARCHIVE)

though it is *his* birthday. After distributing presents, he sits down with his back to the camera, while each daughter opens her gift and reacts (fig. 5.7). Again, this seems to be some sort of test, like a biblical parable. The full frontal presentational aspect is striking: four lovely daughters on display. "Four thousand gold," as the Chinese title says, suggests a beguiling treasury of feminine charm, but also four very willful, fractious, and not entirely dutiful offspring anxious to find individual happiness, not just the family's. Display and incipient discord, nubility and filial piety, charming daughters and scheming sisters who compete for attention, even stealing boyfriends . . . such dichotomies are clearly transmitted in this portrait of a modern, urban, and very refined Chinese family.

A decade later we find variations on this sorority pattern. In Shaw Brothers' *Hong Kong Nocturne* (1967, dir. Inoue Umetsugu), three rival sisters collide with father due to individual ambitions. The three singing, dancing assistants to father's magic act present an ambivalent spectacle. They are at once talented performers who upstage Papa, and they are tempting objects of male fantasy. In a weak moment Papa even tries to force the most loyal daughter (Zheng Peipei) to revive his fortunes with a striptease. Inoue, a Japanese veteran of every studio and genre, injects a risqué subtext into what is essentially a prodigal family reunion story. *Hong Kong Nocturne*, a big hit for Shaws, was a remake of Inoue's 1963 Japanese film *Odoritai yoru* (Tonight we'll dance), but he made several variations on it for Shaws,

5.7 Father with his "four thousand gold," *Our Sister Hedy* (COURTESY HONG KONG FILM ARCHIVE)

having outlined the original widower–three daughters premise in 1957, with *Odoru taiyo* (Dancing sun; Nikkatsu).[67]

The motif of the sisters' imminent marriage bound to a widower's inevitable loneliness is a staple of Asian cinema, like the films of Li Xing (see chapter 1) and Japanese director Yasujiro Ozu. Compared to Ang Lee's film, *Our Sister Hedy*'s sibling differentiations are stark, ingeniously putting up the girls for scrutiny on the same "block." The sisters' display betrays a patriarchal, masculine ideology; note the reverse-angle close-up of Papa admiring his daughters. Perhaps Tao's film should have been called "My Daughter Hedy." However, the film is based on a popular dime novel by woman author Zheng Hui.[68] Also, with four sisters, not three, Tao Qin divides the sisters into pairs, with No. 1 and 3 (Hedy, played by Jeanette Lin Cui) as "good" girls while the second and fourth are "bad." This pairing allows for many interesting structural parallels, displacements, and reversals. Ang Lee's introduction of his three sisters is comparatively simple, with a sequence showing each daughter in characteristic activity: the eldest, Jialian, listening to hymns on a faulty Walkman; Jiaqian in a high-rise office checking spreadsheets; and Jianing working at a branch of Wendy's, an American burger chain. Lee shrewdly conceals the introduction of Jinrong, the neighbor, who may as well be the fourth daughter in her affinities with the Zhu girls and her close relationship to Zhu. She is the one who speaks to him by phone while he is busy preparing the Sunday feast. He dispenses advice on the freshness of the fish, suggesting a professional, not a personal matter. In contrast to Tao Qin's emphasis on sorority display, it is Chef Zhu who receives a grand, theatrical introduction, along with his culinary martial arts.

The parallels between *EDMW* and *CTHD* are the Chinese stories, and traditions like cooking and martial arts, with their greater ambition and scale. The appropriation of canonical works in Chinese popular culture is a key touchstone, even though *Hedy* is about as far from martial arts as it is possible to go. Neither *Eat Drink* nor *Crouching Tiger* is nationalist in any overt way, but both capitalize on a vernacular tradition known primarily, if not exclusively, to *Chinese* audiences. Appropriating well-known film and literary classics, Lee reactivates traditions which had been consigned to collectors, catalogs, and film courses, delivering a new, improved commodity in accessible terms. He adds value and range to the critical and commercial reputation of Chinese cinema as a whole. An additional bonus is to stimulate a market on home video for the old classics and directors.

To recapitulate, *EDMW* is both transitional and transpositional. A transposition is different from a remake. Transposition takes liberties with essential narrative premises while remakes basically repackage for a new generation, leaving the central narrative intact. Transposition allows filmmakers to draw on a treasury of film culture, including house styles, genres, cycles, and ideology, then mixing and rearranging these ingredients for different uses. What makes *EDMW* important is its ambition of reworking a model film and a cinematic tradition: the Golden Age of Mandarin films of the 1950s and 1960s.[69] Lee attempts to revisit classic Chinese family melodrama and recuperate it within a contemporary Taipei setting. This makes the film much different from the apprenticeship of his first two films, despite their thematic continuities. Ang Lee adjusts the colonial modernity of *Hedy* and the ultrafeminine quality of the Cathay line, but goes even further, twisting and even deforming these elements to articulate his Confucian complex. The breezy, British colonialism is replaced with a cosmopolitan hodgepodge (Wendy's, Toys R Us, French language labs); modernity turns to neoclassical nostalgia, and Cathay's urban femininity becomes patriarchal anxiety and hysteria. Lee's evocation of *Chinese* film traditions from the past, *despite never having worked in the Chinese film industry*, is a potent sense of historical custody. It allows him to lay claim to a historical and authorial authenticity. It is as if Lee is re-Confucianizing film history, as well as Confucianizing Hollywood.

SEGMENTATION

Crouching Tiger, Hidden Dragon

1. Yu Xiulian meets Li Mubai, who has cut short his retreat. Gives away Green Destiny sword.

2. Trip to Peking
   a. Sir Te's compound: he takes the sword, reluctantly. Worries about Yu Xiulian's happiness.
   b. Yu meets Jen, a girl infatuated with the *jianghu*.
   c. Sir Te gives advice on *jianghu* to Governor Yu (Jen's father).
   d. Jen's chambers; her governess discourages her from talking to Yu.

3. FIGHT ONE (16m). That night, Green Destiny is stolen. Yu tries to catch thief.

4. Next day, Te, Bo and Yu discuss theft.

5. Flyer implicating Jade Fox. Bo investigates.

6. Yu and Jen, "sisters." Yu reveals killing of her fiancé (Jen's desert flashback).

7. Tsai's story. Dart-message from Jade Fox.

8. Li Mubai arrives at Sir Te's. Li hints that he came to see her, but is interrupted.

9. FIGHT TWO (36m). Night. Grudge fight between Fox, Tsai, May, and Bo. Li arrives, about to avenge his master by killing Fox. Jen arrives, fights Li. Tsai is killed. Fox, Jen retreat.

10. Next day, Te, Yu and Li discuss what to do. Yu's "fox trap" idea.

11. To Jen's mother, Yu obliquely suggests returning stolen item. She informs Jen that a policeman was murdered. (Tea cup business) Li is introduced to Jen and congratulates her.

12. Night. Bo and May wait for Fox. Jen returns sword only to be caught by Li. After a chase and a "lesson," he offers to teach her. She angrily refuses.

13. Jen, now revealed as thief, argues with Fox. Background on Wudang manual, which Jen (not Fox) has mastered. (*Major turning point*)

14. Fox leaves, and Li vows to kill her with Green Destiny. Refers to Jen as "poisoned dragon."

15. Lo steals into Jen's room.

16. FLASHBACK: FOUR YEARS EARLIER. DESERT.
    a. Bandits attack. Jen chases Lo. She confronts bandits. Another chase, then they collapse.
    b. In a cave, Jen eats, then knocks out Lo. She escapes, gets lost, passes out.
    c. Cave. Jen is tied up, later takes a bath. Lo sings, they argue, then make love.
    d. Jen and Lo wander the wilderness. Reluctantly, they agree to separate. END FLASHBACK.

17. Jen's room. She breaks up with Lo.

18. Jen's wedding. Lo tries to disrupt it. He escapes, but is caught by Li.

19. Lo questioned by Li and Yu. Lo agrees to go to Wudang Monastery.

20. Sir Te's compound. Green Destiny is stolen again. Jen has run away. (*Major turning point*)

21. Jen confronted by country thugs.

22. Yu and Li on country road. He takes her hand. Yu: "repressed feelings only get stronger."

23. FIGHT THREE (1 hr 22m). Inn. For fun, Jen thrashes a whole roomful of thugs.

24. FIGHT FOUR (1 hr 30m). Yu's headquarters. Yu: "you're no sister of mine." Yu fights Jen, and is wounded. (*Major turning point*)

25. FIGHT FIVE (1 hr 36m). Li intervenes. After a chase, he fights Jen in bamboo grove. Disarming her, he throws away the sword. She dives after it, then is rescued.

26. Jade Fox's lair, an abandoned kiln. Her plans for Jen.

27. At headquarters, Yu's wound is dressed.

28. Li finds Jen, drugged. Yu and Bo arrive. Li kills Jade Fox who, in return, poisons Li. (Fox calls Jen "poison, an 8-year-old girl, full of deceit.")

29. Jen arrives at Headquarters to get antidote.

30. Li, dying, confesses love to Yu. (Jen rides through woods)

31. Li Mubai is dead. Yu sends chastened Jen to Wudang.

32. Wudang Monastery. Jen together with Lo. He makes a wish and she leaps into clouds.

Camping Out with Tsai Ming-liang

Ah Liang the Panhandler

Chen Kuo-fu, the director of *Treasure Island* (1993), *The Personals* (1998), and *Double Vision* (2002), used the strange behavior of Tsai Ming-liang to illustrate the parlous state of Taiwan's film industry. Chen was sitting on a panel called "The Global Reception of Taiwan Cinema" at an American conference in late 2003.[1] Despite the recent success of his cross-cultural horror thriller (*Double Vision*), Chen showed little optimism for the future of Taiwan-made films. People in Taiwan just do not care anymore about Taiwan cinema, he asserted. He then told an extraordinary story about the methods used by Tsai Ming-liang to drum up interest in his work. Tsai would go to theater box offices and announce who he was and why people should buy tickets to see his film. Sometimes he would hand out leaflets or postcards, like a smalltime political candidate. Ah Liang, the diminutive version of his given name Ming-liang (clear and bright), would always explain to the curious why he was reduced to this: the indifference of local distributors to Taiwan films meant they actively blocked promotion of his film. This was an argument Tsai would consistently make at press screenings, festivals, and ordinary cinemas to whomever would listen. He would beseech his audience, asking patrons to urge their friends to come see his film. Like the signature barker in Edward Yang's animated Web site, Miluku.com, Ah Liang would park himself on the street, calling out "Lai kanxi, ah!" (Come see the show!).

At this point, Chen said, Tsai would become emotional and shed tears. An uncertain, embarrassed silence would settle over the audience, as it did over Chen's because, although Chen smiled, we were unsure how to take this. Was this for real?

A month later, Ah Liang himself was in action at another academic conference in Taipei. He greeted the assembly of professors, students, and cinephiles, telling them about his new film, *Goodbye, Dragon Inn*, and how well it had been received at the Pusan Film Festival. He was sure we would enjoy it, he said, but just to make sure, he was giving away free copies of his short, *The Skywalk Is Gone*, with every ticket purchase. This was his gift to supporters in Taiwan, to thank them for their interest in local films in the absence of press, radio, and television coverage, all media where you might expect to hear about a new Taiwan film—but no, all we can hope for in this world, my friends, is a little goodwill, and your good opinion of my films.

And as if on cue, Tsai Ming-liang started to cry. Was he for real?

This was a performative act, which by now had become a trademark routine that was gaining fame on the festival circuit and college campuses in Taiwan and the West.[2] It had a curious effect, eliciting stares, sympathetic nods, and giggles of recognition. The emotional scene created an intimacy that broke down the usual discursive barriers in a "meet the director" session. It hardly mattered whether the audience thought Tsai was sincerely breaking down, was pulling its leg, or just needed a drink. Tsai's point was sharply made, in that it

1. Held up to ridicule established ways of film marketing, promotion, and distribution.
2. Questioned the norms of filmmakers' appearances by brazenly asking for support directly from the public.
3. Evoked *song*, a tacky, working-class behavior typical of street markets, hustlers, and buskers ("Lai kanxi, ah!").
4. Was maudlin, camp, possibly insincere, but still riveting and over-the-top, all the more so in the semi-intellectual atmosphere of a conference or film festival.
5. Called forth a variety of responses, because those for whom it was intended saw a display of heartfelt emotion, while others, having seen or heard about it before, recognized it as part of a repertoire or signature performance.

Ah Liang was making a spectacle of himself, betraying an uncontrollable passion for the handmade production, and promotion, of his films. It is also a defiant act, this loss of dignity, a preemptive strike against distributors and audiences' habitual rejection of locally made films. The spectacularization and even excess of Tsai's emotional exposure seem at odds with the cool restraint in his films. The game being played is both "shame on you" and "spot the imposter." If it was a posture, it was not quite convincing (perhaps on purpose). The affectation of Tsai's outburst raised doubts about his inner motivations, as if outer excess indicates concealment of an inward lack of conviction.[3] And when postures are being struck, with or without the recognition of an audience, we are in the realm of camp.

Tsai Ming-liang's films are camp because they play a game of black humorous role-playing, planting in the most private seat of human subjectivity seeds of doubt. These germinate in the dark, in fantasy, sexuality, and in moments alone, undermining the distinctions between family life/romance, convictions of personal authenticity, and the whole spatiotemporal structure of Taiwan's working-class life encapsulated in a single word: *song*. *Song* (the Taiwanese pronunciation of *su*, "earthy") is loud—in voice, color, manner—the usual way to describe a bumpkin in the city. As an epithet of condescension it indicates a "typically" Taiwanese vulgarity. But it also has connotations of hearty vitality, the relaxed but hardy vernacular of working-class/peasant behavior. Tsai's films are not usually camp in the flamboyant way of "exaggeration, theatricality, parody and bitching."[4] This is not the world of John Waters or the Kuchar brothers. Tsai's films are deadpan, a bit like Jim Jarmusch, their camp quality emerging from a wily gay aesthetic whose manipulations twist the *song* of Taiwan urban life into something queer—clearly recognizable but not easily classified.

As transgressive posturing and role-playing, camp lends a new perspective on Tsai's films, but the films also complicate prevailing notions of camp, through cultural and class difference, and through film style. The films are shot through with camp incongruity: between the earthy world of *song* and its meticulous, otherworldly evocations in film. In other words, slatternly *song* is conjured by ascetic techniques of the art film, like the weeping panhandler Ah Liang and Tsai Mingliang, auteur and winner of prizes at Venice and Berlin, who sit rather uncomfortably together. This discomfort, like an itch refusing to go away, indicates camp sensibility. It invites camp as viewing strategy, even if it does not automatically entail that Tsai is a camp artist.

Why Camp?

Most writings on Tsai recycle ideas relating to the modernity syndrome, such as the dialectics of intimacy and alienation, collapse of the nuclear family, contradictory feelings of loneliness and cravings for love, all represented in persistent urban imagery of water and doors, entrances and exits, passageways such as lifts, escalators, holes, and so on.[5] Sexuality, the body and spatiality, the peculiar assimilation of the private and the public, nostalgia for the songs and movies of the 1960s, and documentary-like techniques of objectivity round out the catalog of Tsai's themes and effects.[6] Another angle on Tsai is the millenarian one of apocalypse, contagion, and the end of history, tied in with fears of global homogenization and/or collapse.[7] All these take Tsai's work very seriously, though there is general acknowledgment of the sly humor.

These are thematic readings of Tsai's films. They make the films approachable, easily comprehended within modernist frameworks. But such criticism by and large assimilates Tsai's work within Western modernism, which is not wrong but too general to account for what makes Tsai special, funny, and entertaining. In other words, despite its gravity this kind of critical discourse dilutes Tsai's rich texts for easy digestion. This may be compensation or even reprisal for the eventlessness—effectively, Boredom—in most of Tsai's stories. Worse, it is too literal, assuming Tsai's films are a cinema of pain, alienation, and cruelty instead of seeing them as an attitude, a situation, a setup or put-on, as outrageous, subversive camp. Some writers appeal to Japanese psychoanalytical notions to explain Tsai's work.[8] From time to time, prevailing discourse even spins a mystical aura around the films, especially in French writing, because the more specific, localized contexts fail to catch the eyes of these critics.[9] This doesn't bother Tsai, who usually expresses delight in the ingenuity of French critical fancies.[10]

Strange, too, that most critics seem diffident toward the gay quality of Tsai's films, which is the more patent and sometimes confronting aspect.[11] Is it because Tsai structures gay practices ambivalently, often in the closet, consistent with his repeated distancing of himself from the label of "gay film director"?[12] On the gayness of Lee Kang-sheng (Li Kangsheng) in *Vive l'amour*, Tsai says, "Lee Kang-sheng's character was the most difficult to write because most audiences are interested in gay characters. They think it's a sensational topic. In this regard I have to be cautious when I write a character like this because I do not want the audience to come to the film because it's a gay film."[13] Like most directors, Tsai is afraid of being labeled; he implies also a wish to avoid sensationalizing gay sexuality. Camp allows a resistance to being pinned down. Far from diluting gayness, camp provides a greater role for Tsai's gay elements, especially when they are lodged together with competing sexual and class affiliations. Camp allows gay characters, behavior, and style more freedom to be eccentric, unpredictable, and human. Gayness is wedged, not amalgamated, into various social roles and vocations in the films. It is not the province of a subcultural particular, but for Tsai gay is a plural identity and the attendant politics are similarly stirred up. In Tsai's films camp does not displace gay practices but instead compounds the ironies and contradictions of straight, normative society.

Why camp? Put simply, because of class, ethnicity, and black humor. As a gay filmmaker celebrating *song*, Tsai's films stage a critique, or at least a mockery, of "bourgeois assimilationism" and middle-class fantasies of belonging.[14] There's always a gap between the drifters that populate Tsai's films and the trappings of family and community life surrounding them. Of course camp is not the same as irony, sarcasm, satire, travesty, and so forth. But the space between characters' imagination and their material circumstances forms a camp site. Gay yearnings in the films often come down on the side of imagination, including ideology and self-delusion. This may explain why Tsai is reluctant to identify as a "gay film director." Consider a simple example of cross-dressing.

In *Vive l'amour* there's a moment when Xiao Kang dons women's clothing and flounces about in front of a mirror, appreciating himself. What is Xiao Kang doing? It seems to be a brief drag queen performance, camping up the budding sensuality of a young girl (as if to sing "I feel pretty . . . "). Is he for real? Despite his gay abandon, is this "a specifically queer discourse," an instance of queer sexual parody?[15] Or rather, is it a burlesque of domesticity? Like casually tossing dirty laundry into a churning Jacuzzi, Xiao Kang is doing improv. He's an impersonator playing at being a house-wife, happily feeding and washing his oblivious male love object while squatting in a vacant luxury flat. The camp effect here centers on bourgeois domesticity and the insouciant pleasures of home ownership, like children playing house. (Recall Charlie Chaplin's casual boredom as he expertly prepares to carve a boiled shoe in *The Gold Rush*). In camping domesticity, Tsai and alter ego Xiao Kang conjure a blissful aspiration of residence, right of abode, and household labor, much like a realtor's pitch ("Picture yourself . . . "). Xiao Kang's fantasy also accommodates the fact that his love object is heterosexual, motivating his transvestite narcissism. Women, straight and gay, are indispensable in Tsai's world. Every one of his films includes heterosexual desire, but always spliced in with gay or bisexual relations. In his first two films, women mediate unconsummated sexual urges between male protagonists. Later, women "act up" autonomous sexual performances for, by, and between themselves (*What Time Is It There?*, *Goodbye, Dragon Inn*). Camp presents itself in awkward or indeterminate sexual–class–ethnic postures, foregrounding arbitrariness and arbitration, negotiating and parrying the demands of dominating social roles.

Camp questions the peculiar depoliticizing of criticism that tiptoes over the gay, queer, bi, and trans in favor of the Aesthetic. It also does this with class and ethnicity (as we will see in the next section). Camp reveals important ethnic dimensions of Tsai's perennial scenes, much as it touches, sometimes roughly, on Jewish, black, Latino, and other "marginal social identities in general."[16] As Pamela Robertson Wojcik writes of the confluences of sexuality and ethnicity: "camp relies on various essentialist tropes of racial and ethnic difference to construct a porous and mobile queer identity."[17]

In Tsai's first film, *Rebels of the Neon God* (1992), the protagonist secretly destroys a character's motorbike, then spray-paints "AIDS" over it like a malicious tagger. The gesture is highly ironic, a salute of contempt, but it is also camp. Why? First, in this film Xiao Kang is a young boy coming to terms with his gay predilections, along with his dislike of studying and his fascination with hoodlums. Xiao Kang's act is a double repetition of two earlier gestures: the bike's owner had casually vandalized his father's cab (which makes it a revenge gesture). And it reprises the biker's casual *heterosexual* promiscuity, another object of Xiao Kang's fascination, which also makes the AIDS tag a gesture of envy. When the biker smashed his father's mirror and caused a traffic accident, he was riding with a sexy young pickup. It is hard to avoid concluding that the biker boy was showing off for his new girl. As if aware of the drunken threesome (almost) performed by the trio in a recycled "love hotel" room—on sheets still wet from the previous tryst—Xiao Kang happily inscribes on the bike his target's worst fear. This "act of god" excites him, as we shall see.

Though Tsai himself may be shy of political critique within and about his work, a camp approach encourages it. Some writers play down Tsai's homosexual camp in favor of more straightforward, "serious" literary properties.[18] But why diminish a capacity for play in favor of metaphor and symbol, particularly when playfulness is political? Camp enables recognition of the mischievousness and elaborate irony of Xiao Kang's gesture, one of defacement by a homophobic schoolboy. Tsai relies on the prejudicial associations of AIDS by installing "essentialist tropes" of homosexuality in an anonymous, cowardly act. In a delirium, Xiao Kang dances madly when he sees Chen discover the vandalized bike. Later he comes up behind and gently asks if his victim needs help. Whether or not he has homosexual urges toward his handsome antagonist, it is a delicious irony since the working class to which they both belong takes for granted the stigma of AIDS as a "gay disease." In this act Xiao Kang plays the role of a gay-baiting punk, a closeted fairy hiding behind a lewd macho gesture. This in turn is attributed to the folk god Nezha, a supernatural dispenser of bad luck.

Camp is rarely discussed in Asian cinema, let alone Taiwan film.[19] It is daunting because of the implications and stakes in using the concept. Whether camp is exclusive to gay men is a hotly contentious issue.[20] Must it have a sharp political edge, or can it be a sensibility (whose?) indulged in "just" for fun? Must camp be confrontational? If so, what is Barry Humphries' Dame Edna doing selling "oh what a feeling Toyota" on network television? Commercial camp? Or a variation on the appropriations of pop camp? Would this even qualify for what Margaret Thompson Drewal calls "the camp trace," exemplified by Liberace, "America's blue-collar royalty"?[21] What to do with reactionary and misogynist camp? Is camp a traveling show? Does it rely on shared knowledge, unable to cross linguistic and cultural boundaries? Do these boundaries have camp patrols? Given the prominence of impersonation and caricature, as well as stereotyping, purloined mannerisms, and gross exaggeration, it would seem camp is well suited for international passage.

This chapter attempts, as an essay or experiment, to take Taiwan cinema to an unfamiliar domain—camping out—and to bring camp to a foreign territory—camping in. By evoking camp, we hope to illuminate the most intriguing features of Tsai Ming-liang's creative strategies relating to traditions of Chinese popular culture and cinema. We also argue the need to take a converging perspective—camp strategies, canons of film history, and the Taiwan working-class context—on the aesthetic, the cinematic, the local, and the sexual, to examine Tsai's films in their rich textual and historical operations.

Aestheticizing the Local Working Class

Tsai Ming-liang's films are noticeably "provincial"—provincial in respect to his working-class characters and environment, and Tsai's astute audiovisual design that builds an organic world of aesthetic artificiality that can roughly be called Taiwan camp. We chose for discussion areas such as characterization, the mise-en-scène, and folk ritual practices.

The working class element is a highly visible attribute in Tsai's characters. Taxi drivers, petty thieves, roller skating attendants (Miao Tian, Chen Zhaorong, Wang Yuwen in *Rebels*); street hawkers, real estate agents, columbarium salesmen (Chen Zhaorong, Yang Guimei, and Li Kangsheng in *Vive l'amour*), ex-KMT soldiers (Miao Tian in *What Time Is It There?*), elevator operator, pornographer (Lu Xiaoling and her lover in *The River*), film projectionist and ticket girl in *Goodbye, Dragon Inn*. Vocational placement is enhanced by costuming and surroundings. Women's dresses are often markedly tacky and retro: the mother in *The River* dresses like the young girl at the film shoot—cheerleader miniskirt, see-through blouse that reveals the black bra coquettishly worn underneath. Mother seems to have had a checkered background, with her pornographer boyfriend, her restaurant hostess job, and her superstitions. Men nearly always wear white underwear at home; Xiao Kang wears tight T-shirts, loud aloha shirts, and white shoes while Miao Tian's white shirt from the 1960s clearly betrays his background as a retired KMT soldier, called *bebe* (or "old uncles") in the Taiwanese colloquial.

The ethnicity of these old men reveals key aspects of *song*. Distinctions are maintained between mainlander and islander, Mandarin and Hokkien dialect, civil servant and merchant, as well as distinct neighborhoods in the city, like Ximending (West Gate District), Taipei's old entertainment quarter. While these ethnic distinctions are visible, they rarely amount to much dramatic tension, but instead cohabit within the colorful but fading life of *song*. Mainland immigrants and Taiwan natives coexist in Tsai's films, just as they do within Xiao Kang's household. In *The River* (1997), Xiao Kang's mother subjects him to all kinds of Taiwanese folk rituals while his *bebe* father takes him to Western doctors and chiropractors. But in *Rebels* the parents have a row when Mother thinks Xiao Kang is the god Nezha reincarnated. Father in turn finds consolation in the food court, a place for loitering by displaced *bebe* whose haunts have been redeveloped by the government. It's striking that Tsai Ming-liang manages to co-opt the bright yellow arches of McDonald's into the camp aesthetic of *song*.

These characters move around the city doing specific things: visiting stands that sell watermelons and durians, eating tropical fruits (seeds and rinds tossed on the floor), having traditional breakfast at street stalls, patronizing old movie theaters, old department stores, and video arcades. Yet the routines are all aimless; their sense of purpose seems forgotten somewhere, like a lost umbrella.

Much has been said about the relationship between Tsai Ming-liang and Taipei, the capital city of Taiwan. A particular focus of critical scrutiny is the demolition of the former squatters' villages and the ruthless redevelopment of the city, which indicates Tsai's elegy for the disappearance of the old townships.[22] While discourses on the relations between a sensitive artist and his environment are familiar, it remains unclear as to how exactly to consider and understand Tsai's work as city films. If they are about the temporal and spatial dislocations of contemporary Taipei, how do they compare to those urban comedies and thrillers of Edward Yang? What makes their urban scenarios different?

Tsai's cityscape is symbiotic, combining the popular and the marginal: the gaudy, the *song*, the conspicuous, and subliminal as well as the invisible. Instead of panoramic establishing views of the capital, Tsai shows anonymous cubical spaces where people spend most of their time, boxed in: empty, cold, leaking apartments where strangers meet and exchange sex (like Edward Yang's crime thrillers); thief-infested video parlors in which teenagers jiggle their joysticks; plastic McDonald's where retired folks gather and initiate pickups (contrasting with the company's more sterile image as a family and children's fast-food restaurant); cheap gay saunas and "love hotels" for casual sexual contact; claustrophic, haunted elevators, stairwells, and public toilets where inmates shelter, and perform (Yang Guimei's cabaret in *The Hole*) or work (Lu Xiaoling operates the elevator for a Cantonese restaurant in Taipei).

These confined places all share a distinctly shabby, working-class aura, judging from their décor. Even the McDonald's gives off a shady emanation different from the restaurant settings of Edward Yang (like T.G.I. Friday's and the Hard Rock Cafe). In *The River*, Xiao Kang just misses meeting his father in a gay sauna whose décor reflects the cultural tastes of Taiwan's working class. The scene where the father

6.1 The postal service sign, *The River* (1997)

and his pickup (Chen Zhaorong, Tsai's ultimate gay sex object) are about to consummate their sexual contact is crosscut with a spastic Xiao Kang getting dressed for a night out. Xiao Kang's back is to the camera and so his bright green aloha shirt occupies a large portion of the mirror framed-within-the frame. Xiao Kang is next seen walking on an empty skywalk and in the background is an enormous flashing green neon sign for the post office, which reads: friendly and reliable (fig. 6.1). As Xiao Kang enters the sauna, we see a New Year's greeting "gongxi facai" (Wishing you a prosperous New Year) posted on the wall near the entrance. When Xiao Kang passes Chen on his way out, we have a clear picture of the inner partition of the sauna, which is simply a beaded curtain made up of a kitsch Chinese sketch of two birds against a bright red sun. Xiao Kang sees no one attending to the business and he leaves. Back on the skywalk, Chen and Xiao Kang cross paths again, and we see him approach yet another large billboard with "Big Cheap Sale" and a flashing KTV neon sign in the near distance.

A previous scene depicting Miao Tian picking up Chen Zhaorong features another typical cubical setting: a shopping arcade dominated by McDonald's. This scene is rendered with a vivid camp theatricality orchestrated by neon and the choreography of gay cruising. The scene begins with a wide-angle shot of Miao Tian and some other *bebe* sitting inside a McDonald's. When Chen enters the scene, he faces away from the camera, and he gazes through a large glass panel into the food court. Miao returns Chen's look with an active, searching gaze. Chen walks away, and the camera pans left as Miao gets up, exiting the McDonald's. The panning reveals a spectacular

6.2 Neon McDonald's chic, *The River*

array (fig. 6.2). A rectangular boxlike arcade with an iconic yellow M on the up-per right, a red electronic bulletin board flashing commercial blurbs in the middle ground, and far to the back is a small square of fluorescent light with two girls casu-ally shopping. What is stunning about this deep-focus scene is a twisting blue neon light that runs across the ceiling of the shopping arcade, producing a strongly reces-sive composition that guides the eye along the corridor top, bottom, and both sides, to the vanishing point. This space resembles an ornate, intimate theater where two gay men intensely size each other up. "Cruising" appears vividly as sexually focused, articulated gazes.[23] Body movements, lighting up cigarettes, measured pacing, and casual pauses—all build to a peculiar but discreet queer aura.

This beautiful composition bears comparison with Edward Yang's tunnel visions (chapter 3), lending historical depth through lighting and compositional gauntlets. Where Yang uses amber tungsten, flickering in and out due to the brownouts of the early 1960s, Tsai emphasizes neon, which never falters or blinks, unlike the conventional melancholy of film noir neon. Tunnel visions in Yang's films (as well as in Hou Hsiao-hsien's), drag the eyes into a vortex of possibilities. Deep space as set up by Tsai is repellent, shining with a glassy, inanimate chill. Tsai's staging of a gay pickup in such "anywhere" places shows sophisticated high-fashion artifice tinged with threat. As they stalk the food court, the wariness of these two men has the precision of a tableau vivant by Prada. Any quality of human connection or heat is missing from this ritual, having more to do with design than desire. Tsai's treat-ment turns *song* into an elaborate rite of gay style.

Fetish Objects

A few more recurring visual motifs can be drawn from the mise-en-scène. The first shot of *What Time Is It There?* has a singular familiarity to Tsai's fans. Father Miao Tian sits in front of the dining table, getting ready to eat his dumplings. A green Ta-tung (Datong, "everyone the same") brand rice cooker is on display in this domestic scene of the Taiwanese family. Ta-tung rice cookers are arguably the most useful and used *Taiwanese* household appliances. Locally made, the rice cooker is a multifunctional appliance that can steam rice, fry vegetables, cook seafood, and heat leftovers. Its simple design makes it easy to use, for whole families as well as singles. Long before the Crock-Pot or microwave ovens, Ta-tung rice cookers were a must-have electrical device for Taiwanese when they went abroad.

If we recall the beginning of *Rebels of the Neon God*, the domestic setting is identical, with the rice cooker (this time in red) located in exactly the same spot inside exactly the same apartment. In *The River*, Tsai's most accomplished film, the Ta-tung cooker is again placed on the dining table of Xiao Kang's home. Its prominence in the home invites a semiotic account. On the one hand, it serves as an important prop because it is cast as the family kitchen or hearth. Nowhere in the film is the family seen cooking their food, although there is a brief cooking scene in *Rebels*. But in *The River* each of the family members eats alone, and when they do they eat pretty much the same food from the same rice cooker—rice and leftover barbequed meat from the mother's restaurant.

On a different level, the rice cooker can be seen as a crucial visual motif, pointing toward aesthetic and stylistic motivations (figs. 6.3, 6.4, and 6.5). The Ta-tung rice cooker, precisely because of its quotidian familiarity and uniformity, opens for stylistic business: transformation into something extraordinary. The cooker is framed insistently, not for the characters but for spectators who are invited to appreciate Tsai's aesthetic stunt. To what extent can a humble rice cooker be presented as an aesthetic fetish? As the name says, all Ta-tung rice cookers are supposed to be the same except when they alternate in color between green and red (originally the rice cooker was released in white). Perhaps the alternation shows the cooker needs to be replaced every few years, anticipating obsolescence. Green and red are the colors that Tsai often uses to construct a garishly camp but alienated family environment. We call this camp because Tsai defamiliarizes—or better, *deforms*—the familiar and the everyday. The Ta-tung cooker sits there innocently, which Susan Sontag calls "naïve camp,"[24] yet it's transformed from daily household item to an aesthetic object, morphing across several films from an unnoticeable piece to a thing of distinction calling for our attention. It is notable, furthermore, that this camp device is nostalgic, resting on the concept of time warp, or even pastoral— linked with old and forgotten household items, be they appliances, kitsch décor,

6.3, 6.4, and 6.5 Rice cookers in *Rebels of the Neon God* (1992), *The River* (1997), and *What Time Is It There?* (2001)   (COURTESY LIN MENGSHAN)

6.4

6.5

people, or films. This temporal development unfolds between Tsai's early and late films. By *What Time Is It There?* (2001), the director's fifth feature, the rice cooker will have accumulated a certain aura, just like Tsai's repeated use of the same apartment, furnishings, and cast. In *Goodbye, Dragon Inn*, a rice cooker keeps company with the lame ticket girl in her lonely booth. She uses it to steam a birthday peach bun (*shoutao*) for Xiao Kang, the oblivious projectionist upstairs. Wrapped in plastic, the peach bun initially fails to catch Xiao Kang's attention. But when the ticket girl puts it back into the rice cooker, which she leaves for Xiao Kang as her farewell token on her final day at work, Xiao Kang discovers it and brings the cooker and a piece of her heart home with him.

A similar camp object is seen in the Chinese calligraphy, part of the household décor. In *What Time Is It There?*, a piece of black-and-white calligraphy is hung up in the living room. *Qinai jingcheng* (kinship, love, devotion, and sincerity) is a four-character motto used by Taiwan's late president Chiang Kai-shek to lift military morale in the good old anti-Communist days. But in the context of Taiwan society of the 1990s and onward, this calligraphy would appear utterly outmoded even though it was, again, a common household item in many KMT-affiliated families. Here it is treated as kitsch, an article that has a specific historical resonance but now completely discredited. It recalls the immediate postwar period, and also signifies regression to a cult of personality. Generalissimo Chiang used to be the definitive symbol of patriarchy, of semidivine masculinity for the KMT soldiers—like Miao, the father character who settled on the island in the name of the fatherland.

It is appropriate then to see the picture of the deceased Miao Tian juxtaposed with Chiang Kai-shek in kitsch form, a round dish stamped with Chiang's face. This juxtaposition occurs in one of the most campy, uncanny scenes in *What Time Is It There?* When the mother (Lu Yijing, formerly known as Lu Xiaoling) enters the father's room one night in her nicest dress (a *qipao* with a conspicuous floral pattern, a pearl necklace, and coiffure (a flower in her head) (fig. 6.6), the camera pans to the picture of Miao Tian at the desk, sitting next to that of Chiang Kai-shek. The mother lies on the bed, rubbing the father's rattan pillow against her thighs. This uncovers the mother's frustration and longing. Stylistically, Tsai orchestrates it in the campiest mode. The mother performs a masquerade, making herself up like a lascivious teahouse lady, pouring wine to the deceased husband and his old generalissimo. After the toast, she crawls onto his bed, making love to herself.

When—through various apparitions—the mother believes that the father has returned to the family, she becomes infatuated with the fat white fish in the tank. One sleepless night, she kisses the fish through the glass. The act fuses superstition, sexual desire, and surreal artificiality in a working-class setting. This allows Tsai to frame a moment of extreme privacy in exaggerated fashion. Under glassy

6.6 Lu Yijing in mourning, *What Time Is It There?* (2001)   (COURTESY LIN MENGSHAN)

blue light, the mother's face is bisected by the edge of the tank; and though she talks longingly to the fish, it may be its liquid world that attracts her, a languid, watery realm that gently cradles and appears to flow through the creature's body. There is nothing strange about a woman grieving for her spouse, feeling desolate. But Tsai's treatment makes it uncomfortably intimate, like a séance, evoking plaintive calls of the dead and hocus-pocus. Again, a gap is opened between the outer and inner worlds, leading once more to doubts about emotional excess, affect: "Shun affectation! [writes physiognomist John Bulwer in 1644] for all affectation is odious; and then others are most moved with our actions when they perceive all things to flow, as it were, out of the liquid current of nature."[25] The lady's intimacy also seems absurd because of the fish's unwitting role in this transfer of affect.

Folk Rituals and Their Aesthetic Sediment

By deforming the everyday, it becomes aestheticized, pronounced, and enlivened. This stylistic strategy comes across in all Tsai's films. The everyday includes peculiar living spaces, unusual places of work and, especially, practices of Taiwan's folk rituals. Well aware of their curiosity to outsiders (because he is, or once was one), Tsai is drawn to rituals such as shamanism and folk remedies for their everyday otherworldliness. They are special opportunities for Tsai to synthesize camp and ethnography. Tsai's first film, *Rebels of the Neon God*, literally records folk beliefs and forecasts Tsai's repeated presentation of these practices. These fascinate in their sheer spectacle, as well as their value to a significant segment of Taiwan's working class, predominantly women. Like Pentecostals and faith healers, Taiwan folk religion presents a theater of faith, "just in case" cynicism, and ethnographic exoticism. In *Rebels* we see a traditional folk ritual in a Taoist temple performed on a frightened little boy, with Xiao Kang's mother in the background looking impressed.

What's translated in the title as "Neon god" (Nezha), in most Chinese folklore is a young prince known to be feisty, rebellious, and impetuous. In *Rebels*, Xiao Kang's parody of Nezha is a hilarious practical joke played on his parents. They argue about whether Xiao Kang is Nezha's reincarnation because Nezha hates his father for trying to imprison him. Xiao Kang's father has no patience whatsoever for such superstition. In a wide-angle, high shot down onto the familiar table, we see Xiao Kang in a hallway in the background. Barely visible, he faces the wall and starts to wiggle. At first he appears to be handling himself, breathing hard. Alarmed, his parents jump up from the table and question him. Then Xiao Kang goes into a wild dance, kicking off his slippers and prancing about in what he thinks might look like spirit possession. Cut to a close-up of Xiao Kang, his terrified parents in the background. He starts to whoop like a savage, shaking his head and flapping his arms. Instead of laughing, his parents are mortified. Miao Tian only ends the performance by hurling a rice bowl, which shatters next to Xiao Kang's head. For a doleful exposé of Taipei youth, this small comic outburst from the normally taciturn Xiao Kang is a camp gem.

The best example of turning folk religious rituals to aesthetic purpose comes from the series of unorthodox medical practices in *The River*. The folk remedies that Xiao Kang undergoes in order to cure his strange illness include shamanism, two kinds of Taiwanese chiropractic massage, vibrators, and acupuncture (fig. 6.7). These curing scenes are like ethnographic spectacles in which the doctors perform specialized skills, much like kung fu. The patient endures excruciating pain as the treatment becomes worse than the illness itself. When Xiao Kang's family takes over in a story of diagnosis and increasingly radical treatments, illness and healing start to compete in outlandishness. There is no reason to suppose the clattering, automatic writing of the Taoist soothsayer is staged. Indeed, the narrative premise may only be a pretext for the presentation of a series of exorcisms each more bizarre than the last. Nevertheless, Tsai's procession of Taiwanese cures *is* exotic, and possibly camp, just as the presentation of Xiao Kang's contorted symptoms is. These are themselves darkly comic, in that the exaggerated grimaces and contortions, not to mention his spasmodic movements, are so excessive. They are reminiscent of a Chaplinesque parody of mechanization.

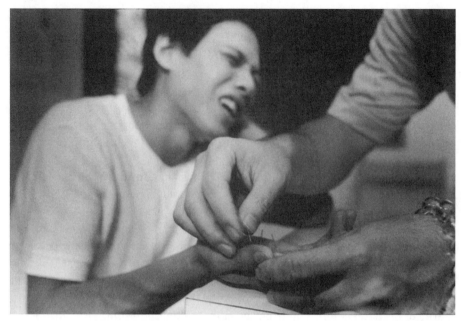

6.7 Xiao Kang and his ritual treatment, *The River*   (COURTESY LIN MENGSHAN)

The Hole

Tsai's most obvious use of camp comes in the musical fantasies that pepper this film. In its narrative premise, *The Hole* (1998) is unrelentingly bleak. It is a simple tale of survival within a quarantined neighborhood sometime in the near future. The locale, a public housing block, is both familiar and uncanny, depopulated, plagued, and evacuated. Residents have either died of the mysterious, cockroach-borne Taiwan flu, or they have abandoned ship. Not only have authorities shut off the water supply, something is wrong with the climate. The deluge is constant, along with the occasional garbage bag flung down from an upper unit. With a diluvian gloom shrouding the action, there is hardly any distinction between night and day; nothing is left to do except wait, and sometimes go fetch supplies from an abandoned wet market (traditional Asian market with livestock, fish, produce). But one day a plumber arrives and inexplicably leaves a gaping hole in the floor of Xiao Kang's flat, opening an aperture onto the life below, that of May (Yang Guimei).

We might say "straight" camp is at play here because the fumbling encounters between protagonists are mediated by five garish production numbers. These cabaret numbers are taken from the popular songs of Grace Chang (aka Ge Lan), a major Hong Kong movie and singing star of the late 1950s and 1960s. The dank, dystopian setting is abruptly interrupted by nostalgic Technicolor hues of outmoded Mandarin pop music. Like a mirage, these numbers are generated by May's

6.8 May's camp production number, *The Hole* (1999) (COURTESY LIN MENGSHAN)

fantasies (or delirium) because at one point she shows signs of the dreaded Taiwan flu (scrabbling on a filthy floor among the soaked wastepaper). The contrast between her material plight and the fantasy sequences could not be more stark. The point of the film is the contradiction between the predicament of the apartment dwellers and the outlandish projections of the frustrated, waterlogged woman. Her appearance as the glamorous showgirl in each of the camp numbers indicates the fantasies are hers (fig. 6.8), running a range of nightclub hits like "Oh, Calypso," "Gesundheit!" and the famous 1958 Shanghai hit "Wo yao nide ai" (I want your love), with English lyrics by J. Hendricks: "Listen to your mama and you never will regret it and if anybody wonders you can tell them that I said it. . . . It's time for you to give me a little turtle loving baby, hold me tight, and do what I tell you." Each song-and-dance is sillier and more extravagant than the last. The fantasies are heterosexual, with May pursuing a ludicrously pomaded Xiao Kang, flapping his arms in a white tuxedo as he pretends to flee.

But the production numbers' feverish hunger not only for sexual gratification but for grand, glam style ironizes the performance and takes it way over the top—not just because of the dark, pestilential setting but because of how May presents the songs. By herself, and with a number of female and male dancers, May's lip-synch camps up the songs with outrageous feathery boas, coquettish, not-quite-professional moves, and come-hither mugging for the camera. *Niurou chang*, "beefsteak songs," is what Taiwanese viewers might call them, referring to the scantily clad girls who shimmy and sing at funeral folk processions in the countryside. Needless to say, May's rendition of Grace Chang is quintessentially *song*: gaudy, vulgar, tawdry, saucy, loose, ersatz, smelling of the street if not the gutter, and very Taiwanese. This is despite the songs' colonial associations, calling to mind other worlds, the glitter of Shanghai and Hong Kong nightclubs, movie musicals, and ultimately Hollywood.

Like a karaoke routine, these interludes have an expressive, cathartic function. Tsai got permission from EMI Records to use its music only by promising to allow the company to use his film clips to make karaoke videos (KTV). When Tsai met Grace Chang, she was surprised at his choices because they are not her best-known songs. [26] According to Tsai,

> The musical numbers play a different role here than they do in other musicals. For me it's more like the statement of the inner world, particularly of the female character. This woman is apparently very cold, on the surface she has to be very fierce to fight her environment, she's very defensive. But her inner world is very passionate and she craves somebody to love her. . . . I think that toward the end of the century a lot of qualities—such as passionate desire, naïve simplicity—have been suppressed. The musicals contain those qualities. It's something that I use psychologically to confront the world.[27]

Within the fantasy sequences, then, there's a gap between sound and image, between Chang's recorded singing and the tacky Vegas-revue choreography, which amounts to burlesque. The songs are great fun but they are changed in the performance, made *song* in the way they are staged, costumed, mimed, and danced. Not very respectful, this appropriation is actually an affectionate send-up of Grace Chang, though Tsai's epigraph to the film duly reads: "Comes the year 2000, and we are grateful that we still have Grace Chang's singing to keep us company." The chasm between the narrative diegesis and the fantasy numbers is matched by an internal bifurcation between the songs themselves, carried by Grace's elegant voice, and their staging as outrageous, trampy camp.

This spectacle clashes with the indelible star image of Grace Chang within the history of Mandarin popular film and music. With a single exception (as the sultry nightclub performer in *The Wild Wild Rose*, 1960), Grace Chang's star image was that of a wholesome girl-next-door type. She was a cheerful, classically trained beauty who appealed to both women and men. A thoroughly modern star, Chang embodies an impeccable image of modern Chinese femininity. She did not have the ethereal, tragic beauty of Lucilla You Min that might have been deemed too "Chinese," or the aggressive sexuality of Linda Lin Dai that seemed too "Western." Chang is a bit of both, without undue theatricality, the perfect blend of ingénue and siren, of activity and stylish grace. This dual quality is exemplified in her starring film roles. In *Mambo Girl*, she is the eponymous teenager who sings and dances to the latest Western pop music. But she is utterly innocent, devoid of sexual interest in men or pursuit of fame. In *Sun, Moon, and Star* (1961), Grace is cast as the moon, a synthesis of the blazing sun played by Julie Yeh Feng and the twinkling, fading star Lucilla You Min.

None of these visual cues is evoked in Tsai's rendition of the songs in *The Hole*, as part of his playful nostalgia for the 1950s and '60s. What we see is an irreverent appropriation of Shanghai/Hong Kong Mandarin popular music à la Grace Chang, scored to a localized image, the indigenous working-class culture of Taiwan. The class distinction of camp, working-class *song* comes forward at the expense of classy star image. Grace Chang is replaced with May's sultry, beefy *song*, carrying the aroma of working-class Taiwan, tinged with torrid masculinity. A sunny colonial metropolis is substituted by the disease-bearing monsoon of Taipei. The cozy bourgeois villas of Hong Kong are transformed into anonymous working-class "citizens' residences" (*guomin zhuzai*). Lively, chattering families have faded to black, and a silent, solitary cubicle becomes the only way of living. In all his films, Tsai evokes "the emotional weather of the closet," Michael Moon's lovely phrase for the damp moldiness of Jack Smith's funky swamp-thing performance-films.[28]

Tsai, like Smith, appropriates pop culture idols of the past in order to both celebrate and lampoon. Writing of Bette Davis and Joan Crawford in *What Ever Happened to Baby Jane?*, Andrew Ross argues that, "The camp effect . . . is created not simply by a change in the mode of cultural production (and the contradictions attendant on that change), but rather when the products (stars, in this case) of a much earlier mode of production, which has lost its power to produce and dominate cultural meanings, become available, in the present, for redefinition according to contemporary codes of taste."[29]

For a 1998 film about the millennium, Tsai's redefinition of 1960s Chinese film stars is a prediction about an emptied-out city whose inhabitants are similarly hollow. Traveling forward into a bleak future, Tsai matches pseudo-science fiction with nostalgic retrojections of an obsolete popular culture. This makes for an ingenious but quite artificial generic synthesis, cobbling together future and past, apocalypse and sweet memory. Like Stanley Kubrick's *Dr. Strangelove*, the incongruity of these audiovisual combinations promotes an extravagant sense of the absurd, together with a haunting evocation that Fredric Jameson has called "nostalgia for the present."[30] Tsai's recombinant genre performance redefines a musical and cinematic tradition as camp, while holding out for its therapeutic power in a cold, clammy world.

Goodbye, Dragon Inn

If *The Hole* is a straightforward use of camp as bulwark or inoculation, *Goodbye, Dragon Inn* is more of a commentary and an elegy. Like *The Hole*, the film has a simple premise. In an old working-class neighborhood, a Japanese tourist runs into a decrepit movie palace to get out of the rain. He finds himself in King Hu's *Dragon Inn* (see chapter 1) on the theater's final day. Inside the hall, patrons loiter and roam, except for two old men, Miao Tian and Shi Jun. These are the actors who appeared in the 1967 *Dragon Inn*, and they rather quizzically watch themselves up on the big screen. Other than this strange pair, people come to the cinema to kill time, to use the toilet, to eat, smoke, and cruise. A subplot concerns a not-quite-budding love story between a lame ticket girl and the projectionist upstairs, played by Tsai's alter ego Xiao Kang.

Tsai incorporates lengthy clips from King Hu's classic film to evoke once again the 1960s and a brighter day of popular mass culture. But again, these martial arts clips are juxtaposed with a present-day urban environment containing a homosexual ghost story. Male sexuality is the thread that links the two worlds. This is a variation on the pattern established in *The Hole*. The Japanese tourist, apparently seeking a liaison, encounters potential partners as well as the perennial Yang Guimei in her most *song* outfit and behavior (methodically cracking and spitting watermelon seeds) and a few other lost souls who appear to be ghosts. The film touches on superstition, contagion, and transport back to a more robust era of popular Chinese culture, specifically through the martial arts genre. In this respect Tsai's film is similar to those of Ang Lee through the activation of latent meanings in martial arts. Past stars and present spectators, foreigners and ghosts, gay sexuality and homophobic combat all coexist in Tsai's peculiar time-warped world. If *The Hole* is spiked by five camp production numbers, and *What Time Is It There?* includes two brief clips from Truffaut's *The Four Hundred Blows*, then *Goodbye, Dragon Inn* gives much more time to its titular text, which functions almost as a host, through which the contemporary vignettes unfold parasitically. The vigor and ferocity of King Hu's characters clash with the anemic shadows fumbling in the dark, nearly empty rows of the theater. Almost a reversal of a movies/life dichotomy, life is insubstantial and halting, while the movies dazzle with heroic action. Like *The Hole*, the film's aesthetic rests primarily on the stark duality between a glittering fantasy and the projection's shabby, pedestrian source. But the colorful spectacle projected by *Dragon Inn* is so powerfully sustained that it threatens to overpower the present-day *Goodbye* part, spilling over its screen and drenching the gray lives of its contemporary spectators.[31]

Anachronism, Eroticism: Disappearance of the Movie Palace

The old-time cavernous movie theater, here a place for wandering apparitions, has seen its days as a collective pleasure palace come to an end. It is populated now by hungry ghosts haunting the place where they once reigned, seeking anonymous consolation. Whereas Tsai usually devotes long takes in his other films to characters in

6.9 Surprised by time, *What Time Is It There?* (2001)   (COURTESY LIN MENGSHAN)

private moments (e.g., Miao Tian's endless urination in *The River* and Yang Guimei's weeping at the end of *Vive l'amour*), *Goodbye* features lengthy takes on collective moments: men gathered in a public toilet, washing hands or urinating without any attempt to stop. But Tsai also utilizes the long take to eulogize the sensuous bygone feel of the movie palace. The camera is transfixed by rows of empty seats in the enormous theater on its final day. With an almost intolerable immobility and duration (lasting in fact for two minutes, eighteen seconds), this long take is a farewell to cinema itself as a collective experience of absorption. Writing of *Goodbye's* companion film *The Missing* (2003, dir. Li Kangsheng), Kim Ji-seok says that "familiar surroundings suddenly become unfamiliar through long takes. As a result, the main characters' confusion is palpable to the audience."[32] This palpable confusion clearly indicates an elegiac lingering. It almost defies understanding with its suspension of the diegesis. But it also bids goodbye to King Hu, as an essential part of Tsai's diegesis and a version of dynamic, dynastic Chinese cinema whose popularity partly depends on its obvious homophobia.[33] Mass culture, sustained by a heterosexist norm of masculinity, turns finally into a rather listless subculture of gay cruising.

It's worth noting that this old movie palace, strongly personified in *Goodbye, Dragon Inn*, also makes an appearance in *What Time Is It There?* as the place where Xiao Kang is pursued by a wacky homosexual (fig. 6.9). What in the latter film was only a setting for an amusing encounter (the fat boy pops out of a stall, holding a stolen outsized clock over his [outsized?] cock) is now the major conceit, a grand theater of loss and fond remembrance. A comic gag in the earlier film here becomes the center of attention and thematic basis. Tsai always wants to alert us to the "action" behind the screen. The old movie palace works as a metonymy for a classic screen tradition, an incubator of proscribed practices facilitated by the collective trance of eroticism. This is an eroticism of imminent disappearance, feeding on forbidden (time) zones, trespassing into condemned spaces.

While a mass audience once enjoyed watching films on big screens, the movie palace now provides gay men and ghosts a place to wander. This too will pass. Demolition of the movie palace is more than the loss of the cinema, it is also disappearance of a shelter for gay communities. If Miao Tian and Shi Jun are no longer remembered as stars from the past, the cruising men are themselves now ghosts, roaming deserted nooks and crannies of the old theater. So we see this Japanese gay tourist lost in space and time. Coming all the way to Taiwan, he has entered this old theater, only to find himself hitting on the wrong targets—righteous hero Shi Jun and Chen Zhaorong, who politely reveals that he might be a ghost.

Incongruity

As we've seen in many other films, especially those of Edward Yang, there is a discrepancy between the film's English and Chinese title, *Busan* ("inseparable"), indicating the lingering presence of ghosts within the medium and venue. The English "goodbye" is a fond farewell to classics, to the works of the old fathers saturated with heroic homophobia, and to the cinema. There is palpable ambivalence and incongruity between tenacious nostalgia and the need to part from outgrown practices. In this regard, *Busan/Goodbye* is, like Tsai's previous films, fractured by duality: between reality and fantasy, social norms and psychosexual fancy; between hetero- and homosexuality; between camp and the classics.

Yet this duality has a sense of balance, a delicate coexistence. The divided terms remain bound in tension, and do not assimilate or resolve into a greater synthesis. One of the most memorable moments of *Vive l'amour* is when homosexual Xiao Kang masturbates under the bed, directly beneath a heterosexual coupling. *The River* is about a family living like housemates, suspended uncomfortably rather than in conventional kinship relations. In acute denial, Xiao Kang and his father sleep in the same motel bed, pretending nothing has happened after sexual contact with each other. In *What Time Is It There?* sex occurs simultaneously in three different places, in various forms, as attempted release from loneliness. In *The Hole*, Grace Chang's heavenly voice accompanies Yang Guimei's earthy burlesque. But what lies underneath this coexistence and co-incidence are unsettling moments when libido boils over. Defense mechanisms fail to arrest anxiety's surge up and out into the social body, through homo/hetero/auto-sexual contact. These encounters are always temporary, sublimatory, and they offer no solutions. Thus we see a Sisyphean equilibrium constantly resumed in a kind of perpetual loop.

Unlike *The Hole*, in *Goodbye, Dragon Inn* the long clips from King Hu's film imply criticism. The straight camp of *The Hole* is replaced by a cutting accusation targeting representations of the eunuch. Power in the eunuch comes from a constitutive lack, a fetish for absence. Eunuchs have a special place in Chinese popular cinema, from King Hu and Li Hanxiang to Tsui Hark. In *Swordsman* and *Swordsman II*, Tsui dubs the eunuchs with female voices to enhance their freakish quality. The quasi-demonic eunuch is not a rarity in art cinema either. Recall the staging of the traumatic rape that little Cheng Dieyi (Leslie Cheung) endures in Chen Kaige's *Farewell My Concubine* (1993). Dieyi is brought to the bed of an aging but powerful eunuch one night. What was meant to be an avuncular chat turns into a terrible nightmare. The drunken eunuch wears a *du dou* (traditional underwear to cover women's breasts), with his long gray hair draping down, like a vampire eager to devour the little opera boy as if he were a tasty morsel.

Eunuchs are often stigmatized as sadistic, brazenly androgynous, and very powerful. They are invariably, utterly evil. Their kung fu is practically unassailable, lending them the most masculine proficiency in the martial arts world ("gender without genitals").[34] Like the soaring voice of the castrato, eunuchs' power derives precisely from their lack of ordinary mortal equipment. Such demonization mobilizes a narrative and ritual impulse to kill off eunuchs onscreen. In *Goodbye*, Tsai Ming-liang particularly highlights the conversation in the final battle scene between the great Eunuch Cao and the righteous warriors to uncover the patent homophobia in Chinese classics. After cutting off the ornament of Cao's official headgear, the warriors tease him: "Ah, Eunuch Cao, not only have you already lost your lower part, you can't even keep your upper parts!" Here Tsai promotes an active, resistant reading of the scene, but he does so in the camp style—humorous, playful, tongue-in-cheek. He allows the film to flaunt its prejudices in an old movie theater flooded with all manner of subliminal exchanges and displays of desire.

As elegy for the cinema, *Goodbye, Dragon Inn* embodies contradiction: can't let go (*bu san*, "inseparable") but must, because there is no choice. The movie palace will close down because there is no more audience. Martial arts, the king genre of Chinese popular films, are consigned to the ghostly world of late night TV and video games. King Hu is about to be forgotten, but he is actively appropriated, revivified, and reinterpreted by a younger generation. Ang Lee did it in *Crouching Tiger* and now Tsai has done it even more explicitly, "coming out" from a once dominant but now closeted tradition. Their uses of King Hu work like an homage, but also a critique. They resuscitate "forgotten forms of labor," creating surplus value through "rediscovery of history's waste."[35] Their interventions are nostalgic, but also a salvage and update for twenty-first-century audiences, questioning conventions like the didacticism and homophobia that have outlived their time. These conventions are irresistible, overripe for camp treatment.

the river

Perverse Camp: Rewriting the Chinese "Family Ethical Drama"

Tsai Ming-liang's version of the Family Romance is characteristically twisted. The warped family relations are not bent by black, sarcastic humor so much as a series of structural inversions and displacements. In Tsai's films the triadic relationship is not Oedipal (boy-loves-mother) but anti-Oedipal. Oedipal romance is a sort of family rehearsal for the exchange value of women within patriarchy, but Tsai reverses this. Instead of the son desiring his mother, junior loves his dad. The father does not desire the mother and therefore frustrates the classic competition between father and son. Mother, in turn, may still want to lean on her son as surrogate. Son responds, but in a condensation-displacement of libido he unconsciously transfers onto himself a desire for the father, represses it, and tries to persuade himself that they simply don't get along.

Why is this camp?

One possibility is that Tsai is trying to rewrite family melodrama, which forms the core of the dramatic ethos in Chinese theater, television, and film. *Jiating lunli ju* (literally, "family ethical drama") builds upon Confucian doctrines of the family: hierarchy, unity, and filial piety. *Fu ci zi xiao* (benevolent father–filial son), *xiong you di gong* (respect your elder brother and be a friend to your young brother) constitute the core of Confucian family ethical hierarchy. *Tian lun* ("the order of heaven") is the code often used to describe the family regime where every member assumes her role, where each must behave according to the proper place set for them by Confucian teaching (see also chapter 5).

In the history of modern Chinese dramatic tradition, family ethical drama arose to handle the dilemmas of Confucian family ethics in the modern world. Hierarchy, unity, and filial piety are all under siege by ideas such as personal independence, the headlong pursuit of wealth, and the rise of women's rights. In Chinese drama, crises of the family often appear in the form of a death in the family, the waywardness of a parent, or juvenile delinquency. The happy ending for the Chinese family melodrama is re-union accompanied by a new understanding of parents and children, husbands and wives, together with their mutual obligations.

In Tsai Ming-liang's films we can find the basics of family ethical drama–the problems of relating, failures of communication, personality and perhaps generational conflicts, clashing pursuits, and so on. But the means of reaching an understanding or solution is quite shocking and subversive. Sex, homosexuality, perversion, topics not normally broached in the Chinese family . . . these become the only possible way out. This shock treatment or "coming out" is in stark contrast to the depiction provided by Ang Lee in his Confucian melodramas. Lee acknowledges the awkward relations in his dramas are mostly due to fear of talking, and frankly admitting sexual desire. In this Lee and Tsai share some common ground. And the source is often the aging, repressed father. But Lee's oeuvre is mostly heterosexual where Tsai's is mostly homosexual. In *Eat Drink Man Woman*, father marries the daughter-figure to regain his masculinity (see chapter 5). In *The Wedding Banquet*, father tacitly accepts the gay marriage of his son. In Tsai's *The River*, father literally has sex with his son, unbeknownst to either in an anonymous encounter. The result: Xiao Kang's illness is cured and the family is (temporarily) reunited.

Lee's rewriting of Chinese family melodrama is disturbing but still acceptable to the mainstream because it is heterosexual and patriarchal. *The Wedding Banquet* is heterosexual too because it requires the illegal alien bride as a prop, even while it winks at the naughty firstborn son. Tsai's rewriting is gay, subversive, and mind-boggling in its anti-Oedipal implications. After weeks of physicians, Chinese medicine, acupuncture, chiropractors, folk doctors, and shamans, Xiao Kang hits on the miracle cure: the healing power of homosexual incest. This might be funny, as his ailment itself is darkly humorous, if it weren't such a nasty shock.[36]

The scene takes place in darkness. Two bodies are just visible, but what is most salient are the long hands creeping over and around the body in front. The dark composition creates strong chiaroscuro while the sinister fingernails shine out. Figure placement is identical to an early scene in a bathhouse. Here Miao Tian was trying to push young Chen to perform fellatio. Chen resists. In this later climactic moment the setup and lighting are identical, though the action happens in a different town, where father and son are visiting a temple. Both bathhouse scenes have a strange classical quality, composed like a pietà painting, a sacrificial Christ being held from behind by his distraught mother (fig. 6.10).

Can we call this "camp"? Indeed we can, when we also recall what initiated Xiao Kang's ailment in the first place. It is commonly assumed that he is stricken because he reluctantly becomes a body double for a film, playing a corpse floating in the filthy Tanshui River. But what happens next? He gets a hot shower in a nearby motel, some refreshments, and then Xiao Kang couples with the young woman (Chen Xianqi) who invited him to the shoot. She disappears, and Xiao Kang soon starts to grimace, screw up his neck, and crash his motorbike. Can she be the cause of his illness? From this point on, Xiao Kang's whole body is a rictus of suffering and humiliation. His frame seizes up, twisting itself into painful contortions. One cannot but feel Tsai's diabolical instructions, all in the name of convincing behavior that's camera-ready. We are set up for this at the beginning. The perfection-

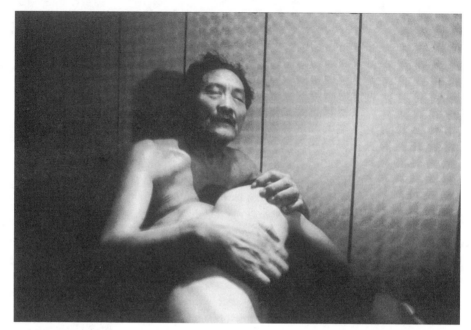

6.10 Reverse Oedipal romance, *The River*　　　　　(COURTESY LIN MENGSHAN)

ism of Hong Kong film director Ann Hui who, playing herself, rejects a floating dummy and cajoles Xiao Kang to enter the water, is matched by Tsai's. Like Hui, he too implicitly casts himself as cajoling puppet master. There is sadomasochistic humor here, since the symptoms manifested by Xiao Kang may be acted, simulated—*but not his immersion in the river.* The act of floating facedown in the Tanshui River is the same, whether committed by the character of Xiao Kang or actor Lee Kang-sheng. This early scene puts him—character and actor—in harm's way.

The river stunt straddles the border between fact and simulation, fudging distinctions between performance as agency and as make-believe. It casts Xiao Kang as a living dummy on which desires of directors, spectators, and other characters are inscribed.[37] Yet the river itself might well be a red herring, if we weigh other suspects in the etiology of Xiao Kang's illness. Heterosexual fornication may be a culprit, given Xiao Kang's latent homo- or bisexuality. But it could be anything, even an allergy. Perhaps it's the water he drinks or the lunch box he devours at the shoot before he enters the filthy water. Is it because he sits under the tail of a great stone lion, feeding stray dogs? The river stunt itself is an excuse, invitation, or even seduction, proffering a rush to judgment. Just as the river is used as "coverage" for any number of causes, so Ann Hui is cast as a demanding, castrating film director, a stand-in for Tsai himself. Finally, the series of treatments are delinked from any connection to Xiao Kang's symptoms because they are scattershot, approaching various trouble spots from different premises, all assuming different lines of cause and effect (physical, chemical, energies, auras, evil spirits, etc.). Tsai is a trickster, offering various possibilities, some wildly implausible, for understanding the dynamics of pathology.

There's a certain humor with which Tsai handles duration. His extra-long takes show morbid, puerile curiosity for the body's natural functions. How much did Miao Tian drink in order to urinate for as long as he does in a transitional shot in *The River*? The camera patiently continues to run along with the old man's seemingly endless flow. In *Vivre l'amour* the close-up of May crying in the park runs for nearly six minutes while the shot of rows of empty theater seats in *Goodbye, Dragon Inn* seems to run forever. This is real time, issuing from the director's interest in duration itself, at the expense of breaking diegetic flow and driving spectators to distraction. "How far will you follow me?" Tsai seems to ask. It also seems to be a pushing of generic boundaries, a cryptic form of parody, à la Jacques Tati, which skewers a technical hallmark of the New Cinema and art films in general.

Camp Economy

Tsai Ming-liang plunders the world's library of moving images. His explicit citation of film traditions, both Chinese and European, gives the films a strong paratextuality. This distinguishes Tsai from other intertextual Taiwan directors, though we have just compared him with Ang Lee, whose homage to King Hu in *Crouching Tiger* can be understood as more deferent, though renovative. In his incorporation of other filmmakers and performers (King Hu, François Truffaut, Grace Chang), Tsai could be seen as derivative, frivolous, even parasitical, leaning perhaps too heavily on styles and themes of the past. He does this repeatedly, as if he is running out of ideas. At the same time, the films do a great service to their source material, encouraging (re)discovery of a classic period and showing impeccable taste in their choice cuts. Tsai's selections are meticulously chosen and painstakingly matched with the progress of his story. This gives the films camp value, as well as contemporary referentiality by including moving images and narratives that surround him and his characters.

Just as Tsai's walls and doors seem always festooned with kitsch greetings wishing a "Prosperous Lunar New Year" (*Gongxi facai*), his characters inhabit a world of moving images from cinema, television, and video. Given their closeted, alienated lives, it is plausible characterization to integrate long clips of film, video, or porn into the diegesis. Where does this impulse to infuse images come from? Why do these specters from the past form such an important part of Tsai Ming-liang's space? Rather than answer this categorically, we might consider Tsai Ming-liang's background.

Although his films are always contemporary, the references to film and popular culture derive from Tsai's childhood memories of Kuching (1957–1978), his days working in avant-garde theater (1982–1984); his job as a television writer (1982–1987), and miniseries director (1989–1991).[38] In Malaysia, Tsai's father and grandfather both ran a street noodle stall all their lives. But this did not mean Ah Liang had a boyhood of privation. A spoiled child, he was always being taken to the movies by his grandparents. They even did his homework for him. Instead of studying, Ah Liang enjoyed the dream world of Mandarin musicals produced by Cathay Pictures and Shaw Brothers expressly for the greater Chinese diaspora.

As a fresh college graduate, Tsai showed a gift for experimental theater in his first three plays: *Instant bean sauce noodles* (Sushi zajiang mian, 1982), *A sealed door in the dark* (Heian li dabukai de yi shan meng, 1983), and *The closet in the room* (Fangjian li de yigui, 1984). *A sealed door* depicts a contradictory relationship between two inmates kept in the same prison cell. A young inmate arrives at the cell of an older prisoner, who immediately takes advantage of the new roommate by stealing his clothes. The two gradually become friends and their relationship changes from territorial rivalry to sharing a rapport as well as a cell. Without warning, the older inmate rapes his cohort. Their relationship becomes tense once more. The young inmate is later released, only to return again to the same cell, with the same old friend. It seems to be a story of compulsion, futility, and endless returns. *The closet in the room* is about a love crisis that a writer undergoes while completing a script in his tiny bedroom. The writer receives a phone call from his lover, who is getting married. The desperate protagonist then discovers someone living in his closet. He begins to react, and the closet reciprocates. Tsai directed, wrote, and acted in the apparently autobiographical *The closet in the room*.[39]

Clearly, in the early days when Tsai was a young theater director, he had already embraced a vanguard, minimalist style along with a wry undertone. In these plays, he explores issues of gay love, sadomasochistic power relations, spatial confinement, affection for the closet, passing, double identity, the loneliness of writing and writer's block, and queer identity. We may conclude that queer-minimalist style is one of Tsai's main creative impulses, drawing in the dank "moldiness" of the closet.[40] It should be remembered, though, that for Tsai the closet is not just a confining lockup but also enveloping and familiar. Much as the outside world may entice, the closet is secure, warm, like a womb. Recall, after all, the etymology of the "camera," an enclosed room.[41]

Another of Tsai's impulses can be traced back to his exertions for television, as writer and director. Tsai was hired by the military-owned Chinese Television System to write thirty episodes of a prime-time soap called *Endless love* (Bu liao qing, 1989).

It was a huge success, and Tsai asked his producer to allow him to direct a six-episode series called *The sky of the little people* (Xiao zhimin de tiankong). Here, Tsai no longer dwells on the closet or the prison cell. He goes to those seedy pockets where young girls work as prostitutes and a little boy helps the family business by hustling in the street. One episode called "All the corners of the world" (Haijiao tianya) is particularly brilliant. It was noted by Tony Rayns as the world's best TV program in 1989.[42]

Tsai Ming-liang's films indicate a synthesis of these two impulses: experimental avant-garde crossed with queer issues and the *song*; the Taiwanese working class and their daily, sometimes preposterous conundrums. If the former can be seen as universal, as part of an international art movement, the latter is particular, provincial, and Taiwanese. Put together, we find a peculiar form of camp, with the cool, wry humor of queer minimalism intersecting with a warm regard for the vitality of street life. Given Tsai's background as an outsider from Southeast Asia, his detachment is tinged with nostalgia for his noodle stand–matinee movie provinciality. Now educated, experienced, and living in a cosmopolitan city, Tsai embraces the charm, backwardness, and imminent obsolescence of *song* not as native Taiwanese but as a fellow traveler. In this Tsai is something of an ethnographer, salvaging bits and pieces of what is increasingly a lost Taipei.

Tsai's background as a second-generation Chinese immigrant in Malaysia and his émigré status in Taiwan helps account for his outsider observation of people and the physical environment around them. It goes part way toward explaining the films' aesthetic of loneliness. As a child, Tsai saw his grandmother turn their home into a private gambling den. He was mortified by this, but he was also able to observe all kinds of people who patronized the grandmother's business.[43] At one time Tsai was living much like his drifting, feckless characters: before college, he worked as an obituary salesman for a local Chinese newspaper in Kuching;[44] as an overseas college student (*qiaosheng*) in Taiwan, he did all kinds of odd jobs to support himself, like delivering lunch boxes; he always lived a hand-to-mouth existence in several low-income neighborhoods in Taipei.[45] These experiences placed Tsai in the lower depths of Taiwan's society, immersing him in the working class and the streets. Tsai was not slumming, or doing fieldwork. The special street life of places like Ximending and public housing *guomin zhuzai* really is Tsai's element. Like a rich floating theater of life, it provided him with potent ingredients as he went on to transcribe this living theater to the screen.

Song as Foreign Country

What can we make of all this? How can this unruly heterogeneous experience comprise the meticulous film aesthetic of Tsai Ming-liang? Does camp organize or unify the preoccupations of this filmmaker, or help explain his style?

Three propositions may serve to summarize how camp concerns Tsai Ming-liang's films. These touch on geographical, temporal, and colonial movement, concerning upward mobility, salvage, and aesthetic reconstruction. Camp typically opens and exploits a gap or distance between its practitioner and its object, subjected to a select parodic play. That this parody must be gay, or queer, is a point of contention in the literature. Tsai the artist *is* gay and his films, seen with a camp sensibility, do seem queer, with respect to working-class Taiwan *song* as well as sexual fantasy, genre, and what we have called paratextuality. The gap may be historical, cultural, gendered, or sexual but it is always initiated and inflected by the camper, not the "campee." The camp performer, skillfully or not, exploits the distance between himself and mock-up, animating the straight material at hand. Inducing it to speak a queer language, the camp artist is, at least for a while, in full control. This is the basis for the aristocracy of taste in the notion of camp, that the marginalized are the elite when they exercise camp performance.[46]

Here we may find a point of difference between Tsai and camp. Most camp performance is an active reclaiming of things mainstream society denies. Tsai is more passive. In other words, he is himself a product of *song*—which is itself camp—and he waits for something elusive, recognizing fugitive versions of it in a rapidly modernizing Taipei. Crass, unpresentable *song* is what the dominant classes of Taipei would rather not face and, in any case, it is going the way of the rickshaw. The gap, but also the resonance between cosmopolitan Taipei and sleepy Kuching, is precisely what facilitates Tsai's cinematic rendering of working-class *song*. Tsai has actually suffered for this, losing out on prizes because he remains a permanent resident, not a citizen of Taiwan.[47] It also accounts for the films' modesty, which is completely at odds with the camp aristocracy, so derisory and bitchy. Unlike the assertive strategy of queer self-invention through parody, camp inhabits the structure of *song* in which Tsai is immersed. He is more like a medium than a drag queen. The marginality, obsolescence, and backstreet invisibility are inherent in the subject matter and filmmaker so the task of the camp filmmaker is to explore and somehow capture it. Because of Tsai's affinity for the Taiwan *song*, his films project a displaced version of his own history, tracing elements of his childhood experiences in a new place and time.

While his features are not documentaries, Tsai has considerable experience with nonfiction film and television.[48] The films are richly stylized and the characters are stately, even in their lonely shells. This topicality and compassion enhances Tsai's surrealist ethnography of Taiwan's *song* demimonde. Accordingly, the first proposition is this: the idea of upward mobility finds camp expression in Tsai Ming-liang. This refers to a geographical movement. In the first instance, it involves class and its respective neighborhoods. The Taiwan middle class lords it over the small shops and arcades of the old neighborhoods, dominating the city's public life. Its domination will eventually exterminate the *song* but, meanwhile, Tsai vividly inscribes it. More individually, Tsai's own upward mobility ascends from the tropics (Malaysia), up into the temperate zone of the contemporary metropolis. Once there, however, he does not fully assimilate but discovers remnants of the old *song*, muddling along in the margins and gutters. Wherever Tsai goes, *he brings it with him* (even to Paris) because he is always searching for it.

Second, a temporal movement: by salvaging *song*, Tsai resurrects his own lost youth. Salvage ethnography is a key tradition in modern anthropology, involving documentation of cultures that are about to disappear. Edward Curtis, Robert Flaherty, Jean Rouch, and many others used film and photography to record tribal practices they knew to be vanishing. Tsai Ming-liang, too, salvages, or rescues, precious objects and moments of Taiwan's forgotten culture of *song*. The difference is that unlike Western anthropological motivations ("eldest daughter of colonialism," admitted Jean Rouch), Tsai's is personal and existential.[49] He finds great comfort in discovering pockets of superstition, moldy objects, or tacky costumes because these arouse emotional (not scientific) links to the past. While such pockets as a derelict movie theater are very personal to Tsai, they are remnants that middle-class consumer society would much rather forget because they interfere with the business of modernity. Especially in its indifference to action and event, Tsai's privileging of "empty" moments, salvaging *song*, is contrary and narcissistic, and more than a little perverse. It betrays fetishism and, because of its stress on loss and extinction, its method is disintegrative, discontinued, taxidermic. Salvage, even when collecting images that resonate personally, is activity based on pathological, even necrophilic, premises.[50] Anthropologist Jacob W. Gruber explains this in a paper published in 1959: "The fact was that the very notion of salvage insisted on the investigation of those sociocultural systems already in an advanced state of destruction; as with the development of medicine itself it was the abnormal that set the norm of investigation."[51]

Third, camp in Tsai's films has a colonial movement in that *song* is reconstructed through style. Salvage depends on recognition of disappearance and desire for preservation. The pathology of salvage points to the regression of imperial desire and nostalgia. This may be experienced not only by aging imperialists but by ex-colonials as well.[52] We have noted the upward mobility (geographical/class), the salvage (temporal), and now, camp style as a response to the colonial. In its meandering pace, its long takes, artificial cinematography and acting, genre-bending, and paratextual quotation, Tsai's film style renders *song* ascetic, like the example of the McDonald's food court. This is camp because an ascetic film style is incongruous, ill-suited, generating a sense of inappropriateness and misfit. The idea can be stated simply, if oxymoronically: *song* chic.

Why is this colonial? First, because the basic materials of *song* always feel out-of-date and hailing from periods outgrown and under erasure. By analogy these echoes recollect the stages of Taiwan's containment within martial law (KMT), the Cold War (United States and the PRC), and imperial occupation (Japan). Tsai's bending and twisting of his lowly materials inevitably changes them, turning them in the direction of queer minimalism. The ascetic, critical presentation of King Hu and the decline of the movie palace not only underlines their deterioration but glorifies it. It is as if Tsai were a sculptor using carcasses or corpses in various states of decay (cf. Dali and Buñuel). If this sounds unpleasant and regressive, consider the witty imagination with which Tsai stylizes his stock characters and situations. The ingenuity with which extravagant style occupies humble surroundings makes both stand out, enlivening through decomposition (e.g., the Ta-Tung rice cooker). To say Tsai occupies or colonizes typically Taiwanese material means he reconstructs the local in a sophisticated, international art form. Quite plainly, Tsai's audience is not the kind of people he writes about and films. It is at once a cultural transformation, opening small things out onto an expansive stage, and a transposition from a sociocultural onto an aesthetic platform. It might be more fitting to call this a postcolonial camp gesture because it changes mainstream pop camp (or camp trace) appropriations of queer discourse, not to return to antagonistic homosexuality but to resituate camp—gay and queer—within style and experiment, opening up forms that will effect thought-change.

"I do not want the audience to come to the film because it's a gay film," Tsai has divulged (see note 13). Is he for real? Instead of playing identity politics, Tsai's films toy with us, keeping us guessing about his motivations but, more importantly, puzzling out the mechanics of emotional discharge in a boxed-in world. Recall one of the signature images from his first film, *Rebels of the Neon God*: wastewater bubbling up against a rag hastily stuffed into a drain. From the camp aristocracy of taste to a more mysterious absorption into overlooked aesthetic sediment, and sentiment, Tsai Ming-liang's camp site is a slippery place.

Postscript

TRACKING LOOSE ENDS

Historical and Cultural Collective

Tsai Ming-liang's camp aesthetic signals a distinctly eccentric pose in both narrative and visual design. We have tried to anchor it within a fascination for working-class *song*, crossed by warped play-time and queer critique. With their languid, yet structured pace, Tsai's films show a strong ritual quality, even in moments that by rights should be most private, idiosyncratic, or obtuse. They have a stateliness that belies the squalor of their settings and characters' inarticulate poverty. Despite the constant loneliness, Tsai's rhythms, rites, and rituals testify to a social network within which human subjectivity necessarily constitutes itself, even as people struggle with chronic solitude. Oddly enough, it might be Tsai Ming-liang whose film style expresses best a Chinese decorum (Confucian *li*), because he is able to contemporize a fading vernacular culture. If the New Cinema tried to liberate a suppressed linguistic and political minority, Tsai Ming-liang as post–New Cinema resurrects a largely forgotten subculture.

Of all the filmmakers we've surveyed, Tsai is probably the most singular, with a reputation for a peculiar, highly individual style. Though he has been criticized for repeating himself, that style is indebted to specifically Taiwan-based ethnic and class affiliations. Though contemporary, these affiliations are also retrospective, incorporating obsolete, nearly forgotten vernaculars like songs, superstitions, and classic films. Therefore the isolation and alienation inherent in Tsai's world, like the squalor and poverty, seem gratuitous, cut off from the real motivation underlying this style. We can see, as the characters cannot, the social and institutional skeins in which they are entangled. These lend a measure of comfort to a near future of environmental disaster (*The Hole*), bereavement (*What Time is It There?*), or unrequited love (*Goodbye, Dragon Inn*). The Taiwanese folk superstitions in *The River* are paralleled with gay rituals of the bathhouse, culminating in sacrilegious imagery of filial sex. This is more disturbing than comforting, but Tsai's *pietá* of father and son, drawing on sacred iconography, emphasizes the intersubjective, transitive quality of isolation. While Tsai's is indeed a cinema of loneliness, there is also a community of shared experience, drawing on a history of common memory if not common cause. There is nostalgia here, but also critique: an insistent pull toward the routine, the quotidian, as silent touchstones of everyday living. There is a deep collective appeal in Tsai's films based not only on the ethnic and class aesthetic of *song* but also on the mindset of a collector, a refusal to let go of detritus (*Bu san*, as in the Chinese title of *Goodbye, Dragon Inn*), as our consumerist logic commands. It refuses because it is valuable cultural detritus; it binds us to others and helps explain who and what we are.

This conviction can be found in all four of the contemporary directors we have studied at length—Lee, Hou, and even Edward Yang—because each acknowledges a Taiwan past that must not only be preserved but reauthorized. Ang Lee wanted to rehabilitate the reputation of a genre identified with Chinese popular culture—martial arts; Hou Hsiao-hsien appropriated forms of Chinese autobiography and brilliantly transposed them into cinematic narratives; most pointedly, Yang interrogated and punctured orthodoxies of affiliation based on clichés of Chinese socio-economic advancement. Edward Yang's films explicitly engage the anachronism of Confucian doctrines, though their rejection indicates a too-literal (perhaps straw man) understanding. In Yang's world a contemporary, viable, and authentic version of the Confucian *li* is impossible. *Li* organizes and mobilizes a central network of human relations. Relations in Chinese traditions must be observed according to class, gender, and age hierarchies. But in modern Taipei since the 1960s, these relations are reified, a form of capital and a potentially unlimited resource.

Speaking of resource, as mentioned in chapter 2, the concept of nativism, "root-land ideology" (*buntu zhuyi*), is a narrative and psychological resource for Taiwan directors. Root-land ideology, the idea of returning to a native cultural and historical past, proves to be a rich treasury. It underlies a shift from authority-guided to author-centered cinema in the late-twentieth century. Root-land ideology bridges the New Cinema directors and native-soil literature, and it allows Taiwan filmmakers to locate their cultural lineage within a specific Taiwan as well as intra-Chinese reference. Nativism is both a break with the mainland-oriented proscriptions of the KMT as well as an idea reclaimed from the pre-Communist mainland (as we have seen with Hou Hsiao-hsien, inspired by the work of Shen Congwen). Nativism therefore is not the exclusive thing it might appear at first, a binary dividing Taiwan and China, or a break between classical and popular forms of storytelling.

Note that the return to the soil and cultural patrimony is not necessarily nostalgic. Instead, it asserts a new authorship, especially one with a cultural pedigree, edging out national or pedagogical motivations. When Hou Hsiao-hsien affirms his Shen Congwen influence, he has re-created a new form that appropriates the prestige of a world-renowned literary figure together with the immediacy of eyewitness to history. It is both creative and reproductive, integrating literary tropes with archival recording. But consider Hou's engagement with cinematic masters during his apprenticeship to "Lai san" (Lai Chengying) and Li Xing. Here, Hou straddled the healthy realist impulses of pastoral-environmentalism in order to play with an intuitive personal style. These took the form of long takes, unusual framing, and visual gags based on the antics of children, hoodlums, and young naifs. Tsai, in contrast, outlines a dystopic environment of pestilence and pollution, while experimenting with similar technical attenuations of time and space. Hou's and Tsai's imagination and utilization of a Taiwan "root-land" are very different, one leaning toward autobiographical acts and the other, quasi-surrealist camp.

Authority and authorial figures, in comparison, appear as perpetual problems in Edward Yang's oeuvre, which includes not only the story itself but methods and modes of production. In nearly every one of Yang's films, the diegetic father figure is dwarfed either by a totalitarian political system or an overpowering economic totality. Yang's epic *A Brighter Summer Day* illustrates his constant preoccupation with the monstrous insidiousness of authority. In his modes of production Yang was never shy about his dislike of the old school of CMPC. Unlike other directors in Taiwan, who like to maintain an ambiguous relationship with the film establishment, Yang has long cut himself loose. His self-sufficiency has recently found a new site, and a new medium—the Web animation of Miluku.com. Taiwan cinema, in its most traditional mode of operation, proves to be too sick for resuscitation, and Yang would rather invest his creative energy in a postcinematic form. Admittedly, this is a return to old forms, because they recall Yang's earliest experiments with comics and caricatures.

If we turn the same comparative framework to Ang Lee, we find Lee's handling of authority is more underhanded and sly, with a twisted sense of humor. Evidently, Lee is the most ardent and explicit about his debts to the precursors of Chinese cinema. Li Xing, King Hu, and Li Hanxiang are the old masters from which Lee has drawn his inspiration. But he points out their institutional stodginess, observing that the types and recipes they relied on are no longer acceptable to a younger, more cosmopolitan audience. Lee is also concerned about the perceived vulgarity of martial arts (something happily paraded by other prominent auteurs) and as a result injected a dose of romance into the genre. Unbeknownst to most of Lee's fans, this was an element already utilized by Wang Dulu, who gained fame and fortune for his synthetic "tragic warrior romance." Here too Ang Lee relies on major popular fiction of the past. Working in a global market, Lee actively resolves to synthesize classical elements of his cinematic memory with contemporary American dialogue, narrative structure, action, and emotion. In addition, like Edward Yang, Lee has moved on to postcinematic comic book forms. His Herculean efforts to produce a summer blockbuster with *The Hulk* failed, though the experiments with editing and rhythm, as well as his perennial father complex, are breathtaking.

Hollywood and Negotiated Creativity

Ang Lee's *Crouching Tiger, Hidden Dragon* was a major media event in Chinese-speaking and Chinese American communities. But the attention sparked a backlash. Lee and the film were attacked for selling out Chinese culture and its cinematic treasures to the West. The underlying critique was that *CTHD* is a Hollywood infringement, not a Chinese film. Since Hollywood is the ultimate, unvanquishable villain for every national cinema, Lee was cast as a borderline Judas and his film a hybrid creature, a bastard born of a shotgun wedding. But Hollywood is also an opportunity, and a challenge. In the mainstream media coverage, Lee's portrayal as a "Chinese prodigy" was based on his success in "Confucianizing Hollywood," because it is notoriously resistant to providing footholds for Chinese filmmakers and talent. As we have argued, "Confucianizing" goes beyond getting the keys to the city; it is also a reorientation of American genres and work practices around certain perceived values, such as sincerity and diligence. Critics in Taiwan were most receptive to the Ang Lee phenomenon for they believed that *CTHD* might change the industrial order of things by actually bringing in capital, know-how, and further access to Hollywood distribution and promotional mechanisms. This did happen, but with unexpected results.

The backlash that Ang Lee received, especially the snipes from Hong Kong and mainland critics, discouraged him from capitalizing on a sequel to *CTHD*, which apparently leaves an open ended "to be continued." But a crack in the door has also opened for local Taiwan filmmakers, even as Hollywood has fully co-opted local exhibition. Like their launches of independent divisions, Hollywood majors went ahead to extend patronage to local production in foreign markets. In 2002, Columbia-Asia, a regional subsidiary of Columbia, released *Double Vision*. Completely funded by Columbia, but directed and cowritten by Chen Kuo-fu, *Double Vision* is at once

"The [Sour] Taste of [American] Apples" (1983, dir. Wan Ren)

(COURTESY KWANG HWA INFORMATION AND CULTURE CENTER, HONG KONG)

a detective thriller and supernatural film noir. It was commonly pitched in the media as "Taoist *Se7en*," referring to the popular David Fincher film of 1995. An intriguing thing about all Chen Kuo-fu's films is his use of popular Taiwanese superstitions, only this time the rituals are sinister, not just mysterious, practiced by a secret society of retired dot-comers disillusioned with the fruits of Taiwan's new economic power. They trade this for an underground Taoist cult of immortality based on blood sacrifice. A clever script, convincing special effects, fine performances, and some gruesome staging of carnage elevated this trashy premise, along with the presence of American character actor David Morse. The film was the highest-budgeted production in Taiwan film history. With Chen's crafty promotional campaign, it topped the year's box office at almost NT$ 37 million, outperforming Hong Kong blockbuster *Infernal Affairs,* and *Red Dragon*, sequel to *Silence of the Lambs*. The reception of *Double Vision* took the Hollywood executives by surprise. A straight-to-video film became a local hit.

A documentary called *Transfer* (Guojing) by a well-known nonfiction filmmaker, Yang Lizhou, was completed as part of the promotional package for viewers who bought tickets for *Double Vision*. It is clear why Chen Kuo-fu commissioned this "making-of" documentary: as a record of what might have been an inaugural transnational production in Taiwan; as a witness to cross-cultural miscommunication and to the arrogance, incompetence, and abuse of the foreign crew (from Australia, Hong Kong, and the United States); and finally to suggest that the new patronage from Los Angeles does not come without strings attached. Columbia's motivation was not completely straightforward, but pursued a dual strategy of outsourcing B-grade features for the U.S. video-cable market while simultaneously trumpeting its support of local production. Like the film itself, American support came with a double vision, and how astonishing it must have been that its cover version paid such handsome returns in Taiwan.

Yang Lizhou's short film questions what impact this offshore production patronage may have on the defunct local industry. The package cover wittily flashes the "double-vision sign," a large eye with two pupils inside (like the eyes of the sacrificial Taoist victim); one is white, the other black, suggesting two opposite, irreconcilable views. One pupil seems to confirm the richness of film consumption on the Treasure Island and that Taiwan is still capable of making popular entertainment pictures for its own people. The other signals a new authority, master not only of Taiwan audiences but also a dictator of its production slate as well. Taiwan is not only a colony of exported Hollywood pictures and a place to produce world-class art cinema; it is also a low-cost offshore center for Hollywood productions, provided the studio scouts the right talent. This has been standard operating procedure for American animated cartoons for many years. In 2004, *20:30:40*, a Taiwan/Hong Kong coproduction directed by Sylvia Chang, was again acquired by Columbia for global distribution. Unlike *Double Vision*, the film was a negative pickup. Still, it did well in both Hong Kong and Taiwan, compared with most other locally made Chinese-language films. *Double Vision* and *20:30:40* raise the question of popularity, the sore spot of Taiwan film, especially when the question really being asked is, whither Taiwan cinema? Where to from here?

For decades it seemed that Taiwan cinema was no longer capable of making popular films. Hence, the domination of Hong Kong films in the 1990s and Hollywood at present. An antagonism developed against filmmakers like Yang, Tsai, and Hou, who in fact did try making films to draw audiences back to the homeland theaters. A more entertaining slate of pictures was also the policy of CMPC, under the supervision of producer Xu Ligong. In the films of Ang Lee, Chen Kuo-fu, and Sylvia Chang we see semi-endogenous popular cinema has yet to completely vanish from the Treasure Island. In the early new millennium, Taiwan cinema is no longer synonymous with the names we have discussed at length in this book.

New directors are burgeoning with a conviction to revive Taiwan film by tracing yet another dark history of the Treasure Island—the disfranchised aborigines and the usurpation (by the Europeans, the Chinese, and the Japanese) they have endured for more than three centuries. The new pluralism of Taiwan culture and society has also opened doors to gay filmmakers by bringing gay and lesbian stories to television and film, not as minority issues but as entertainment for all. Xu Ligong, Ang Lee's Taiwan producer, has completed several series of mainland-made television projects, all literary adaptations. The combination of literary material, a new talent pool, and economical production locations points the way to greater audiovisual integration between Taiwan and China.

Taiwan's entertainment industry may yet recover its senses, seizing the potential rewards from niche marketing to global audiences, not only online but through specialized programs devoted to animation, documentary, digital cinema, and hitherto marginal forms. Taiwan filmmakers, producers, and festival programmers have already discovered the riches of cooperation with their counterparts around Asia, Europe, and the United States. Will distributors follow their lead? Is more connection with the PRC to follow, as is rapidly occurring in Hong Kong? Can regional, multilateral production and distribution counter Hollywood's monopolistic tendencies? Will Taiwan ever enjoy the sort of cinematic vitality demonstrated by South Korea, with its popular, locally made blockbusters balanced by a burgeoning art cinema? Many more chapters about Taiwan—this Treasure Island—await further diagnosis and reflection.

Notes

Introduction: Treasure Island

1. The festival screened forty-two New Cinema films and published a who's who of film-makers and critics, a chrononology, and seven retrospective essays on the movement. Two are cited below, in note 7.

2. Besides Peggy Chiao and Huang Jianye, Li Youxin, Zhang Changyan, Chen Yuhang, and Liu Senyao were all very outspoken critics of the New Cinema. See Li Youxin, ed., *Six major directors from Hong Kong and Taiwan* (Gangtai liu da daoyan) (Taipei: Independent Evening Post, 1986), and Li Youxin, ed., *Films, film people, and film magazines* (Dianying, dianyingren, dianying kanwu) (Taipei: Independent Evening Post, 1988).

3. Peggy Chiao, *Taiwan New Cinema* (Taiwan xin dianying) (Taipei: China Times, 1988); Huang Jianye, *Studies on films by Edward Yang—A critical thinker in Taiwan's New Cinema* (Yang dechang dianying yanjiu—taiwan xin dianying de zhixing sibian jia) (Taipei: Yuan-liou, 1995).

4. On *taiyu pian*, see Huang Ren, *The sadness of Taiwanese-language films* (Beiqing taiyu pian) (Taipei: Variety, 1994); and also *The era of Taiwanese-language films* (Taiyu pian shidai yi) (Taipei: Taipei Film Archive, 1994); and Liao Jingfeng, *Disappearing images: cultural identity and filmic representations of Taiwanese-language films* (Xiaoshi de yingxiang: taiyu pian de dianying zaixian yu wenhua rentong) (Taipei: Yuan-liou, 2001). For historical overviews, see Ye Longyan, *The history of Taiwan film from the return to China* (Guangfu chuqi taiwan dianying shi) (Taipei: Taipei Film Archive, 1995); *Fifty years*

of the Taiwan Film Company (Taiying wushinian) (Taipei: Taipei Film Archive, 1996); *Conversations on the film past* (Dianying suiyue congheng tan), 2 vols. (Taipei: Taipei Film Archive, 1994); Sha Rongfeng, *Seventy years of splendor: a memoir by Sha Rongfeng* (Binfen dianying qishinian: Sha Rongfeng huiyilu) (Taipei: Taipei Film Archive, 1994); and Huang Ren, *Film and political propaganda* (Dianying yu zhengzhi xuanchuan) (Taipei: Variety, 1994).

5. The basic model is Du Yunzhi's three-volume *A history of Chinese cinema* (Zhongguo dianying shi) (Taipei: Taiwan Commercial Press, 1972).

6. Lu Feiyi, *Taiwan cinema, 1949–1994: politics, economy, and aesthetics* (Taiwan dianying: zhengzhi, jingji, meixue) (Taipei: Yuan-liou, 1998), Lu Feiyi's book is available in an English translation from Hong Kong University Press.

7. Ti Wei, "Reassessing the Historical Significance of Taiwan New Cinema in the Context of Globalization," in Ya-mei Li, ed., *20th Anniversary of Taiwan New Cinema* (Taipei: Golden Horse Film Festival, 2002), 8–20, and Shih-lun Chang, "Taiwanese New Cinema and the International Film Festival Approach," ibid., 21–39.

1. Parallel Cinemas: Postwar History and Major Directors

1. E. Patricia Tsurumi, *Japanese Colonial Education in Taiwan* (Cambridge: Harvard University Press, 1977), 109.

2. Robert L. Jarman, ed., *Taiwan: Political and Economic Reports, 1861–1960*, 10 vols. (Slough, U.K.: Archive Editions, 1997), 8:125.

3. For Taiwan's transition from Japan's colonial rule to Kuomingtang's martial law, see Markus Abe-Nornes and Yeh Yueh-yu, "Behind *City of Sadness*," in their article *Narrating National Sadness: Cinematic Mapping and Hypertextual Dispersion* (University of California, Berkeley: Film Studies Program, 1998). See the *CinemaSpace* Web site (at http://cinemaspace.berkeley.edu/Papers/CityOfSadness/table.html).

   See also Darrell W. Davis, "Borrowing Postcolonial: Wu Nien-chen's *Dou-san* and the Memory Mine," *Post Script: Essays on Film and the Humanities* 20.2–3 (Winter / Spring / Summer 2001): 94–114. See also D. W. Davis, "A New Taiwan Person? A Conversation with Wu Nien-chen," *Positions: east asia cultures critique* 11.3 (Winter 2003): 717–34.

4. Lü Sushang, *The history of cinema and drama in Taiwan* (Taiwan dianying xiju shi) (Taipei: Yinhua, 1961), 1–16.

5. For more on *kokusaku-eiga*, see Darrell William Davis, *Picturing Japaneseness: Monumental Style, National Identity, Japanese Film* (New York: Columbia University Press, 1996). For Japanese film production in the empire, see also Michael Baskett's doctoral thesis, "The Attractive Empire: Colonial Asia in Japanese Imperial Film Culture, 1931–1953" (University of California, Los Angeles, 2000).

6. Li Xianglan is the stage name of the China-born Japanese star Yamaguchi Yoshiko, who starred in many national policy films for the Manchurian Film Company (*Manying*, or *Man'ei* in Japanese) during the 15-year war between China and Japan. She was known by the stage name "Ri Koran" to the Japanese audience—a Chinese star who spoke

fluent Japanese though in reality she was the opposite. See Yamaguchi Takeshi, *Film apparitions of the Manchurian Film Company* (Maboroshi no kinema Man'ei) (Tokyo: Heibonsha, 1990). See also Yamaguchi's memoir in Chinese translation, Shankou Shuzi and Tanyuan Zuomi, trans. Jin Ruojing, *Days in china: half of my life* (Zai zhongguo de rizi: wo de bansheng) (Hong Kong: Baixing, 1989).

7. For the production background of *Bell of Sayon*, see a special issue of *Film Appreciation* devoted to this film. This was published on the occasion of a memorial screening, including a restored print, invitations to the aging participants, and associated oral histories about the film. "Tracing the footsteps of *Bell of Sayon*" (Zuisuo *shayuan zhi zhong* de jiaozhong), *Film Appreciation* (Dianying xinshang shuang yuekan) 12.3 (May-June 1994): 15–39.

8. Lü, *The history of cinema*, 32. See also Ye Longyan, *The history of Taiwan film from the return to China* (Guangfu chuqi taiwan dianying shi) (Taipei: Taipei Film Archive, 1995), 88–95.

9. Abe-Nornes and Yeh, "Behind *City of Sadness.*"

10. The term *parallel cinemas* comes from the history of Indian cinema, which sustains a variety of geographically, linguistically, and commercially distinct film practices, such as Hindi ("Bollywood"), Bengali, Malayam, Tamil, and so on. These practices also vary in their relations to commercial and artistic motives and therefore in their modes of address to audiences. In general, parallel cinema refers to any nonmainstream film practice but especially to those postwar impulses, both commercial (Raj Kapoor) and artistically motivated (Satyajit Ray), that were inspired by Italian neorealism. See Sumita S. Chakravarty, *National Identity in Indian Popular Cinema, 1947–1987* (Austin: University of Texas Press, 1993), 235–36; Maithili Rao, "Looking Beyond Bollywood," *Film Comment* 39.1(January-February, 2003): 12; and Roy Armes, *Third World Filmmaking and the West* (Berkeley: University of California Press, 1987), 121–27.

11. Du Yunzhi, *A history of Chinese cinema* (Zhongguo dianying shi), 3 vols. (Taipei: Taiwan Commercial Press, 1972), 1:127–28.

12. Du, *A history of Chinese cinema* 2:5–19.

13. Ibid., 3:50.

14. *Fifty years of the Taiwan Film Company* (Taiying wushinian) (Taipei: Taipei Film Archive, 1996), 10.

15. Huang Ren, *Film and political propaganda* (Dianying yu zhengzhi xuanchuan) (Taipei: Variety, 1994), 34.

16. "Interview with Zhang Ying," *Conversations on the film past*, 2 vols. (Dianying suiyue zongheng tan) (Taipei: Taipei Film Archive, 1994), 2: 406–407.

17. Du, *A history of Chinese cinema* 3:27–37.

18. Ibid., 3:39.

19. Ibid., 3:39–45.

20. Before 1965, Taiwan's Top Ten films had been dominated by either Shaw Brothers or Cathay productions. See Huang Ren, "The glorious days of domestic films" (Guopian de fengguang shengshi), in Cai Guorong, ed., *A selection of famous Chinese directors and films of the 1960s* (Liushi niandai guopian mingdao mingzuo xuan) (Taipei: Motion

Picture Development Foundation of the ROC, 1982), 18–22. For the imports of *minnan* films from Hong Kong, see Yu Moyun, *Eighty years of Hong Kong cinema* (Xianggang dianying bashinian) (Hong Kong: Urban Council, 1993), 36.

21. The ban on Japanese films was lifted in 1951, five years after its initial imposition. Conditions for allowing Japanese films to reenter Taiwan applied only to those films that were anti-Communist with educational values. See Sha Rongfeng, *Seventy years of splendor: a memoir by Sha Rongfeng* (Binfen dianying qishinian: Sha Rongfeng huiyilu) (Taipei: Taipei Film Archive, 1994), 118.

22. Veteran critic Huang Ren divides *taiyu pian* into three stages. See Huang Ren, *The sadness of Taiwanese-language films* (Beiqing taiyu pian) (Taipei: Variety, 1994).

23. Lu Feiyi, *Taiwan cinema: politics, economy, aesthetics* (Taiwan dianying: zhengzhi, jingji, meixue) (Taipei: Yuan-liou, 1998), table 11a.

24. "Interview with Liang Zhefu," *The era of Taiwanese-language films* (Taiyu pian shidai) (Taipei: Taipei Film Archive, 1994), 238. Until Mel Gibson's Christ film, Ang Lee's film was the highest-grossing non-English-language foreign film of all time.

25. "Interview with He Jiming," *The era*, 134–44.

26. "Interview with Li Quanxi," *The era*, 54.

27. On *rensageki* see Hiroshi Komatsu, "Some Characteristics of Japanese Cinema Before World War I," in Arthur Nolletti and David Desser, eds., *Reframing Japanese Cinema: Authorship, Genre, History* (Bloomington: Indiana University Press, 1992), 247–48; and Joseph Anderson, "Spoken Silents . . . ," in Nolletti and Desser, eds., *Reframing*, 270–72. A different perspective can be seen in the older Joseph Anderson and Donald Richie, *Japanese Film: Art and Industry* (Princeton: Princeton University Press, 1982), 27–28. Unlike Taiwan, *rensageki* in Japan was not a folk art but was part of a modernist movement experimenting with new techniques of theatrical presentation.

28. "Interview with Li Quanxi," *The era*, 54

29. "Interview with Liang Zhefu," *The era*, 225–42.

30. Liao Jingfeng writes about the prominence of popular music in *taiyu pian*, partly because of their reliance on radio hits. See Liao, *Disappearing images: cultural identity and filmic representations of Taiwanese dialect films* (Xiaoshi de yingxiang: taiyu pian de dianying zaixian yu wenhua rentong) (Taipei: Yuan-liou, 2001), 82.

31. "Interview with Li Quanxi," *The era*, 54.

32. See "Interview with Zhang Ying," *Conversations on the film past* 2:420; and "Interview with Li Jia," *The era*, 166–67.

33. Stephen Teo, "The 1970s: Movement and Transition," in Poshek Fu and David Desser, eds., *The Cinema of Hong Kong: History, Arts, Identity* (Cambridge: Cambridge University Press, 2001), 90–110.

34. The language policy in broadcast television stipulated that *minnan* language was not to exceed more than one hour in the prime-time slot.

35. The year 1970 is when the number of *taiyu pian* being produced began to drop significantly—from 84 in 1969 to 18 in 1970. See Lu, *Taiwan cinema*, table 11a.

36. Li's *Laurel and Hardy's Taiwan grand tour* and two films from the same series were commercially successful. See "Yige zhongguo daoyan de gaobai: li xing zuopin yanjiu"

(Confessions of a Chinese director: studies on Li Xing's work), in *A film pilgrim: a collection of retrospective writings on the fiftieth anniversary of Li Xing's career* (Dianying xingzhe: li xing congying wushi zhounian huigu wenxuan) (Taipei: Taipei Society for the Historical Research on Chinese Film, 1999), 12.

37. Japanese films were the models for many Taiwan directors at this time. Li Xing specifically mentions the influence of *Rashomon* (see *A film pilgrim*, 12).

38. *A film pilgrim*, 11.

39. Liang Liang, "Li Xing: honest, unbending, inherited" (Li xing: xingqing gengjie, jianshou daotong), in Cai, ed., *A selection of famous Chinese directors and films of the 1960s*, 80.

40. In a symposium held in 1968 to honor Li Xing, leftist writer-critic Chen Yingzhen questioned Li Xing's compromise in *The Road*. See *A film pilgrim*, 23–24.

41. *A film pilgrim*, 19.

42. Bai Jingrui, "On 'Lonely Seventeen,' " in Cai, ed., *A selection*, 75.

43. Huang Ren, "The glorious days of domestic films," in Cai, ed., *A selection*, 21.

44. Liang Liang, "Bai Jingrui," in Cai, ed., *A selection*, 75.

45. For a discussion on the battle over film markets between Cathay and Shaw Brothers, see Yeh Yueh-yu's "Taiwan: The Transnational Battlefield of Cathay and Shaw Brothers," in Wong Ain-ling and Sam Ho, eds., *The Cathay Story* (Hong Kong: Hong Kong Film Archive, 2002), 142–49.

46. Chen Feibao, *Musings on Taiwan film history* (Taiwan dianying shihua) (Beijing: China Film Press, 1988), 140.

47. See Liang, "Li Xing," in Cai, ed., *A selection*, 20–21.

48. See the appendix compiled by Xue Hueiling in Peggy Chiao, *Grand pictures: the five years that changed history* (Guolian dianying: gaibian lishi de wunian) (Taipei: Variety, 1994), 170–82.

49. Huang Ren, ed., *The world of King Hu* (Hu jinquan de shijie) (Taipei: Yatai, 1999), 158.

50. The film earned NT$ 4,385,512 and sold a total of 320,843 tickets. The box office was about NT$ 2 million more than the second best earner of 1967. Lin Wenchi, "Reconstructing *Dragon Gate Inn*'s Spectatorship in Taiwan," paper presented at the Conference on Action Cinema, Lingnan University, Hong Kong, January 7, 2003.

51. "King Hu's Last Interview," in Law Kar, ed., *Transcending the Times: King Hu and Eileen Chang* (Hong Kong: Provisional Urban Council of Hong Kong, 1998), 76. Here, Hu compares his films with what he considers a "real martial arts picture," Kurosawa's *Seven Samurai*.

52. Stephen Teo, "Only the Valiant: King Hu and his *Cinema Opera*," in Law, ed., *Transcending the Times*, 13–25.

53. With the designation of Han Yingjie as the first one to hold this position("King Hu's Last Interview," 75).

54. Tony Williams, "Under 'Western Eyes': The Personal Odyssey of Huang Fei-Hong in *Once Upon a Time in China*," *Cinema Journal* 41.1 (Fall 2000): 3–24.

55. Lau Shing-hon, ed., *A Study of the Hong Kong Martial Arts Film* (Hong Kong: Hong Kong International Film Festival / Urban Council, 1980), 12 and 175.

56. Davis, *Picturing Japaneseness*, 73–82.

57. Tony Rayns, "King Hu: Shall We Dance?" in Lau, ed., *The Hong Kong Martial Arts Film*, 103–106.

58. Teo, "Only the Valiant," 23.

59. Stephen Teo, "Cathay and the *Wuxia* Movie," *The Cathay Story* (Hong Kong Film Archive, 2002), 116.

60. Hector Rodriguez, "Questions of Chinese Aesthetics: Film Form and Narrative Space in the Cinema of King Hu," *Cinema Journal* 38.1 (Fall 1998): 73–96.

61. David Bordwell, "Richness Through Imperfection," in Law, ed., *Transcending the Times*, 32.

62. Huang, ed., *The world of King Hu*, 115–16.

63. Paul Willemen, "Action Cinema, Labour Power, and the Video Shop," paper presented at the Conference on Action Cinema, Lingnan University, Hong Kong (January 6–9, 2003), 23.

2. Challenges and Controversies of the Taiwan New Cinema

1. Hua Jingjiang, "Overview of domestic film production" (Guopian zhizuo gaikuang), in *Cinema in the Republic of China: 1984 Yearbook* (Taipei: Motion Picture Development Foundation of the ROC, 1984), 10.

2. Five features and eight documentaries were sent, along with a delegation of fifty-eight people. Not a single prize was taken due to a change in the festival's operation. From an event that handed out prizes to nearly every "contestant," the new procedure was to go on merit alone, awarding prizes only to the best films "based on technique and artistic expression, rather than themes or ideology." *Cinema in the Republic of China: 1983 Yearbook* (Taipei: Motion Picture Development Foundation of the ROC, 1983), 87.

3. Ang Lee also belongs in this group of U.S.-trained directors targeted by CMPC. The studio (or more specifically, Wu Nianzhen) invited him to begin his directing career under the newcomer policy, but Lee had contractual obligations back in New York. D. W. Davis, "A New Taiwan Person: A Conversation with Wu Nien-chen," *positions: east asia cultures critique* 11.3 (Winter 2003): 719.

4. In 1983, CMPC allocated NT$ 50 million as seed capital to launch ten coproduction projects in the next few years. Liang Liang, ed., "Chronicles of major film events" (Dianying dashiji), in *Cinema in the Republic of China: 1984 Yearbook*, 92.

5. GIO announced that NT$ 10 million would be awarded to the film that won first prize while NT$ 1.5 million would be awarded to films that won any nominations. This shows that cinema in Taiwan functions more than simply a capitalist medium but also serves as a diplomatic vehicle. Ibid., 89.

6. The budget for King Hu's *The Invincible Ones* was four times bigger than the ones carried out by the newcomer policy, which cost on average NT$ 6 million.

7. Historically, all CMPC's projects had to be approved by KMT's "culture work committee" before they could begin production. This rule lasted until 1985 when James Soong was appointed the new head of the committee. Lan Zuwei, "Chronicles of major film

events" (Dianying dashiji), in *Cinema in the Republic of China: 1986 Yearbook* (Taipei: Motion Picture Development Foundation of the ROC, 1986), 158.

8. "To tell a little lie" (Xiaoxiao sa ge huang), in Yang Ze, ed., *The high-speed eighties* (Kuang-biao bashi) (Taipei: China Times, 1999), 132–40.

9. *Cinema in the Republic of China: 1983 Yearbook*, 86.

10. Huang Chunming, "The Taste of Apples," trans. Howard Goldblatt, *The Taste of Apples* (New York: Columbia University Press, 2001), 156.

11. Yang Shiqi, "Our son almost lost his doll" (Erzi xianxie shiqu wan'ou), *United Daily News*, August 15, 1983.

12. Interview with Xiao Ye, Wu Nianzhen, and Wan Ren in "Roaring Waves" (Langchao xiongyong), *Re-viewing old pictures* (Jiuying chongwen), Episode 5. Public Television Taiwan, 1995.

13. Yang Shiqi was heralded as the "patron saint" of the New Cinema for her fervent support of the new directors. Edward Yang dedicated his 1984 *Taipei Story* to Yang Shiqi after her premature death in 1983.

14. Tu Wei-ming, ed., *The Living Tree: The Changing Meaning of Being Chinese Today* (Stanford: Stanford University Press, 1994), is exemplary of this sinocentricity, otherwise known as cultural nationalism.

15. Yvonne Chang Sung-seng, *Modernism and the Nativist Resistance: Contemporary Chinese Fiction from Taiwan* (Durham: Duke University Press, 1993). For nativist literature, see Howard Goldblatt's translation of Huang Chunming's "The Taste of Apples," and of Wang Zhenhe's *Rose, Rose I Love You* (New York: Columbia University Press, 1998).

16. Xiao Ye, "A befuddled patriot" (Hulihutu de aiguozhe), in Yang Ze, ed., *The seventies: a collection of confessions (*Qishiniandai chanhuilu) (Taipei: China Times, 1994), 126.

17. Interview with Xiao Ye in "Roaring Waves" (Public Television Taiwan, 1995).

18. Xiao Ye, "A befuddled patriot," 124–25.

19. A famous example: Tang Shuxuan's *China Behind* (1972), a film about the defecting Red Guards, which was banned for too many shots of Mao, the PRC flag, and revolutionary songs.

20. Huang Jianye, "A retrospective of films of the year 1983" (Yijiubasan nian taiwan dianying huigu), in Peggy Chiao, ed., *Taiwan New Cinema* (Taiwan xin dianying) (Taipei: China Times, 1988), 52.

21. Huang, "A retrospective," 52.

22. "Film Law, article 39," *Cinema in the Republic of China: 1984 Yearbook*, 117.

23. *Cinema in the Republic of China: 1984 Yearbook*, 86.

24. Interview with Xiao Ye in John Lent, *The Asian Film Industry* (Austin: University of Texas Press, 1990), 86.

25. Interview with Wan Ren in Lent, *The Asian Film Industry*, 84.

26. Davis, "A New Taiwan Person," 722.

27. Ibid., 718–19.

28. The collaboration and division of labor among Hou Hsiao-hsien, Zhu Tianwen, and Wu Nianzhen is described in the published script of *Dust in the Wind*. See Wu Nian-

zhen and Zhu Tianwen, *Dust in the Wind* (Lianlian fengchen) (Taipei: Yuan-liou, 1989), 47–48.

29. *City of Sadness* (Era Productions, 1989; LD version), English subtitles by Stan Lai and Jia Peilin.

30. If you wish to page someone in a movie theater in Taiwan, the projectionist will oblige by inserting a slide projected on the edge of the screen notifying your party to meet you: "Mr. Wu, there's someone waiting for you outside."

31. The film is the trilogy *What is your name?* (Kimi no Na wa, 1953–54; dir. Oba Hideo; Shochiku). Asian popular storytelling is exemplified by such Japanese stage practices as *rakugo* (stand-up comedy impressions and caricatures accompanied by *samisen*); *joruri* is the chanted narration accompanying Bunraku puppet theater; *yose* are ballads sung in a variety hall. All were Japanese performing arts widely patronized up to the early Showa period.

32. Joseph Anderson, "Spoken Silents in the Japanese Cinema; or, Talking to Pictures: Essaying the Katsuben, Contextualizing the Texts," in Arthur Nolletti Jr. and David Desser, eds., *Reframing Japanese Cinema: Authorship, Genre, History* (Bloomington: Indiana University Press, 1992), 259–310.

33. Chaoyang Liao, "Borrowed Modernity: History and the Subject in *A Borrowed Life*," *boundary 2* 24.3 (1997): 236.

34. Davis, "A New Taiwan Person," 731.

35. "People of the year: Yu Kanping" (Niandu renwu: yu kanping), in *Cinema in the Republic of China: 1984 Yearbook*, 77.

36. Huang Jianye, "Review of *Moonlight*," in Chiao, ed., *Taiwan New Cinema*, 373.

37. For more on Wu Nianzhen and *Dou-san*, see Darrell W. Davis's "Borrowing Postcolonial: Wu Nianzhen's *Dou-san* and the Memory Mine," *Post Script* 20.2–3 (Winter-Spring 2001): 94–114. Reprinted in Sheldon Lu and Emilie Yeh Yueh-yu, eds., *Chinese-language Cinema's Historiography, Poetics, Politics* (Honolulu: University of Hawaii Press, 2005): 237–66.

38. Wang Tong, interview by authors, Taipei, July 16, 2002.

39. Wang indicated his friendship with nativist writers in the 1960s, before nativist literature was recognized as an important literary movement. Wang Tong, interview, July 16, 2002.

40. According to Wang Tong, several directors were keen on this novel, including Li Xing. Ibid.

41. Ibid.

42. "Wang Tong Overview," in *Taiwan Films* (Taipei: Variety, 1993), 5–20.

43. *The 1984 Yearbook* does not contain any significant review of the film. Only one very short, impressionistic review by Tang Wenbiao was included in Peggy Chiao's *Taiwan New Cinema*, 221–22. In the same volume, Zhan made his remark on *Flower* in "The way the new cinema has come and the way it goes" (Taiwan xin dianying de lailu yu qulu), 30. For Chen Kuo-fu's observation, see "Hong Kong doesn't have it but Taiwan does" (Xianggang meiyou, taiwan you) in his *One-sided view* (Pianmian zhiyan) (Taipei: Taipei Film Library, 1985), 220.

44. Derek Elley, "Taiwan Cinema," *International Film Guide* (New York: A. S. Barnes, 1984), 297.

45. Wang Tong, interview, July 16, 2002.

46. Ibid.

47. Ibid.

48. Ibid.

49. Wan Ren, interview by authors, Taipei, October 21, 2002.

50. There is an anachronism here because the clown is carrying a billboard for *Oyster Girl*, which wasn't released until 1964.

51. Wan Ren, interview, October 21, 2002.

52. Huang Jianye, "Super Citizen" (Chaoji shimin), in Chiao, ed., *Taiwan New Cinema*, 214–18.

53. Wan Ren, interview, October 21, 2002.

54. This information was provided by Hou Hsiao-hsien during his talk at the symposium on the 20th Anniversary of Taiwan New Cinema. Taipei Golden Horse Film Festival, Westin Hotel, Taipei, October 18, 2002.

55. Wan Ren, interview, October 21, 2002.

56. Ibid.

57. Ibid.

58. Li Yamei et al., "Wan Ren on *Connection by Fate*," *Film Appreciation* 17, no. 2 (March/April, 1999): 90.

59. Wan Ren, interview, October 21, 2002.

60. Dan Lanyu, "1996 Box office of domestic film" (Yijiujiuliunian guopian piaofang tongji), in *Cinema in the Republic of China: 1997 Yearbook* (Taipei: Motion Picture Development Foundation of the ROC, 1984), 35–38.

61. Luo Xiulian, "Film review index" (Yingpian lei dianying pinglun), in *Cinema in the Republic of China: 1997 Yearbook*, 181.

3. Navigating the House of Yang

1. A misconception about Yang's USC film education, unlike other success stories in film history, is that he finished his MFA program in Los Angeles. On many occasions, Yang refers to his time at USC as extremely painful and unproductive. Huang Jianye, *Studies on films by Edward Yang: a critical thinker in Taiwan's New Cinema* (Yang dechang dianying yanjiu: Taiwan xin dianying de zhixing sibian jia) (Taipei: Yuanliu, 1995), 202.

2. Huang, *Studies on films by Edward Yang*, 203.

3. Tony Rayns, "*YiYi*: Interviews," April 16, 2000, Hong Kong. *Asian Film Connections*. *See* www.usc.edu/isd/archives/asianfilm/taiwan/yiyi/interviews.html (accessed December 13, 2003).

4. Shelly Kraicer and Lisa Roosen-Runge, "Edward Yang: A Taiwanese Independent Filmmaker in Conversation," *CineAction* 47: *Anything But Hollywood* (October 1998): 48–55.

5. SY Shen, "Permutations of the Foreign/er: A Study of the Works of Edward Yang,

Stan Lai, Chang Yi, and Hou Hsiao-hsien" (Ph.D. diss., Cornell University, 1995), 14 and 25.

6. See Emilie Yueh-yu Yeh, "Elvis, Allow Me to Introduce Myself: American Music and Neocolonialism in Taiwan Cinema," *Modern Chinese Literature and Culture* 15.1 (Spring 2003): 1–28.

7. *Cinedossier: Edward Yang* (Taipei: Golden Horse Film Festival, 1991), 34.

8. Andrew Wilson, *The "Ever-Victorious Army": A History of the Chinese Campaign under Lt.-Col. C. G. Gordon C.B.R.E., and of the Suppression of the Tai-ping Rebellion* (Edinburgh: William Blackwood, 1868), 21.

9. Fredric Jameson, "Remapping Taipei," in *The Geopolitical Aesthetic: Cinema and Space in the World System* (Bloomington and London: Indiana University Press/BFI, 1992), 114–57.

10. Huang, *Studies on films by Edward Yang*, 128; see also Leo Changjen Chen, "The Frustrated Architect," *New Left Review* 11 (September-October 2001): 118.

11. The film grossed over NT$ 10 million in Taipei and was considered very successful compared to many other New Cinema films, which often made no money at all. Given the cold reception to his previous two features and his frustrations on the set, this was a welcome consolation. See Ye Hua, "Overview of the domestic film industry," in *Cinema of the Republic of China: 1987 Yearbook* (Taipei: Motion Picture Development Foundation of the ROC, 1988), 96–99.

12. Tongling Lu makes a useful distinction between internal and exterior terror, corresponding to private boredom and public violence. *Confronting Modernity in the Cinema of Taiwan and Mainland China* (Cambridge: Cambridge University Press, 2002), 139.

13. Edward Yang, *A Confucian Confusion: Edward Yang's energetic comedy* (Duli shidai: yang dechang de huoli xiju) (Taipei: Variety, 1994), 139. These words are given to the writer, when he says that a reincarnated Confucius would be surprised to learn that his audience wants to know the secret not of his teachings, but of his put-on job.

14. Jameson, "Remapping Taipei," 140, and "Totality as Conspiracy," in *Geopolitical Aesthetic*, 83–84.

15. In the epic theater, the goal is not reproduction of life in the naturalist sense, but "to alienate [*verfremden*] them. This discovery (alienation) of conditions takes place through the interruption of happenings." Walter Benjamin, "What Is Epic Theater?" in *Illuminations: Essays and Reflections* (New York: Schocken, 1968), 150.

16. For example, Annette Michelson on Stanley Kubrick, where she writes that "the film medium itself . . . characteristically heightens the spectator's 'perception of being physical to the level of apperception: one becomes conscious of the modes of consciousness.'" Quoted in Greg Taylor, *Artists in the Audience* (Princeton: Princeton University Press, 1999), 132.

17. Yang is critical of Theo Angelopolous, putting him in the category of those who are unsure of what they want to say in their films. *Cinedossier: Edward Yang*, 34.

18. Ti Wei, "Reassessing the Historical Significance of Taiwan New Cinema in the Context of Globalization," in Ya-mei Li, ed., *20th Anniversary of Taiwan New Cinema* (Taipei: Golden Horse Film Festival, 2002), 16.

19. In 1992, Taiwan's film production fell even further, with only twenty-two films. F. Y. Wang, "Flowers Blooming in Barren Soil," *Free China Review* 45.2 (1995): 4–17.

20. See the three symposia organized by *China Times Literary Supplement* and *Liberty Times Literary Supplement*: Luo Zhicheng, Zhan Hongzhi, Liu Daren, Peggy Chiao, Yang Du, and Hou Hsiao-hsien, "A generation anxious to reconstruct the past" (Jiyu chongjian guoqu de yidai), *China Times*, July 12, 1991, Taipei; Yang Ze, Liu Daren, Huang Jianye, Zhang Dachun, and Shu Guozhi, "An allegory of innocence and power" (Tianzhen yu quanli de yuyan), *China Times Evening*, July 15, 1991, Taipei; Lü Zhenghui, Zheng Peikai, Wu Zhenghuan, Qi Rongren, Huang Yuxiu, "Secrets of the magic box: Reinterpreting *A Brighter Summer Day*" (Moshu fanghe de mimi: chongjie gulingjie shaonian sharen shijian), *Liberty Times*, September 3–4, 1991.

21. *Cinema in the Republic of China: 1992 Yearbook* (Taipei: Motion Picture Development Foundation of the ROC, 1993), 155.

22. Hou's *City of Sadness* (1989) and *Good Men, Good Women* (1995) each contain fine examples of tunnel vision: long shots down the corridor of a prison hallway, as if waiting for judgment. These have a paradigmatic quality, arising from an awareness of all the cells on both sides of the corridor, each containing its own inmates, stories, and fates. Wu Nianzhen's *Dou-san: A Borrowed Life* (1994) has similar moments. Xu Xiaoming's *Heartbreak Island* (1995), a film about the Formosa incident of 1979, contains almost identical shots. Furthermore, several tunnel vision scenes appear in the blind alleyways of a veterans' village (*juancun*). Shots taken down the alley exploit the corners of intersecting walls, where people or bicycles unexpectedly pop into sight. This not only creates surprise, it installs expectations of sudden appearances (apparitions), as well as a persistent feeling of being watched, or listened to.

23. Kien Ket Lim of National Taiwan Jiaotong University proposed that *BSD* was a film noir, complete with shady underworld, slick city streets, femmes fatale, and nihilistic urban angst. This prompted lively discussion. "Focus on Taiwan Cinema" conference, National Taiwan Arts University, Taipei, November 28–30, 2003.

24. Bordwell, "Transcultural Spaces: Toward a Poetics of Chinese Film," *PostScript: Essays in Film and the Humanities* 20.2–3 (Winter-Spring and Summer 2001): 16–23.

25. Bordwell updated his earlier article with a talk on "Taiwan Cinema and the Telephoto Aesthetic" ("Focus on Taiwan Cinema" conference, Taipei, November 28–30, 2003). See also Bordwell's *Figures Traced in Light: On Cinematic Staging* (University of California Press, 2005), for elaboration in comparison with three other major directors.

26. Jameson, "Totality as Conspiracy," in *Geopolitical Aesthetic*, 9.

27. Military officers were assigned to every school in Taiwan until the late 1990s, to inculcate discipline and readiness for invasion by the Red Chinese. They also doubled as proxies for school administrators and representatives of the party.

28. Wu Xide, quoted in Yang, *A Confucian Confusion*, 143.

29. Lu, *Confronting Modernity*, 139; Huang, *Studies on films by Edward Yang*, 175.

30. In the interview with Huang, Yang expressed his admiration toward Alain Resnais, especially his highly theatrical *Melo* (1986). Huang, *Studies on films by Edward Yang*, 230.

31. Yang, "Director's Statement," *A Confucian Confusion*, 138; Jonathan Rosenbaum, "Exiles in Modernity: The Films of Edward Yang," *Chicago Reader* (November 7, 1997, sec. 1). *See* www.chireader.com/movies/archives/1197/11077.html (accessed online December 15, 2003).

32. Jameson, "Remapping Taipei," in *Geopolitical Aesthetic*, 141.

33. Stephen Teo considers the European connection between Yang and Antonioni (and Godard) in "A New Kind of Alienation: Edward Yang's *A Brighter Summer Day*," *Cinemaya* 13 (1991): 41–44. Teo's follow-up appears in "The Four-Hour Version Reviewed and Reassessed," *Cinemaya* 14 (1992): 44–47.

34. Fredric Jameson, "Is a National Cinema Possible?" Keynote at "Double Vision: Taiwan's New Cinema, Here and There" Conference, Yale University, October 31, 2003. Here Jameson invoked the Antonioni parallel again, only this time the European director suffers in comparison. See also Fran Martin, "The European Undead: Tsai Ming-liang's *What Time Is It There?*" *Senses of Cinema* 27 (July-August 2003) (*see* www.sensesofcinema.com/contents/03/27/tsai_european_undead.html).

35. Huang, "Interview with Edward Yang," *Studies on films by Edward Yang*, 229.

36. "Island of Light: Symposium on Taiwan Cinema and Popular Culture," University of Wisconsin–Madison, March 2002 (with guest appearance by Wu Nianzhen). "Focus on Taiwan Cinema" Conference, Taipei, November 28–30, 2003 (guest appearance by Tsai Ming-liang). See note 34 above for the Yale conference, which hosted Chen Kuo-fu (director of *Double Vision*), Peggy Chiao, and Fredric Jameson.

37. Michael Walsh, "Jameson and 'Global Aesthetics'" in David Bordwell and Noel Carroll, eds., *Post-Theory: Reconstructing Film Studies* (Madison: University of Wisconsin Press, 1996), 483 (his emphasis).

38. A critique of Jameson's use of Kidlat Tahimik is Felicidad Cua Lim's "Perfumed Nightmare and the Perils of Jameson's 'New Political Culture,'" *Philippines Critical Forum* 1.1 (1995): 24–37.

39. Jameson, "Introduction: Beyond Landscape," *Geopolitical Aesthetic*, 5.

40. Jameson, "Remapping Taipei," *Geopolitical Aesthetic*, 117.

41. Jameson, "Introduction," *Geopolitical Aesthetic*, 5.

42. Jameson, "Remapping Taipei," *Geopolitical Aesthetic*, 155.

43. Jameson, "Introduction," *Geopolitical Aesthetic*, 4.

44. Edward Said, *The World, the Text, and the Critic* (Cambridge: Harvard University Press, 1983), 50.

45. Jameson, "Introduction," *Geopolitical Aesthetic*, 1.

46. Jameson, "Remapping Taipei," *Geopolitical Aesthetic*, 151.

47. Though Jameson's talk was advertised as "Is a National Cinema Possible?" he said he was changing it to something less categorical, like "Thoughts on New Waves."

48. Benedict Anderson, *Imagined Communities*, rev. ed. (London: Verso, 1991). "Machineries of representation" is Jameson's phrase from "Third World Literature in the Age of Multinational Capitalism," *Social Text* 15 (Fall 1986): 65–88. Benjamin's references to empty, homogeneous time comes from "Theses on the Philosophy of History," nos. 13, 14, 17, and 18B in *Illuminations*, 261–62, 264.

49. There is always at least one student who sees *The Terrorizers* (1986) and says, "so what, films playing with time and alternation have been around since *Pulp Fiction*" (made in 1994, someone is obliged to add).

50. Wang Geng'yu, ed., *Notebook on my new film* (Yang dechang dianying biji) (Taipei: China Times, 1991), 41.

51. Fredric Jameson, "An Overview," in Tak-wai Wong and M. A. Abbas, eds., *Rewriting Literary History*. Proceedings of the Second International Conference on Literary Theory, Hong Kong, December 16–21, 1982 (Hong Kong: Hong Kong University Press, 1984), 338–47. It's worth recalling that Jameson has published criticism on Chinese literature and culture since the early 1980s. In these overview remarks, Jameson makes an interesting distinction between modernist faith in the prophetic, or transformative, possibilities of aesthetic experience while postmodernism rejects them (340).

4. Trisecting Taiwan Cinema with Hou Hsiao-hsien

1. Yeh Yueh-yu, "Politics and Poetics of Hou Hsiao-hsien's Films," *PostScript: Essays in Film and Humanities* 20.2–3 (Winter-Spring-Summer 2001): 61–76, reprinted as "Poetics and Politics of Hou Hsiao-hsien's Films," in Sheldon Lu and Emilie Yeh, eds., *Chinese-language Film: Historiography, Poetics, Politics* (Honolulu: Hawaii University Press, 2004), 163–85.

2. Book length-studies include Berenice Reynaud's *City of Sadness* (London: BFI, 2002); the French anthology *Hou Hsiao-hsien* (Paris: Cahiers du cinema, 2000) and its Chinese translation under the same title (Taipei: Taipei Film Archive, 2001); a Chinese anthology from Lin Wenchi et al., eds., *Passionate detachment: films of Hou Hsiao-hsien* (Xilian rensheng hou xiaoxian dianying yanjiu) (Taipei: Rye Field, 2000). Doctoral theses exclusively or devoting chapters on Hou include Jean Yen-chun Ma's "Time Without Measure, Sadness Without Cure: Hou Hsiao-hsien's Films of History" (University of Chicago, 2003); James Udden, "Hou Hsiao-hsien and the Aesthetics of Historical Experience" (University of Wisconsin-Madison, 2003); SY Shen, "Permutations of the Foreign/er: A Study of the Works of Edward Yang, Stan Lai, Chang Yi, and Hou Hsiao-hsien" (Cornell University, 1995); June Chun Yip's "Colonialism and Its Counter-discourse: On the Use of 'Nation' in Modern Taiwanese Literature and Film" (Princeton University, 1996); Young-jeong Chae's "Film Space and Chinese Visual Tradition (New York University, 1997); and I-fen Wu's "Taiwanese New Wave Cinema: Historical Representation and Cultural Landscape" (University of Essex, 2002). For a concise bibliography on English, Chinese, and Japanese writings on Hou, consult Lin et al., eds., *Passionate detachment*, 351–70.

3. Yeh, "Poetics and Politics," in Lu and Yeh, *Chinese-language Film*, 163–74.

4. For instance, PRC critic Meng Hongfeng proposed "gripping the oriental (*dongfang*) Hou Hsiao-hsien with an oriental method." Meng Hongfeng, "On the Hou Hsiao-hsien style" (Hou xiaoxian fengge lun) in Lin et al., eds., *Passionate detachment*, 30 (our translation). This essay was first published in *Contemporary film monthly* (Dan-

dai dianying) 52 (September 1993), reprinted in Lin et al., eds., *Passionate detachment*, 29–59.

5. Zhu Tianwen, "Give alternative cinema a space to survive" (Gei ling yizhong dianying shengcun de kongjian), in Wu Nianzhen and Zhu Tianwen, *Dust in the Wind* (Lianlian fengchen) (Taipei: Yuan-liou, 1989), 4–5, 42.

6. Meng Hongfeng also indicates that Hou's space is made to express, not to tell. Meng goes further to liken Hou's film art to the classical Chinese theory of artistic conception (*yijing*), a term indebted to Buddhism's ultimate enlightenment. Meng, " On the Hou Hsiao-hsien style," in Lin et al.., eds, *Passionate detachment*, 47.

7. Peggy Chiao, "History's Subtle Shadows: Hou Hsiao-hsien's *The Puppetmaster*," *Cinemaya* 21 (1993): 10.

8. Yeh, "Politics and Poetics," *PostScript*, 62–65.

9. Ni Luo, "Hou xiaoxian: The cultural ambassador making the rounds on international film circuits" (Chiming guoji yingtan de wenhua dashi hou xiaoxian), in *Cinema of the Republic of China: 1987 Yearbook* (Taipei: Motion Picture Development Foundation of the ROC, 1998), 4–5.

10. Wu and Zhu, *Dust in the Wind*. See Yeh's "Politics and Poetics" for details.

11. One of the best essays on historical representation and *City of Sadness* is Robert Chi's "Getting It on Film: Representing and Understanding History in *A City of Sadness*," *Tamkang Review* 29.4 (Summer 1994): 43–84.

12. See David Bordwell, "Transcultural Spaces: Toward a Poetics of Chinese Film," *PostScript* 20.2–3 (Winter-Spring-Summer 2001): 9–24. See also *Figures Traced in Light*, ch. 5.

13. See James Udden's two articles: "Hou Hsiao-hsien and the Question of a Chinese Style," *Asian Cinema* 13.2 (Fall-Winter 2002): 54–75, and "Taiwanese Popular Cinema and the Strange Apprenticeship of Hou Hsiao-hsien," *Modern Chinese Literature and Culture* 15.1 (Spring 2003): 120–45.

14. The connection with the old school is not limited to Hou Hsiao-hsien. Christopher Doyle, for instance, was once an apprentice to Chen Kunhou on Li Xing's *Story of a Small Town* (1979). Before shooting Edward Yang's *That Day, on the Beach* (1983), Doyle cut his teeth on some creaky healthy realist films like *The Land of the Brave* (Long de chuanren, 1980; dir. Li Xing).

15. An interesting result of mixing healthy realism with romance or vice versa is a clean, didactic configuration of romantic melodrama (see chapter 1). It mixes the interior/private mise-en-scène specific to melodrama with the civil/public space to accommodate government policy, enabling integration with the state ideological apparatus.

16. Huang Zhuohan, *My life in film production: a memoir* (Dianying rensheng: huang zhuohan weiyi lu) (Taipei: Variety, 1994), 196.

17. James Udden suggests that in order to overcome the difficulty of directing children, Hou had to employ longer takes to allow child actors to improvise rather than to act. See "Taiwanese Popular Cinema and the Strange Apprenticeship," 137–39.

18. Lin Wenchi, "Narrative and realist style in Hou Hsiao-hsien's early films" (Hou xiaox-

ian zaoqi dianying zhong de xieshi fengge yu xushi) in Lin et al., eds., *Passionate detachment*, 93–111.

19. Elizabeth W. Bruss, *Autobiographical Acts: The Changing Situation of a Literary Genre* (Baltimore and London: Johns Hopkins University Press, 1977).

20. John Paul Eakin, *Fictions in Autobiography: Studies in the Art of Self-Invention* (Princeton: Princeton University Press, 1985), 5.

21. Eakin, *Fictions in Autobiography*, 3.

22. Ibid.

23. Ibid., 7.

24. Ira B. Nadel, "The Biographer's Secret," in James Olney, ed., *Studies in Autobiography* (Oxford: Oxford University Press, 1988), 26.

25. Hwei-cheng Cho, "Zhu Tianwen: Writing 'Decadent' Fiction in Contemporary Taiwan" (Ph.D. diss., University of London, 1998), 28.

26. Cho, "Zhu Tianwen," 8–111.

27. For more on the collaboration between Zhu Tianwen and Hou Hsiao-hsien, see an excellent interview by Michael Berry, "Words and Images: A Conversation with Hou Hsiao-hsien and Chu Ti'en-wen," *positions: east asia cultures critique* 11.3 (Winter 2003): 675–716.

28. Zhu Tianwen, *The Story of Xiaobi* (Xiaobi de gushi), new ed. (Taipei: Yuan-liou, 1992), 100 (our translation).

29. For an insightful essay on Taipei's changing urban geography, see Yomi Braester's "If We Could Remember Everything, We Would Be Able to Fly: Taipei's Cinematic Poetics of Demolition," *Modern Chinese Literature and Culture* 15.1 (Spring 2003): 29–62.

30. Li Dayi, "Film life of Hou Hsiao-hsien" (Hou xiaoxian de dianying rensheng), *Film Appreciation* 17.3 (May-June 1999): 81–82. Excerpt translated by Jacob Wong for "Taiwan Film Festival: A Tribute to Hou Hsiao-hsien" (Hong Kong Arts Centre, June 1999), 21.

31. The eminent Chang Aileen once complimented Zhu Xi'ning with the endearment, "to me, you're always the private in Shen Congwen's best stories." Zhu Tianwen, "Introduction" (Daodu), in Zhu Xi'ning, *The best of Zhu Xi'ning's fiction* (Zhu Xi'ning xiaoshuo jingpin) (Taipei: Camel Press, 1998), viii.

32. Shen Congwen, *Congwen's Autobiography* (Congwen zizhuan), 5th ed. (Taipei: United Literature, 1987).

33. Jeffrey C. Kinkley, *The Odyssey of Shen Congwen* (Stanford: Stanford University Press, 1987), 1–3.

34. David Der-wei Wang, *Fictional Realism in Twentieth-Century China: Mao Dun, Lao She, Shen Congwen* (New York: Columbia University Press, 1992), 19.

35. Wang, *Fictional Realism*, 271–74.

36. Shen, *Congwen's Autobiography*, 74.

37. Ibid., 7–19.

38. Ibid., 74.

39. Ibid., 75.

40. Kinkley, *The Odyssey*, 4.

41. Wu and Zhu, *Dust in the Wind*, 216.

42. Cf. *The I Ching or Book of Changes*, Richard Wilhelm translation rendered into English by Cary F. Bayes, 3d ed. (Princeton: Princeton University Press, 1968). See also Nick Browne, "Hou's *Puppetmaster*: The Poetics of Landscape," *Asian Cinema* 8.1 (Spring 1996): 28–38.

43. Wu and Zhu, *Dust in the Wind*, 23.

44. See Darrell W. Davis, "Borrowing Postcolonial: Wu Nien-chen's *Dou-san* and the Memory Mine," *PostScript* 20.2–3 (Winter / Spring / Summer 2001): 94–114.

45. Wu and Zhu, *Dust in the Wind*, 208.

46. See Davis, "A New Taiwan Person? A Conversation with Wu Nianzhen," *Positions* 11.3 (Winter 2003): 717–34.

47. Wu and Zhu, *Dust in the Wind*, 179, 208, 210.

48. Ibid., 180, 210.

49. Ibid., 211.

50. Davis, "A New Taiwan Person?" 732.

51. See "Behind *City of Sadness*: Context III," in Markus Abe-Nornes and Yeh Yueh-yu, *Narrating National Sadness: Cinematic Mapping and Hypertextual Dispersion* (University of California, Berkeley: Film Studies Program, 1998). See the *CinemaSpace* Web site (at http://cinemaspace.berkeley.edu/Papers/CityOfSadness/table.html).

52. Li Tianlu and Zeng Yuwen, *Drama, dream, and life: Li Tianlu's memoir* (Xi meng rensheng: li tianlu huiyi lu) (Taipei: Yuan-liou, 1991), 252.

53. "Writing," in Abe-Nornes and Yeh, *Narrating National Sadness*.

54. Davis, "A New Taiwan Person?" 733.

55. Li and Zeng, *Drama, dream, and life*, 187–240.

56. Browne, "*The Puppetmaster*: The Poetics of Landscape," 32.

57. Wang, *Fictional Realism*, ch. 6.

58. Homi Bhabha, "DissemiNation: Time, Narrative, and the Margins of the Modern Nation," in Homi Bhabha, ed., *Nation and Narration* (London: Routledge, 1990), 297.

59. Wan-you Chou, "The Kominka Movement in Taiwan and Korea: Comparisons and Interpretations," in P. Duus, R. Myers, and M. Peattie, eds., *The Japanese Wartime Empire, 1931–1945* (Princeton: Princeton University Press, 1996), 68.

60. Li and Zeng, *Drama, dream, and life*, 100.

61. Browne, "*The Puppetmaster*: The Poetics of Landscape," 35.

62. Li and Zeng, *Drama, dream, and life*, 87, 95–97.

63. *My Life as a Dream on the Stage* is an alternate English-language title suggested by Nick Browne (" *The Puppetmaster*: The Poetics of Landscape," 35).

64. Browne, "*The Puppetmaster*: The Poetics of Landscape," 32.

65. Li Tianlu was awarded "National Master of Arts" in 1989 by the Ministry of Education as part of a nationwide recognition and institutionalization of "cultural heritage." Li and Zeng, *Drama, dream, and life*, 257.

66. Li and Zeng, *Drama, dream, and life*, 49 (our translation). Instead of the Japanese term "yoshi" (adopted son), Li refers to the matrilineal union as "getting a sow."

67. Wang, *Fictional Realism*, 22–23.
68. *The Taiwan New Cinema* (1998, dir. Zhou De Yung; CMPC production).

5. Confucianizing Hollywood: Films of Ang Lee

1. Perhaps with the exception of Wayne Wang's Hong Kong handover film *Chinese Box* (1997), shot on location and uniting Hong Kong stars Maggie Cheung, Michael Hui, PRC star Gong Li, and Jeremy Irons representing the West.
2. Vivid examples are films about the industry: Robert Altman's *The Player* (1992), the independent *Swimming with Sharks* (George Huang, 1994), *Living in Oblivion* (Tom DiCillo, 1994), and *Bulworth* (Warren Beatty, 1998). It is hard to imagine Ang Lee presiding over sets like these.
3. Edward Yang, "Director's Statement," *A Confucian Confusion: Edward Yang's energetic comedy* (Duli shidai: yang dechang de huoli xiju) (Taipei: Variety, 1994), 137–39 (our translation).
4. John Lahr, "Becoming the Hulk," *The New Yorker* (June 30, 2003): 79; Zhang Jingpei and Ang Lee, *My ten-year dream as a filmmaker* (Zhinian yi jiao dianying meng) (Taipei: China Times, 2003), 138.
5. A genre of Chinese literature on the student-immigrant experience of the West is called "overseas student literature" (*liuxuesheng wenxue*). Lee's trilogy of "father-knows-best" films has been located in this tradition by Sheng-mei Ma, "Ang Lee's Domestic Tragicomedy: Immigrant Nostalgia, Exotic/Ethnic Tour, Global Market," *Journal of Popular Culture* 30.1 (1996): 191–201.
6. Ang Lee, "My Own Direction," *Reader's Digest* (Far East edition) 81.483 (June 2003): 54.
7. Lahr, "Becoming the Hulk," 78.
8. Ang Lee and James Schamus, *Crouching Tiger, Hidden Dragon: A Portrait of the Ang Lee Film* (New York: Newmarket, 2000), 7, quoted in Chia-chi Wu, "*Crouching Tiger, Hidden Dragon* is not a Chinese Film," *Spectator: USC Journal of Film and Television Criticism* 22.1 (Spring 2002): 67. See also Ken-fang Lee's "Far Away, So Close: Cultural Translation in Ang Lee's *Crouching Tiger, Hidden Dragon*," *Inter-Asia Cultural Studies* 4.2 (2003): 281–95.
9. Patrick Frater, "Chasing the Dragon," *Screen International* (September 19, 2003): 29.
10. See David Bordwell on transplanting Hong Kong to Hollywood and vice versa in his *Planet Hong Kong: Popular Cinema and the Art of Entertainment* (Cambridge: Harvard University Press, 2000), 1–25.
11. Zhang Yingjin, "Transregional Imagination in Hong Kong Cinema: Questions of Culture, Identity and Industry" (unpublished MS, 2003, p. 11).
12. Stephen Teo, *Hong Kong Cinema: The Extra Dimensions* (London: BFI, 1997), 111–12.
13. "New school" martial arts is distinct from the Cantonese martial arts fantasy films derived from Shanghai *wuxia* costume films from the 1920s and '30s. The new school, indebted to Japanese samurai, spaghetti Westerns, and the James Bond action genres, sprang up in the mid-1960s, beginning with Zhang Che and King Hu. The "new

school" phrase comes from a cycle of martial arts novels by Jin Yong, Ni Kuang, and Liang Yusheng that were adapted to the screen. Law Kar, "The Origin and Development of Shaws' Colour *Wuxia* Century," in Wong Ain-ling and Sam Ho, eds., *The Shaw Screen: A Preliminary Study* (Hong Kong: Hong Kong Film Archive, 2003), 130.

14. Stephen Teo, "'We Kicked Jackie Chan's Ass!' An Interview with James Schamus." *Senses of Cinema* 13 (March-April 2001); *see* www.sensesofcinema.com/contents/01/13/schamus.html.

15. Hao Jian, "Heroes continue to live but people end up dying" (Yingxiong huozhe ren zi le), *Film Appreciation* 21.2 (Winter 2003): 115–17.

16. Elley, quoted in Teo, "'We Kicked Jackie Chan's Ass!'"

17. Zhang and Lee, *My ten-year dream*, 434–39.

18. Ibid., 330–31.

19. Ibid., 329.

20. It is no coincidence that early 2002 saw the regional rerelease of the Shaw Brothers library with the 1966 *Come Drink with Me*, featuring Zheng Peipei on tour, shortly after the triumph of *CTHD*. Smaller distributors followed Celestial's suit in capitalizing on the interest in classic martial arts in Hong Kong and around the region.

21. Zhang and Lee, *My ten-year dream*, 291–92.

22. For an insightful account of the film's reception, see Wu, "*Crouching Tiger* Is Not a Chinese Film," 67–70.

23. Sam Ho, "One Jolts, the Other Orchestrates: Two Transitional Shaw Brothers Figures," in Wong and Ho, eds., *The Shaw Screen*, 114.

24. Another version of dubbing is the exaggerated sound effects of blows, kicks, knuckle-cracking, and the snapping of sleeves, as fighters prepare themselves in precombat-ready stances.

25. Zhang and Lee, *My ten-year dream*, 305–306 (our translation).

26. The China Film Co-production Corp. was one of the entities formed to make the film (in order to get permission to film on the mainland) and to hold Asian copyright, which was never protected on the mainland because of a two-month delay in releasing the film. Teo, "'We Kicked Jackie Chan's Ass!'"

27. Dade Hayes, "'Tiger' Earns Oscar Stripes," *Daily Variety* (March 26, 2001): 1. In Lee's memoir, he says the film had a U.S. $12 million production budget.

28. Frater, "Chasing the Dragon," 29.

29. Scott Hettrick, "'Tiger' Leaps to Vid, DVD," *Daily Variety* (March 27, 2001): 24.

30. Shelly Kraicer, review of David Bordwell's *Planet Hong Kong; see* www.chinesecinemas.org/planethk.html.

31. Lahr, "Becoming the Hulk," 79.

32. "The martial arts form externalizes the elements of restraint and exhilaration. . . . In a family drama there is a verbal fight. Here you kick butt." Lee and Schamus, *CTHD: A Portrait of the Ang Lee Film*, 83.

33. Zhang Zhen, "Bodies in the Air: The Magic of Science and the Fate of the Early 'Martial Arts' Film in China," *PostScript* 20.2–3 (Winter-Spring-Summer 2001): 55.

34. On Mandarin duck and butterfly fiction, see Perry E. Link, *Mandarin Ducks and Butterflies: Popular Fiction in Early Twentieth-Century Chinese Cities* (Berkeley: University of California Press,1981); and Rey Chow, *Women and Chinese Modernity: The Politics of Reading Between East and West* (Minneapolis: University of Minnesota Press, 1991).

35. Ye Hongshen, "Introduction," in Wang Dulu, *Crouching tiger, hidden dragon* (Wohu canglong), 2 vols. (Taipei: United Literature, 1985) , 1:46–47.

36. Ye, "Introduction," in Wang, *Crouching tiger* 1:46.

37. Ibid., 1:83.

38. Ibid., 1:83–84.

39. Lee and Schamus, *CTHD: Portrait of the Ang Lee Film,* 64.

40. Wang, *Crouching tiger* 2:756–74.

41. Wang, *Crouching tiger* 2:774–75 (our translation).

42. Stephen Teo, "Love and Swords: The Dialectics of Martial Arts Romance," *Senses of Cinema* 11 (December 2000–January 2001); *see* www.sensesofcinema.com/contents/00/11/crouching.html.

43. The film made a global return of $32 million on a $750,000 investment. With this ratio it was the single most profitable film of 1993, surpassing even *Jurassic Park.* See Zhang and Lee, *My ten-year dream as a filmmaker,* 117; Lahr, "Becoming the Hulk," 78.

44. "A Feast for the Eyes: Ang Lee in Taipei," making-of featurette, *Eat Drink Man Woman* (MGM Home Video, 2002).

45. "A Feast for the Eyes" featurette.

46. Compared to the month-long shooting schedule for Lee's first two films, *EDWM* took forty-seven days. Wang Huiling, Ang Lee, James Shamus, and Chen Baoxu, *Eat, drink, man, woman: film script and shooting process* (Yinshi nannü: dianying jubun yu paishe guocheng) (Taipei: Yuan-liou, 1994), 174.

47. Zhang and Lee, *My ten-year dream,* 128.

48. Ma, "Ang Lee's Domestic Tragicomedy," 198.

49. "A Feast for the Eyes" featurette.

50. Brooke Comer, "*Eat Drink Man Woman*: A Feast for the Eyes," *American Cinematographer* (January 1995): 62; quoted in Ma, "Ang Lee's Domestic Tragicomedy," 195.

51. A maxim stated outright in *Crouching Tiger, Hidden Dragon:* "To repress one's feelings only makes them stronger."

52. Lahr, "Becoming the Hulk," 79.

53. Shu-mei Shih, "Globalization and Minoritisation: Ang Lee and the Politics of Flexibility," *New Formations: A Journal of Culture/Theory/Politics* 40 (Spring 2000): 87–101. "Resuscitated patriarchs" is attributed to Cynthia Lew's " 'To Love, Honor, and Dismay': Subverting the Feminine in Ang Lee's Trilogy of Resuscitated Patriarchs," in *Hitting Critical Mass: A Journal of Asian American Cultural Criticism* 3.1 (Winter 1995): 1–60 (Shih, "Globalization and Minoritisation," 96).

54. "You become a Westerner and you betray your parents. Something you feel unable to deal with: total guilt." Quoted in Lahr, "Becoming the Hulk," 78.

55. Ma, "Ang Lee's Domestic Tragicomedy," 193.

56. Epigraph to introduction of Gary Alan Fine's *Kitchens: The Culture of Restaurant Work* (Berkeley: University of California Press, 1996), 1.
57. Ma, "Ang Lee's Domestic Tragicomedy," 198.
58. Lahr, "Becoming the Hulk," 74.
59. Zhang Daqian (1899–1983) is regarded as a national painter, one of the leading artists in twentieth-century China, especially for his creation of a synthesis of contemporary Western and traditional Chinese techniques.
60. "A Feast for the Eyes" featurette.
61. Wang et al., *Eat, drink, man, woman*, 189.
62. Zhang and Lee, *My ten-year dream*, 128–29.
63. Steve Fore, "Jackie Chan and the Cultural Dynamics of Global Entertainment," in Sheldon Lu, ed., *Transnational Chinese Cinema* (Honolulu: University of Hawaii Press, 1997), 241.
64. Sheng-mei Ma in "Ang Lee's Domestic Tragicomedy" uses the term "tourist-friendly" to describe Lee's films, which "appeal to bourgeois taste and the subsuming of class" (192). See also Shu-mei Shih, "Globalization and Minoritisation."
65. SY Shen, "Permutations of the Foreign/er: A Study of the Works of Edward Yang, Stan Lai, Chang Yi, and Hou Hsiao-hsien" (Ph.D. diss., Cornell University, 1995), 27–28. On controversies of the Fifth Generation, see Ni Zhen, *Memoirs from the Beijing Film Academy: Genesis of China's Fifth Generation*, trans. Chris Berry (Durham, N.C.: Duke University Press, 2003), 194 ff.
66. As noted, Jiaqian works for a national airline, while Jialian, the eldest, is a teacher at a top city high school. The youngest daughter, Jianing, works a McJob at Wendys, indicating both consumer globalization and international proletarianization. Yet of all the sisters she is the most easygoing, freely taking the initiative in love and sex.
67. D. W. Davis and Emilie Y. Y. Yeh, "Inoue at Shaws: The Wellspring of Youth," in Wong and Ho, eds., *The Shaw Screen*, 255–71. This father-daughter premise is like an international storehouse, indebted to such films as the various remakes of *Little Women*, *Young at Heart*, *Four Daughters*, *Make Way for Tomorrow*, and even D. W. Griffith's *Broken Blossoms* and *Birth of a Nation*.
68. The original property was so popular that Cathay issued a 4,000-word brochure explaining changes made to the story, including a statement from Zheng expressing admiration for Tao Qin's work. See Shu Kei, "Notes on MP&GI," in Wong Ain-ling and Sam Ho, eds., *The Cathay Story* (Hong Kong: Hong Kong Film Archive, 2002), 96–97. Zheng's original story is much darker than Tao's comic melodrama. The siren Helen has an affair with Hilda's widower husband and feels so guilty that she simply disappears. Hedy becomes a nun because of a flying accident, which kills her boyfriend, and for which she feels responsible. Hazel, a young mother struggling with diapers, barely maintains the household on her husband's meager wage.
69. In this, Lee mediates between ordinary remakes and true homages like those of Tsai Ming-liang, whose direct references to classic films and performers are foundational to his own idiosyncratic works. See chapter 6.

6. Camping Out with Tsai Ming-liang

1. "Double Vision: Taiwan's New Cinema, Here and There," Yale University, November 1, 2003.

2. Beginning with *What Time Is It There?* (2001), Tsai used the college film festival model to promote his films, with excellent results. This is a throwback to the early days of the New Cinema (see chapter 2).

3. Thomas A. King, "Performing 'Akimbo': Queer Pride and Epistemological Prejudice," in Moe Meyer, ed., *Poetics and Politics of Camp* (London and New York: Routledge, 1994), 26. Meyer himself reiterates this dialectic in his essay "Under the Sign of Wilde," *Poetics and Politics*, 76.

4. Andy Medhurst, "Camp," in Andy Medhurst and S. Munt, eds., *Lesbian and Gay Studies: A Critical Introduction* (London: Cassell, 1997), 276.

5. See the overview and list of sources by Darren Hughes, "Great Directors" database, *Senses of Cinema* (*see* www.sensesofcinema.com).

6. Carlos Rojas, "'Nezha Was Here': Structures of Dis/placement in Tsai Ming-liang's *Rebels of the Neon God*," *Modern Chinese Literature and Culture* 15.1 (Spring 2003): 63–89.

7. Ban Wang, "Black Holes of Globalization: Critique of the New Millennium in Taiwan Cinema," *Modern Chinese Literature and Culture* 15.1 (Spring 2003): 90–106.

8. Chris Berry, "Where Is the Love? The Paradox of Performing Loneliness in *Vive l'amour*," in Leslie Stern and George Kouvaros, eds., *Falling for You: Essays on Performance* (Sydney: Power, 1999), 147–76.

9. Jean-Pierre Rehm, Olivier Joyard, and Daniele Riviere, *Tsai Ming-liang* (Paris: Dis Voir, 1999).

10. "You also draw attention in *Vive l'amour* to the odour of May's under-arm sweat. Do these bodily manifestations signify that the body is escaping from itself, becoming diluted, dematerialized, or on the contrary, does this oozing show that it is still alive?" [*Laughter*] "That's something I've never wondered about!" in Rehm, Joyard, and Riviere, *Tsai Ming-liang*, 114.

11. One exception is Ji Dawei, "Wo kan gu wo zai: chengzhang dianying yu shenfen rentong" (I see therefore I am: Films of development and identity recognition), *Youshi wenyi* 510 (June 1996): 95–105; cited in Rojas, "'Nezha Was Here,'"89.

12. Peggy Chiao and Tsai Ming-liang, *The River* (Heliu) (Taipei: Huangguan, 1997), 18; cited in Rojas, 64.

13. Wen Tianxiang, *Framing the light and shadow: Tsai Ming-liang's spiritual terrain* (Guangying dingge: tsai ming-liang de xinling changyu) (Taipei: Hengxing, 2002), 111 (our translation).

14. Meyer, "Introduction: Reclaiming the Discourse of Camp," in *Poetics and Politics*, 2.

15. After Moe Meyer's concise definition of camp: "strategies and tactics of queer parody." Meyer, "Introduction," 9, 14.

16. Meyer, "Introduction," 3.

17. Wojcik, "A Star Is Born Again or, How Streisand Recycles Garland," in Stern and Kouvaros, eds., *Falling for You*, 206.

18. In reading the AIDS inscription as a general metaphor of contagion, Carlos Rojas pre-emptively writes: "In treating AIDS here as a metaphor, I neither deny nor downplay the devastating social impact of the disease itself or the ways in which misleading gen-eralizations about how the virus is contracted and spread have been used to increase prejudice against various specific social groups" ("'Nezha Was Here,'" 65).

19. One exception is Julian Stringer, "Problems with the Treatment of Hong Kong Cinema as Camp," *Asian Cinema* 8 (Winter 1996–97): 44–65.

20. Meyer, "Introduction," 1–22. See also the critique by Greg Smith, *Artists in the Audi-ence: Cults, Camp, and American Film Criticism* (Princeton: Princeton University Press, 1999), 167; and Medhurst, "Camp," 274–93.

21. Margaret Thompson Drewal, "The Camp Trace in Corporate America: Liberace and the Rockettes at Radio City Music Hall," in Meyer, ed., *Poetics and Politics*, 149–81.

22. Yomi Braester, "If We Could Remember Everything, We Would Be Able to Fly: Taipei's Cinematic Poetics of Demolition," *Modern Chinese Literature and Culture* 15.1 (Spring 2003): 29–62.

23. Michael Moon, "Flaming Closets," in Corey Creekmur and Alexander Doty, eds., *Out in Culture: Gay, Lesbian, and Queer Essays on Popular Culture* (Durham, N.C.: Duke University Press 1995), 295.

24. Susan Sontag: "One must distinguish between naïve and deliberate camp. Pure Camp is always naïve . . . most campy objects are urban. (Yet they often have a serenity—or a naivete—which is the equivalent of pastoral.)" Sontag, "Notes on Camp," in Fabio Cleto, ed., *Camp: Queer Aesthetics and the Performing Subject: A Reader* (Ann Arbor: University of Michigan Press, 1999), 58, 55.

25. James Cleary, ed., *Chirologia; Or, the Natural Language of the Hand* and *Chironomia; Or, the Art of Manual Rhetoric* (Carbondale: Southern Illinois University Press, 1974); cited in King, "Performing 'Akimbo,'" 25.

26. Wen, *Framing the light and shadow*, 230.

27. David Walsh, "An interview with Tsai Ming-liang, director of *The Hole*," World Socialist Web Site (October 7, 1998); *see* www.wsws.org/arts/1998/oct1998/tsai-007.shtml.

28. Moon, "Flaming Closets," 299.

29. Andrew Ross, "Uses of Camp," in *No Respect: Intellectuals and Popular Culture* (New York and London: Routledge, 1989), 139; originally published in *Yale Journal of Criti-cism* 2.1 (Fall 1988).

30. Fredric Jameson, "Nostalgia for the Present," *South Atlantic Quarterly* 88.2 (Spring 1989): 517–37. Essay also appears in *Postmodernism; Or, the Cultural Logic of Late Capi-talism* (1991), and is reprinted in Jane Gaines, ed., *Classical Hollywood Narrative: The Paradigm Wars* (Durham, N.C.: Duke University Press, 1992), 253–73.

31. This may be an outsized impression due to the fact this film was viewed from the first row of a sold-out festival screening. The extra-large spectacle and sound, almost distorted in its proximity, lent an appropriate sense of otherworldliness to Tsai's ap-propriations of King Hu.

32. Kim Ji-seok, "The Missing (Bu Jian)," *The 8th Pusan International Film Festival Cata-logue* (October 2–10, 2003), 73.

33. Both King Hu and Li Hanxiang, masters of Chinese cinema of the 1960s, made their

mark as directors of historical drama. Li is the expert on the Qing dynasty (1644–1911) while Hu specializes in the Ming dynasty (1368–1644). What is uncanny in their respective areas is a common interest in eunuchs, who are often blamed for the destruction of the dynasties.

34. Philip Core, "The Lie That Tells the Truth," in Cleto, ed., *Camp,* 81.

35. Ross, "Uses of Camp," 151.

36. Tsai has said he earned considerable hostility from this turn of the narrative screw: "That scene in *The River* brought me a lot of criticism . . . in some cases, outright insults. They say there are three groups of people who hate the film: First, there are those who only remember the incest scene. Then, homosexuals who ask: 'Why does he have to show homosexuals in such a sad, dark setting?' Finally, feminists who dislike a film, which shows a world full of men who reject women." Rehm, Joyard, and Riviere, *Tsai Ming-liang,* 98.

37. Moe Meyer, "Under the Sign of Wilde: An Archaeology of Posing," in Meyer, ed., *Poetics and Politics,* 83 ff.

38. Wen, *Framing the light and shadow,* 14–64.

39. Ibid., 32–37.

40. Moon, "Flaming Closets," 299.

41. Ibid., 294–95. Here we find the idea of mirror-as-camera, along with the studio (particularly Universal's B-lot, where Maria Montez worked) as closet.

42. Wen, *Framing the light and shadow,* 55.

43. Ibid., 18.

44. Ibid., 21.

45. Wang Xiaodi, "Look! This Foreigner," in Tsai Ming-liang et al., *Vive l'amour* (Aiqing wansui) (Taipei: Variety, 1994), 180.

46. King, "Performing 'Akimbo,'" 24–26.

47. In 1998, Wang Yingxiang, the most powerful Taiwan local distributor, filed a complaint against Tsai Ming-liang. Wang questioned the granting of subsidy funds to filmmakers without Taiwan citizenship. In August 1999, the Government Information Office passed an amendment to the film subsidy fund that stipulates citizenship as one of the application criteria. *Cinema in the Republic of China: 2000 Yearbook* (Taipei: Motion Picture Development Foundation of ROC, 2001), 260.

48. *My New Friends* (Wo xin renshi de pengyou, 1995) is a television documentary Tsai contributed to a series of public-funded programs to address issues of AIDS in Asia. In 2001, with funding from Korea's Jeonju Film Festival, Tsai made another nonfiction DV called *Conversations with God* (Yushen duihua, aka *Fish, Underground*). This video is about a shaman and dead fish in a contaminated river. When Tsai was making *The River,* he came across a woman *jitong* (shaman) with whom he was intrigued. He wanted to document her and her daily routine as a shaman.

49. Jean Rouch, quoted in Brian Winston, "Documentary Film as Scientific Inscription," in Michael Renov, ed., *Theorizing Documentary: A Reader* (Routledge/American Film Institute, 1993), 51. Admittedly, Flaherty also was "salvaging" something personal, romantic, and not very authentic.

50. This is similar to Moe Meyer's brilliant critique of Andrew Ross, an attack on the

bourgeois appropriation of camp as "a bizarre love affair with a dead queer . . . safely contained within the coffin of a distancing metaphorical historicization" (Meyer, "Introduction," 16). But Tsai Ming-liang is now the queer lover reanimating queer, bi, and heterosexual curiosities and perversities, and this is emancipatory, resurrecting suppressed practices rather than containing and co-opting them. The resurrection of *song* is affirmative, for as Meyer writes, "the power of Camp lies in its ability to be conscious of its future as an appropriated commodity" (ibid., 17).

51. Jacob W. Gruber, "Ethnographic Salvage and the Shaping of Anthropology," originally published in *American Anthropologist* 61 (1959): 379–89.

52. A vivid example of this can be found in Wu Nianzhen's *Dou-san: A Borrowed Life* (1994), though there are hints of it in Hou's Taiwan trilogy, especially *The Puppetmaster* (1993).

Index

Personal names are alphabetized by family name, whether traditional or westernized, with no comma in traditional names. Film and book titles are in *italic*. Capitalization of English translations of Chinese-language titles follows the authors' usage. Film title under director's name is major discussion; see title of film for additional references.

Film and Culture / A SERIES OF COLUMBIA UNIVERSITY PRESS

EDITED BY JOHN BELTON